NGO INVOLVEME
ORGA

A LEGAL ANALYSIS

NGO INVOLVEMENT IN INTERNATIONAL ORGANIZATIONS

A Legal Analysis

SERGEY RIPINSKY
and
PETER VAN DEN BOSSCHE

British Institute of
International and
Comparative Law

Published and Distributed by
British Institute of International and Comparative Law
Charles Clore House, 17 Russell Square, London WC1B 5JP

© Sergey Ripinsky and Peter Van den Bossche 2007

British Library Cataloguing in Publication Data
A Catalogue record of this book is available from the British Library

ISBN 978-1-905221-19-6

Typeset by Cambrian Typesetters
Camberley, Surrey
Printed in Great Britain by Biddles Ltd
King's Lynn

Contents

Acknowledgements   xi

Introduction   xiii

Chapter 1: NGOs as International Actors   1
  I.   Emergence of NGOs as International Actors   1
  II.   What is an NGO?   4
  III. Main Types of NGOs   7
  IV.   Roles and Functions of NGOs   9
  V.   Pros and Cons of NGO Involvement   11
  VI.   The Problem of NGO Legitimacy   13
  VII. The Place of NGOs in International Governance   15

Chapter 2: United Nations Economic and Social Council
          (UN ECOSOC)   19
  I.   Legal and Institutional Framework   19
        A. Scope of NGO Involvement in UN Activities   19
        B. Economic and Social Council   21
        C. ECOSOC Resolution 1996/31   22
  II.   Types of Consultative Status   24
        A. General Consultative Status   24
        B. Special Consultative Status   26
        C. Roster   27
        D. Comparative Table and Additional Remarks   28
  III. Accreditation Criteria   30
        A. Common Criteria for Accreditation   31
        B. Criteria Determining the Type of Consultative Status 34
  IV.   Procedures for Accreditation   36
  V.   Monitoring of NGOs   40
        A. Quadrennial Reports   40
        B. Suspension and Withdrawal of Consultative Status   41
  VI.   NGO Participation in UN Conferences   44
  VII. Probable Changes to the UN Accreditation System   49

Chapter 3: United Nations Conference on Trade and
          Development (UNCTAD)   51
  I   Introduction   51
  II.   Legal Basis   52

III. Forms of Involvement   53
    A. Categories of NGOs   54
    B. Participation in UNCTAD's Intergovernmental Meetings   55
    C. Civil Society Forums   57
    D. Civil Society Hearings   58
IV. Accreditation Criteria and Procedures   59
    A. Criteria for the Observer Status with UNCTAD   59
    B. Procedures for Obtaining Observer Status   62
    C. Quadrennial Conferences   64
    D. Civil Society Hearings   66
V.   Monitoring of NGOs   66

Chapter 4: International Labour Organization (ILO)   67
I.   Introduction   67
II.   Scope of this Chapter   68
III. Legal Basis   69
IV.   Forms of Involvement   70
    A. NGOs in General and Regional Consultative Status   70
    B. NGOs on the Special List   72
    C. Remaining International NGOs   73
    D. Conclusion   73
V.   Accreditation Criteria and Procedures   74
    A. General and Regional Consultative Status   74
    B. Special List   75
    C. Accreditation to the Conference   78
    D. Accreditation to Conference Committees   80
    E. Accreditation to Other ILO Meetings   81
VI.   Monitoring of NGOs   82

Chapter 5: World Intellectual Property Organization (WIPO)   83
I.   Introduction   83
II.   Legal Basis   85
III. Forms of Involvement   86
    A. Types of NGO Observers   87
    B. NGO Participation in WIPO Meetings   88
IV.   Accreditation Criteria   89
    A. Permanent Observer Status   89
    B. Ad Hoc Observer Status   92
V.   Accreditation Procedures   93
    A. Permanent Observer Status   93
    B. Ad Hoc Observer Status   94
VI.   Monitoring of NGOs   95

Chapter 6: World Health Organization (WHO) 97
I. Introduction 97
II. Legal Framework 98
III. Forms of NGO Involvement 100
    A. Health Assembly 102
    B. Executive Board 105
    C. Other Rights 106
    D. Regional and Country Level 107
IV. Criteria for Obtaining OR Status 108
V. Procedure for Obtaining the OR Status 112
    A. First Contacts 113
    B. Working Relations 114
    C. Admission into the OR Status 115
VI. Monitoring of NGOs 116

Chapter 7: United Nations Environment Programme (UNEP) 119
I. Introduction 119
II. Legal Framework and Forms of Involvement 120
III. Policy Development 122
    A. GC/GMEF Sessions 123
    B. Global Civil Society Forum (GCSF) 129
IV. Implementation of the UNEP's Work Programme 131
    A. Modalities of NGO Involvement 131
    B. Selection Criteria and Procedures 133
V. Monitoring of NGOs 133

Chapter 8: United Nations Development Programme (UNDP) 135
I. Introduction 135
II. Legal Framework 136
III. Forms of NGO Involvement 138
    A. UNDP CSO Advisory Committee to the Administrator 140
    B. UNDP Executive Board 143
    C. Project Execution 143

Chapter 9: World Bank 151
I. Introduction 151
II. Legal Basis and Forms of Involvement 152
III. Involvement in Bank Policy Development 157
    A. Introduction 157
    B. History 159
    C. Annual and Spring Meetings 160
    D. World Bank–Civil Society Forum 164

IV.   Participation in Bank-Financed Projects   164
      A. Legal Framework and Forms of Involvement   164
      B. Selection Criteria and Procedures   167
V.   Role in Dispute Settlement (Bank Accountability
      Mechanism)   170
      A. Introduction   170
      B. Procedure   170
      C. NGO Involvement   171
VI.   Conclusion   173

Chapter 10: International Monetary Fund (IMF)   177
I.   Introduction   177
II.   Legal Basis and Forms of NGO Involvement   178
      A. Legal Basis   178
      B. Opportunities for NGO Involvement   179
      C. Format of Participation   183
III. Accreditation/Selection Criteria and Procedures   184

Chapter 11: World Trade Organization (WTO)   189
I.   Introduction   189
II.   Legal Basis   190
III. Forms of Involvement   192
      A. Attendance of the Ministerial Conference Sessions   194
      B. Public Symposia or Forums   196
      C. Improved Access to WTO Information and
         Opportunities for Information Exchange   198
      D. Informal Meetings with NGOs   199
      E. Prospects   199
IV.   NGO Involvement in Dispute Settlement   201
      A. Attendance of Proceedings   201
      B. *Amicus Curiae* Briefs   202
      C. Experts and Legal Counsel   204

Chapter 12: Comparative Analysis   207
I.   Legal Basis   207
II.   Forms of NGO Involvement and Participatory Rights   210
III. Accreditation Criteria   216
IV.   Accreditation Procedures   220
V.   Monitoring NGOs   222
VI.   Concluding Remarks   223

Appendix I: UN ECOSOC 225
  Charter of the United Nations 225
  Resolution 1996/31 on Consultative Relationship Between
    the United Nations and Non-Governmental Organizations 225

Appendix II: UNCTAD 243
  Resolution of the United Nations General Assembly 1995
    (XIX), 'Establishment of the United Nations Conference on
    Trade and Development as an Organ of the General Assembly' 243
  Rules of Procedure of the Trade and Development Board 243
  Rules of Procedure of the Conference 244
  Rules of Procedure of the Main Committees of the
  Trade and Development Board 245
  Arrangements for the Participation of Non-Governmental
    Organizations in the Activities of the United Nations
    Conference on Trade and Development 245

Appendix III: ILO 249
  Constitution of the International Labour Organization 249
  Report of the Committee on Legal Issues and International
    Labour Standards 249

Appendix IV: WIPO 259
  Convention Establishing the World Intellectual Property
    Organization 259
  Admission of Observers 259

Appendix V: WHO 263
  Constitution of the World Health Organization 263
  Principles Governing Relations between WHO and
    Non-Governmental Organizations 263
  Draft Policy for Relations with Non-Governmental Organizations 269

Appendix VI: UNEP 277
  Resolution of the United Nations General Assembly 2997 (XXVII)
    'Institutional and Financial Arrangements for International
    Environmental Co-operation' 277
  Rules of Procedure of the Governing Council of UNEP 277
  Accreditation of Non-Governmental Organizations at UNEP 278
  Modalities for Accredited International Non-Governmental
    Organizations to UNEP to Submit Written Inputs into the
    Unedited Working Documents of the UNEP'S GC/GMEF
    and to Submit Written Statements to the GC/GMEF of UNEP 281

Enhancing Civil Society Engagement in the Work of the United
    Nations Environment Programme Implementation of
    GCSS.VII/5   282

Appendix VII: UNDP   297
    UNDP and Civil Society Organizations: A Policy Note on
        Engagement   297
    Concept Paper on the Establishment of a CSO Advisory
        Committee to UNDP   315
    UNDP Programming Manual: Chapter 6: Operations of
        Programmes and Projects   318
    Framework of Selection Criteria to Asssess CSO Capacity   325
    Simplification of NGO Execution for Crisis and Post Conflict
        Situations   331

Appendix VIII: World Bank   335
    Involving Non-Governmental Organizations in Bank-Supported
    Activities   335

Appendix IX: IMF   345
    Guide for Staff Relations with Civil Society Organizations   345

Appendix X: WTO   361
    Agreement Establishing the World Trade Organization   361
    Guidelines for Arrangements on Relations with
        Non-Governmental Organizations   361

Acknowledgements

This study on *NGO Involvement in International Organizations: A Legal Analysis* was carried out in the context of the multidisciplinary research project on *Globalization and the Legitimacy of Power of Non-Governmental Organizations* financed by the Netherlands Organization for Scientific Research. The authors wish to thank the Netherlands Organization for Scientific Research for its generous financial support. The authors are grateful to Jill Roche, Andrea Bruns, Marijn Blok and Astrid Van den Bossche for their assistance in preparing this study for publication, as well as to Gemma Parsons and Orla Fee for producing it as a book. Finally, the authors wish to thank the many officials of international organizations in Geneva, New York and Washington, who generously volunteered their time to be interviewed and shared documents and information. Without their help, this study would not have been possible.

Sergey Ripinsky and Peter Van den Bossche
London & Maastricht, May 2007

Introduction

This book deals with the legal arrangements for the involvement of non-governmental organizations (NGOs) in the activities of international institutions.[1] In recent years, the increasing participation of NGOs in international diplomacy and governance has received considerable attention from the international community and academia. A prime example of this attention is the Cardoso Report of June 2004, *We the People: Civil Society, the United Nations and Global Governance*, which examined the relationship between NGOs and the United Nations system and made a number of proposals for improving this relationship.[2] Also the Sutherland Report of January 2005 on *The Future of the World Trade Organization: Addressing Institutional Challenges in the New Millennium* discussed the issue of the role of NGOs in the deliberations and processes of the WTO.[3] The similarities and differences in the relevant conclusions of the Cardoso and Sutherland Reports reveal the continued controversy regarding the appropriate role of NGOs in international organizations.[4] These and other reports and studies focus primarily on the political aspects of the involvement of NGOs in the activities of international organizations. To date, surprisingly little has been done to comprehensively describe and analyse the existing legal arrangements for NGO participation in international organizations.[5] This study aspires to fill this gap.

---

[1] In this study, the terms 'international institution' and 'international organization' are used interchangeably to mean 'international inter-governmental organizations'.

[2] Report of the Panel of Eminent Persons on United Nations–Civil Society Relations, *We the People, Civil Society, the United Nations and Global Governance* (Cardoso Report) A/58/817 (11 June 2004), available at <http://documents-dds-ny.un.org/doc/UNDOC/GEN/N04/376/41/pdf/N0437641.pdf?OpenElement>, visited 1 Apr 2005.

[3] Report by the Consultative Board to the Director-General Supachai Panitchpakdi, *The Future of the WTO: Addressing Institutional Challenges in the New Millennium* (Jan 2005), available at <http://www.wto.org/english/thewto_e/10anniv_e/10anniv_e.htm#future>, visited 7 June 2005.

[4] This controversy also became apparent during the debate on the Cardoso Report in the UN General Assembly in Oct 2004. See the plenary meeting transcripts available at <http://www.un.org/ga/59/pv.html>, visited 9 Apr 2006.

[5] Notable exceptions are A Lindblom, *Non-Governmental Organisations in International Law* (CUP, Cambridge, 2006), and a 2002 Report prepared by Ecologic and FIELD, entitled *Participation of Non-Governmental Organisations in International Environmental Governance: Legal Basis and Practical Experience*, available at <http://www.ecologic.de/download/projekte/1850-1899/1890/report_ngos_en.pdf>. Note, however, that the scope of the book by Lindblom is both wider and narrower than the present study. It is wider in that it is concerned with the legal status of NGOs in international law and not 'merely' with the legal arrangements of their involvement in the activities of international organizations. It is narrower in that it examines the legal status of NGOs in international law, with an emphasis on human rights law. The present study does not have such emphasis. The 2002 Report prepared by Ecologic and FIELD is an extremely useful study but is mostly confined to *environmental* governance and does not include many of the international organizations covered in this study.

To do so, it looks at a number of selected international organizations with the aim to reveal the legal basis and practices of NGO involvement in the activities of these organizations. It concentrates on the forms of NGO involvement, on existing criteria for NGO accreditation with international institutions and on procedures for obtaining accreditation and for subsequent monitoring of accredited NGOs. Taking into account the large number of international organizations, it is hardly possible to cover them all. Therefore, a number of organizations with a high international profile have been chosen. These organizations deal with issues which have an important impact on different aspects of the lives of people all around the world (economic development, labour, environment, health, etc) and which, for this reason, attract much attention from NGOs. The selection of international organizations has also been determined by this study's aim to discuss a broad range of different types, degrees and mechanisms of NGO engagement. This study does not deal with international organizations in the fields of human rights or gender issues (the focus of many NGOs), leaving this area for a separate study.

The following international organizations are covered in the present study:

- the United Nations Economic and Social Council (UN ECOSOC);
- the United Nations Conference on Trade and Development (UNCTAD);
- the International Labour Organization (ILO);
- the World Intellectual Property Organization (WIPO);
- the World Health Organization (WHO);
- the United Nations Environment Programme (UNEP);
- the United Nations Development Programme (UNDP);
- the International Bank for Reconstruction and Development (IBRD or World Bank);
- the International Monetary Fund (IMF); and
- the World Trade Organization (WTO).

A separate chapter is devoted to each of the selected international organizations. Although the structure of these chapters may differ, all of them are built around the same elements. They include:

1. An introduction on the activities and governance structure of the international organizations concerned.
2. The legal basis for NGO involvement.
3. Forms of NGO involvement and their participatory rights.
4. Criteria employed to accredit NGOs, where accreditation schemes are in place, or to select them for other forms of cooperation (where available).

5. Procedures applicable to accreditation/selection of NGOs (where available).
6. Arrangements for monitoring of accredited/selected NGOs (where available).

The study is based on the constitutive treaties, secondary rules (resolutions, decisions and guidelines), other documents of the international organizations concerned and information available on their official websites and in academic and other literature. To make the review more comprehensive a number of interviews were conducted with officials from the international organizations concerned.

The main focus of the study is NGO involvement in the policy deliberations and decision-making processes of the international institutions concerned. In addition, where appropriate, it covers NGO participation in projects and programmes carried out by some international organizations and NGO participation in dispute settlement.

The *practical use* of this study is threefold. First, it may serve as an information tool for NGOs to learn about opportunities for engagement with prominent international organizations. Secondly, it can help international organizations to compare the rules and practices on NGO involvement in order to distil 'best practices' and consider improvements to their own systems. Thirdly, being fact-specific and with few value judgments, the study may be further used by specialists in the fields of political science and international relations to make their assessments on the relative effectiveness of different modalities for engagement with NGOs. Since the relevant information is currently rather scattered, it is useful to compile it and set it out in a systematic fashion in one publication.

The participation of NGOs in the activities of international organizations is a dynamic issue. The rules on such participation have been undergoing changes and will undergo further transformation. This study describes the current situation in order to see where we stand now and where the way forward lies.[6]

---

[6] This study reflects the state of relevant rules and practices in 2006. Later developments have not been considered systematically. To the best of the authors' knowledge, these developments did not result in substantial changes to the rules and practices discussed in this study.

CHAPTER 1

NGOs as International Actors

I. EMERGENCE OF NGOS AS INTERNATIONAL ACTORS

NGOs are an important factor to consider for a full understanding of contemporary international legal and political processes. The importance of NGOs as international actors has increased significantly over the last decades—they have developed and spread their influence all over the globe. Since the mid-20th century, when NGOs were formally recognized as international actors in Article 71 of the UN Charter, they have become a powerful force in international policy-making and compliance monitoring. Engagement between civil society and international organizations has especially intensified since the early 1990s. At present, an ever-growing number of NGOs participate, or aspire to participate, in the work of international organizations. As noted by Kal Raustiala, many commentators believe that:

> this growth of NGO activity may indicate an emerging transformation of the international legal and political system—a decline in the importance of the sovereign state and the state system and an accompanying rise of governance by a dynamic global civil society.[1]

Whether this is indeed the case, today NGOs can surely be called fully-fledged actors in international governance.[2]

Perhaps the most important reason for the empowerment of NGOs on the international plane is the phenomenon of globalization and the growing need to find global solutions for global problems. This need has encouraged governments to engage in more negotiation, policy formation and decision-making at the international level, which, in turn, has had obvious and profound effects on domestic policy and legislation. At the start of the 21st century, regulatory activities are no longer wholly centred on the national territorial State. Much governance directly affecting a wide range of people has shifted to the supranational level, ie to international institutions. NGOs

---

[1] K Raustiala, 'The "Participatory Revolution" in International Environmental Law' (1997) 21 The Harvard Environmental L Rev 537, 539.

[2] For example, P Willets sees events in any area of contemporary global policy-making as 'complex systems, containing governments, companies and NGOs interacting in a variety of international organizations'. See P Willets, 'Transnational Actors and International Organizations in Global Politics' in J Baylis and S Smith (eds), *The Globalization of World Politics* (OUP, Oxford, 1997) 287.

have adapted to this shift of regulatory activities from the national to the international level. Many formerly domestic NGOs have 'internationalized' in order to maintain their ability to pressure governments and affect policy decisions.[3] As NGOs have become increasingly widely connected and organized into global networks, their visibility has also enhanced.

As suggested in the Cardoso Report on the UN relationship with civil society, globalization engenders the disparity in modern politics that renders traditional forms of representation increasingly less relevant. This is because economics, trade, communications and culture are becoming more global, with more decisions being reached in international forums and organizations, whereas representative democracy remains essentially national and local. The Report suggests that this leads to a radical transformation, namely that:

> Representative democracy, in which citizens periodically elect their representatives across the full spectrum of political issues, is now supplemented by participatory democracy, in which anyone can enter the debates that most interest them, through advocacy, protest and in other ways.[4]

People are using new channels to express their political interests, through global civil-society networks and global social movements. This is why the support for many international policy-oriented NGOs has soared.[5]

Other, related factors for the 'internationalization' of NGOs include:

- The growing number of multinational corporations with world-wide operations—this has entailed the internationalization of actors such as trade unions, consumer groups, environmental organizations, etc, who would like to retain their influence on corporations;
- new developments in telecommunications and information technologies that have made the exchange of information very fast and inexpensive, and have thus facilitated the creation of global information networks—it has become almost as easy for advocacy groups to be global as local; and
- the resultant integration of the world, the increased sense of the inter-

---

[3] See K Nowrot, 'Symposium, The Rule of Law in the Era of Globalization: Legal Consequences of Globalization: The Status of Non-Governmental Organizations under International Law' (1999) 6 Indiana J of Global Legal Studies 579, 586–7.

[4] Report of the Panel of Eminent Persons on United Nations-Civil Society Relations, *We the People, Civil Society, the United Nations and Global Governance* (Cardoso Report) A/58/817 (11 June 2004) para 13, <http://documents-dds-ny.un.org/doc/UNDOC/GEN/N04/376/41/pdf/N0437641.pdf?OpenElement>, visited 15 Aug 2005.

[5] See ibid paras 10–13.

connectedness of human beings, the growing feeling of solidarity and the need for pursuing the public interest on the global level.[6]

The activities of today's international NGOs spread over a vast range of issues including, but not limited to: the environment, economic and social development, labour conditions, human rights, consumer protection, legal and judicial matters, business and industry, international peace and security, women's rights, indigenous peoples, children and youth, health, religion, education, refugees, charity and emergency relief activities. Because many of these issues today increasingly are affected by the activities of international intergovernmental organizations, it is natural that NGOs have been looking for ways to exert influence within these organizations. Diplomacy and international negotiations traditionally have been associated with a higher level of confidentiality and secrecy as compared to domestic politics. Under the growing pressure from NGOs such processes are increasingly confronted with raised expectations regarding transparency and the opportunity they provide for public participation through, inter alia, international NGOs.[7] As a result, both intergovernmental organizations such as the United Nations and the foreign ministries of individual States are now increasingly accustomed (however reluctantly) to the presence of NGOs wherever diplomatic agendas are being set, foreign policies implemented, treaties negotiated, or compliance monitored.[8] The growing presence and importance of NGOs at global and national levels has motivated both national governments and global institutions to establish more formal mechanisms for listening and responding to claims made from within civil society.[9] Raustalia suggested that:

> NGOs have been increasingly incorporated into what were previously 'states only' governance activities, and the scope, type, and scale of their activities are much greater today then ever before. This shift in

---

[6] See Nowrot (n 3) 587–9.

[7] See D Wirth, 'Public Participation in International Processes: Environmental Case Studies at the National and International Levels' (1996) 7 Colorado J of Intl Environmental L & Policy 1, 1–5.

[8] See DC Thomas, 'International NGOs, State Sovereignty, and Democratic Values' (2001) 2 Chinese J of Intl L 389.

[9] According to Kathryn Sikkink, many NGOs exercise soft power within international organizations even without being formal actors. She calls this influence 'hidden'—not in the sense of being illicit or secret but rather in the sense of being informal or behind the scenes. Even NGOs with formal consultative status carry out roles above and beyond the roles envisaged for NGOs with such status. See K Sikkink, 'Restructuring World Politics: The Limits and Asymmetries of Soft Power' in S Khagram, J Riker, and K Sikkink (eds), *Restructuring World Politics: Transnational Social Movements, Networks and Norms* (University of Minnesota Press, Minneapolis, 2002) 304–5.

both formal and informal participation represents a notable evolution when contrasted with historical practice.[10]

Other authors, however, have observed that there is 'a paradox between the unquestioning acceptance of the importance of NGOs in international life, and the meager formal recognition and provisions for their influence in international institutions'.[11] NGOs have, indeed, been allowed certain forms of access and participation (to be analysed below) that make them increasingly visible and important players in the process of international cooperation. NGOs are justly credited with raising national and international awareness and with opening international organizations to the scrutiny of public opinion. However, as John Gamble and Charlotte Ku noted, 'NGOs have had difficulty finding a seat at the table of authoritative decision-making'.[12] In other words, while NGOs play an important role in decision-making, both through their influence on governments and international organizations, and by providing information, they have certainly not (yet) attained the function of authoritative decision-maker.[13] In addition, the picture is far from homogeneous because, as discussed below, NGO involvement differs substantially from one international organization to another.

The Cardoso Report stated that:

> Effective engagement with civil society and other constituencies is no longer an option—it is a necessity in order for the United Nations to meet its objectives and remain relevant in the twenty-first century. [14]

As Jan Scholte confirmed, '[a] broad consensus has by now emerged that civil society bodies and global governance institutions should have relations with each other'. [15] However, Scholte also noted that 'there is far less clarity, let alone agreement, on how these relations should be conducted, and to what ends'.[16]

II. WHAT IS AN NGO?

It is not the purpose of this study to engage in the long quest for the definition of the term 'non-governmental organization'. Rather than looking for

---

[10] Raustiala (n 1) 542. [11] Sikkink (n 9) 304.
[12] JK Gamble and C Ku, 'International Law—New Actors and New Technologies: Center Stage for NGOs?' (2000) 31 L and Policy in Int Business 221, 236–7.
[13] See ibid. [14] Cardoso Report (n 4) para 38.
[15] JA Scholte, 'The WTO and Civil Society' in S McGuire and B Hocking (eds), *Trade Politics* (2nd edn, Routledge, London, 2004) 147.
[16] ibid.

a precise and comprehensive definition—which, in view of the number of competing definitions, is a daunting task—this study has opted for identifying the most characteristic features of NGOs.

The difficulty in giving one uniform definition stems from the fact that there are a great variety of organizations that are, strictly speaking, 'non-governmental'. The term itself is constructed as negative—'*non*-governmental'—which contrasts NGOs with entities created by States. This reflects the history of the term's conception. After the term was introduced in the UN Charter, the UN Economic and Social Council (ECOSOC) defined it to mean 'any international organization which is not established by inter-governmental agreement'.[17] Moreover, the term was intended by ECOSOC to designate only those organizations having consultative status with the United Nations.[18] However, with time, the term became popularly used also to refer to organizations that did not have UN consultative status.

Several international institutions treat NGOs as one type of civil society organization (CSO). Others use the term NGOs as a synonym of CSOs. To clarify, civil society is usually seen as a social sphere separate from both the State and market. The increasingly accepted understanding of the term 'civil society organizations' is that of non-State, non-profit, voluntary organizations formed by people within the social sphere of civil society. They cover a variety of organizational interests and forms, ranging from formal organizations registered with authorities to informal social movements rallying around a common cause, including faith-based associations, labour movements, local community groups, indigenous peoples' organizations, philanthropic foundations, research institutions, think tanks and others. CSOs do not include, however, political parties, sub-national authorities, commercial media and for-profit entities. The term NGO is also commonly used to describe non-State, non-profit, voluntary organizations. However, contrary to many CSOs, they usually have a formal structure and are, in most cases, registered with national authorities.

Although there is 'no generally accepted definition of an NGO and the term carries different connotations in different circumstances',[19] the main features usually ascribed to NGOs in literature include the following:

- NGOs are not established by States but, rather, formed at the initiative of private, natural or juridical persons (voluntarily). They are, therefore, part of 'civil society'.

---

[17] UN ESCOR, ESC Res 288B, 10th Sess, Supp No 1 (1950) 25. Before the UN Charter and the ECOSOC definition, international NGOs were called international associations, institutes, unions or simply organizations. See P Willetts, 'What is a Non-Governmental Organization?' (2002), <http://www.staff.city.ac.uk/p.willetts/CS-NTWKS/NGO-ART.HTM>, visited 15 Aug 2005.
[18] On NGO consultative status with the UN see below, pp 19–49.
[19] Willetts (n 17).

- Following logically from the first feature, a further characteristic element of an NGO is its general independence from governmental influence.[20]
- The objectives of NGOs are mostly public in nature, such as, for example, poverty alleviation or protection of the environment. At the same time, many NGOs represent a more narrow set of private interests (for example, industry associations).
- NGOs do not pursue the objective of earning profit. This feature distinguishes NGOs from corporations, which are profit-oriented economic entities. At the same time, NGOs may have self-earned income to finance their main activities.[21]
- NGOs cannot be constituted as political parties; they do not seek political power as political parties do.
- It is usually affirmed that an NGO must be generally law-abiding, in order to exclude from their ranks terrorist or organized criminal groups.[22]

The list of features above is not meant to be exhaustive or definitive. It is intended to provide a better picture of the examined phenomenon. Additionally, to a certain extent these features reflect the ECOSOC conditions for recognition of organizations as NGOs, thus generating not only theoretical, but also practical value.[23] At the same time, other international organizations may have somewhat different definitions of what constitutes an NGO.[24]

NGOs do not have special legal status under international law. There are no regulations under international law governing the establishment,

---

[20] See S Hobe, 'Global Challenges to Statehood: The Increasingly Important Role of Nongovernmental Organizations' (1997) 5 Indiana J of Global Legal Studies 191, 194.

[21] Traditionally, membership dues have provided the main source, but today NGOs tap many other sources including grants or contracts from governments and international institutions, fees for services, profits from sales of goods and funding from private foundations, corporations and wealthy individuals. Public grants represented 1.5 per cent of NGO income in 1970 and 35 per cent in 1988. Such grants probably accounted for more than 40 per cent of NGO income by the end of the century. This trend inevitably exposes NGOs to pressure from governments and limits their capacity to act independently. See J Paul, 'NGOs and Global Policy-Making' (June 2000), <http://www.globalpolicy.org/ngos/analysis/anal00.htm>, visited 1 Oct 2005.

[22] For a more detailed discussion of these and some other features, see Nowrot (n 3) 615–20.

[23] The ECOSOC conditions for recognition and accreditation are discussed in more detail below, see p pp 30–5.

[24] For a brief account of definitions of the term 'NGO' applied by different international institutions see Ecologic and FIELD, *Participation of Non-Governmental Organisations in International Environmental Governance: Legal Basis and Practical Experience* (2002) 22–5, <http://www.ecologic.de/download/projekte/1850-1899/1890/report_ngos_en.pdf>, visited 15 Aug 2005.

requirements and legal status of NGOs. Several attempts at drafting a multilateral treaty on NGOs have been made, but all of them failed because of the lack of the consent of States.[25] Being created by private, natural or legal persons, NGOs are governed by national laws of the State in which they have been established and where they are based. Consequently, there is no uniform legal regime for international NGOs; their recognition, rights and duties depend on the respective national conditions.[26] In this respect, the gap between the international activism of NGOs and their legal standing in terms of international rights and duties is growing.[27]

III. MAIN TYPES OF NGOS

There is a large number, as well as a great variety of NGOs active on the international plane. According to the *Yearbook of International Organizations*, the number of NGOs was already as high as 44,000 in 1999.[28] For the same year, the World Bank—employing different criteria—estimated that were about 26,000 international NGOs.[29] These high numbers are explained by the vast range of issues covered and interests represented by NGOs. The latter also explains the great variety of NGOs. As James Paul put it:

> In addition to the great organizations dealing with human rights, environmental protection and humanitarian assistance, there are NGOs representing industry associations like soap and chemicals, narrowly zealous religious organizations and advocates of obscure causes like Esperanto and space colonization. While some NGOs are fiercely independent, others are known as the creatures of governments, businesses or even criminal interests. Some have hundreds of thousands of members around the world while others speak for only a handful of people. Some have large central secretariats and some are very decentralized. With such diversity, generalizations about NGOs can be difficult.[30]

---

[25] See K Martens, 'Examining the Non-Status of NGOs in International Law' (2003) 10 Indiana J of Global Legal Studies 1, 20.

[26] See ibid 21.

[27] See M Noortmann, 'Non-State Actors in International Law' in B Arts, M Noortmann, and B Reinalda (eds), *Non-State Actors in International Relations* (Ashgate, Aldershot, 2001) 71.

[28] See *Yearbook of International Organizations*, 1999–2000, 550.

[29] See *Working Together: World Bank–Civil Society Relations* (The World Bank, Washington, DC, 2003) 22. The World Bank also indicated an increase in the numbers of international NGOs between 1990 and 1999 from 6,000 to 26,000.

[30] J Paul, 'NGOs and Global Policy-Making' (June 2000), <http://www.globalpolicy.org/ngos/analysis/anal00.htm>, visited 1 Oct 2005.

There are three common classifications of NGOs. First, NGOs can be classified according to their primary aims, interests or motivations. For example, business and industry NGOs (BINGOs) represent the interests of a certain economic sector; public interest NGOs (PINGOs) pursue more general interests (improvement of healthcare and education, peace, global economic fairness and reduction of poverty, humanitarian assistance in emergencies, etc). Professional associations, trade unions, religious groups, scientific organizations, etc—all of them have a particular interest, or a group of interests they work towards. Due to such variety, it is common to have strong divisions, clashes, and conflicts among NGOs.

Secondly, NGOs can be local (grassroots, or community-based), national or international in nature. International organizations mainly engage with international NGOs, although there are exceptions. An NGO is normally considered international if it has members or branches in more than one country and if its objectives are not limited to one State.[31] Frequently NGOs become international through the formation of umbrella organizations made of national/local NGOs (federations with national chapters, for example, Oxfam International). Others may acquire a centralized structure with local offices accountable to a central body (for example, Greenpeace). Networks and coalitions of NGOs without a formal umbrella organization are not considered international NGOs.

Thirdly, one can make a distinction between operational (or service provision) NGOs and advocacy (or campaigning) NGOs. Operational NGOs provide relief in emergencies, primary healthcare, non-formal education, housing, legal services and micro-credit, as well as training to other service providers. Advocacy includes lobbying, as well as public mobilization and campaigning around particular issues such as debt relief or the protection of tropical rainforests.[32] To look at it from a different angle, operational NGOs aim at small-scale change achieved directly through projects, while advocacy NGOs work towards a large-scale change indirectly through influence on the political system.[33] Frequently, NGOs combine the two types of activities.

[31] Under another definition, an international NGO is the one that has a decision-making structure with voting members from at least three countries, and whose aims are cross-national and/or international in scope. See S Khagram, J Riker, and K Sikkink, 'From Santiago to Seattle: Transnational Advocacy Groups Restructuring World Politics' in Khagram, Riker, and Sikkink (n 9) 6. International organizations may have their own definitions of international NGOs.

[32] See M Kaldor, 'Civil Society and Accountability' (2003) 4 J of Human Development 5, 16.

[33] See Willetts (n 17).

IV. ROLES AND FUNCTIONS OF NGOS

Roles that NGOs can play in the context of world politics and global governance are numerous. NGOs create and mobilize networks, gather information on local conditions and mount pressure both within States and transnationally. They may serve as sources of information and technical expertise on particular issues, enhance public participation, mobilize individuals and groups to undertake political action and/or monitor government and corporate behaviour. They influence political discourse, push issues onto national and international agendas, strive to participate in decision-making and in the creation of new norms, as well as in monitoring their implementation, and the settlement of international disputes.

In order to play these and other roles, NGOs need access to the places where States endeavour to achieve consensus on norms and principles, agree on the texts of treaties and conventions, coordinate policies, resolve disputes, and allocate resources to implement programmes and activities. Often these activities take place within the framework of international organizations.[34] Functions of NGOs in the context of their involvement with international organizations may be broadly classified as follows:

1. Participation in policy deliberations and decision-making processes of international organizations by advocating their interests and by providing expert knowledge and advice (including molding the treaty language in the course of international negotiations).
2. Participation in planning, implementing and monitoring of projects undertaken/financed by international organizations (policy implementation).
3. Monitoring compliance and implementation of international commitments undertaken by States (compliance monitoring).
4. Participation in dispute settlement procedures within the framework of international organizations.

A somewhat different, more detailed classification of functions, activities and channels of NGO influence can be found, in table form, in the 2002 Report by Ecologic and FIELD on 'Participation of Non-Governmental Organisations in International Environmental Governance'. This excellent classification is relevant not only for environmental governance, but for other fields of international governance as well, and is worthy of reproducing in full.

---

[34] See M Karns and K Mingst, *International Organizations: The Politics and Processes of Global Governance* (Lynne Rienner Publishers, Boulder, CO, 2004) 230.

Table 1: Functions, Activities and Channels of Influence of NGOs in International Environmental Cooperation Functions: Illustrative List of Activities and Channels of Influence[35]

Functions	Illustrative List of Activities and Channels of Influence
Enhancing the knowledge base (science, policy and law)	• gather, compile and disseminate information • conduct and publish studies and reports • distribute information and organize side-events at major conferences
Advocacy and lobbying[36]	• informal contacts with government delegates (side-events, workshops, conferences, in the corridors, modern telecommunication technology) • formal participation in inter-governmental negotiations (official written submissions, unofficial written position papers, statements in meetings) • provision of advice to 'friendly' delegations • campaigns outside the negotiating arena (e.g. media and public information, protests) to enhance influence
Membership in national delegations	• receipt of inside information about governmental negotiations • provision of advice to governments • negotiate on behalf of governments
Contribution to compliance review and enforcement as well as dispute settlement procedures	• submission of *amicus curiae* briefs • provision of information on implementation/alerting delegations and institutions of non-compliance
Ensuring transparency	• reports from negotiations • 'naming and shaming' of laggard countries • public relations work (media) • reports on effectiveness of implementation
Supporting international secretariats	• provide Secretariat functions • provide advice and expertise to Secretariats
Broader functions of NGOs in international environmental governance	• shaping the opinions of individuals and groups (campaigns and training) • co-operation between environmental groups and business and industry • networking, including integrating levels of governance • 'globalisation' of values and preferences

[35] Ecologic and FIELD (n 24) 52.
[36] For an alternative useful list of NGO advocacy and lobbying activities see B Arts, 'The Impact of Environmental NGOs on International Conventions' in Arts, Noortmann and Reinalda (n 27) 199–200.

The Report notes that the identified NGO activities go 'far beyond' the opportunities formally provided for in the relevant rules of international organizations.[37] The exact content of these rules and relevant practices with regard to different international institutions will be analysed in the chapters that follow.

V. PROS AND CONS OF NGO INVOLVEMENT[38]

There are valid arguments both in favour and against the participation of NGOs in international governance, especially policy-making. Summarizing the abundant literature and research on this issue, the four main arguments *in favour* of NGO involvement are the following:

1. NGO participation enhances the decision-making process because NGOs provide information, arguments and perspectives that governments do not bring forward. NGOs have a wealth of specialized knowledge, resources and analytical capacity. As Daniel Esty noted, NGOs can and should function as 'intellectual competitors' to governments in the quest for optimal policies.[39] In fact, governments often lack the resources and specific expertise necessary to investigate certain issues. NGOs may frequently be of help, enhancing the resources and expertise available and, thereby, enriching the policy debate.
2. NGO participation increases the legitimacy of international organizations as NGOs are seen to introduce elements of democratic governance by representing the interests of a global constituency. Some consider NGOs the conscience of international civil society, and public confidence in international organizations increases when NGOs have the opportunity to observe and be heard in the policy deliberation and decision-making processes. NGOs contribute to ensuring that decisions result from the open and transparent exchange of rational arguments rather than from shady bargaining. Moreover, NGOs can play an important role in disseminating information at the national level, ensuring broader public support and understanding.
3. Certain transnational interests and concerns may not be adequately represented by any national government. By involving NGOs in their deliberations and processes, international organizations are more likely

---

[37] See ibid 51.
[38] This section draws upon P Van den Bossche, *The Law and Policy of the World Trade Organization* (CUP, Cambridge, 2005) 156–7.
[39] See D Esty, 'Non-Governmental Organizations at the World Trade Organization: Cooperation, Competition, or Exclusion' (1998) 1 J of Intl Economic L 123, 136.

to hear about important issues which national governments have less interest in putting on the agenda.

4. Civil society participation in the debate at the national level is only an option among those States with open and democratic processes at the national level. Hearing NGOs at international organizations can compensate for the fact that NGOs are not always and everywhere heard at the national level.

There are also four main arguments *against* the involvement of NGOs in the activities of international organizations:

1. NGO involvement may lead to the capture of the policy-making process by special interests.[40] NGOs seeking access to international organizations are often entities representing special interests, not the interests of the general public. By allowing for the participation of NGOs in the work of international organizations, special interests may gain undue influence.

2. NGOs may lack necessary legitimacy, meaning that they are neither accountable to an electorate nor representative in a general way. NGOs typically advocate relatively narrow interests. Unlike governments, they do not balance all of society's interests. It is legitimate to ask questions regarding the actual constituency of an NGO.

3. The involvement of NGOs in the work of international organizations may contribute to the marginalization of developing countries in some international organizations. NGOs, and in particular NGOs focusing on environmental or labour issues, regularly take positions that developing countries consider to be inimical to their (short- and medium-term) interests. Moreover, NGOs of industrialized countries tend to be better organized and financed than NGOs of developing countries. Allowing for NGO participation may thus tilt the negotiating balance (further) to the disadvantage of developing countries.[41]

4. NGO involvement makes decision-making in large international organizations, which is already very difficult, even more challenging. In the language of the Cardoso Report, '[i]f the United Nations brought everyone relevant into each debate, it would have endless meetings without conclusion. And governments would find other forums for negotiations, as they already do in the areas of trade and economics'.[42]

---

[40] See J Dunoff, 'The Misguided Debate over NGO Participation at the WTO' (1998) 1 J of Intl Economic L 433, 437.

[41] It should be noted, however, that NGOs from developed countries may also work in coalition with developing countries and support these countries in the realization of their policy objectives.

[42] Cardoso Report (n 4) 23.

As summarized in a 2003 Background Paper for the Cardoso Report, the well-handled involvement of NGOs:

> enhances the quality of decision-making, increases ownership of the decisions, improves accountability and transparency of the process and enriches outcomes through a variety of views and experiences. But—handled badly—it can confuse choices, hamper the intergovernmental search for common ground, erode the privacy needed for sensitive discussions, over-crowd agendas and present distractions at important meetings.[43]

Consequently, the challenge for international organizations and NGOs is to build the kind of relationship that will maximize the benefits and minimize the drawbacks. The chapters to follow provide the information for analysis of whether and how the existing rules and practices for NGO involvement contribute to finding this proper balance.

VI. THE PROBLEM OF NGO LEGITIMACY

A close reading of the pros and cons of NGO involvement in international governance reveals that the term 'legitimacy' appears under both headings. On the one hand, NGOs as representatives of 'global civil society' are considered to enhance the legitimacy of international decision-making through broader public participation and the promotion of transparency. On the other hand, NGOs themselves are often said to lack the legitimacy necessary to claim participatory rights in international institutions.

Whom do NGOs represent? Who appoints them as spokespersons for world society? To whom are they accountable? These questions turn on the issues of legitimacy. Governments distinguish themselves from NGOs by pointing to their legitimacy as (elected) representatives of the people to whom they are accountable, and for whom they are responsible. Governments sometimes prefer to present NGOs as organizations with 'narrow, self-serving interests ... driven by the personal egos and ambitions of a few frustrated individuals'.[44]

When analysed, the two main problems with NGO legitimacy relate to an apparent lack of (1) a democratic mandate and 'representativity'; and (2)

---

[43] *UN System and Civil Society: An Inventory and Analysis of Practices*, Background Paper for the Secretary-General's Panel of Eminent Persons on United Nations Relations with Civil Society (May 2003) Introduction, <http://www.un.org/reform/pdfs/hlp9.htm>, visited 7 Sept 2005.

[44] H Agam, 'Working with NGOs: A Developing World Perspective' (2002) 13 Colorado J of Intl Environmental L & Policy 39, 42.

internal democracy, transparency and public accountability. Analysis of these arguable deficiencies falls outside the scope of this study.[45] Suffice it to say that the picture is not black and white, and that arguably mechanisms exist to ensure NGOs' legitimacy, although in a manner different from democratic States.[46]

To a large extent, the problem of legitimacy stems from the great variety of NGOs in existence. As noted by Paul Wapner, '[t]o be an NGO these days, it seems one needs only a fax machine and internet access'.[47] At the same time, the world knows NGOs with memberships outnumbering the populations of many States, and with democratic inner structures. NGOs of the latter type would seem to have more political legitimacy than those of the former. As will be seen below, many international organizations, when establishing the criteria for NGO accreditation, take this into account and include criteria (particularly concerning the internal governance of NGOs) that ensure a certain 'degree' of legitimacy.[48] For example, as stated in the Cardoso Report, it would be reasonable to:

> expect the UN Secretariat to ensure that actors engaging in their deliberative processes meet at least some basic standards of governance and demonstrate their credentials, whether they are based on experience, expertise, membership or a base of support.[49]

The rules and practices of international organizations on engagement with NGOs contribute to the enhancement of regulatory legitimacy of NGO involvement.[50] Moreover, looking from a different angle, the very fact that international organizations (and, therefore, States) formally recognize NGOs helps to promote their legitimacy.

---

[45] For such analysis see, for example, Ecologic and FIELD (n 24) 217–23.

[46] For the defence of NGOs' accountability see P Wapner, 'The Democratic Accountability of Non-Governmental Organizations: Defending Accountability in NGOs' (2002) 3 Chinese J of Intl L 197, 197–205. See also M Kaldor (n 32) 20–6; and M Edwards, 'NGOs and International Economic Policy-Making: Rights and Responsibilities in the Global Arena' (2001) 2 World Economics 127.

[47] P Wapner, 'The Democratic Accountability of Non-Governmental Organizations: Introductory Essay: Paradise Lost? NGOs and Global Accountability' (2002) 3 Chinese J of Intl L 155, 157.

[48] See below, p 32.

[49] Cardoso Report (n 4) para 18.

[50] See also P Van den Bossche, 'Regulatory Legitimacy of the Role of NGOs in Global Governance: Legal Status and Accreditation' in A Vedder, P Van den Bossche, V Collingwood, A van Gorp, M Kamminga, L Logister, and C Prins, *NGO Involvement in International Governance and Policy: Sources of Legitimacy.* (Brill/Martinus Nijhoff, Leiden, forthcoming).

VII. THE PLACE OF NGOS IN INTERNATIONAL GOVERNANCE

As outlined above, the emergence of NGOs as international actors poses the problem of constructing an adequate place for them in international governance, and, particularly, within international institutions. When approaching this subject, one should bear in mind the existing distinction between formal and informal ways of NGO participation. This study will mainly focus on formal means of involvement, although it recognizes that often the 'informal' strategies used by NGOs to promote their goals may be even more important and successful. Informal means include direct personal appeals to, and contacts with, responsible decision-makers in international organizations and national governments, as well as circulation of expert documents and proposals, etc.[51] Among proponents of enlarging the opportunities for NGOs to become officially recognized within intergovernmental organizations there is recognition that the informal strategies used by NGOs have a strong influence on decision-making.[52] However, as pointed out in one report on NGO participation, 'informal practices have an inherent danger of being easily eroded in future'.[53] As this report suggests, formalization of the rules governing NGO participation and providing a legal basis would prevent the rights gained over the last decade from being weakened by States attempting to limit NGO involvement in international governance.[54] Furthermore, as suggested above, formalization of NGO status within the relevant international bodies makes their participation more legitimate.

Although the international system remains State based, the growth of powerful non-State actors has placed a greater demand on international organizations to accommodate their interests and improve collaboration with them. However, the ways in which this State-based system is to integrate non-State actors is a hotly debated topic. The main viewpoints on formal NGO involvement can be divided into two competing schools of thought, the 'accommodationists' and the 'restrictionists'.[55]

The accommodationist school wants greater NGO participation in the international system. They believe an increased role would lead to better international governance. Some theorists of this school go so far as to

---

[51] See Nowrot (n 3) 594–5; and W Schoener, 'Non-Governmental Organizations and Global Activism: Legal and Informal Approaches' (1997) 4 Indiana J of Global Legal Studies 537, 550–1.
[52] See Schoener, ibid 552.
[53] Ecologic and FIELD (n 24) 9.
[54] See ibid.
[55] See JA Hartwick, 'Non-Governmental Organizations at United Nations-Sponsored World Conferences: A Framework for Participation Reform' (2003) 26 Loyola of Los Angeles Intl & Comparative L Rev 217, 243–50.

suggest that NGOs should be on an equal ground with States and inter-governmental institutions (including the UN General Assembly) and should have voting rights on a par with States. This view is radical and politically impracticable as States are unlikely to permit such a dramatic increase in NGO power any time soon. The more moderate accommoda-tionists argue simply for a fuller integration of NGOs into the system of international governance. To achieve this, they propose granting NGOs some form of legal personality, more participatory rights (including the right to make written and oral statements in the relevant fora) and the right to file *amicus curiae* submissions in international tribunals.[56] Accommodationists argue that integration would permit better use of NGO expertise, increase accountability, and further NGO legitimacy in the world order.

Contrary to the adherents of the accommodationist school, restriction-ists maintain that NGOs are a problem for a State-centric international system, and that they may disrupt and impede the international decision-making processes (mostly, for the reasons indicated above as 'cons' of NGO involvement). They argue, therefore, that NGOs should be constrained. Restrictionists suggest, for example, that an NGO complaint system (for governments to document alleged abuse of position by NGOs) should be instituted, that NGO accreditation should be limited, as should access to meetings and participatory rights, and that NGO participation on State delegations should be prohibited.[57]

It is not the purpose of this study to argue for or against one of these schools of thought. Instead, the perspective taken here attempts to reflect a realistic point of view. It is hardly disputable that in spite of the increasing influence of NGOs, States are and will continue to be the principal actors on the world stage, at least for the foreseeable future. It is also evident that States are generally reluctant to share power with non-State actors such as NGOs since this diminishes State power. The desire of NGOs to have greater acceptance, influence and access to international institutions places them on a collision course with States, as States fear an encroachment on their power and sovereignty.[58] It is important to bear in mind that the rules of NGO participation in international institutions are set by States. Therefore, one may hardly expect a fast leap forward in terms of NGO participation. Rather, what one would expect is the gradual enhancement of NGO involvement in various international fora through a series of small

---

[56] See, for example, PJ Spiro, 'The Democratic Accountability of Non-Governmental Organizations: Accounting for NGOs' (2002) 3 Chinese J of Intl L 161, 167; Nowrot (n 3) 614.
[57] See Hartwick (n 55) 250–70.
[58] See Spiro (n 56) 166–7.

concessions from States under pressure from global civil society. The probability of such development is evidenced by the current trend and further demonstrated by the status of NGOs within various international institutions as documented in this study.

CHAPTER 2

United Nations Economic and Social Council (UN ECOSOC)

I. LEGAL AND INSTITUTIONAL FRAMEWORK

A. Scope of NGO Involvement in UN Activities

Currently there are four primary ways of formal UN–NGO cooperation:[1]

- NGOs may obtain consultative status with ECOSOC (engagement in policy deliberations).
- NGOs may be accredited to particular UN conferences (policy deliberations with a possible follow-up/implementation stage)
- NGOs may establish relations with particular UN programmes or specialized agencies (policy deliberations and project implementation).
- NGOs may become associated with the UN Department of Public Information (DPI) (dissemination of information).

The first three ways of involvement are reviewed in this study.[2] NGO association with the UN DPI is not addressed because this type of association does not entail NGO involvement in policy deliberations, project implementation or dispute settlement.[3]

The only article in the UN Charter that deals with NGO involvement is Article 71. This Article states:

> The Economic and Social Council may make suitable arrangements for consultation with non-governmental organizations which are concerned with matters within its competence. Such arrangements

---

[1] See UN Secretariat, Department of Economic and Social Affairs, NGO Section, *Guidelines for Association between the United Nations and Non-Governmental Organizations (NGOs)* (undated) 3, <http://www.un.org/esa/coordination/ngo/>, visited 7 Sept 2005.

[2] ECOSOC relations with NGOs are discussed immediately below. The review of NGO participation in UN conferences can be found in this chapter under a separate heading (see p 44). For information on NGO involvement with other UN programmes and specialized agencies (UNEP, UNCTAD, WIPO, etc) see separate chapters of this handbook.

[3] For information on NGO association with the UN DPI see the DPI website at <http://www.un.org/dpi/ngosection/index.html>; see also UN Secretariat, *Guidelines for Association* (n 1) 12–15.

may be made with international organizations and, where appropriate, with national organizations after consultation with the Member of the United Nations concerned.

Article 71 is found in Chapter X of the UN Charter, 'Economic and Social Council'. Taken together with the language of the provision, this has two important legal consequences for the scope of the application of Article 71.

First, Article 71 is limited to 'matters within the competence' of the Economic and Social Council (hereinafter, ECOSOC, or the Council). In other words, Article 71 limits NGO involvement only to the activities of the ECOSOC itself. Article 71 *cannot* be interpreted to mean that ECOSOC may make suitable arrangements for NGO participation in the work of the other UN organs, in particular, the UN General Assembly—an organ with general competence to debate all issues falling within the ambit of the UN Charter, and the Security Council.[4] There have been calls for formal recognition of NGO involvement beyond economic and social matters; this idea was also supported in the Cardoso Report.[5]

Secondly, Article 71 does not apply to other UN organizations and specialized agencies. They have their own arrangements for relations with NGOs. Nonetheless, it is considered that Article 71 set a benchmark for other UN agencies.[6] The latter generally have a formal consultative system for engagement with NGOs similar to that of ECOSOC, but work with a smaller number of more specialized NGOs. In recent years, many UN organizations have been undertaking reviews of their relations with NGOs.[7]

---

[4] Over time practice has evolved to allow a certain degree of informal participation by NGOs in the work of the General Assembly's main committees and several of its subsidiary bodies, as well as in special sessions of the Assembly. For a useful review of modalities of NGO participation in special sessions of the General Assembly in the late 1990s, see United Nations, *Reference document on the participation of civil society in United Nations conferences and special sessions of the General Assembly during the 1990s*, version 1 (August 2001) prepared by the Office of the President of the Millennium Assembly, 55th session of the United Nations General Assembly, sections 13–20, <http://www.un.org/ga/president/55/speech/civilsociety1.htm>, visited 10 Sept 2005. However, these practices lack the degree of legitimacy that NGOs enjoy in their relation with ECOSOC without a clear legal basis in the UN Charter.

[5] See Report of the Panel of Eminent Persons on United Nations-Civil Society Relations, *We the People, Civil Society, the United Nations and Global Governance* (Cardoso Report), A/58/817 (11 June 2004) para 124, <http://documents-dds-ny.un.org/doc/UNDOC/GEN/N04/376/41/pdf/N0443764.1.pdf?OpenElement>, visited 15 Aug 2005.

[6] See S Charnovitz, 'Two Centuries of Participation: NGOs and International Governance' (1997) 18 Michigan J of Intl L 183, 253.

[7] See T Hill, 'UNCTAD and NGOs: An Evolving Cooperation' in *UNCTAD–Civil Society Dialogue on Selected Development Issues Being Addressed by the United Nations System* (United Nations, New York, 2002) 56.

B. Economic and Social Council

The Cardoso Report confirmed that ECOSOC is the major gateway for the entry of civil society into the United Nations.[8] ECOSOC oversees the work of the UN on economic and social questions. Also, the UN's work on human rights and on the environment comes under its mandate. The Council meets in regular sessions twice a year and in special sessions when the majority of its members so requests.

ECOSOC was constituted in 1946 as a relatively small executive council of 18 governments, elected by the General Assembly. In 1965 it was expanded to 27 members and in 1971 expanded further to 54 members. This growing expansion of the Council has made it too large to act as an effective executive. The Council is able to effectively review broad policy questions but because of its size it has difficulty negotiating the details of policy implementation. Most of the Council's resolutions and decisions repeat the exact texts, or slightly amend the texts, as recommended by its subsidiary organs.[9]

Among ECOSOC subsidiary organs, there are functional commissions, each dealing with a single policy domain (for example, the Commission on Human Rights and the Commission on Sustainable Development). Additionally, there are five regional commissions on a continental basis (for example, Economic Commission for Africa). A myriad of intergovernmental committees and committees of experts have been added to these two types of commissions.

One of the ECOSOC subsidiary organs—the Committee on Non-Governmental Organizations (the NGO Committee)—specifically deals with matters of ECOSOC relations with NGOs. In fact, it is the only intergovernmental Committee in the UN that focuses exclusively on relations with NGOs. It consists of 19 Member States elected by ECOSOC on the basis of equitable geographical representation with a term of office of four years.[10] The Committee's decisions are considered recommendations, often in the form of draft decisions calling for action by the Council. The Committee meets annually for three weeks. These three weeks of meetings are usually divided into two sessions—one (regular) in January and the other (resumed) in May. When in session, and also before sessions, the NGO Committee may also meet informally. Sometimes, informal meetings

---

[8] See Cardoso Report (n 5) para 122.
[9] See P Willetts, 'NGOs and the Structure of the United Nations System' in P Willetts (ed), *The Conscience of the World: The Influence of Non-Governmental Organisations in the UN System* (The Brookings Institution, Washington, DC, 1996) 280.
[10] Currently, the Committee consists of representatives of five African States; four Asian States; two Eastern European States; four Latin American and Caribbean States; and four Western European and other States. Terms of reference of the NGO Committee are contained in Part IX of the ECOSOC Resolution 1996/31.

include only members of the Bureau of the NGO Committee, that is, the chairperson and four vice-chairpersons of the Committee—this format facilitates discussions and effective consensus building.[11] Technical support to the NGO Committee is provided by the NGO Section of the Department of Economic and Social Affairs, a unit of the UN Secretariat.[12]

C. ECOSOC Resolution 1996/31

Pursuant to its mandate under Article 71, ECOSOC adopted on 25 July 1996 the currently applicable Resolution 1996/31 on the 'Consultative Relationship between the United Nations and Non-Governmental Organizations'.[13] The Resolution establishes three types of consultative relationships that NGOs may enter into, enumerates participatory rights enjoyed by NGOs in ECOSOC and its subsidiary organs, sets out NGO accreditation criteria, lays down rules for NGO participation in UN conferences, provides for suspension and withdrawal of consultative status and sets out other rules on ECOSOC relations with NGOs.

Resolution 1996/31 updated the arrangements earlier set out in Resolution 1296 (XLIV) of 23 May 1968. Most importantly, the updated rules opened the UN process to national NGOs. Before, under the Resolution of 1968, only international NGOs could be admitted. Although some other minor pro-NGO innovations were introduced in 1996 (see below), the dichotomy that had characterized the presence of civil society in the UN system—willingness of the Member States to allow participation on the one hand and their desire to keep it firmly under control on the other—persisted.[14]

Resolution 1996/31 defines an NGO as any 'organization that is not established by a governmental entity or intergovernmental agreement ... including organizations that accept members designated by governmental authorities, provided that such membership does not interfere with the free expression of views of the organization'.[15] Thus, ECOSOC adopted a definition with a very broad scope—in particular, it does not exclude profit-

[11] Information from the NGO Section of the Department of Economic and Social Affairs, 17 Jan 2006.
[12] The NGO Section maintains a website which contains information and documents relevant to ECOSOC relations with NGOs, see <http://www.un.org/esa/coordination.ngo/>, visited 7 Sept 2005.
[13] UN Economic and Social Council, *Consultative Relationship between the United Nations and non-governmental organizations* Res 1996/31 (25 July 1996) E/1996/31, <http://www.un.org/documents/ecosoc/res/1996/eres1996-31.htm>, visited 2 Apr 2005. See also Appendix I to this book, p 225.
[14] See *UN System and Civil Society: An Inventory and Analysis of Practices*, Background Paper for the Secretary-General's Panel of Eminent Persons on United Nations Relations with Civil Society (May 2003), <http://www.un.org/reform/pdfs/hlp9.htm>, visited 7 Sept 2005.
[15] ECOSOC Resolution 1996/31 (n 13) para 12.

making organizations. However, the substantive requirements for granting consultative status to NGOs established by the Resolution somewhat narrow the circle of eligible organizations—in particular, the 'funding requirement' effectively excludes profit-making entities.[16]

Article 71 of the UN Charter refers to 'consultation' with NGOs, and accordingly, Resolution 1996/31 provides for the granting of 'consultative status' to NGOs. According to Resolution 1996/31, the purpose of consultative arrangements is dual: (1) to enable the Council to secure expert information or advice from organizations that have special competence in the relevant subjects; and (2) to enable NGOs representing important elements of public opinion to express their views.[17]

NGOs may be granted one of three types of consultative status: general consultative status, special consultative status, and inclusion on the Roster. Which relationship may be entered into depends on the nature of the NGO concerned, its scope of activity, and the contribution it can be expected to make to the work of the Council. Each type of status corresponds to a certain bundle of rights.[18]

In setting out the principles governing NGO involvement in ECOSOC's work, Resolution 1996/31 makes clear that the rights granted to NGOs, in any type of consultative status, should *not* be the same as the rights pertaining to non-Member States of the Council or the rights of the representatives of UN specialized agencies.[19] The two latter categories can 'participate, without vote' in the deliberations of the Council (Articles 69 and 70 of the UN Charter). Thus, in the conception of Resolution 1996/31, the rights of NGOs may not amount to 'participation without vote'; they constitute something less.

To further shape the role of NGOs in policy deliberations of the Council, the Resolution states that '[t]he arrangements should not be such as to overburden the Council or transform it from a body for coordination of policy and action, as contemplated in the Charter, into a general forum for discussion'.[20] This is ECOSOC's response to the concern that enhanced NGO participation may paralyse the decision-making process.

Guided by the mentioned principles, the ECOSOC has adopted a rather cautious attitude towards the arrangements with NGOs by carefully circumscribing the extent of NGO involvement in the policy deliberations of the Council. This is manifested in the rights afforded to NGOs and the conditions attached to these rights in order to retain ECOSOC's full control over NGO participation.

---

[16] On accreditation criteria see below, pp 30–5.
[17] See ECOSOC Resolution 1996/31 (n 13) para 20.
[18] See below, pp 24–30.
[19] See ECOSOC Resolution 1996/31 (n 13) para 18.
[20] ibid para 19.

The three types of consultative status are reviewed in turn. Rights associated with each type of consultative status are additionally summarized in Table 2 below.[21]

A. General Consultative Status

General consultative status can be requested by any organization that is concerned with most of the activities of ECOSOC and its subsidiary bodies, from which substantive and sustained contributions can be expected, and whose membership is broadly representative of major segments of society in a large number of countries in different regions of the world.[22] The rights and privileges pertaining to this status are the most far-reaching of the three types of consultative relationship. Resolution 1996/31 differentiates between the arrangements for consultation (1) with the Council itself, and (2) with commissions and other subsidiary organs of the Council. Respective NGO rights are slightly different.

As far as the *Council itself* is concerned, an NGO in general consultative status:

- is informed of the provisional agenda of the Council;[23]
- may propose to the NGO Committee that the Committee request the UN Secretary-General to place items of special interest on the provisional agenda of the Council (the NGO cannot make this proposal directly to the Secretary-General);[24]
- may designate representatives to attend public meetings of the Council;[25]
- may submit written statements to be circulated to the members of the Council.[26] Such statements should not exceed 2,000 words; if they do, they should have a summary for circulation. Submissions of more than 2,000 words can still be circulated if either the NGO provides a sufficient number of copies, or upon the specific request of the Council or

---

[21] See p 29.

[22] See ECOSOC Resolution 1996/31(n 13) para 22.

[23] See ibid para 27.

[24] See ibid para 28. Para 62 sets out a non-exhaustive list of points that the NGO Committee must consider when reviewing the request of an NGO. They are: (a) the adequacy of the documentation submitted by the organization; (b) the extent to which it is considered that the item lends itself to early and constructive action by the Council; (c) the possibility that the item might be more appropriately dealt with elsewhere than in the Council. Any decision of the NGO Committee is final unless the Council decides otherwise (para 63).

[25] See ibid para 29.

[26] See ibid para 30.

its NGO Committee. Written statements have to be submitted in sufficient time to give the Secretary-General the possibility to comment on
them. An NGO has to give due consideration to such comments;[27]
- may make oral statements to the Council on particular agenda items
  (if recommended by the NGO Committee and approved by the
  Council).[28] NGOs are heard after government delegates; and
- may present orally to the Council introductory statements of an
  expository nature on items included in the agenda of the Council upon
  the NGO's proposition. The same NGO may further be invited by the
  President of the Council to make, in the course of the discussion, an
  additional oral statement for the purposes of clarification.[29]

With regard to *commissions and other subsidiary organs* of the Council,
Resolution 1996/31 grants NGOs in general consultative status the following rights:

- to be informed of the provisional agenda of the subsidiary organs;[30]
- to propose items for the provisional agenda of commissions (without
  the involvement of the NGO Committee), approval for which must be
  adopted by a two-thirds majority of present commission members);[31]
- to attend public meetings of the subsidiary organs;[32]
- to submit written statements for circulation to members of the
  subsidiary organ concerned. The requirements are similar to those
  relating to written statements for the Council;[33]
- to 'consult' with subsidiary organs (either directly with the subsidiary
  organ or through committee(s) established for this purpose).[34] In practice, this right has been interpreted as enabling NGOs to make oral
  statements at meetings of subsidiary organs;[35] and
- to undertake, upon request of a subsidiary organ, specific studies or
  investigations or prepare specific papers.[36]

[27] See ibid para 31.
[28] See ibid para 32 (a). The NGO Committee considers requests from NGOs to address the
ECOSOC high-level segment as part of its agenda during its sessions. For example, in 2005
the NGO Committee approved the request of eight coalitions of NGOs and 24 organizations
to be heard by the Economic and Social Council at its high-level segment. See Economic and
Social Council, *Report of the Committee on Non-Governmental Organizations on its resumed
2005 session (New York, 5–20 May 2005)* (15 June 2005) E/2005/32 (Part II) para 52.
[29] See ECOSOC Resolution 1996/31(n 13) para 32(b).
[30] See ibid para 33.
[31] See ibid para 34.
[32] See ibid para 35.
[33] See ibid paras 37(a)–(d).
[34] See ibid para 38(a).
[35] NGOs wishing to make oral statements at meetings submit their requests to the unit of
the UN Secretariat servicing the subsidiary organ concerned.
[36] See ECOSOC Resolution 1996/31 (n 13) para 39.

The right to propose items for the provisional agenda of meetings is an exclusive right of NGOs in general consultative status and renders them different from all other NGOs in consultative status. However, in practice NGOs almost never make use of this right.[37]

As of 2004, 134 NGOs qualified for the general consultative status,[38] including, for example, the World Wide Fund for Nature (WWF), the African-American Institute, the International Youth and Student Movement for the UN and the Muslim World League.[39]

B. Special Consultative Status

Special consultative status can be requested by organizations whose scope of competence and activity is limited to only a few of the fields of activity covered by the Council and its subsidiary bodies.[40] NGOs in special consultative status enjoy *some* of the same privileges as those enjoyed by NGOs in general consultative status. In particular, they:

- are informed of the provisional agenda of the Council and its subsidiary organs;[41]
- may attend public meetings of the Council and its subsidiary organs;[42]
- may submit written statements for circulation to the members of the Council. Such statements should not exceed 500 words for the Council (1,500 words for subsidiary organs); if they do, they should have a summary for circulation. The submission of more than 500 (1,500) words can still be circulated if requested by the Council or its NGO Committee (or the subsidiary organ);[43]
- may be heard by the Council (upon the recommendation of the NGO Committee and only in cases where there is no subsidiary organ with jurisdiction over the subject-matter concerned);[44]
- may 'consult' with subsidiary organs (either directly with the subsidiary organ or through committee(s) established for this purpose).[45] In practice, this right has been interpreted as enabling NGOs to make oral statements at meetings of subsidiary organs;[46] and

---

[37] Information from the NGO Section of the Department of Economic and Social Affairs, 17 Jan 2006.

[38] See <http://www.un.org/esa/coordination/ngo/>, visited 18 May 2005.

[39] See <http://habitat.igc.org/ngo-rev/status.html.general>, visited 18 May 2005.

[40] See ECOSOC Resolution 1996/31 (n 13) para 23.

[41] See ibid paras 27 and 33.   [42] See ibid paras 29 and 35.

[43] See ibid para 31(e).   [44] See ibid para 32(a).

[45] See ibid para 38(a).

[46] NGOs wishing to make oral statements at meetings submit their requests to the unit of the UN Secretariat servicing the subsidiary organ concerned.

- may undertake, upon request of a subsidiary organ, specific studies or investigations or prepare specific papers.[47]

However, NGOs in special consultative status cannot propose to place items of interest on the agenda of the Council or of its subsidiary bodies.[48] Their opportunity to make oral statements at meetings of the Council is very restricted.

As of 2004, 1474 NGOs were registered under the special consultative status.[49] Examples include Amnesty International and ActionAid.[50]

C. Roster

Organizations which do not fulfil the criteria for either general or special consultative status but which, in the opinion of the Council or the UN Secretary-General, can make occasional useful contributions to the work of the Council are put on a list known as the Roster.[51] Many NGOs are on the Roster by virtue of their consultative status with specialized agencies and other UN bodies.[52] NGOs on the Roster:

- are informed of the provisional agenda of the Council and its subsidiary organs;[53]
- may attend meetings of the Council and its subsidiary organs concerned with matters within their field of competence;[54]
- may submit written statements to the Council (only upon invitation of the Secretary-General, the Council, or its NGO Committee) and to the subsidiary organs (only upon invitation of the Secretary-General or the subsidiary organ itself). Requirements for these written submissions are the same as for submissions of NGOs in special consultative status;[55]
- may be heard by a subsidiary organ (on the recommendation of the Secretary-General and at the request of the subsidiary organ);[56] and
- may undertake, upon request of a subsidiary organ, specific studies or investigations or prepare specific papers.[57]

[47] See ECOSOC Resolution 1996/31 (n 13) para 39.
[48] See ibid paras 28 and 34. These paragraphs apply only to NGOs in general consultative status.
[49] See <http://www.un.org/esa/coordination/ngo/>, visited 18 May 2005.
[50] See <http://habitat.igc.org/ngo-rev/status.html.general>, visited 18 May 2005.
[51] See ECOSOC Resolution 1996/31 (n 13) para 24. Note that the UN Secretary-General acts in this context only in consultation with the Council or its NGO Committee.
[52] See ibid para 24.   [53] See ibid paras 27 and 33.
[54] See ibid para 29.   [55] See ibid paras 31(f) and 37(f).
[56] See ibid para 38(b). NGOs wishing to make oral statements at meetings submit their requests to the unit of the UN Secretariat servicing the subsidiary organ concerned.
[57] See ibid para 39.

NGOs on the Roster cannot make proposals with regard to the provisional agenda of the Council or its subsidiary organs. They have a very limited opportunity to submit written statements and cannot make oral presentations to the Council (they may only speak at the meetings of the ECOSOCs subsidiary organs).

As of 2004, 923 NGOs were listed under Roster status,[58] including, for example, the American Foreign Law Association, the International Association of Gerontology and the International Iron and Steel Institute.[59]

D. *Comparative Table and Additional Remarks*

The following table demonstrates the difference in rights of NGOs in the three types of consultative status. As shown, the difference lies mainly in the right to propose to place items on the agenda, in the maximum allowed length of written statements and in the possibility to make oral statements.

Aside from involvement with ECOSOC and its subsidiary organs, Resolution 1996/31 authorizes NGOs in any type of consultative status to consult with officers of the UN Secretariat. Such consultations may be conducted upon the request of the NGO or upon the request of the Secretary-General.[60] Also, the Secretary-General may request an accredited NGO to carry out specific studies or prepare specific papers, subject to the relevant financial regulations.[61] At meetings NGOs are allowed to distribute their publications/materials outside the meeting rooms; usually a number of tables are provided. Additionally, the Secretary-General is authorized to offer facilities to accredited NGOs including:

(a) access to UN grounds and facilities;
(b) arrangement of informal discussions on matters of special interest to groups or organizations;
(c) accommodation for conferences or smaller meetings of consultative organizations on the work of the ECOSOC; and
(d) appropriate seating arrangements and facilities for obtaining documents during public meetings.[62]

The rules of Resolution 1996/31 do not extend NGO participatory rights to the preparatory processes that precede public meetings. For example, the current rules allow NGO admission only to public meetings, which means that they are excluded from the preparatory meetings. They are informed of

---

[58] See <http://www.un.org.esa/coordination/ngp/>, visited 18 May 2005.
[59] See <http://habitat.igc.org/ngo-rev/status.html.general>, visited 18 May 2005.
[60] See ECOSOC Resolution 1996/31(n 13) para 65.
[61] See ibid para 66.
[62] See ibid para 67.

Table 2: Rights of NGOs in Different Types of Consultative Status

Rights	General consultative status	Special consultative status	Roster
Council			
To receive provisional agenda of the Council	Yes	Yes	Yes
To propose to place additional items on the provisional agenda of the Council (through the NGO Committee)	Yes	No	No
To attend public meetings of the Council	Yes	Yes	Yes
To submit written statements relevant to the work of the Council	Yes (generally of no more than 2000 words)	Yes (generally of no more than 500 words)	Only upon invitation (generally of no more than 500 words)
To make oral statements to the Council	Yes (upon recommendation and approval)	Yes (upon recommendation and in the absence of the relevant subsidiary organ)	No
To make oral presentations of an expository nature on items included into the agenda of the Council upon the proposition of this NGO	Yes	No	No
Subsidiary organs			
To receive provisional agenda of the subsidiary organs	Yes	Yes	Yes
To propose to place additional items on the provisional agenda of commissions	Yes	No	No
To attend public meetings of the subsidiary organs	Yes	Yes	Yes
To submit written statements to the subsidiary organs	Yes (generally of no more than 2,000 words)	Yes (generally of no more than 1,500 words)	Only upon invitation (generally of no more than 1,500 words)
To be consulted by the subsidiary organ (includes making oral statements)	Yes	Yes	Only at the request of the subsidiary organ
To undertake specific studies or investigations or prepare specific papers, upon request of a subsidiary organ	Yes	Yes	Yes

the provisional agenda, but are not provided with the preparatory working documents distributed to State delegations. The Resolution rarely specifies the timeframes required for different actions. For example, there is no mention of how much time in advance of the meeting the provisional agenda must be communicated, or what period of time would be deemed 'sufficient' in order for NGOs to submit their written submissions. These matters are left to the discretion of ECOSOC, its subsidiary organs and the UN Secretariat officials. In many cases, NGOs cannot use their rights without recommendations, approvals and requests of ECOSOC or other organs. This is also a limiting factor for participation.

A study conducted by Kerstin Martens reveals that NGOs mainly value consultative status as a means to freely access UN buildings and offices. A UN badge and pass allow direct contact with government delegates and UN representatives. This access is of highest importance, since it enables NGOs to keep themselves informed about current discussions, projects and decisions, participate in meetings and hearings, and lobby officials informally.[63] In addition, consultative status allows NGOs to receive all official documents and informational materials issued by the UN; accredited NGOs are put on various distribution lists and are kept informed about future and ongoing events at the UN.[64]

III. ACCREDITATION CRITERIA

ECOSOC Resolution 1996/31 on the 'Consultative Relationship between the United Nations and Non-Governmental Organizations' sets out substantive requirements which an NGO must meet in order to be eligible for one of the three types of consultative status (general, special and inclusion on the Roster). Here, the act of conferring consultative status is also referred to as 'accreditation'.[65]

---

[63] See K Martens, *NGOs and the United Nations: Institutionalization, Professionalization and Adaptation* (Palgrave Macmillan, Basingstoke, 2005) 134.

[64] See ibid 135–36. According to Martens, advocacy and service NGOs assign different value to consultative status: advocacy NGOs tend to value consultative status more because it gives them direct access to decision-makers and enables participation in UN meetings, whereas for service NGOs consultative status is simply a formality allowing the organization to deal with the UN without additional bureaucratic hurdles—they do not use all possibilities for UN interaction that consultative status offers. See ibid 134–5, 160–1. For an interesting and detailed account of what several prominent NGOs say about their ECOSOC consultative status and what use they make of it, see ibid 135–54.

[65] The reader should not be misled by use of the term 'accreditation'. Normally, in the UN context this term (when applied with respect to NGOs) covers situations where NGOs, even without consultative status, are admitted to particular meetings, or generally to the UN premises; accreditation in such context allows NGOs to attend meetings but not to make use of the rights enshrined in ECOSOC Resolution 1996/31. However, here 'accreditation' means a *permanent* accreditation scheme, ie granting of consultative status.

It should be noted from the outset that it is for the NGO concerned (and not for the ECOSOC NGO Committee) to prove that the NGO meets the requirements set out in Resolution 1996/31. The basic criteria that need to be met in order to receive accreditation are the same for all types of consultative status. These basic criteria will be examined first. Subsequently, factors determining the type of consultative status that an NGO should be granted will be reviewed.

A. Common Criteria for Accreditation

To be admitted to any type of consultative status, an NGO (whether national, sub-regional, regional or international) must meet a number of basic requirements.[66] For convenience, the requirements are classified into four groups: (1) activities, (2) democratic legitimacy and accountability, (3) organizational, and (4) funding.

Activities

1. The NGOs must be concerned with matters falling within the competence of the Council and its subsidiary bodies.[67] These matters are quite broad and include international economic, social, cultural, educational, health, and related matters (Article 62 of the UN Charter).
2. The aims and purposes of the NGO must be in conformity with the spirit, purposes and principles of the UN Charter.[68] The said purposes and principles are set out in Articles 1 and 2 of the UN Charter. For example, on the basis of this requirement, ECOSOC can refuse accreditation to NGOs that call for violence or advocate race discrimination or disrespect for recognized human rights.
3. The NGO must be able to demonstrate that its programme of work is of direct relevance to the aims and purposes of the UN.[69] This requirement is in place to ensure that the link between the activities of the NGO and the UN activities is sufficiently close, so that NGOs whose activities have only cursory relevance could not claim consultative status.
4. The NGO must also be of recognized standing within its field of competence or of a representative character.[70] The first part of this requirement ('recognized standing') seems quite subjective and difficult to assess. The fact that the NGO has already been recognized by another international organization (including UN specialized agencies) can be relevant in this context. If a national government commissioned

---

[66] See ECOSOC Resolution 1996/31 (n 13) para 5.
[68] See ibid para 2.
[70] See ibid para 9.

[67] See ibid para 1.
[69] See ibid para 8.

certain work to an NGO or if the latter has been successfully involved in projects on the national or international level, this would also be evidence of recognized standing. An NGO can provide references to its publications to show that they are perceived as an authoritative and/or reliable source of information by others. However, even if an NGO (for example, a small grassroots organization) cannot provide any such evidence of recognition, the requirement is considered to be satisfied if the NGO shows that it is, in fact, active in its field.[71] 'Representative character' seems to suggest that the NGO has a substantial support base (for example, broad membership). An NGO's representative character can also be viewed as a sign of recognition—recognition not by governments or international institutions but by people. This is perhaps why these two criteria are joined.

Democratic Legitimacy and Accountability

5. The NGO must have a democratically adopted constitution, which shall provide for the determination of policy by a conference, congress or other representative body, and for an executive organ responsible to the policy-making body.[72] Apparently, a 'democratically adopted constitution' means a constitution adopted by the conference of the NGO's members or by another body representative of members. This requirement also ensures that the internal governance structure of the NGO meets the basic democratic principles, namely that there is an internal division of powers between a policy-making body and an executive organ.

6. The NGO must have the authority to speak for its members through its authorized representatives.[73] Such authority can be provided for in the NGO's constitution or by-laws.

7. The NGO must have a representative structure and possess appropriate mechanisms of accountability to its members who shall exercise effective control over its policies and actions through the exercise of voting rights or other appropriate democratic and transparent decision-making processes.[74] This is the last in the set of three requirements relating to the democratic structure/legitimacy/accountability of NGOs. Although the term 'appropriate mechanisms of accountability' is as vague as can be, it is helpfully illustrated by one (most common) mechanism—the control over policies and actions through voting rights of members. This requirement overlaps with requirement 5

---

[71] Information from the NGO Section of the Department of Economic and Social Affairs, 17 Jan 2006.

[72] See ECOSOC Resolution 1996/31 (n 13) para 10; a copy of which must be deposited with the UN Secretary-General.

[73] See ibid para 11.　　　　[74] See ibid para 12.

above—if an NGO meets one of them, it would seem to meet the other as well.

Organizational
8. The NGO must have an established headquarters with an executive officer.[75]
9. The NGO must attest that it has been in existence for at least two years at the date of receipt of its application for consultative status.[76]

Funding
10. Regarding the funding of the NGO, its basic resources must be derived in the main part from contributions of the national affiliates or other components, or from individual members.[77] The NGO may be accredited without meeting this requirement if it provides satisfactory information and explanations in accordance with further provisions of paragraph 13 of Resolution 1996/31.

Additionally, national NGOs can be accredited only after consultation with the Member State concerned.[78]

As the common criteria for accreditation are quite numerous, some of them, in practice, may be more important than others in the sense that some draw more attention from the organs that process the NGO applications and make decisions on accreditation. For example, in several documents of the NGO Section, which processes the applications from NGOs, only four criteria are indicated, namely:

(i) the applying organization's activities must be relevant to the work of ECOSOC;
(ii) the NGO must have a democratic decision-making mechanism;
(iii) the NGO must have been in existence (officially registered with the appropriate government authorities as an NGO/non-profit) for at least two years; and
(iv) the major portion of the organization's funds should be derived from contributions of national affiliates, individual members, or other components.[79]

---

[75] See ibid para 10.
[76] See ibid para 61(h).
[77] See ibid para 13.
[78] See Article 71 of the UN Charter; ECOSOC Resolution 1996/31 (n 13) para 8.
[79] See UN Secretariat, *Guidelines for Association* (n 1) 6. See also the NGO Section's webpage 'How to obtain consultative status with ECOSOC', and the 'Questions and Answers' section, <http://www.un.org/esa/coordination/ngo/>, visited 7 Sept 2005.

Although the NGO Section notes that these are criteria 'among others', the fact that they are singled out probably means that these are the criteria that the NGO Section and the NGO Committee primarily look at. According to a competent official of the NGO Section, the NGO Committee treats the following two criteria as the most essential when considering applications for consultative status:

1. funding—the NGO Committee wants to see, first, that on the sources-of-income side, the NGO is independent from governments and is not a profit-making entity, and secondly, that on the expenditure side, the NGO spends the major portion of its funds on relevant activities (not on its own administration) and that its funds are sufficient to enable the NGO to participate in the work of the ECOSOC and its subsidiary bodies;
2. whether the NGO can practically contribute to the work of ECOSOC and its subsidiary bodies.[80]

B. Criteria Determining the Type of Consultative Status

As mentioned, the above-examined criteria are common for NGOs applying for any type of consultative status. But since Resolution 1996/31 differentiates between the three types of status, it is useful to examine which criteria guide the decision of ECOSOC in conferring a certain type of status on a particular NGO.

Judging from the text of Resolution 1996/31, to be admitted to the *general* consultative status, an NGO must:

- be concerned with most of the activities of the ECOSOC and its subsidiary bodies;
- have substantive and sustained contributions to make to the achievement of the objectives of the United Nations;
- be closely involved with the economic and social life of the peoples in the areas they represent; and
- have a considerable membership broadly representative of major segments of society in a large number of countries in different regions of the world.[81]

For the *special* consultative status:

---

[80] Information from the NGO Section of the Department of Economic and Social Affairs, 17 Jan 2006.
[81] See ECOSOC Resolution 1996/31 (n 13) para 22.

- The NGO's scope of competence and activity is limited to only a few of the fields of activity covered by the Council and its subsidiary bodies; and
- the NGO must be known within the fields for which it seeks consultative status.[82]

Conditions for admittance to the *Roster* are the following:

- An NGO does not fulfill the criteria for either general or special consultative status; and
- it can make occasional and useful contributions to the work of the Council, its subsidiary bodies or other UN bodies. Whether the NGO is able, in principle, to make the said contributions, is determined by the Council or by the UN Secretary-General in consultation with the Council or its NGO Committee.[83]

The dividing lines between the three types of status are not very clear. However, the decisive factor is evident—it is the scope of an NGO's activities and competence. For the general status, it has to be as broad as, or at least comparable to, that of ECOSOC; for the special status it has to cover 'a few' relevant fields; for the Roster the coverage may apparently be even narrower. At the same time, the criteria listed in the second and third points under general status are simply unworkable, and, most probably, they are disregarded. The borderline between the special status and the Roster is blurred because of the undefined nature of 'a few' relevant fields.

It is helpful to look at how the NGO Section, which processes the applications for consultative status from NGOs, explains the difference between consultative categories. Beyond the criteria listed in the Resolution, the NGO Section notes that NGOs granted general consultative status 'tend to be fairly large, established international NGOs with a broad geographical reach'; those with special consultative status not only 'have a special competence', but are also 'smaller and more recently established'. Finally, the NGO Section highlights that NGOs included on the Roster 'tend to have a rather narrow and/or technical focus'.[84] As a matter of practice, special consultative status is a 'default' status granted to approved NGOs.[85]

---

[82] See ibid para 23.   [83] See ibid para 24.
[84] See the 'Questions and Answers' section on the website of the online NGO Section, specifically the answer to the question 'What is the difference between General category, Special category and Roster?', <http://www.un.org/esa/coordination/ngo/>, visited 7 Sept 2005.
[85] Information from the NGO Section of the Department of Economic and Social Affairs, 17 Jan 2006.

IV. PROCEDURES FOR ACCREDITATION

Resolution 1996/31 on the 'Consultative Relationship between the United Nations and Non-Governmental Organizations' sets out the procedure for obtaining consultative status with ECOSOC. In order to be accredited, an NGO must submit an application, which will be reviewed by the NGO Committee. The Committee recommends to the Council which NGOs should be admitted and what status they should be accorded. The final decision is taken by the Council itself.

In more detail, the procedure looks as follows.[86] To begin the process of applying for consultative status, an NGO must address a written letter of intent to the NGO Section of the Department of Economic and Social Affairs (NGO Section), which provides technical support to the NGO Committee. Once the NGO Section receives the letter of intent, it will mail the application package containing the questionnaire and all the background materials to the organization. The application and questionnaire is then completed and submitted by the NGO.

The following documents are required from applicants:

1. A copy of the NGO's constitution/charter and/or its statutes/by-laws.
2. Registration papers from the country where the NGO is incorporated or holds tax-exempt or non-profit status or, for NGOs based in countries where there is no legal requirement to register, the NGO Section needs evidence that the NGO is a non-profit organization.
3. A copy of the most recent completed financial statement, preferably a statement that has been audited. The financial statement should clearly indicate the sources of income.
4. A list of associations and groups affiliated with the NGO.
5. A sample of the NGO's publications and articles concerning the NGO's activities that are related to UN activities.
6. A completed questionnaire.[87]
7. A completed summary of the application.

Completed applications must be received by 1 June of the year preceding the year the NGO wants to be considered for recommendation by the NGO Committee. For example, complete applications received by the NGO Section before 1 June 2005, will be taken up by the NGO Committee in the year 2006.

---

[86] Based on UN Secretariat, *Guidelines for Association* (n 1) 5–7 and interviews with competent officials from the NGO Section of the Department of Economic and Social Affairs. See also the website of the online NGO Section titled 'How to obtain consultative status with ECOSOC', <http://www.un.org/esa/coordination/ngo/>, visited 7 Sept 2005.

[87] The questionnaire is available at <http://www.un.org/esa/coordination/ngo/>, visited 7 Sept 2005.

In the period between 1 June and the date the NGO Committee meets, the NGO Section reviews the applications to ensure that all necessary information has been submitted and that the applicant meets the technical requirements mandated by ECOSOC (eg that the NGO has been in existence for at least two years, that it has a headquarters, etc). During this time the NGO may be contacted and asked for more information or clarifications. Only after an application has been reviewed and is considered complete will it be submitted to the NGO Committee.

When submitting an application to the NGO Committee, the NGO Section does not give its opinion on whether the NGO concerned should be granted consultative status or on the type of consultative status to be granted. However, it is understood that if the NGO Section transmits the application of the NGO, it deems that the NGO satisfies the accreditation criteria. The NGO Section may decline an application without submitting it to the NGO Committee if it considers that the NGO concerned does not satisfy the criteria.[88]

The NGO Committee meets twice a year to decide which NGOs applying for consultative status it will recommend to the Council. As a matter of practice, the NGO Committee pre-discusses all new applications for consultative status at informal meetings, which precede its formal sessions. After these informal meetings, NGO applications are grouped into two lists. List 1 includes 'unproblematic' NGOs; List 2 features those NGOs that gave rise to questions from one or more delegations.[89] These questions are sent to the NGOs concerned, so that they may respond until the beginning of the formal session of the NGO Committee.[90]

At its formal session, the NGO Committee first considers all NGOs from List 1, spending 3–5 minutes on each, and then goes on to consider NGOs on List 2, which usually take more time. If Member States are not satisfied with answers received from a particular NGO, its application is deferred and additional questions are posed. After deliberations on each NGO, the chairperson of the meeting usually suggests granting it special consultative status and if there are no objections or proposals to change the type of

---

[88] Information from the NGO Section of the Department of Economic and Social Affairs, 17 January 2006.

[89] For example, 99 NGOs were considered during the January 2006 session of the NGO Committee—60 were put on List 1 and 39 on List 2.

[90] In many instances, these questions have little to do with the compliance of the NGO with the established accreditation criteria, but have more to do with political sensitivities of particular States. To give just one example, at the January 2006 session of the NGO Committee, Cuba posed the question to an NGO that focused on human rights violations in the Global South whether this NGO considered that there were no human rights violations in the Global North. Although this NGO eventually was granted special consultative status, the example is illustrative.

status (into general or Roster) from Member States, special status is granted. In difficult cases, the NGO Committee may resort to voting.

When an application becomes part of the agenda of the NGO Committee, a letter is sent to the NGO informing it of the upcoming session and inviting it to send no more than two representatives to be present during the session. In its explanations, the NGO Section emphasizes that the presence of NGO representatives in the room 'is in no way mandatory and it does not imply any advantages. NGOs simply have the right to be present when their applications are being considered'.[91] However, an NGO representative has an opportunity to reply in person to questions of the NGO Committee, if they arise. In any case, any NGO applying for accreditation has a right to respond in writing to any objections being raised in the NGO Committee before the Committee makes its decision.[92] If the NGO does not respond until the end of the session of the NGO Committee,[93] the review of its application is deferred until the next session.

After each session, the recommendations of the NGO Committee are published in a report and submitted to the next ECOSOC meeting for final approval.[94] Official notification is sent to all reviewed NGOs, informing them of the Committee's recommendation. When the Council finally approves the Committee recommendation, official notification is sent by the Secretariat.

If a *national* NGO applies for consultative status, a decision on granting this status will only be taken after consultation with the Member State concerned.[95] While only consultation with, and not the consent of, the Member State is required, the Council is unlikely to accredit a national NGO when the Member State concerned has serious reservations with regard to the granting of the consultative status. Resolution 1996/31 provides that the views expressed by the Member State, if any, shall be communicated to the NGO concerned, which shall have the opportunity to respond to those views through the NGO Committee.[96]

The NGO Committee may recommend a type of consultative status different from the one requested by the NGO, as it is guided by the criteria

---

[91] See <http://www.un.org/esa/coordination/ngo/>, visited 7 Sept 2005.

[92] See ECOSOC Resolution 1996/31(n 13) para 15.

[93] Sessions of the NGO Committee normally last for 8–10 days.

[94] The NGO Committee has been criticized for not acting, on a number of occasions, in conformity with the strict terms of Resolution 1996/31: '[s]ometimes this has been the result of internal political considerations or horsetrading; sometimes of willful (mis)interpretation of the wording of the Resolution; sometimes simple ignorance of precedent; sometimes unawareness of rich variety of NGO strictures, procedures, purposes and terminology'. However, the author does not give specific examples of inappropriate actions on part of the NGO Committee. See C Ritchie, 'Collaboration among Entities of the UN System and of Civil Society, Notably NGOs' (2003) 55 Transnational Associations 207, 211.

[95] See Art 71 of the UN Charter; ECOSOC Resolution 1996/31 (n 13) para 8.

[96] See ECOSOC Resolution 1996/31 (n 13) para 8.

reviewed above. Subsequently, an NGO may request reclassification. According to the NGO Section, when the NGO Committee considers a request for reclassification it will want to know if the NGO has increased its geographical distribution and the scope of its activities in the fields with which ECOSOC is concerned.[97] Every year, the NGO Committee recommends about 3–5 NGOs for reclassification (upgrading the status) upon NGO requests.[98]

To date, more than 2,700 NGOs have received consultative status with the ECOSOC. In the 1970s and 1980s, there were 20–30 new applications to ECOSOC per year. This had risen to 200 in 1998–99, 400 in 2000–01 and 500 in 2002–03, resulting in a mounting backlog of applications.[99] For the NGO Committee, this dramatic increase has made it extremely difficult to verify in depth whether the applicants truly fulfil the substantive requirements for conferring of consultative status. In 2005, consultative status was granted to 192 NGOs (two NGOs were granted general consultative status; 167 NGOs given special consultative status; and 23 NGOs were included on the Roster).[100]

Compared to the number of accredited NGOs, the number of those refused consultative status is small. For example, in 2005 there were no such organizations. In 2004, the NGO Committee refused recommendation to four NGOs. To give an example, Alliance Vietnam Liberté was refused accreditation because of the statements of the Vietnamese delegation that the organization had committed acts of sabotage in Vietnam, and was featured in a 1992 FBI list of criminal organizations. Another NGO, a Ghana-based organization called Thirty-First December Women's Movement, was rejected because it allegedly had functioned as an integral part of one of the political parties in Ghana.[101] In addition to the four rejected NGOs, consideration of applications from two other NGOs was closed because the host government did not recognize the existence of the organizations concerned.[102]

---

[97] See UN Secretariat, *Guidelines for Association* (n 1) 10.
[98] See the annual reports of the NGO Committee to ECOSOC.
[99] *UN System and Civil Society: An Inventory and Analysis of Practices.* The backlog also remains considerable because of the inability of many NGOs to submit all information requested from them by the NGO Section. Information from the NGO Section of the Department of Economic and Social Affairs, 17 Jan 2006.
[100] See Economic and Social Council, *Report of the Committee on Non-Governmental Organizations on its 2005 regular session (New York, 5–14 January 2005)* E/2005/32 (Part I) (15 Feb 2005); and Economic and Social Council, *Report of the Committee on Non-Governmental Organizations on its resumed 2005 session (New York, 5–20 May 2005)* E/2005/32 (Part II) (15 June 2005).
[101] For details, see Economic and Social Council, *Report of the Committee on Non-Governmental Organizations on the 2004 regular session (New York, 10–28 May and 23 June 2004)* E/2004/32 (13 Aug 2004) paras 10–26.
[102] See ibid paras 8–9.

V. MONITORING OF NGOS

A. *Quadrennial Reports*

NGOs in general or special consultative status are under an obligation to submit, every four years, a brief report on their activities to the NGO Committee (the quadrennial report).[103] NGOs on the Roster do not have this obligation. In exceptional circumstances, the NGO Committee may request a report from any NGO (including those on the Roster) between the regular reporting dates.[104]

Quadrennial reports should be brief (strictly limited to four pages) and contain the following information:

1. Brief introductory statement recalling the aims and purposes of the NGO.
2. Indication of whether there have been any changes in: (i) increase in geographical membership; (ii) substantial changes in sources of funding; (iii) any affiliations to NGOs in consultative status.
3. Participation in conferences of ECOSOC or other UN entities (including attendance, presentation of oral or written statements, dates and places of meetings).
4. Description of how the NGO has cooperated with UN entities and agencies.
5. Description of any other relevant activities such as:
   a. Implementation of UN resolutions at international, national or regional level;
   b. Consultations and cooperation with UN officials;
   c. Preparation of papers and/or materials requested by ECOSOC or the other UN entities;
   d. Other examples of activities involving consultative status, eg financial assistance received from or given to the UN, joint-level collaboration, sponsorship of meetings, seminars studies, etc.

Annexes or other supplementary material (publications, texts of statements, updated financial statements, revised membership lists and the number of members by country, etc) can be submitted along with the report.[105]

---

[103] See ECOSOC Resolution 1996/31 (n 13) para 61(c).
[104] See ibid.
[105] See UN Secretariat, *Guidelines for Association* (n 1) 9; UN Secretariat (Department of Economic and Social Affairs), NGO Section, *Guidelines for Submission of Quadrennial Reports for Non-Governmental Organizations in General and Special Consultative Status with the Economic and Social Council*, <http://www.un.org/esa/coordination/ngo/>, visited 7 Sept 2005.

Quadrennial reports are a tool for the NGO Committee to determine whether the NGO concerned continues to satisfy the substantive criteria of consultative status. If the Committee is of the opinion that this is not the case, it can recommend to the Council to reclassify or even withdraw the consultative status.[106] However, in past years such cases have been practically non-existent, turning the practice of quadrennial reporting into a formality. The delegates to the NGO Committee have admitted that due to the high workload, particularly as a result of the increasing number of NGOs already in consultative status, 'it is impossible to read thoroughly the reports, if at all'.[107] Additionally, the Committee has to rely on information provided by individual NGOs, as there is no independent investigation to verify the information in the report. Without a mechanism for independent verification the process may be susceptible to abuse.[108]

At the same time, statistics show that the process of approval of reports by the NGO Committee is not automatic. For example, in 2005, the NGO Committee reviewed 138 quadrennial reports. Out of this number, the Committee took note of 116 reports, while consideration of the remaining 22 reports was deferred pending responses from relevant NGOs to the additional questions posed by the Committee.[109]

B. Suspension and Withdrawal of Consultative Status

Accredited NGOs are under a general obligation to 'conform at all times to the principles governing the establishment and nature of their consultative relations with the Council'.[110] There are, in fact, three cases in which the consultative status of an NGO may be suspended for up to three years *or* withdrawn:

1. If an NGO, either directly or through its affiliates or representatives acting on its behalf, clearly abuses its status by engaging in a pattern of acts contrary to the purposes and principles of the UN Charter including unsubstantiated or politically motivated acts against Member States incompatible with those purposes and principles.

---

[106] See ECOSOC Resolution 1996/31 (n 13) paras 61(c) and 56(c).
[107] J Aston, 'The United Nations Committee on Non-Governmental Organizations: Guarding the Entrance to a Politically Divided House' (2001) 12 Eur J of Intl L 943, 961.
[108] See J Hartwick, 'Non-Governmental Organizations at United Nations-Sponsored World Conferences: A Framework for Participation Reform' (2003) 26 Loyola of Los Angeles Intl & Comparative L Rev 217, 227–8.
[109] See Economic and Social Council, *Report of the Committee on Non-Governmental Organizations on its 2005 regular session (New York, 5–14 January 2005)* E/2005/32 (Part I) (15 Feb 2005) paras 26–9; and Economic and Social Council, *Report of the Committee on Non-Governmental Organizations on its resumed 2005 session (New York, 5–20 May 2005)* E/2005/32 (Part II) (15 June 2005) paras 33–7.
[110] See ECOSOC Resolution 1996/31 (n 13) para 55.

2. If there exists substantiated evidence of influence from proceeds resulting from internationally recognized criminal activities such as the illicit drugs trade, money-laundering or the illegal arms trade.
3. If, within the preceding three years, an NGO did not make any positive or effective contribution to the work of the United Nations and, in particular, of the Council or its commissions or other subsidiary organs.[111]

An NGO whose accreditation has been withdrawn may only reapply for consultative status after three years.[112] As in the case with granting consultative status, it is the Council itself—upon the recommendation of the NGO Committee—that makes the decision on suspension/withdrawal of accreditation.[113]

After decades in which no NGO was deprived of its consultative status, several NGOs have been stripped of this status since 1996.[114] Complaints by States do not necessarily result in a recommendation to suspend/withdraw consultative status from an NGO. In 2001–02, for example, the Committee did not recommend a single suspension or withdrawal measure although there had been several complaints by States.[115] In 2003, consultative status of one NGO—Reporters without Borders—was suspended for one year for disrupting the opening of the session of the Commission on Human Rights by throwing flyers, which contained abusive language.[116] In 2004, the NGO Committee recommended the suspension of consultative status for two NGOs: Transnational Radical Party for three years (this NGO allowed a member of an alleged terrorist group to address the Commission on Human Rights and subsequently accredited him to various meetings of the ECOSOC) and the Indian Movement 'Tupaj Amaru' for one year (its representatives unfurled, at a session of the Commission on Human Rights, a banner with the word 'PACE' on it and chanted anti-

---

[111] See ibid para 57.
[112] See ibid para 59. Also, an NGO whose listing on the Roster is withdrawn may only reapply for listing after three years.
[113] See ibid para 59.
[114] See M Kamminga, 'The Evolving Status of NGOs under International Law: A Threat to the Inter-State System?' in P Alston (ed), *Non-State Actors and Human Rights* (Oxford University Press, Oxford, 2005) 110.
[115] See Economic and Social Council, *Report of the Committee on Non-Governmental Organizations on its resumed 2002 session* E/2003/11 (18 Mar 2003); Economic and Social Council, *Report of the Committee on Non-Governmental Organizations on its resumed 2001 session* E/2002/10 (1 Mar 2002); and Economic and Social Council, *Report of the Committee on Non-Governmental Organizations on its 2001 regular session* E/2001/86 (15 June 2001).
[116] See Economic and Social Council, *Report of the Committee on Non-Governmental Organizations on its 2003 regular session (New York, 5–23 May 2003)* E/2003/32 (Part II) (26 Aug 2003) paras 82–96.

American slogans).[117] In 2005 the NGO Committee recommended a one-year suspension of the consultative status of one NGO—A Woman's Voice International—following the incident where a representative of the NGO produced and activated a taser gun while delivering his statement to the Commission on Human Rights.[118]

To give one more detailed example, the Spanish-based human rights organization International Council of the Association for Peace in the Continents (ASOPAZCO) had its consultative status suspended for three years in 2000. Initially, Cuba requested that the consultative status of ASOPAZCO be withdrawn, alleging that this NGO was engaging in activities aimed at the overthrow of the Cuban Government.[119] The special report submitted by the NGO at the request of the Committee denied these accusations. Cuba then changed its strategy to request a three-year suspension of ASOPAZCO's consultative status. Cuba was able to convince a sufficient number of hesitant members of the NGO Committee to go along with this less severe measure. On the basis of the recommendation of the Committee, a divided Economic and Social Council eventually decided (25 votes for, to 18 votes against, with nine abstentions) to suspend the consultative status of ASOPAZCO for three years.[120] After the years of suspension elapsed, ASOPAZCO submitted an updated application for its reinstatement in status and additionally, as requested by the NGO Committee, a special report on its activities during its three-year suspension explaining how it had overcome the reasons for the suspension. Despite the legal opinion of the UN Office of Legal Affairs, according to which reinstatement in status should be automatic upon the expiration of the suspension period, Cuba and several other delegations insisted on definitive withdrawal of consultative status. A divided NGO Committee adopted the Cuban proposal in 2005. This proposal was subsequently adopted by the Council.[121]

Generally, on the matter of the reinstatement of an NGO whose consultative status was suspended, it should be noted that ECOSOC Resolution 1996/31 does not set out any procedures for the reinstatement of consultative

[117] See Economic and Social Council, *Report of the Committee on Non-Governmental Organizations on the 2004 regular session* E/2004/32 (13 Aug 2004) paras 98–127.
[118] See Economic and Social Council, *Report of the Committee on Non-Governmental Organizations on its resumed 2005 session (New York, 5–20 May 2005)* E/2005/32 (Part II) (15 June 2005) paras 58–70.
[119] See Economic and Social Council, *Report of the Committee on Non-Governmental Organizations on the First and Second Part of its 2000 Session* E/2000/88 (Part I) (5 July 2000) and E/2000/88 (Part II) (13 July 2000) paras 71–93.
[120] Council Decision of 18 Oct 2000, UN Doc E/2000/307; see also UN Doc A/55/3/Add.2, para 5, et seq.
[121] See Economic and Social Council, *Report of the Committee on Non-Governmental Organizations on its resumed 2005 session* E/2005/32 (Part II) (15 June 2005) paras 14–32.

status following suspension, unlike in cases of withdrawal. This legal lacuna entailed controversy in the NGO Committee. To date, reinstatement had not been automatic, and the NGO Committee has decided on a case-by-case basis whether a particular organization should have its status reinstated.

Some believe that the 'misbehaviour' of an NGO brought to the attention of the NGO Committee is often merely a pretext for 'muzzling critical voices' in the UN forum and that in reality, withdrawal or suspension of the consultative status of an NGO is frequently requested on the grounds of having criticized the human rights record of a Member State of the NGO Committee.[122] Additionally, although Resolution 1996/31 requires a *'pattern* of acts', in practice, as some of the above examples show, a single unacceptable act can be considered sufficient to suspend or withdraw consultative status.

VI. NGO PARTICIPATION IN UN CONFERENCES

UN-sponsored international conferences are gatherings of States, international organizations and NGOs that hold meetings and discussions on important world topics, such as the global environment, human rights, social development, women's rights, racism and discrimination, HIV/AIDS, new technologies, etc. The main reason for holding major UN specialized conferences is to shift a particular issue higher up in public and formal agendas.[123] The three-fold purpose of UN-sponsored international conferences has been identified as: (1) to promote international awareness of important issues; (2) to achieve an international consensus in formulating solutions; and (3) to interface with civil society to achieve conference objectives.[124] World conferences are usually called by the UN General Assembly or ECOSOC.

During the 1990s, the UN conferences acquired such regularity to become a part of global governance processes. The conference process includes preparatory meetings on regional and thematic areas, the main conference and a follow-up process ('Plus 5s' and 'Plus 10s') on a topic of concern. The objectives of the main conference are for all attending States to reach agreement on the issue of concern and to develop a plan of action, which, although not necessarily binding, can have strong moral and political value. The 'Plus 5s' and 'Plus10s' should, ideally, monitor the realiza-

---

[122] See Aston (n 107) 956. On the high level of politicization of the NGO Committee, see also Martens (n 63) 131–3.
[123] See Willetts (n 9) 280.   [124] See Hartwick (n 108) 230.

tion of the commitments made, though sometimes they may also involve some renegotiation of commitments.[125]

The regular and active role of UN conferences in global governance make them attractive for civil society since they provide a chance to pressure States, raise consciousness on relevant issues and, more broadly, to influence global policy debates.[126] As one observer put it, global conferences give NGOs 'unprecedented opportunities for organising, media attention and lobbying'.[127] Frequently, NGOs organize parallel conferences in the same location to make their voice stronger.

Each UN-sponsored event is unique and has its own rules governing NGO participation agreed to by the NGO Section of the UN Secretariat and the UN entities most related to the main themes of the event.[128] A useful review of rules on NGO participation in major UN conferences and summits of the 1990s can be found in the lengthy 'Reference document', prepared by the Office of the President of the Millennium Assembly.[129] Resolution 1996/31 establishes only the essential framework for NGO participation common to all international conferences convened by the United Nations and their preparatory processes.

The basic rule is that to be able to participate, an NGO has to be accredited to the conference. Accredited NGOs are not divided into categories (as in the case of ECOSOC); all organizations have the same rights. Because ECOSOC itself is not involved in UN conferences, Resolution 1996/31 provides that NGO accreditation to UN conferences is the prerogative of Member States. This prerogative is exercised through the preparatory committee of the conference with support from the secretariat of the conference.[130]

An NGO that has been granted accreditation may attend the conference and its preparatory sessions. However, in recognition of the intergovernmental nature of any conference and its preparatory process, participation of NGOs therein 'does not entail a negotiating role'.[131] Nevertheless, NGOs accredited to the conference may be given an opportunity to briefly address the preparatory committee and the conference in plenary meetings and their subsidiary bodies (at the discretion of the chairperson and the

[125] See C Tabbush, 'Civil Society in United Nations Conferences: A Literature Review', United Nations Research Institute for Social Development, Civil Society and Social Movements Programme Paper Number 17 (Aug 2005) 4.
[126] See ibid 4 and 6.
[127] K Sikkink, 'Restructuring World Politics: The Limits and Asymmetries of Soft Power' in S Khagram, J Riker, and K Sikkink (eds), *Restructuring World Politics: Transnational Social Movements, Networks and Norms* (University of Minnesota Press, Minneapolis, 2002) 305.
[128] See UN Secretariat, *Guidelines for Association* 10.
[129] See United Nations, *Reference document on the participation of civil society* sections 2–12.
[130] See ECOSOC Resolution 1996/31 (n 13) para 41.
[131] ibid para 50.

consent of the body concerned).[132] NGOs accredited to the conference may also make written presentations during the preparatory process.[133] As a matter of fact, each particular conference has been free to adopt its own rules for NGO participation and to broaden, or narrow, room for NGO involvement.

On the matter of *accreditation criteria*, it should be noted at the beginning that NGOs in general consultative status, special consultative status and on the Roster, that express their wish to attend the conference and/or meetings of its preparatory bodies, shall *as a rule* be accredited for participation.[134] Perhaps, the words 'as a rule' were inserted to serve as a barrier to those NGOs whose participation is strongly objected to by a State or States, or whose fields of activities are absolutely irrelevant to the subject of the conference. Note, however, that in practice conference accreditation of NGOs in consultative status with ECOSOC has been automatic.

Other NGOs wishing to be accredited may apply to the secretariat of the conference and satisfy the requirements set out in the Resolution. In fact, only one criterion has been made explicit in this regard—namely, the competence of the NGO and the 'relevance of its activities to the work of the conference'.[135] However, the list of documents required from NGOs in order to be accredited shows that other factors can also be taken into account. The required documents include, inter alia, financial statements, a list of financial sources and contributions, a description of the membership of the organization (with indication of the total number of members and their geographical distribution) and a copy of the constitution and/or by-laws of the organization.[136] It appears that, similarly to the criteria for obtaining consultative status with ECOSOC, NGOs have to meet certain minimum requirements as to their funding, representative character, or internal governance structure. The fact that these criteria have not been made explicit may mean, on the one hand, that it is more difficult to refuse NGOs from being accredited, but on the other hand, that the conference preparatory committee has more discretion when assessing NGOs' eligibility in the absence of precisely formulated requirements. In practice, each conference has established different rules for accrediting NGOs that do not have consultative status, particularly grassroots national NGOs.[137]

[132] See ibid para 51.
[133] See ibid para 52.
[134] See ibid para 42.
[135] See ibid para 44. In the provision that follows, this is referred to as the 'background [of the NGO] and [its] involvement in the subject areas of the conference'. See ibid para 45.
[136] For the full list of required documents see ibid para 44.
[137] See M Karns and K Mingst, *International Organizations: The Politics and Processes of Global Governance* (Lynne Rienner Publishers, Boulder, CO, 2004) 231.

As mentioned above, the accreditation of NGOs is the prerogative of Member States, exercised through the preparatory committee of the conference. The secretariat of the conference is responsible for the receipt and preliminary evaluation of requests from NGOs for accreditation to the conference and its preparatory process.[138] Periodically, the secretariat publishes and disseminates to Member States the updated list of applications received. Member States may submit comments on any of the applications on the list within a 14-day time limit. The comments of Member States, if any, must be communicated to the NGO concerned, which must be given the opportunity to respond.[139]

In cases where the secretariat believes that the NGO has established its competence and the relevance of its activities to the work of the preparatory committee, it recommends to the preparatory committee that the NGO be accredited. In cases where the secretariat does not recommend accreditation, it has to make available to the preparatory committee its reasons for not doing so. The secretariat must also notify unsuccessful applicants of the reasons for non-recommendation, must provide an opportunity to respond to objections and must furnish additional information as may be required.[140]

The preparatory committee must decide on all recommendations for accreditation within 24 hours after the recommendations of the secretariat have been taken up by the preparatory committee in plenary meeting. In the event a decision is not made within this period, interim accreditation must be accorded until such time as a decision is taken.[141]

One commentator observed that the admission of a non-ECOSOC-approved NGO to a UN conference is not guaranteed since accreditation flexibility varies from conference to conference.[142] At the same time, practice shows that very few applications are actually rejected (for example, three in the case of the 1992 UN Conference on Environment and Development in Rio de Janeiro, one for the 1995 World Summit on Social Development in Copenhagen, and two for the 2002 World Summit for Sustainable Development in Johannesburg).[143] To see how small these figures are, one has to compare them with numbers of NGO participation in major UN conferences (Table 3).

Resolution 1996/31 also provides that the accreditation of NGOs may be suspended or withdrawn. The suspension/withdrawal of accreditation is

[138] See ECOSOC Resolution 1996/31 (n 13) para 43.
[139] See ibid para 46.
[140] See ibid para 47.
[141] See ibid para 48.
[142] See Hartwick (n 108) 227.
[143] See *UN System and Civil Society: An Inventory and Analysis of Practices*, Background Paper for the Secretary-General's Panel of Eminent Persons on United Nations Relations with Civil Society.

Table 3: NGO Participation (numbers) in Major UN Conferences[144]

Year	Venue	Conference Issue	New NGOs Accredited	Parallel NGO Forum Participants
1968	Tehran	Human Rights	57	None
1972	Stockholm	Human Environment	>300	Not known
1975	Mexico City	International Women's Year	114	6000
1985	Nairobi	End of Women's Decade	163	13,500
1992	Rio de Janeiro	Environment & Development	1378	18,000
1993	Vienna	Human Rights	841	c 1000
1994	Cairo	Population & Development	934	Unknown
1995	Copenhagen	Social Development	1138	c 30,000
1995	Beijing	4th World Conf. on Women	2600	30,000
2001	Durban	Racism	1290	c 15,000
2002	Monterrey	Financing for Development	107	Unknown
2002	Johannesburg	Sustainable Development	737	35,000

subject to the relevant rules applicable to the suspension/withdrawal of the ECOSOC consultative status discussed above.[145]

If NGOs accredited to an international conference subsequently want to apply for consultative status, they must follow normal procedures. However, the NGO Committee—in recognition of the importance of their participation in the conference follow-up process—has to review such applications 'as expeditiously as possible' and use documentation already submitted by NGOs for the conference accreditation.[146] While these applications are pending, ECOSOC has to decide on the participation of NGOs accredited to the conference in the work of the relevant functional commission on the follow up to and implementation of that conference.[147] This means that NGOs can become involved in the work of the relevant commission before formally receiving ECOSOC consultative status.

[144] See ibid.
[145] See ECOSOC Resolution 1996/31 (n 13) para 54. See above, pp 41–44.
[146] See ibid para 53. Perhaps somewhat misleadingly, when mentioning 'normal procedures' for obtaining consultative status, Resolution 1996/31 refers to the old ECOSOC Resolution 1296 (XLIV), which was adopted in 1968. The solution is that Resolution 1296 (XLIV) is referred to 'as updated', and it was updated precisely by Resolution 1996/31 (as evident from the last paragraph of the preamble of Resolution 1996/31). Thus, this is a rather strange legal technique to refer, in effect, to the provisions of the 'present Resolution', that is, to the provisions of the Resolution 1996/31.
[147] See ibid.

VII. PROBABLE CHANGES TO THE UN ACCREDITATION SYSTEM

Examining the existing mechanisms for UN accreditation, the Cardoso Report has pointed out the following problems:

- They are often driven by the political concerns of Member States, rather than the expertise and inputs that the non-State actors may offer;
- They vary greatly across the United Nations system, and so are confusing and time-consuming for all;
- They are often costly (in time and money) and are disconnected (without system-wide information-sharing), rather than streamlined through information technology links;
- They are not transparent or responsive, from the review of applications to the final decision-making stage.[148]

To remedy these drawbacks, the Cardoso Report offers a number of measures, such as:

- streamlining the process of UN accreditation by merging the current procedures of ECOSOC, the Department of Public Information, conferences, and their follow up into a single UN accreditation process, with responsibility for accreditation assumed by an existing committee of the General Assembly;
- formally extending participatory rights of NGOs beyond social and economic matters and, in particular, formally involving NGOs in the work of the General Assembly;
- shifting the main responsibility for reviewing NGO applications from the political body (currently the NGO Committee) to the UN Secretariat so as to reduce time inefficiencies and increase the technical focus, as well as transparency of the review;
- improving standards of governance for NGOs, such as those for transparency and accountability;
- more consistently requiring periodic reviews, monitoring contributions of accredited organizations and routinely de-accrediting inactive NGOs; and
- given the large number of NGOs currently accredited to ECOSOC, providing incentives for forming NGO networks so that civil society speaks with fewer, but more professional and more compelling voices.[149]

These may be some ideas that will guide the development of the UN accreditation system for NGOs in the foreseeable future.

---

[148] See Cardoso Report (n 5) para 124.   [149] See ibid ch VII.

CHAPTER 3

United Nations Conference on Trade and Development (UNCTAD)

I. INTRODUCTION

The United Nations Conference on Trade and Development (UNCTAD) was established in 1964 by the UN General Assembly to deal with trade, investment and development issues. Its main goal is to maximize the trade, investment and development opportunities of developing countries and to assist these countries in their effort to integrate into the world economy on an equitable basis. UNCTAD functions as a forum for intergovernmental deliberations, supported by discussions with experts and exchanges of experiences aimed at consensus building on issues of economic development. Furthermore, it undertakes research, policy analysis and data collection for the debates of government representatives and experts. It also provides technical assistance to developing countries.[1]

Nominally, UNCTAD is a subsidiary body of the UN General Assembly established by a General Assembly resolution,[2] but in practice it acts as a separate international organization. It is composed of 192 Member States.

The highest decision-making body of UNCTAD is the Quadrennial Conference, at which Member States (on a ministerial level) make assessments of current trade and development issues, discuss policy options and formulate global policy responses. The Conference also sets the organization's mandate and work priorities. In the four years between the meetings of the Conference, UNCTAD's work is guided by the Trade and Development Board (TDB). The TDB is responsible for ensuring the overall consistency of UNCTAD's activities with agreed priorities. Membership of the TDB is open to all Member States of UNCTAD. The TDB meets in Geneva once a year in a regular session, and up to three times a year in executive sessions to deal with ad hoc policy and institutional issues. The TDB has three commissions that meet once a year to address policy issues

---

[1] See <http://www.unctad.org/Templates/Page.asp?intItemID=1530&lang=1>, visited 1 Apr 2005.
[2] See UN General Assembly Resolution 1995 (XIX), 'Establishment of the United Nations Conference on Trade and Development as an Organ of the General Assembly' (30 Dec 1964), <http://www.un.org/documents/resga.htm>, visited 12 Sept 2005.

in specific areas and provide guidance for the work of the Secretariat.[3] In order to benefit from a higher level of technical expertise, each commission may convene *expert meetings*. Up to 10 such expert meetings are convened by the commissions every year.[4] Decisions in UNCTAD intergovernmental organs are taken by consensus. The Secretary-General heads the UNCTAD Secretariat located in Geneva.

II. LEGAL BASIS

UN General Assembly Resolution 1995 (XIX), by which UNCTAD was established, provides that the Trade and Development Board may offer to NGOs concerned with matters of trade and trade as related to development the opportunity to participate, without vote, in its deliberations and those of the subsidiary bodies and working groups established by it.[5]

The TDB made use of this mandate by including in its rules of procedure Rule 77 on relations with NGOs.[6] Rule 77 established a legal basis for granting NGOs observer status with UNCTAD and also provided for substantive participatory rights of NGOs.

Norms on NGO participation were subsequently also included in the Rules of Procedure of the Conference (Rule 81),[7] and in the Rules of Procedure of the Main Committees of the TDB (Rule 75).[8] The text of these two provisions was modelled on Rule 77 of the TDB Rules of Procedure.

Matters of UNCTAD's relations with NGOs are further regulated by TDB Decision 43 (VII) of 20 September 1968, 'Arrangements for the participation of non-governmental organizations in the activities of the United Nations Conference on Trade and Development'.[9] Most importantly,

---

[3] Commission on Trade in Goods and Services, and Commodities; Commission on Investment, Technology and Related Financial Issues; and Commission on Enterprise, Business Facilitation and Development.

[4] For more on UNCTAD and its organizational structure see <http://www.unctad.org/Templates/Page.asp?intItemID=3360&lang=1>, visited 10 Sept 2005.

[5] See UN General Assembly Resolution 1995 (XIX) (n 2) para 11. See also appendix II to this book, p 243.

[6] See UNCTAD, 'Rules of Procedure of the Trade and Development Board', TD/B/16/Rev.4, adopted by the TDB on 27 April 1965, with subsequent amendments. See also appendix II of this book, p 243.

[7] See UNCTAD, 'Rules of Procedure', TD/63/Rev.2, adopted by the Conference on 1 Feb 1968, with subsequent amendments. See also appendix II of this book, p 244.

[8] See UNCTAD, 'Rules of Procedure of the Main Committees of the Trade and Development Board', TD/B/740, approved by the TDB on 8 September 1978. At present, these Rules of Procedure govern the meetings of the three UNCTAD Commissions. See also appendix II of this book, p 245.

[9] This Decision is included as Annex II to the Rules of the Procedure of the Conference and Annex III of the Rules of Procedure of the TDB. See also appendix II of this book, p 245.

Decision 43 (VIII) established criteria and procedures for granting observer status to NGOs.

Within the UNCTAD Secretariat there is a special unit—the Civil Society Outreach (CSO)—responsible for liaison between UNCTAD and civil society. Established in 2000, it works to enhance civil society involvement in the activities of UNCTAD and to develop new ways of engaging with civil society in a useful and constructive manner.

III. FORMS OF INVOLVEMENT

The purpose of UNCTAD's relations with NGOs is, on the one hand, to enable the TDB and/or its subsidiary organs to secure information or advice from organizations having special competence and, on the other hand, to enable organizations which represent important elements of public opinion to express their views.[10]

UNCTAD's relations with NGOs may be divided into two major types. First, there are forms of involvement that facilitate NGO input into the work of UNCTAD's intergovernmental organs. These forms are, in particular:

- participation of NGOs in meetings of UNCTAD's intergovernmental organs;
- civil society forums; and
- civil society hearings.

The second type encompasses various modes of cooperation between the UNCTAD Secretariat and NGOs. Such cooperation may involve NGO participation in meetings, workshops and seminars, producing co-publications, information-sharing and policy analysis through an informal exchange of ideas and implementation of technical cooperation programmes. These forms of NGO involvement fall outside the UNCTAD intergovernmental machinery and are carried out by the UNCTAD Secretariat. They are informal and occur on an ad hoc basis. Sometimes, they may become formalized through memoranda of understanding, letters of agreement, letters of intent or other similar documents.[11]

This chapter focuses on mechanisms that enable NGOs to contribute to the work of UNCTAD's intergovernmental organs. It identifies the three categories of NGOs established by UNCTAD, reviews rules for NGO

[10] See Trade and Development Board Decision 43 (VII), 'Arrangements for the participation of non-governmental organizations in the activities of the United Nations Conference on Trade and Development' (20 September 1968) para I:2.
[11] Information from UNCTAD Civil Society Outreach, 16 Nov 2005.

participation in UNCTAD's intergovernmental organs and describes civil society forums and civil society hearings. Finally, this chapter examines the NGO accreditation criteria and procedures applied by UNCTAD.

A. Categories of NGOs

All NGOs officially recognized by UNCTAD are placed in one of the three categories established by Decision 43 (VII). The *General Category* refers to international NGOs that exercise functions and have a basic interest in most of the activities of UNCTAD—nearly all development-related NGOs officially recognized by UNCTAD are found in this category.[12] The *Special Category* covers those international NGOs that have special competence in one or two areas of UNCTAD activities falling within the terms of reference of one or two of the commissions.[13] The NGOs in these first two categories are called 'NGOs with observer status' (or NGOs in status). The third category includes *national* NGOs of recognized standing, which are deemed to have a significant contribution to make to UNCTAD's work. The UNCTAD Secretary-General may enter these NGOs on the *Register* after consultation with the Member State concerned.[14]

The rights of NGOs in each of these categories will be described below. Note that these rights relate solely to NGO participation in UNCTAD's intergovernmental meetings. The official status is also relevant for participating in civil society forums and civil society hearings. By contrast, the fact that a particular NGO is not officially recognized by UNCTAD does not exclude the possibility of the NGO's cooperation with UNCTAD Secretariat on projects of mutual interest.

In August 2005, there were 194 NGOs approved by the TDB: 106 in the General Category, and 88 in the Special Category. In addition, the Secretary-General of UNCTAD entered 16 national NGOs on the Register.[15]

NGOs in status, ie NGOs in the General or Special Category, include development-related bodies, umbrella associations representing a wide range of national and international member organizations, chambers of commerce, trade unions, professional associations and specialized bodies in specific sectors such as trade, sustainable development, transport, banking, insurance, environment and commodities.[16] Among the NGOs in the

---

[12] See Decision 43 (VII), para I:12(a).
[13] See ibid para I:12(b).
[14] See ibid Part III.
[15] See UNCTAD, 'List of Non-Governmental Organizations Participating in the Activities of UNCTAD' TD/B/NGO/LIST/7/Add.1 (2 Aug 2005) para 5.
[16] See <http://www.unctad.org/Templates/Page.asp?intItemID=3476&lang=1>, visited 10 Sept 2005.

General Category are, for example, the International Chamber of Commerce, the International Law Association, Oxfam International and Third World Network. The NGOs in the Special Category include, among others, the Bureau of International Recycling, the European Apparel and Textile Organization, the General Arab Insurance Federation and the International Council of Nurses. Included on the Register are, for example, the All India Association of Industries and the Association of Financial and Industrial Groups of Russia.[17]

B. Participation in UNCTAD's Intergovernmental Meetings

Formal arrangements for NGO involvement in UNCTAD's policy deliberations extend to the Quadrennial Conferences, the Trade and Development Board meetings and the three Commissions. NGO participation in respective meetings is governed by the rules of procedure of the organ concerned.

The Rules of Procedure of the Conference, of the TDB and of the Commissions, all confer on NGOs identical participatory rights. In particular, Rule 77 of the TDB Rules of Procedure provides:

1. Non-governmental organizations concerned with matters of trade and of trade as related to development, referred to in paragraph 11 of General Assembly Resolution 1995 (XIX), may designate representatives to sit as observers at public meetings of the board, its sessional committees and subsidiary organs. The Secretary General of the Conference, in consultation with the Bureau of the Board, shall from time to time prepare a list of such organizations for the approval of the Board. Upon the invitation of the President or Chairman, as the case may be, and subject to the approval of the board or of the subsidiary organ concerned, non-governmental organizations may make oral statements on matters within the scope of their activities.
2. Written statements provided by non-governmental bodies referred to in paragraph 1 above, related to items on the agenda of the Board or of its subsidiary organs, shall be circulated by the secretariat to the members of the Board or the subsidiary organ concerned.

Rule 77 states that in order to participate in the activities of UNCTAD, NGOs must be approved by the Board. Rule 77 confers specific rights on NGOs with observer status:

- The right to designate representatives to sit as observers at public meetings of the TDB and its subsidiary organs;

---

[17] See ibid 2–14.

- The right to make oral statements on matters within the scope of activities of an NGO—upon the invitation of the President/Chairman and subject to the approval of the TDB or of the subsidiary organ concerned; and
- The right to submit written statements related to items on the agenda of the TDB or of its subsidiary organs for circulation to the members of the TDB or the subsidiary organ concerned.

As follows from the text of Rule 77, NGO rights laid down in it apply only to 'public' meetings of the TDB and its subsidiary organs; accordingly, NGOs cannot participate in informal meetings. Also, NGOs are not given an opportunity to influence the agenda-setting for the meetings of the TDB.

In addition to the rights provided for in Rule 77, NGOs in status receive documentation on UNCTAD's ongoing work programmes and projects. This includes studies, publications, documentation and notifications of intergovernmental meetings that they may attend. On request, UNCTAD also disseminates its publications, including occasional papers, periodicals and annual reports.[18]

Rule 81 of the Rules of Procedure of the Conference sets forth the same rights for NGOs.[19] However, in contrast to the TDB meetings where NGOs typically speak on their own behalf or on behalf of several NGOs, at the Conference NGOs usually deliver joint statements agreed to in the course of the civil society forums (see below). In the preparatory process to the Conference, informal meetings are held between the Intergovernmental Preparatory Committee and NGOs that have UNCTAD observer status or have been accredited to the Conference. In the run up to UNCTAD XI, held in 2004, three such informal meetings were convened. Such meetings allow NGOs to influence the shaping of the Conference agenda by raising their issues of concern.

---

[18] See <http://www.unctad.org/Templates/Page.asp?intItemID=3462&lang=1>, visited 10 Sept 2005.

[19] Rule 81 'Observers from Non-Governmental Organizations' provides:

1. Non-governmental organizations concerned with matters of trade and of trade as related to development, referred to in para 11 of General Assembly resolution 1995 (XIX) and included in the list referred to in the *Arrangements for the participation of non-governmental organizations in the activities of the UNCTAD*, may designate representatives to sit as observers at public meetings of the Conference, its main committees and other sessional bodies. Upon the invitation of the President of the Conference or the Chairman of the main committee or of the sessional body, as the case may be, and subject to the approval of the conference or of the sessional body concerned, non-governmental organizations may make oral statements on matters within the scope of their activities.

2. Written statements provided by non-governmental bodies referred to in paragraph 1 above, related to items on the agenda of the Conference shall be circulated by the secretariat to the members of the Conference.

The Rules of Procedure of the Commissions set forth the same NGO rights for participation in meetings of the Commissions and its subsidiary organs (including expert meetings).[20]

As for the difference in rights between NGOs in General and in Special categories, it lies in a range of meetings in which NGOs may participate. NGOs in General Category may participate in all public meetings of *all* UNCTAD intergovernmental organs, including all three Commissions and their subsidiary bodies. NGOs in Special Category may participate in the meetings of the Conference, the TDB and in the meetings of the Commission[21] to which they were assigned at the time of accreditation, as well as the subsidiary bodies of that Commission.[22] Thus, the rights of NGOs in the Special Category are substantively the same, but apply in a narrower circle of intergovernmental organs in accord with the specific area of NGO expertise.

Participatory rights provided for in the Rules of Procedure of the Conference, the TDB and the Commissions do not extend to national NGOs in the Register.[23] For example, these NGOs cannot make written or oral statements to the TDB or its subsidiary organs. Their rights are effectively limited to receiving UNCTAD's documentation.[24] Thus, only international NGOs belonging to the General or Special Category enjoy the mentioned rights.

C. Civil Society Forums

In addition to the involvement described in relevant rules of procedure, beginning in 1996, a practice has emerged to hold global NGO forums linked to UNCTAD Quadrennial Conferences. Formally, these forums are

---

[20] Rule 75 of the Rules of Procedure of the Main Committees of the TDB provides:

1. Non-governmental organizations concerned with matters of trade and of trade as related to development, referred to in paragraph 11 of General Assembly resolution 1995 (XIX) and included in the list referred to in rule [77] of the rules of procedure of the Board, may designate representatives to sit as observers at public meetings of the Committee, its sessional committees and subsidiary bodies. Upon the invitation of the Chairman, and subject to the approval of the body concerned, non-governmental organizations may make oral statements on matters within the scope of their activities.

2. Written statements provided by non-governmental organizations referred to in paragraph 1 of this rule, related to items on the agenda of the Committee or of its subsidiary bodies, shall be circulated by the secretariat to the members of the Committee or the subsidiary body concerned.

[21] Sometimes two Commissions.

[22] See Decision 43 (VII), para I:12.

[23] See Decision 43 (VII), Part V.

[24] See A Haffouz, 'Institutional Framework for Civil Society Cooperation with UNCTAD and Suggestions for its Further Evolution' in *UNCTAD–Civil Society Dialogue on Selected Development Issues Being Addressed by the United Nations System* (United Nations, New York, 2002) 46.

purely NGO (not UNCTAD) events, but UNCTAD facilitates their organization in terms of logistical support by providing meeting space, equipment, interpretation facilities, etc.[25]

NGO forums adopt joint statements embodying NGO views on Conference agenda items. These civil society statements are subsequently delivered to the Conference at the plenary meetings as well as at the meetings on substantive issues, and disseminated as official Conference documents. Consensus for joint statements is built during the preparatory process leading to the forum, which may involve several regional and global preparatory meetings.

In 2004, the Civil Society Forum was convened as part of the official programme of the UNCTAD XI Conference in São Paulo. More than 300 civil society organizations with observer status with UNCTAD organizations accredited by the Preparatory Committee for UNCTAD XI were able to participate. During the Plenary of the Forum (the first two days), participants exchanged information, built consensus and finalized and adopted the Civil Society Declaration which was then presented to the Conference at its Opening Plenary. In the remaining time (6 days) CSOs organized daily workshops, roundtables, debates and side meetings on particular issues of concern. Civil society representatives also had the opportunity to interact and exchange views with representatives of UNCTAD Member States and were able to make contributions to the opening and closing plenaries and the interactive thematic sessions held during the Conference. They were also invited to present their statements during the general debate.[26]

There is no separate accreditation scheme for NGO forums. As they are convened in conjunction with Quadrennial Conferences, NGOs eligible for participation in the Conference take part in the forum.[27]

D. Civil Society Hearings

Since 1988, UNCTAD has held regular consultations with civil society. These consultations have covered a range of topics often of immediate relevance to preparations for upcoming UNCTAD conferences and have provided important opportunities for the UNCTAD Secretariat and NGO representatives to exchange information and analysis on core trade and development issues.[28] In 2001 these meetings developed into the *UNCTAD–Civil Society Dialogues*

[25] Information from UNCTAD Civil Society Outreach, 16 Nov 2005.
[26] See <http://www.unctad.org/Templates/Page.asp?intItemID=3469&lang=1>, visited 10 Sept 2005.
[27] These are the NGOs having UNCTAD observer status and those accredited for the Conference.
[28] See T Hill, 'UNCTAD and NGOs: An Evolving Cooperation', in *UNCTAD–Civil Society Dialogue on Selected Development Issues Being Addressed by the United Nations System* (United Nations, New York, 2002) 55.

and, since 2004, into the *Hearings with Civil Society*. For the first time, this form of cooperation with NGOs was formally institutionalized by the *São Paulo Consensus* adopted by Member States during UNCTAD XI in 2004. Specifically, the TDB was called upon to 'arrange for half-day informal hearings with non-state actors to allow them to express their views on the issues before the Board' (para 117 of the *São Paulo Consensus*). Thus, the Hearings were 'upgraded' in status to become part of the TDB sessions and thus part of UNCTAD's intergovernmental machinery.[29]

Today, the Hearings are held annually in connection with TDB sessions to debate issues before the Board. This is not an inter-NGO event like a civil society forum, but a meeting where NGOs engage in discussions with Member States. Outcomes of the Hearings are summarized by the Secretariat for submission as input into the discussions of the TDB. To participate in the Hearings, an NGO either has to have an observer status with UNCTAD or receive a special accreditation for the Hearings.

IV. ACCREDITATION CRITERIA AND PROCEDURES

A. Criteria for the Observer Status with UNCTAD

To recall, NGOs wishing to take advantage of the rights provided for in the rules of procedure of UNCTAD intergovernmental organs have to be admitted in either the General or the Special Categories (together referred to as NGOs in observer status). Criteria that NGOs must satisfy to receive observer status are set out in TDB Decision 43 (VII) of 20 September 1968. These requirements are common for the General and Special Categories. UNCTAD verifies whether the NGO in question meets the set criteria based on information provided by the NGO in the application questionnaire that is required to be filled out by any NGO applying for the observer status, as well as on the basis of additional materials submitted by the NGO (see below). The criteria are the following (for convenience, they are classified in three groups):

Activities and Membership
1. The NGO must be concerned with matters of trade and of trade as related to development and provide the necessary evidence thereof.[30] UNCTAD undertakes activities in the following main areas:

    * globalization and development;
    * investment, enterprise development and technology;
    * international trade;

---

[29] Information from UNCTAD Civil Society Outreach, 16 Nov 2005.
[30] See Decision 43 (VII), para I:1.

- commodities;
- services infrastructure for development and trade efficiency;
- least developed, landlocked and island developing countries;
- Africa's development; and
- sustainable development.[31]

Evidence of relevant activities of the NGO could include participation in relevant projects, organization of and participation in advocacy campaigns, production of publications, etc.

2. Regard shall be given to the nature and scope of the NGO's activities and to the assistance that may be expected by UNCTAD in carrying out its functions.[32] This criterion facilitates the selection of NGOs whose activities, by their nature, fall in line with those of UNCTAD (primarily policy work, research and technical cooperation).

3. The aims and purposes of the NGO must be in conformity with the spirit, purposes and principles of the UN Charter. [33] The NGO must undertake to support the work of UNCTAD.[34] These basic requirements serve to bar NGOs which could have a destructive impact on UNCTAD activities from admittance (eg violent, extremist, etc).

4. The NGO must be of recognized standing and should represent a substantial proportion of the organized persons within the particular field in which it operates.[35] A Civil Society Outreach official explained that to be of 'recognized standing' means, in UNCTAD context, that the NGO must be officially recognized—that is, registered or incorporated in the country where it was established.[36] The requirement to represent 'a substantial proportion of the organized persons within the particular field' is quite vague. It seems to mean that the NGO has to include in its network (as members or affiliates) a certain number of other NGOs (in particular, national and/or regional NGOs) active in the same field.

5. The NGO must be international in its structure.[37] This criterion is not explained in Decision 43 (VII). It would appear to be satisfied if the NGO has organizations, members and/or affiliates in different countries, or if the NGO has offices and carries out activities in different countries. In assessing the international nature of an NGO, UNCTAD also pays special attention to whether there are representatives of different countries on the governing body of the NGO.[38]

---

[31] See <http://www.unctad.org/Templates/Page.asp?intItemID=3460&lang=1>, visited 10 Sept 2005.
[32] See Decision 43 (VII), para I:11.   [33] See ibid para I:3.
[34] See ibid para I:4.   [35] See ibid para I:5.
[36] Information from UNCTAD Civil Society Outreach, 16 Nov 2005.
[37] See Decision 43 (VII), para 1:8.
[38] Information from UNCTAD Civil Society Outreach, 16 Nov 2005.

6. An international NGO that is a member of a committee or of a group composed of international organizations that has already been accorded observer status will normally not be accredited.[39] This condition is designed to prevent the multiplication of NGOs in observer status that are potentially able to speak in a single voice.

7. Account will be taken of whether or not the field of activity of the organization is wholly or mainly within the field of a specialized agency or another intergovernmental organization.[40] Apparently, such NGOs can be considered ineligible even though their scope of activities may partially coincide with the matters covered by UNCTAD.

Organizational

8. The NGO must have an established headquarters with an executive officer.[41]

Democratic Legitimacy and Accountability

This group of requirements seeks to ensure that NGOs in observer status comply with basic standards of democratic governance, and in particular, that they truly represent their members' interests. These requirements are designed to guarantee that essential (policy) decisions are not taken by a narrow group of individuals (eg, executive officers) but, instead, by a collective organ representative of all members.

9. The NGO must have a conference, convention or other policy-making body.[42]

10. Members of the NGO must exercise voting rights in relation to its policies or action.[43]

11. The NGO must have authority to speak for its members through its authorized representatives.[44]

Decision 43 (VII) does not have any explicit requirements relating to NGOs' independence from national governments or their funding; although, sources of funding must be disclosed in the questionnaire and the annual budget submitted.[45] A Civil Society Outreach official acknowledged in an interview that funding is an important factor that UNCTAD considers. This is explained by the fact that (1) NGOs are non-profit organizations by their nature, (2) they are also 'non-governmental' by their name

---

[39] See Decision 43 (VII), para I:9.
[41] See ibid para I:6.
[43] See ibid para I:8.
[45] See below, p 63.

[40] See ibid para I:10.
[42] See ibid para I:6.
[44] See ibid para I:7.

and thus must be independent—including financially—from governments, and that (3) NGOs must have sufficient financial resources to be sustainable.[46]

Once all common criteria are satisfied, the next step is to decide which of the two types of observer status should be accorded to a particular applicant. To determine this, the only criterion is the extent to which the NGO's scope of activities coincides with those of UNCTAD. According to Decision 43 (VII), NGOs which exercise functions and have a basic interest in most of the activities of the Board are admitted in the General Category;[47] those that have a special competence in, and are concerned with, specific matters falling within the terms of reference of the commissions or of the Board are admitted in the Special Category[48] (for example, NGOs advocating debt relief for poor countries or those concerned with trade in a particular product).

To be entered into the Register, national NGOs are not formally required to meet the common criteria set out above. From Decision 43 (VII) only two conditions for their admission can be discerned:

- They have to be of recognized standing; and
- They must be deemed to have a significant contribution to make to the work of UNCTAD.[49]

National NGOs do not have to be approved by the TDB; they are entered into the Register by the UNCTAD Secretary-General (after consultations with the Member State concerned). Perhaps due to the fact that NGOs in the Register do not have extensive rights, there has not been much interest from national NGOs in obtaining this type of UNCTAD recognition.

B. Procedures for Obtaining Observer Status

To apply for the observer status, NGOs are required to complete an application questionnaire prepared on the basis of the criteria contained in Decision 43 (VII). The questionnaire seeks rather detailed information on the following items:[50]

- *Official name of the organization, its address and the working language;*

---

[46] Information from UNCTAD Civil Society Outreach, 16 Nov 2005.

[47] See Decision 43 (VII), para I:12(a).

[48] See ibid para I:12(b).

[49] However, national NGOs are required to fill out the same questionnaire and submit the same documents as NGOs applying for observer status.

[50] See UNCTAD, Non-Governmental Organizations Questionnaire, 'Application for Status with UNCTAD', available on request from UNCTAD Civil Society Outreach.

- *Membership*: name and address of each national affiliate; method(s) of affiliation and number of members where possible; criteria determining eligibility for membership; and if there are individual members, their number in each country;
- *Officers*: names, nationalities and terms of office of the officers of the international decision-making body and of the senior executive staff;
- *Short history*: events leading to the foundation of the organization, the date of its establishment, the nature of the instrument establishing it and a brief history of the organization;
- *Aims, objectives and activities*: the general aims and objectives of the organization and the activities undertaken to achieve those aims;
- *Structure*: an outline of the structure of the organization and a separate description of each decision-making and administrative body, special commissions, ad hoc bodies, etc; the decision-making process; voting procedures and the manner in which authority is delegated; an explanation of whether the organization has any constitutional, administrative or financial relations with any other organization and whether any aspect of the organization's decision-making process is subject to approval by a related organization;
- *Meetings*: frequency and average attendance; a report of the latest meeting of the principal governing body with the date and place of the next meeting;
- *Finances*: details on all sources of revenue and the basis for assessing membership contributions;
- *Publications*: titles of periodic or other publications issued by the organization;
- *Bibliographical references*: indication of published sources, if any, which make reference to the organization and its work; and
- *Relations with other international organizations*: including ECOSOC, other UN organs/specialized agencies, and other international organizations.

The questionnaire also requests provision of the following supporting documents:

- the NGO's charter, constitution, by-laws and rules of procedure;
- the report of the latest meeting of the principle governing body;
- annual budgets for the past three years;
- one or two examples of the NGO's publications, including annual reports; and
- other documents containing relevant information (at the discretion of the NGO concerned).

The questionnaire and the supporting documents have to be accompanied by a formal request to the Secretary-General of UNCTAD for inclusion on the list provided for in Rule 77 of the TDB Rules of Procedure.

On the basis of the information received from the NGO, the Civil Society Outreach of the UNCTAD Secretariat prepares a document (report) describing the main features of the NGO and submits it for consideration to the Bureau of the TDB.[51] The Secretariat will only make such a report if it is satisfied that the NGO has submitted all required information and satisfies, prima facie, criteria for accreditation.[52] This report is first considered by the Bureau of the TDB.[53] If there are no objections within the Bureau in relation to the particular organization, the candidate NGO is submitted for consideration to the TDB. The Bureau may also return the file to the Secretariat and request additional information about the NGO. The final decision on whether to grant or refuse observer status to an NGO rests with the TDB.[54]

National NGOs do not have to be approved by the TDB; they are entered onto the Register by the UNCTAD Secretary-General after consultations with the Member State concerned.

C. Quadrennial Conferences

NGOs in observer status can take part in Quadrennial Conferences without additional accreditation. Other NGOs (including national NGOs) may also participate in the Conference if they are accredited by the Preparatory Committee (Prepcom) of the Conference. If NGOs on the Register wish to take part, they also have to request accreditation. However, ad hoc accredited NGOs are not entitled to make oral statements in official meetings of the Conference or circulate written statements; they are only entitled to observe the proceedings of the public meetings of the Conference, have access to non-restricted general documentation and use facilities provided for NGOs/CSOs.[55] As an additional benefit, NGOs accredited to the Conference do not have to undergo accreditation for the annual civil society hearings for four years until the next Quadrennial Conference.[56]

---

[51] This report also suggests to classify the NGO into General or Special category.

[52] Information from UNCTAD Civil Society Outreach, 16 Nov 2005.

[53] The Bureau of the TDB consists of 12–15 government representatives elected by the TDB for one year. The main function of the Bureau is to prepare TDB sessions, including setting of the agenda and reviewing of applications for observer status.

[54] Information from UNCTAD Civil Society Outreach, 16 Nov 2005.

[55] See UNCTAD, UNCTAD XI: São Paolo, Brazil, 13–18 June 2004, Accreditation procedures for NGOs/CSOs which do not have observer status with UNCTAD, available on request from Civil Society Outreach.

[56] Information from UNCTAD Civil Society Outreach, 16 Nov 2005.

Criteria for such ad hoc accreditation have not been formalized. The Secretariat makes an assessment of particular NGOs on the basis of the information that NGOs are required to submit in special questionnaires. The information requested by UNCTAD for accreditation to the UNCTAD XI Conference included:

- name and address of the organization;
- structure and geographical coverage (international/regional/national/local);
- membership (total number of members and list of countries; members of the governing body and countries of nationality);
- year of establishment;
- general aims, objectives and activities;
- activities and programmes related to the theme and sub-themes of the Conference;
- finances (sources of revenue and latest annual budget);
- relations with other international organizations; and
- information about whether the NGO has been accredited to an UNCTAD Conference in the past.

This questionnaire is a 'light' version of the one required from NGOs applying for observer status with UNCTAD. Together with the questionnaire, NGOs have to submit copies of their organization's constitution/by-laws/statutes and mission statements, the latest annual report and a financial statement.

Based on the information received, the Civil Society Outreach compiles a report on each NGO applicant and transmits it to the Conference Prepcom for consideration. If no Member State objects, the Prepcom accredits the NGO. In case of objections, there may be a process of consultation and consensus-seeking that will result in a decision either to accredit or to decline accreditation.[57] This process seems to be more political than legal in nature and does not have much to do with the particular NGO's formal compliance, or non-compliance, with the accreditation criteria, especially given the fact that no such criteria have been explicitly established.

Because the UNCTAD Conferences are thematic, the Secretariat and the Prepcom, when assessing applications, pay special attention as to whether the activities and competence of the applicant NGOs correspond to the topic of the Conference. At the same time, the selection is not very strict as this accreditation is just for one event.[58]

---

[57] ibid.   [58] ibid.

D. Civil Society Hearings

According to the UNCTAD website, to participate in the Hearings, NGOs need to be accredited to the Hearings or have observer status with UNCTAD.[59] However, in practice, NGOs on the Register and those accredited to the Quadrennial Conference preceding the Hearings do not need accreditation to participate either.[60]

The criteria that NGOs requesting accreditation have to meet in order to be accredited to the Hearings have not been made explicit. Again, to gather information about applicant NGOs, UNCTAD uses a special questionnaire that is almost identical to the questionnaire that has to be filled out by NGOs applying for accreditation at a Quadrennial Conference. Very few further documents are required from applicants (only copies of constitution/by-laws/statutes and, where available, a mission statement).

Member States are briefed (by email) about NGOs that applied for accreditation to the Hearings. If there are no objections from Member States within the period of time specified by the Secretariat, then the NGOs are accredited. In case of objections, accreditation is declined.[61]

V. MONITORING OF NGOS

UNCTAD rules do not provide for the system of monitoring of NGOs. NGOs are not required to submit periodic reports like in the ECOSOC or WHO systems. Neither do UNCTAD rules envisage a possibility of withdrawing/suspending an observer status. However, it is UNCTAD's policy to exclude NGOs from the list of observers if the contact with a particular NGO has been lost for three years and that NGO does not respond to emails or telephone calls.[62]

Further, as suggested by a Civil Society Outreach official, there is no obstacle for the TDB to make a decision on withdrawal of the observer status from any NGO that manifestly abuses its status or engages in criminal activities. In her view, although the UNCTAD rules do not have explicit provisions in this respect, the relevant powers of the TDB are implicit. However, so far this has never been done.[63]

---

[59] See <http://www.unctad.org/Templates/Page.asp?intItemID=3465&lang=1>, visited 10 Sept 2005.
[60] Information from UNCTAD Civil Society Outreach, 16 Nov 2005.
[61] ibid.
[62] Civil Society Outreach periodically contacts NGOs in order to update basic information about each NGO—concerning, in particular, the head of the organization and its liaison officers, location of headquarters, scope and content of activities, etc.
[63] Information from UNCTAD Civil Society Outreach, 16 Nov 2005.

CHAPTER 4

International Labour Organization (ILO)

I. INTRODUCTION

The International Labour Organization (ILO), established in 1919, is the specialized agency of the United Nations for the promotion of social justice and internationally recognized human and labour rights. The goals of the ILO are to improve working and living conditions of workers, promote and realize human rights at work and enhance employment opportunities. Member States use the ILO as a forum to negotiate and adopt international labour standards in the form of Conventions and Recommendations. The ILO also provides technical assistance to promote and protect basic labour rights.

The ILO is different from other international organizations in the UN system because of its tripartite structure. Whereas in other multilateral institutions Member States are represented only by governments, the ILO has—in each Member State delegation—government, employer and worker representatives.

The two governing organs of the ILO are the International Labour Conference (the ILC, or the Conference) and the Governing Body. The Conference is the organization's annual general assembly with universal country membership. It provides a world forum for discussions on social and labour problems, sets international labour standards, and elects the Governing Body. Every two years, the Conference adopts the ILO's biennial work programme and budget. Each member country has a right to send four delegates to the Conference, two from the government, one representing workers and one representing employers. The worker and employer delegates are selected by the government of their country. However, they cannot be government officials, but must be selected 'in agreement with the industrial organizations, if such organizations exist, which are most representative of employers or workpeople, as the case may be, in their respective countries'.[1] When proposals are voted on, each Member State has two votes for the government, one vote for the workers and one vote for the employers. Worker and employer delegates may speak and vote independently from the government of their country.

---

[1] See Art 3(5) of the ILO Constitution.

The Governing Body is the executive organ of the ILO, comprising 28 government members, 14 worker and 14 employer members. The government members are elected by Member States in the manner prescribed by the ILO Constitution, and employers' and workers' representatives are elected by the employers' and the workers' delegates to the Conference (all for three-year terms).[2] This executive organ of the ILO meets three times a year. It takes decisions on actions to give effect to ILO policies, prepares the draft programme and budget which is then submitted to the Conference for adoption, and elects the Director-General of the ILO.

The permanent secretariat of the ILO is called the International Labour Office (the Office) and is headed by the Director-General, who is elected for a renewable five-year term. Aside from the headquarters in Geneva, the ILO has five regional offices. Regional meetings of the ILO Member States are held periodically to examine matters of special interest to the regions concerned.

II. SCOPE OF THIS CHAPTER

As already mentioned, due to the tripartite structure of the ILO, the Conference and the Governing Body, as well as ILO subsidiary and regional organs and meetings, include representatives of employers' and workers' organizations. The latter two consist of NGOs that are most directly affected by ILO activities. Together, they have equal voting rights with government representatives[3] and thus are organically associated with the work of all ILO decision-making organs.

Accordingly, the ILO Constitution grants unprecedented rights to representatives of these two types of NGOs—workers' and employers' organizations. No other international institution examined in this study grants voting rights to NGOs of any type. Thus, the ILO is unique in directly including non-governmental representatives of national workers' and employers' organizations in its decision-making processes. Note, however, that the worker and employer delegates in the delegation of each Member State represent national organizations and are not accredited by the ILO, but selected by each member government.

The tripartite system of the ILO has been the subject of extensive research and will not be examined in this chapter. The text below will cover only the system of the ILO relations with international NGOs.[4] The latter

---

[2] See Art 7 of the ILO Constitution.

[3] One vote each for the worker and employer representative, two votes for the government.

[4] It must be noted, for the sake of clarity, that ILO relations with international NGOs constitute a smaller part of its relations with civil society as a whole, taking into account the extensive involvement of non-governmental representatives of national workers' and employers' organizations.

do not form part of Member States' delegations but can nevertheless be involved in the ILO processes.

The 1919 Constitution of the International Labour Organization provides for consultative relationships with international NGOs. Article 12(3) of the ILO Constitution states:

> The International Labour Organization may make suitable arrangements for such consultation as it may think desirable with recognized non-governmental international organizations, including international organizations of employers, workers, agriculturists and co-operators.

The ILO Governing Body has adopted, over time, a number of decisions that laid down rules and procedures detailing and classifying the arrangements for NGO involvement. The ILO rules for NGO involvement are not collected in a single document but scattered throughout many Governing Body decisions dating from late 1940s to the present.[5]

Participation of international NGOs in various ILO meetings is further governed by standing orders adopted for each type of meeting, in particular:

- Standing Orders of the International Labour Conference;
- Standing Orders of the Governing Body;
- Rules for Regional Meetings; and
- Standing Orders for Sectoral Meetings.[6]

Within the International Labour Office, the Bureau for Workers' Activities and the Bureau for Employers' Activities deal with trade unions and employers' associations respectively, while the Bureau for External Relations and Partnerships (EXREL) deals with international NGOs that are neither trade unions nor employers' associations. All together, at the headquarters and in the field offices, the ILO has over 80 full-time staff handling relations with non-governmental actors.[7]

---

[5] A useful compilation of a number (but not all) of these decisions can be found in the recent ILO document GB.294/9 (November 2005) 81–89, <http://www.ilo.org/public/english/standards/relm/gb/docs/gb294/pdf/gb-9.pdf>, visited 18 Nov 2005. See also appendix III of this book, p 249.

[6] For the texts of these standing orders, see <http://www.ilo.org/public/english/bureau/leg/reglem.htm>, visited 10 Nov 2005.

[7] This figure includes staff dealing with national workers' and employers' organizations and international NGOs. Source: interview with Ms Yoshie Ichinohe and Mr Dominique Peccoud, ILO Bureau for External Relations and Partnerships (18 Nov 2005).

NGO involvement in ILO activities can be divided into two broad categories:

- involvement in ILO policy deliberations through participation in ILO meetings; and
- involvement in ILO operational, ie technical cooperation, activities.

This chapter focuses on the participation of international NGOs in ILO meetings and policy deliberations. As far as the operational level is concerned, the ILO mainly cooperates with local, national or regional NGOs—professional associations, cooperatives, village development committees, water users' committees, rural or urban credit groups, NGOs concerned with local and national development or human rights, indigenous community organizations, and others.[8] Each technical department of the ILO has discretion to determine whether and to what extent to involve NGOs in its programmes and projects, in accordance with the ILO's financial regulations, and after consulting the department in charge of the relations between the ILO and employers' and workers' organizations.[9] One example of a department with particularly close relations with NGOs is the ILO International Programme on the Elimination of Child Labour (IPEC).[10] NGO involvement in operational activities will not be covered further in this chapter.

The ILO has established, over time, the following three major categories of international NGOs:

- NGOs in general and regional consultative status;
- NGOs included on the 'Special List'; and
- all remaining international NGOs.

These categories will be reviewed in turn.

A. NGOs in General and Regional Consultative Status

NGOs in general or regional consultative status are international NGOs with an important interest in a wide range of the ILO's activities.

---

[8] See <http://www.ilo.org/public/english/comp/civil/ngo/relngios.htm>, visited 15 Oct 2005.

[9] Interview with Ms Yoshie Ichinohe and Mr Dominique Peccoud (n 7).

[10] For more, see <http://www.ilo.org/public/english/standards/ipec/index.htm>, visited 15 Oct 2005.

Depending on their geographic coverage, they are granted either general or regional consultative status. Currently there are eight NGOs in general consultative status[11] and 16 NGOs in regional consultative status.[12]

NGOs granted general consultative status enjoy a standing invitation to all ILO meetings, namely meetings of the Conference, of the Governing Body (including all of their subsidiary organs) and regional meetings.[13] During all meetings, NGOs have the same participatory rights:

- the right to observe;
- the right to make oral statements on questions considered at the meeting other than administrative and financial questions (with the permission of the President/Chairman of the meeting and in agreement with two Vice-Presidents/Vice-Chairmen; if agreement cannot be reached, the matter is referred to the meeting for decision without discussion); and
- the right to circulate written statements on questions considered at the meeting other than administrative and financial questions (conditions for the exercise of this right are the same as for oral statements).

These rights are provided for in the standing orders governing the procedures at various ILO meetings.[14] NGOs are not entitled to participate in the preparatory processes for meetings or influence the setting of meeting agendas.

Regional consultative status was introduced in the 1960s in order to forestall applications for consultative status of regional organizations that were international but did not have a worldwide scope.[15] NGOs granted regional consultative status may participate in all regional meetings subject to the relevant standing orders. In particular, they may attend ILO Regional Conferences and ILO tripartite meetings of a regional nature in their respective regions, as well as make or circulate (with the permission of the Chairperson and Vice-Chairpersons) statements on matters included in the

---

[11] For example, the World Federation of Trade Unions, the International Organisation of Employers and the International Confederation of Free Trade Unions and World Confederation of Labour (the latter two organizations are in the process of being unified into a new world trade union organization).

[12] For example, the International Confederation of Arab Trade Unions, the Inter-American Regional Organization of Workers, and the European Trade Union Confederation.

[13] See Resolution of the ILO Governing Body: *Relations between the International Labour Organisation and Non-Governmental Organisations*, Minutes of the 105th Session of the Governing Body (June 1948) 92.

[14] See Arts 2(3)(j), 14(10) and 56(9) of the Standing Orders of the Conference; Art 7 of the Standing Orders of the Governing Body; Arts 1(7) and 10(4) of the Rules for Regional Meetings; and Art 9(3) of the Standing Orders for Sectoral Meetings. Mentioned documents are available at <http://www.ilo.org/public/english/bureauj/leg/reglem.htm> visited 10 Nov 2005.

[15] See E Osieke, *Constitutional Law and Practice in the International Labour Organisation* (Martinus Nijhoff, Dordrecht, 1985) 70.

agenda and receive ILO documents regularly.[16] NGOs in regional status are *not* automatically invited to global ILO meetings, such as sessions of the Conference and its committees, of the Governing Body, or of any other meetings of general character. If they wish to attend any such meetings, they need to secure an invitation for this purpose, with the exception of the Governing Body meetings which are open *exclusively* to NGOs with general consultative status.[17] To clarify, an 'invitation' in the ILO context means the same as 'accreditation' in the context of other international organizations, that is, permission to participate. The procedures to obtain an invitation are discussed in detail below.

B. NGOs on the Special List

The second category, the Special List of Non-Governmental International Organizations, was set up by the ILO Governing Body in 1956 with a view to establish working relations with international NGOs that are *not* employers' or workers' organizations but whose aims and activities coincide with those of the ILO.[18] These may be NGOs concerned with the promotion of human rights, poverty alleviation, social security, professional rehabilitation, gender issues, youth matters, etc. There are currently 160 NGOs on the Special List, including Amnesty International, Indigenous World Association, International Centre for Human Rights and Democratic Development, International Council of Women, International Council on Social Welfare, World Assembly of Youth.

The NGOs on the Special List are not considered to be in consultative status and do not automatically receive any rights or privileges in terms of participation in the ILO meetings; standing arrangements for their representation have not been made. However, it is made easier for them—as compared to NGOs that do not have any formal relations with the ILO—to obtain an invitation to participate in specific ILO meetings. Having secured an invitation, they can make use of the same rights as NGOs in consultative status.[19] Additionally, they do not need an invitation to the meetings of the Conference if they want to attend simply as observers without additional participatory rights. In this case, it is sufficient for them to announce their intention to attend one month in advance of the Conference.

---

[16] See Report of the Officers of the ILO Governing Body, Minutes of the 160th Session of the Governing Body (17–20 Nov 1964) 147, para 14. See also ILO Rules for Regional Meetings, Arts 1.7 and 10.4, <http://www.ilo.org/public/english/bureau/leg/reglem.htm>, visited 10 Nov 2005.

[17] See Report of the Officers of the ILO Governing Body, Minutes of the 160th Session of the Governing Body (17–20 Nov 1964) 147, para 15.

[18] See ILO Governing Body, *Establishment of a Special List of Non-Governmental Organizations*, GB.132/6/5 (1–2 June 1956) para 4.

[19] See the list of rights above, p 71.

NGOs on the Special List also enjoy the privilege of receiving journals and periodicals published by the ILO, as well as information on forthcoming sessions of the International Labour Conference and other ILO meetings on a regular basis.[20]

C. Remaining International NGOs

All remaining international NGOs do not have any formal relationship with the ILO but they can request the Governing Body to extend invitations to attend specific sessions of the International Labour Conference or other ILO meetings excluding the Governing Body sessions, for which these NGOs have a particular interest. To be invited, NGOs have to satisfy the established criteria.[21] Accordingly, this is, in fact, a system of ad hoc accreditation for particular events. Once invited, these NGOs formally enjoy the same participatory rights as NGOs in consultative status.[22]

D. Conclusion

Under the ILO regime, despite the differentiation between NGOs, there is no formal difference in treatment of NGOs, as long as they are officially invited to be represented at a particular meeting. Whether it is an NGO in general consultative status, regional consultative status, an NGO from the Special List or an NGO without any formal relationship with the ILO, once invited, it will have the same participatory rights.[23] The difference lies only in their admission to meetings.

NGOs in general consultative status can access all ILO meetings without requesting an invitation to a particular meeting. Additionally, those in general consultative status are the only NGOs with the privilege of attending meetings of the Governing Body; other NGOs do not have the possibility of securing such an invitation. NGOs in regional consultative status can access regional ILO meetings of the respective region without requesting an invitation to a particular meeting. NGOs in regional consultative status can also access global ILO meetings if they obtain an invitation (through a simplified procedure). NGOs on the Special List can participate in ILO meetings (whether general or regional) only if they receive an invitation, although through the same simplified procedure. Finally, all other NGOs have to go through a more burdensome accreditation procedure[24] if they

---

[20] Interview with Ms Yoshie Ichinohe and Mr Dominique Pecloud (n 7).

[21] See below pp 78–81.

[22] See the list of rights above, p 71.

[23] Naturally, although all participating NGOs receive formally equal treatment, they do not have the same political influence.

[24] The difference between the simplified accreditation procedure and the regular accreditation procedure is explained below, p 79.

want to be represented in a particular ILO meeting. However, after they are accredited for the first time, accreditation for subsequent Conference meetings becomes simplified for them too.

V. ACCREDITATION CRITERIA AND PROCEDURES

A. *General and Regional Consultative Status*

Speaking broadly, general or regional consultative status is reserved for those NGOs that are considered to be 'social partners' of the ILO, that is, NGOs representing workers and employers.[25]

Article 12(3) of the ILO Constitution, cited above, refers to consultative relationships with 'recognized non-governmental international organizations, including international organizations of employers, workers, agriculturists and co-operators'. From this provision, it follows that any NGO applying for *general* consultative status must be, at a minimum:

- international. The ILO effectively limited the grant of general consultative status to *universal* NGOs, that is, to those that cover all four ILO regions (Africa, Americas, Asia and the Pacific, and Europe). The only exceptions are the Organization of African Trade Union Unity and the Pan-African Employers' Confederation—they were granted general consultative status on the understanding that this decision was based on the special circumstances of the case and would not constitute a precedent for the future;[26]
- recognized. The ILO does not have any officially articulated definition of what 'recognized' means—the term may connote such meanings as 'known' or 'representative'; recognition by other international organizations or by other workers' and employers' movements may also be taken into account;[27] and
- relevant to most ILO matters of competence and with 'an important interest in a wide range of ILO activities',[28] as evidenced by an illustrative list of organizations included in the Article. In fact, this list is now considered exhaustive—thus, *only* organizations of employers, workers, agriculturists and cooperators are eligible for the general consultative status.

---

[25] Interview with Ms Yoshie Ichinohe and Mr Dominique Peccoud (n 7).
[26] See Osieke (n 15) 71.
[27] Interview with Ms Yoshie Ichinohe and Mr Dominique Peccoud (n 7).
[28] Resolution of the ILO Governing Body of 14 June 1948, *Relations between the International Labour Organization and Non-Governmental Organizations*, Minutes of the 105th Session of the Governing Body, 92, para 1.

Regional consultative status can be granted to regional NGOs of employers and workers that are 'broadly representative of interests concerned with a wide range of ILO activities in the region concerned and active there'.[29] Article 12(3) of the ILO Constitution does not apply to NGOs in regional consultative status.[30]

The difference between NGOs in general and regional status lies in their geographical reach. Those whose representation and activities are confined to one of the four ILO regions (Africa, Americas, Asia and the Pacific, and Europe) can only claim regional status, whereas global NGOs are granted general status. It appears that an NGO covering two regions still cannot claim general status—in this case the NGO can be granted regional status in two regions.[31]

An NGO applying for general or regional consultative status must provide to the ILO:

- a copy of its Constitution;
- names and addresses of its officers;
- particulars of its composition and of the membership of affiliated national organizations; and
- a copy of its latest annual report.[32]

Both general and regional statuses are granted by the Governing Body, on the recommendation of its officers. Most NGOs in general and regional consultative status have had such status for decades, and no new organizations of comparable importance and breadth of coverage are expected to emerge in the near future.

B. Special List

There exists a separate set of criteria for admission of NGOs to the Special List. These criteria, established by the Governing Body in 1956, include:[33]

---

[29] See Report of the Officers of the ILO Governing Body, Minutes of the 160th Session of the Governing Body (17–20 Nov 1964) 147, para 13.

[30] Interview with Ms Yoshie Ichinohe and Mr Dominique Peccoud (n 7).

[31] This is currently the case for the International Confederation of Arab Trade Unions and the General Union of Chambers of Commerce, Industry and Agriculture for Arab Countries—these organizations have regional status for both Africa and the Asia and the Pacific regions simultaneously.

[32] For general consultative status, see Resolution of the ILO Governing Body of June 1948, *Relations between the International Labour Organization and Non-Governmental Organizations*, Minutes of the 105th Session of the Governing Body, 92, para 4. For regional consultative status, see Report of the Officers of the ILO Governing Body, Minutes of the 160th Session of the Governing Body (17–20 Nov 1964) 147, para 13.

[33] See *Establishment of a Special List of Non-Governmental Organizations* (n 18) para 5.

- the international nature of the NGO's activities. In the ILO, an 'international NGO' means an NGO international in its structure (having national organizations as members/affiliates), geographical coverage, or its scope of activities.[34] It is clear that for the purposes of the Special List, 'international' does not mean 'universal' or 'world-wide', as is the case with general consultative status;
- the aims of the NGO should be in harmony with the spirit, aims and principles of the ILO Constitution and the Declaration of Philadelphia.[35] This requirement can bar from admission, for example, extremist organizations or those promoting anti-ILO values; and
- the NGO must have an evident interest in at least one of the fields of activity of the ILO. This means that the NGO must demonstrate that its own activities are relevant to the activities of the ILO.

The following factors are also taken into account when reviewing NGOs' applications:

- the length of existence of the NGO;
- membership;
- geographical coverage; and
- practical achievements of the NGO.[36]

These requirements are listed in two groups, as 'criteria' and as 'factors', to underscore the vagueness of the requirements designated as 'factors'. For example, the ILO considers the length of existence of the NGO to be relevant, but it does not specify an acceptable minimum period of existence. Similarly, it is unclear how broad membership and the geographical coverage of an NGO must be to make it eligible. The same is true for the 'practical achievements' factor. These requirements are subject to very flexible interpretation, leaving a wide margin of discretion to the ILO organ reviewing the application from an NGO.

As a matter of practice, these criteria and factors are not exhaustive. In an interview, the ILO officials stated that when considering an NGO for accreditation, they also check whether it is independent from the government, including financially (these requirements follow from the concept of an NGO as a 'non-governmental' organization), and whether the NGO

---

[34] Interview with Ms Yoshie Ichinohe and Mr Dominique Peccoud (n 7).

[35] The full title of the Declaration of Philadelphia is the 'Declaration concerning the aims and purposes of the International Labour Organization'. It was adopted at Philadelphia in 1944 and is annexed to the ILO Constitution.

[36] See *Establishment of a Special List of Non-Governmental Organizations* (n 18) para 5. It is also mentioned that the fact that an organization has already been granted official status with the ECOSOC, or a UN specialized agency, is relevant but does not necessarily lead to the inclusion in the Special List.

concerned adheres to basic principles of democratic governance (for example, that members of the NGO can exercise voting rights and can do it in a non-discriminatory manner).[37] They also take into account the previous and ongoing working relations of applicant NGOs with ILO technical departments. They maintained that admission to the Special List is not a 'mechanical process'; the ILO 'really selects' which NGOs to include by making an overall assessment of each NGO and its activities. As explained by the ILO officials, since admission to the Special List implies an institutionalized relationship with the ILO, when assessing applicant NGOs, they pay more attention to their structure, representativity, sustainability and other institutional matters, rather than purely to the relevance of the NGO to ILO activities, as is the case with ad hoc accreditation for specific meetings.[38]

Documents required from an NGO applying for inclusion to the Special List are basically the same as those required for the granting of consultative status:

- a copy of its statutes;
- a list of the names and addresses of its officers;
- information regarding its composition and the aggregate membership of the national organizations affiliated to it;
- a copy of its latest annual report or detailed and verifiable information about its activities;[39] and
- information on the sources of financing of the NGO.[40]

Upon receiving a request and all required documents, EXREL makes a preliminary assessment of whether the NGO satisfies the criteria. The application can be rejected at this stage if there is a manifest inconsistency with one or more of the requirements.[41] In case the NGO is considered eligible, EXREL compiles general data about this NGO in an information note and circulates it to relevant technical departments of the ILO, asking for their comments.[42] This process of internal consultation results in a recommendation to the Director-General who has power to include or refuse inclusion

---

[37] Interview with Ms Yoshie Ichinohe and Mr Dominique Peccoud (n 7).
[38] ibid.
[39] See <http://www.ilo.org/public/english/comp/civil/ngo/relngios.htm#ol>, visited 15 Sept 2005.
[40] Interview with Ms Yoshie Ichinohe and Mr Dominique Peccoud (n 7).
[41] ibid.
[42] The Information Note is always sent to the Bureau for Employers' Activities, Bureau for Workers' Activities, Office of the Legal Adviser and any concerned technical departments, as identified by EXREL. Source: Interview with Ms Yoshie Ichinohe and Mr Dominique Peccoud (n 7).

of the NGO on the Special List. Usually, the whole procedure does not take more than a year.[43]

During the first 10 years of existence of the Special List, NGOs were admitted to it by the decision of the officers of the Governing Body. However, in 1966 the officers delegated this power to the ILO Director-General who makes a decision on recommendation from EXREL.[44] Usually, two to five NGOs are admitted to the Special List each year.

C. Accreditation to the Conference

The ILO has established a separate set of criteria that must be satisfied by NGOs wishing to be invited to the International Labour Conference. These criteria are less numerous than the ones set for NGOs on the Special List. Again, note that in the context of the ILO, accreditation is referred to as an 'invitation'.

Any NGO wishing to be invited to the Conference:[45]

1. should be international in its composition and activities. It appears that the NGO needs to demonstrate that it is represented or has affiliates in a considerable number of countries;
2. should have aims and objectives that are in harmony with the spirit, aims and principles of the ILO Constitution and the Declaration of Philadelphia; and
3. should formally express a clearly defined interest, supported by its statutes and by explicit reference to its own activities, in at least one of the items on the agenda of the Conference session to which it requests to be invited. The NGO has to provide concrete proof of its interest in an agenda item and of activities actually conducted by it in the field in question.[46] This proof can be in the form of studies, publications, participation in relevant projects, etc.

---

[43] ibid.

[44] See ILO, Report of the Officers of the Governing Body, *Admission to the ILO Special List of Non-Governmental Organizations*, GB.164/18/40 (28 Feb–4 Mar 1966).

[45] See ILO, 'Information Note: Representation of international non-governmental organizations at the International Labour Conference and other ILO meetings' (May 2005) 1, <http://www.ilo.org/public/english/comp/civil/ngo/relngios.htm#ol>, visited 15 Sept 2005 [hereinafter 'Information Note for NGOs']. The same information can be found in the *Conference Guide*, 94th Session of the International Labour Conference (Geneva, 7–23 Feb 2006) Appendix III: Representation of international non-governmental organizations at the International Labour Conference, <http://www.ilo.org/public/english/standards/relm/ilc/ilc94/guide.pdf>, visited 15 Nov 2005 [hereinafter 'Conference Guide'].

[46] See ILO Governing Body, Committee on Standing Orders and the Application of Conventions and Recommendations, *Representation of Non-Governmental International Organizations at the International Labour Conference*, GB.245/SC/2/1 (Feb–Mar 1990) footnote 3.

As the accreditation for the Conference is for one event only and does not entail an institutional relationship between the ILO and admitted NGOs, the examination focuses more on the relevance of the activities of a particular NGO to the agenda item(s) of the Conference.[47]

An NGO applying for the accreditation at the Conference must send with its request:

- a copy of its statutes;
- the names and titles of its officers;
- a description of its composition and the aggregate membership of the national organizations affiliated with it;
- a copy of its latest report; and
- detailed and verifiable information about its sources of financing.[48]

Recall that only NGOs in general consultative status can participate in the Conference without requesting a special invitation. NGOs in regional consultative status, NGOs on the Special List and all other NGOs (without any formal relationship with the ILO) all need to request and secure such an invitation in order to enjoy participatory rights. However, organizations with regional consultative status, those on the Special List and those that have been invited to previous sessions of the Conference are considered to have satisfied conditions (1) and (2) and are exempt from submitting the documents and information otherwise required.[49] For the enumerated organizations, it is sufficient to express, in the request for accreditation, a clearly defined interest in at least one of the items on the agenda of the Conference session and to support this interest by its statutes and by explicit reference to its own activities. This constitutes a *simplified accreditation procedure*.

Accordingly, all of the listed documents need to be submitted only by NGOs applying for Conference accreditation for the first time. The request for accreditation must be submitted at least one month before the opening of the session of the Governing Body preceding the session of the Conference.[50]

The information received by the ILO from each NGO applying for the first time is compiled in an information note, a 'write-up'. The write-up is then circulated among the Office of the Legal Adviser, the Bureau for Employers' and Workers' Activities and any technical departments concerned, for review and comment. If there is no evident lack of confor-

---

[47] Interview with Ms Yoshie Ichinohe and Mr Dominique Peccoud (n 7).
[48] 'Information Note for NGOs' (n 45) 1. The list of this document was originally set out in *Establishment of a Special List of Non-Governmental Organizations* (n 18) para 6.
[49] 'Information Note for NGOs' (n 45) 2; ILO, 'Conference Guide' (n 45) 17.
[50] 'Information Note for NGOs' (n 45) 1.

mity with the agreed criteria, the write-up is then included in the customary note submitted to the officers of the Governing Body for decision.[51] If there are disagreements between the officers as to whether a particular NGO should be accredited, they refer the matter to the Governing Body.[52] NGOs cannot attend the deliberations concerning their admission and cannot appeal the decision.[53]

In 1998 and in 2004, a considerable number of first-time requests for accreditation to the Conference were received and approved due to the highly topical items on the agenda of the Conference in those years (child labour and migrant workers, respectively). In the intervening years only a few, or even no requests at all, were received or approved.[54]

D. Accreditation to Conference Committees

The accreditation to the Conference is sufficient to participate in the plenary sittings of the Conference but does not extend to participation in the Conference committees. For this, an NGO would need a special invitation from the Selection Committee of the Conference.[55] The criteria for a special invitation have not been formalized, but since the NGO has already gone through the Conference accreditation procedure and is deemed to satisfy the basic criteria for participation, the main criterion is the relevance of NGO activities to the work of the particular Conference committee.[56]

The rules governing such decisions by the Selection Committee have not been formalized either, but in practice NGOs are not required to submit any further documents. The explanation of the connection between the committee mandate/agenda and the activities of the NGO is sufficient. Usually, NGOs specify the agenda items that they wish to follow, ie which committee meetings they would like to attend, in their request for accreditation to the Conference.[57]

---

[51] See ILO, Report of the Officers of the Governing Body, *Procedure and criteria applied to initial requests by international non-governmental organizations to be invited to be represented at the International Labour Conference*, GB.292/17/2 (Mar 2005) para 3.

[52] See ibid para 6.

[53] Interview with Ms Yoshie Ichinohe and Mr Dominique Peccoud (n 7).

[54] See ILO, Report of the Officers of the Governing Body, *Procedure and criteria applied to initial requests by international non-governmental organizations to be invited to be represented at the International Labour Conference*, GB.292/17/2 (Mar 2005) para 4

[55] See Standing Orders of the ILC, Article 56(9); and 'Information Note for NGOs' (n 45) 2. The Selection Committee is composed of 28 members appointed by the government group, 14 members appointed by the employers' group, and 14 by the workers' group. Its responsibilities include arranging the programme of the Conference, fixing the time and agenda of its plenary sittings and acting on its behalf on any other routine question. See 'Conference Guide' (n 45) 8.

[56] Interview with Ms Yoshie Ichinohe and Mr Dominique Peccoud (n 7).

[57] ibid.

E. Accreditation to Other ILO Meetings

According to the ILO Information Note for NGOs, requests by international NGOs for invitations to be represented at ILO meetings *other than the Conference* are considered in light of the relevant rules and standing orders governing those meetings.[58] However, for example, the Standing Orders of the Governing Body do not contain any criteria for the admission of NGOs to its meetings.[59] Neither do the Standing Orders for Sectoral Meetings or Rules for Regional Meetings.[60] The only 'relevant rule' that was located suggests that the main criterion for accreditation is the 'special interest [of an NGO] in the matter to be dealt with at the meeting'.[61] In other words, an NGO's competence and activities must be relevant to the subject of the meeting.

With regard to procedures for this form of accreditation, the ILO Information Note refers, once again, to the relevant rules and standing orders governing the meetings in question.[62] However, again the ILO rules and standing orders do not, in fact, set forth lists of required documents; they provide only that the invitations are granted to NGOs by the Governing Body. The Information Note specifies that it is the officers of the Governing Body who make the decision.[63] Before the matter comes to the attention of the officers of the Governing Body, NGOs' requests for accreditation are considered by the ILO technical department responsible for the meeting, or, in case of regional meetings, by ILO regional offices. If there are disagreements among the officers as to whether or not to accredit a particular NGO, they refer the matter to the Governing Body.

Every year, in August–September, the ILO sends to NGOs with which it has formal relations, as well as to other NGOs that have been invited to one or more previous sessions of the Conference, the list of next year's Conference and other ILO meetings that they may be accredited to, so that NGOs can apply for accreditation well in advance.[64] A request for an invitation to a meeting must be submitted by NGOs not later than one month before the Governing Body session preceding the meeting for which the request is made.

---

[58] See 'Information Note for NGOs' (n 45) 2.

[59] See Art 7 of the Standing Orders of the Governing Body on representation of NGOs. As a matter of practice, only NGOs in general consultative status are admitted to meetings of the Governing Body. Source: Interview with Ms Yoshie Ichinohe and Mr Dominique Peccoud (n 7).

[60] See Art 9.3 of the ILO Standing Orders for Sectoral Meetings and Art 1.7 of the ILO Rules for regional Meetings.

[61] Report of the Officers of the ILO Governing Body, Minutes of the 148th Session of the Governing Body (7–10 Mar 1961) 130, para 9.

[62] See 'Information Note for NGOs' (n 45) 2.

[63] See Art 7 of the Standing Orders of the Governing Body; ILO, 'Information Note for NGOs' (n 45) 2.

[64] Interview with Ms Yoshie Ichinohe and Mr Dominique Peccoud (n 7).

VI. MONITORING OF NGOS

The ILO does not have detailed rules on the monitoring of NGOs. NGOs on the Special List have an obligation to submit their annual reports to the ILO,[65] which are not only used to assess relations between the ILO and NGOs, but are also treated as an indication that the NGOs concerned are still in existence and active in the field relevant to the ILO.[66] NGOs in general or regional consultative status are not required to submit annual reports.

The Governing Body Resolution of 14 June 1948 provides that the 'Governing Body may at any time revoke a decision to establish consultative relationships'.[67] The Resolution does not specify what may constitute the grounds for revocation. At the time when this Resolution was adopted, the general consultative status was the only form of official ILO relations with NGOs. Therefore, legally, this norm is applicable only to the NGOs in general consultative status.

So far, no NGO has been deprived of its general or regional consultative status; NGOs have only been removed from the Special List because they ceased to exist or were no longer traceable. An NGO can also be removed if it merges with another NGO(s); if the newly born NGO wishes to be included on the Special List, it must go through a new accreditation procedure.[68] EXREL conducts occasional surveys to see whether the NGOs on the Special List still exist and are active. If EXREL, for whatever reason, finds that an NGO should be removed, it makes a recommendation to the officers of the Governing Body, who make a final decision.[69]

---

[65] See *Establishment of a Special List of Non-Governmental Organizations* (n 18) para 20.
[66] Interview with Ms Yoshie Ichinohe and Mr Dominique Peccoud (n 7).
[67] Resolution of the ILO Governing Body of 14 June 1948, *Relations between the International Labour Organisation and Non-Governmental Organisations*, Minutes of the 105th Session of the Governing Body, 92, para 5.
[68] Interview with Ms Yoshie Ichinohe and Mr Dominique Peccoud (n 7).
[69] ibid.

CHAPTER 5

World Intellectual Property Organization (WIPO)

I. INTRODUCTION

The World Intellectual Property Organization (WIPO), created in 1967 by the Convention Establishing the World Intellectual Property Organization (WIPO Convention), is the specialized agency of the United Nations for the promotion of the use and protection of intellectual property. It administers 23 international intellectual property treaties, the oldest of which are the 1883 Paris Convention for the Protection of Industrial Property and the 1886 Berne Convention for the Protection of Literary and Artistic Works.[1] WIPO assists governments, organizations and the private sector with intellectual property matters. WIPO closely monitors developments in the field of intellectual property and harmonizes and simplifies relevant rules and practices.[2] The three major areas of WIPO activities are (1) registration of certain intellectual property rights; (2) norm-setting work in the field of intellectual property; and (3) technical cooperation with developing countries. WIPO Member States currently include 182 nations.

WIPO is a constitutionally complex organization. Its complexity stems from the fact that most international treaties administered by WIPO establish a legally separate Union of States (meaning that each treaty has its own unique membership), usually with its own administrative organ of Member States. These separate Unions are linked by the common subject-matter of the treaties establishing them (intellectual property) and by a common secretariat. WIPO is thus the umbrella organization that ensures administrative cooperation between the various Unions and provides a secretariat for all of them.

At the time WIPO was created, the administrative structures of existing Unions were modified to render them more uniform.[3] Treaties concluded

---

[1] These 23 treaties include 15 treaties on industrial property, seven on copyright and neighbouring rights, and the WIPO Convention.

[2] See <http://www.wipo.int/about-wipo/en/gib.htm#P6_18>, visited 1 Apr 2005.

[3] The relevant treaties were: the Paris Convention for the Protection of Industrial Property of 1883 (Paris Convention), the Berne Convention for the Protection of Literary and Artistic Works of 1886 (Berne Convention), the Madrid Agreement Concerning the International Registration of Marks of 1891, the Hague Agreement Concerning the International Deposit of Industrial Designs of 1925, the Nice Agreement Concerning the International Classification of

since that time also established governance structures according to this adopted template. Each Union has an Assembly of Member States and, in the case of earlier treaties, may also have a Conference of Representatives. As a general rule, these bodies meet in ordinary session once every two years. In the case of the Paris Convention and the Berne Convention, there are also Executive Committees that meet in the interim year when the Assemblies of those Unions do not meet in ordinary session.

Aside from organs established by treaties governing various substantive aspects of intellectual property, there are also organs established by the WIPO Convention itself. These latter organs include the WIPO General Assembly, the Conference and the Coordination Committee. The General Assembly meets once every second year in ordinary sessions to appoint the Director General, adopt the biennial budget, give instructions to the Coordination Committee, approve measures concerning the administration of the covered international agreements and exercise other functions.[4] Since 2000, as a matter of practice, a session of the General Assembly takes place alongside sessions of other WIPO Assemblies every year.[5] The main function of the Conference, which is convened annually during the same period as the General Assembly and is also open to all WIPO Member States, is to discuss matters of general interest in the field of intellectual property. The Conference may adopt recommendations relating to such matters, having regard for the competence and autonomy of the Unions.[6]

The Coordination Committee is WIPO's executive organ, created to ensure coordination between the Assemblies of the various Unions on matters of common interest. It is formed by Member States of the Executive Committees of the Paris Union and of the Berne Union. The primary tasks of the Coordination Committee are to give advice to the organs of the Unions, the General Assembly, the Conference and the Director General concerning all administrative, financial and other matters of common interest; to prepare the draft agendas of the General Assembly and of the Conference; and to nominate candidates for the position of the Director General.[7] WIPO's intergovernmental organs and the intergovernmental organs of the Unions are supported by the Secretariat (the 'International Bureau').

Aside from the mentioned intergovernmental bodies, WIPO also has a multitude of committees that may be either standing or ad hoc. Committees

Goods and Services for the Purposes of the Registration of Marks of 1957 and the Lisbon Agreement for the Protection of Appellations of Origin and their International Registration of 1958.

[4] See Art 6 of the WIPO Convention.
[5] It thus meets, in turn, in ordinary and extraordinary sessions.
[6] See Art 7 of the WIPO Convention. 'Unions' refers primarily to the Paris Union (International Union established by the Paris Convention) and the Berne Union (International Union established by the Berne Convention), see Art 2 of the WIPO Convention.
[7] See Art 8 of the WIPO Convention.

may be created by a particular treaty, by one of the main organs of WIPO or by a particular Union. For example, ad hoc committees of experts have been traditionally used within WIPO as a vehicle for preparing instruments establishing new norms in the area of intellectual property. If, and when, the work of a committee of experts reaches a sufficiently mature stage, a diplomatic conference will be convened to conclude the treaty on the subject-matter initially considered by the committee of experts.

Another category of bodies within WIPO consists of working groups established by committees. Usually they are created to facilitate the discussion and resolution of particular questions and have both limited missions and existence.

<h2 style="text-align:center">II. LEGAL BASIS</h2>

The 1967 WIPO Convention provides explicitly for consultation and cooperation with international and national NGOs. Article 13(2) of the WIPO Convention states:

> The Organization may, on matters within its competence, make suitable arrangements for consultation and cooperation with international non-governmental organizations and, with the consent of the Governments concerned, with national organizations, governmental or non-governmental. Such arrangements shall be made by the Director General after approval by the Coordination Committee.

The existing WIPO formal arrangements for consultation and cooperation with NGOs apply only to their participation in WIPO meetings. Although NGOs can also be involved in WIPO technical cooperation activities, there are no rules or guidelines whatsoever governing this form of involvement.[8]

Generally, WIPO rules on relations with NGOs are rather scarce. The gaps are filled through actual practice. NGO participation in WIPO meetings is subject to the WIPO General Rules of Procedure,[9] which govern meetings of all bodies convened under the auspices of WIPO, to the extent that any such body does not adopt special rules of procedure.[10] In particular, Rule 8(2) and Rule 24 are relevant for NGOs.

In the run-up to each session of WIPO Assemblies, the WIPO Secretariat prepares a memorandum entitled 'Admission of Observers', which reiterates certain general principles of WIPO relations with NGOs and lists

---

[8] Interview with an official from the WIPO Office of Legal Counsel, 21 Nov 2005.
[9] See WIPO, *General Rules of Procedure*, adopted on 28 Sept 1970, and amended on 27 Nov 1973, 5 Oct 1976 and 2 Oct 1979, WIPO publication No 399 (FE) Rev 3.
[10] See Rule 1(1) of the WIPO *General Rules of Procedure*.

NGOs that have applied for permanent observer status in the year preceding the upcoming session of the Assemblies.[11]

Within the WIPO Secretariat, a number of units deal with NGOs. The Office of Legal Counsel is responsible for initial processing and submission of NGO applications for permanent observer status to WIPO Assemblies. Various secretarial divisions and departments serving particular WIPO bodies (such as standing committees) handle ad hoc accreditation of NGOs. The Sector of External Relations designates a staff member responsible for the coordination of other NGO-related activities. Other secretarial units handle NGO involvement in specific technical cooperation projects.

III. FORMS OF INVOLVEMENT

NGOs may be involved in (1) WIPO policy deliberations, by taking part in meetings of WIPO bodies, and (2) WIPO technical cooperation activities.

To enable NGOs to attend and participate in meetings of WIPO bodies, WIPO may grant to NGOs permanent observer status or may accredit them, on an ad hoc basis, to a particular WIPO body or for a particular event/series of meetings. This form of NGO involvement in WIPO activities will be analysed in more detail below.

NGOs also participate in WIPO technical cooperation activities with developing countries. In particular, NGOs possessing expertise on specific intellectual property matters are frequently invited to share their knowledge at regional meetings and capacity-building seminars for countries—recipients of technical assistance.[12] No rules govern these forms of NGO involvement; relevant WIPO officials appear to have unchecked discretion when dealing with these matters. Therefore, this form of NGO involvement is not covered in this chapter.

Other forms of WIPO–NGO relations include NGO meetings with WIPO staff (bilateral and multilateral) to exchange views and information on particular issues of interest to NGOs. Such meetings are not regular but they take place at least once a year and are usually organized at the request of NGOs.[13] In 2005, WIPO also organized, for the first time, a large interactive meeting with NGOs where more than 500 organizations were invited (permanent and ad hoc observers). The purpose of the meeting was to

---

[11] See, for example, WIPO, Memorandum of the Director General, *Admission of Observers*, A/41/8 (15 Aug 2005), <http://www.wipo.int/meetings/en/archive.jsp>, visited 22 Nov 2005. See also Appendix IV of this book, p 259.

[12] Interview with Ms Joëlle Rogé, Director-Advisor on Non-Governmental Organizations, WIPO Sector of External Relations (23 Nov 2005).

[13] ibid.

debrief NGOs about WIPO activities in the preceding year, as well as to listen to the concerns of NGOs and their proposals for further cooperation. However, the meeting did not arouse much interest in the NGO community, with only about 25 organizations actually attending.[14]

The following sections describe the forms of official recognition of NGOs in WIPO and the opportunities that NGOs have to take part in WIPO policy-making through participation in various WIPO meetings.

A. *Types of NGO Observers*

As mentioned above, WIPO can grant NGOs an observer status of two types. First, NGOs can become permanent observers. Secondly, they can be accredited as ad hoc observers to a particular WIPO body (for example, a Standing Committee) or for an event/series of meetings (for example, for inter-sessional intergovernmental meetings).

There is no difference, in terms of participatory rights, between permanent and ad hoc NGO observers when they are present at a particular meeting. The difference lies only in the scope of meetings that they may attend. Naturally, ad hoc observers can attend only those meetings, or meetings of those WIPO bodies, to which they are accredited. By contrast, permanent NGO observers enjoy a standing invitation to many more, although not all, WIPO meetings.

A further distinction, within the category of permanent NGO observers, is between international and national NGOs. It was only in 2002 that WIPO opened up the possibility for national NGOs to obtain permanent observer status.[15] This distinction between international and national NGOs manifests itself mostly in the rules on their admission. There is no formal difference in treatment between international and national NGO at WIPO meetings.

To date, 202 international and 31 national NGOs enjoy permanent observer status with WIPO. To give some examples, international NGOs include the Afro-Asian Book Council (AABC), the Association of Commercial Television in Europe (ACT), International AntiCounterfeiting Coalition, Inc (IACC), International Association for the Protection of Industrial Property (IAPPI), International Federation of Industrial Property Attorneys (FICPI) and the International Trademark Association (INTA).[16]

---

[14] ibid.
[15] See WIPO, Memorandum of the Director General, *Admission of Observers*, A/37/8 (19 Aug 2002) paras 14–16, <http://www.wipo.int/meetings/en/archive.jsp>, visited 22 Nov 2005.
[16] For a complete list, see WIPO, *Intergovernmental Organizations Admitted as Observers to the Meetings of the Assemblies of the Member State*, BIG/158/17, ANNEX II, <www.wipo.org/directory/en/admission/pdf/observers.pdf>, visited 1 Apr 2005.

The national NGOs with permanent observer status include, for example, the American Association for the Advancement of Science (AAAS) and the South African Institute of Intellectual Property Law (SAIIPL).[17]

Recently, there has been a rise in the number of NGOs applying for permanent observer status at WIPO. For example, in 2005 alone, 40 NGOs (22 international and 18 national) were granted permanent observer status. This sudden increase of NGO interest in WIPO activities is ascribed to the heightened profile of WIPO as an international organization, to the recognition of the relevance of intellectual property issues to the broader problems of economic development, and more specifically, to the WIPO Development Agenda that has been debated in WIPO since 2004 and has attracted a lot of attention from NGOs.[18]

B. NGO Participation in WIPO Meetings

As a matter of practice, NGOs with permanent observer status, whether national or international, are admitted to the following meetings without an additional invitation:

- all WIPO Assemblies;
- diplomatic conferences convened under the auspices of WIPO;
- inter-sessional intergovernmental meetings (IIM);
- the annual WIPO Conference;
- standing and other committees; and
- working groups.[19]

As follows from the list once an international NGO is admitted to attend, as an observer, the meetings of the Assemblies of the Member States of WIPO, it is also invited to attend, as an observer, meetings of committees, working groups, or other bodies subsidiary to the Assemblies, 'if their subject matter seems to be of direct interest to that organisation'.[20] This rule also applies to national observer NGOs.[21] For all meetings that NGOs are eligible to attend, WIPO sends out invitations to each and every NGO by mail.

Meetings that remain closed to NGOs with permanent observer status are meetings of the WIPO Coordination Committee and of Executive

---

[17] ibid.
[18] Interview with an official from the WIPO Office of Legal Counsel (21 Nov 2005).
[19] ibid.
[20] Assemblies of the Member States of WIPO, *Admission of Observers*, Memorandum by the Director General, A/37/8 (19 Aug 2002) para 10.
[21] Interview with an official from the WIPO Office of Legal Counsel (21 Nov 2005).

Committees for the Paris and Berne Conventions.[22] Neither can NGOs be accredited to these meetings on an ad hoc basis. Furthermore, regarding NGOs without permanent observer status, ad hoc accreditation is *not* possible for sessions of the Assemblies, for diplomatic conferences or meetings of the WIPO Conference.[23]

WIPO General Rules of Procedure do not contain detailed norms on modalities of NGO participation in WIPO meetings. Its only relevant provision, Rule 24, states:

(1) Observers may take part in debates at the invitation of the Chairman.
(2) They may not submit proposals, amendments or motions.

Rule 24(2) has been interpreted as *not* precluding NGOs from circulating *any other* written statements to delegates of Member States.[24] Thus, admitted NGOs have the following rights:

• to attend the meeting;
• to make oral statements (at the invitation of the Chairman) (oral statements can also be made on behalf of groups of NGOs; requests for permission to make an oral statement are usually forwarded to the Chairperson in advance of the meeting); and
• to circulate written statements to representatives of the Member States, before or after the meeting (directly to delegates and not through the Secretariat).[25]

WIPO General Rules of Procedure govern all meetings of all bodies convened under the auspices of WIPO, to the extent that any such body does not adopt special rules of procedure.[26] Hence, participating NGOs enjoy the same rights in all WIPO meetings. According to a WIPO official, no WIPO body has so far adopted special rules of procedure that would modify participatory rights of NGO observers.[27]

IV. ACCREDITATION CRITERIA

A. Permanent Observer Status

Article 13(2) of the WIPO Constitution does not contain any guidance as

[22] ibid.   [23] ibid.
[24] ibid.
[25] ibid.
[26] See Rule 1(1) of the WIPO General Rules of Procedure.
[27] Interview with an official from the WIPO Office of Legal Counsel (21 Nov 2005).

to which NGOs can be accredited to WIPO—it only provides that both international and national organizations may be granted observer status. In fact, accreditation criteria have been explicitly established—in 2002—only for national NGOs applying for permanent observer status.[28] As for international NGOs, the WIPO website only lists the documents and information that it requires applicant NGOs to submit, but does not spell out the criteria against which it will assess whether international NGOs will be granted permanent observer status.[29]

1. International NGOs

As confirmed by a WIPO official in an interview, criteria for granting international NGOs permanent observer status do exist; they have been developed through actual practice and the experience of the WIPO Secretariat since the 1970s, but have not been officially formalized.[30] In particular, these criteria include:[31]

1. The NGO must be international. In determining whether a particular NGO is international, WIPO pays attention to whether the NGO has offices in more than one country, whether it has national NGOs as members and whether there are persons of different nationalities among the NGO's officers.
2. The competence and activities of the NGO must be relevant to those of WIPO. This does not mean that the NGO's competence has to cover all intellectual property rights; one or two aspects (for example, copyright issues, or industrial property alone) are sufficient. The proof of relevant activities usually includes studies, position papers, newsletters and other publications produced by the NGO, as well as workshops, seminars and other events organized by the NGO.
3. The NGO must be non-profit, which follows from the generally recognized definition of an NGO.
4. The NGO must be independent from the government, including financially, which also follows from its nature as a *non-governmental* organization.
5. The NGO must have a statute/by-law on the basis of which it functions and must be duly registered in the country where it has its headquarters.

---

[28] For the first time they were listed in the Memorandum of the WIPO Director General, *Admission of Observers*, A/37/8 (19 Aug 2002) para 16, <http://www.wipo.int/meetings/en/archive.jsp>, visited 22 Nov2005.

[29] See <http://www.wipo.int/directory/en/admission.html>, visited 27 Apr 2006.

[30] Interview with an official from the WIPO Office of Legal Counsel (21 Nov 2005).

[31] These criteria were enumerated in an interview by an official from the WIPO Office of Legal Counsel (21 Nov 2005).

International NGOs are required to provide the WIPO Secretariat with the following documents/information:

- a text of its constituent instrument (articles of incorporation, by-laws, etc);
- the date and place where it was established;
- a list of its officers (showing their nationality);
- a complete list of its national groups or members (showing their country of origin);
- a description of the composition of the members of its governing body or bodies (including their geographical distribution);
- a statement of its objectives; and
- an indication of the field or fields of intellectual property (eg, copyright and related rights) of interest to it.[32]

This information helps to establish whether applicant NGOs meet the accreditation criteria applied by WIPO. The Secretariat may employ additional tools to ensure that the criteria are satisfied; in particular, it may do Internet-based research and consult NGO databases.[33]

2. National NGOs
In relation to national NGOs applying for permanent observer status, the WIPO website lists a number of criteria ('principles') that have to be satisfied.[34] They are:

1. The NGO must be essentially concerned with intellectual property matters falling within the competence of WIPO and shall, in the view of the Director General, be able to offer constructive, substantive contributions to the deliberations of the Assemblies of WIPO.
2. The aims and purposes of the NGO must be in conformity with the spirit, purposes and principles of WIPO and the United Nations.
3. The NGO must have an established headquarters. It must have democratically adopted statutes, adopted in conformity with the legislation of the Member State from which the NGO originates.
4. The NGO must have authority to speak for its members through its authorized representatives and in accordance with the rules governing observer status.

---

[32] See <http://www.wipo.int/directory/en/admission.html>, visited 10 Nov 2005. These documents have to be provided, whenever possible, in English, French and Spanish.

[33] Interview with an official from the WIPO Office of Legal Counsel (21 Nov 2005).

[34] See <http://www.wipo.int/directory/en/admission.html>, visited 10 Nov 2005. These criteria were originally set out in the Memorandum of the Director General, *Admission of Observers*, A/37/8 (19 Aug 2002) para 16.

5. The admission of national NGOs to observer status must be the subject of prior consultations between Member States and the Secretariat.[35]

These criteria are quite typical for international organizations that have a system of NGO accreditation. They ensure the relevance of accredited NGOs to the WIPO's matters of competence, exclude NGOs of extremist or violent character[36] and ascertain the legality and observance of basic democratic principles by NGOs.

The documents/information required by WIPO from national NGOs applying for observer status are nearly identical to those required from international NGOs.[37]

B. Ad Hoc Observer Status

Criteria for ad hoc accreditation have not been formalized. As confirmed by a WIPO official in an interview, they are essentially the same criteria as for the permanent observer status but are applied in a 'less strict manner'.[38] To recall, these criteria are unwritten for international NGOs. This, together with the fact (as elaborated below) that NGO requests for permanent and ad hoc observer status are considered by different units of the WIPO Secretariat,[39] may lead to the lack of a uniform and consistent application of accreditation criteria.

It has been suggested by a WIPO official that the principal criterion for obtaining ad hoc accreditation is the relevance of the concerned NGO's activities to the subject-matter of a WIPO body or of an event that accreditation is requested for.[40]

There is no official list of documents/information that NGOs applying for ad hoc accreditation must submit. Typically, NGOs will send a request for accreditation without enclosing any additional documents. It is then for a secretarial unit reviewing the application to decide which documents/information it would like to request. Normally, the list of

---

[35] As a matter of practice, Member States are not consulted by the WIPO Office of Legal Counsel when it reviews the application from a national NGO. A Member State is assumed to be able to raise its objections, if any, at the meetings of the Assemblies that will consider the granting of permanent observer status.

[36] The non-extremist character can be ensured through the requirement to act in accordance with the 'spirit, purposes and principles of WIPO and the United Nations'.

[37] See <http://www.wipo.int/directory/en/admission.html>, visited 10 Nov 2005.

[38] Interview with an official from the WIPO Office of Legal Counsel (21 Nov 2005).

[39] The Office of Legal Counsel is responsible for accreditation of NGOs applying for the permanent observer status. Various secretarial divisions and departments servicing particular WIPO bodies (such as standing committees) handle the ad hoc accreditation of NGOs.

[40] Interview with an official from the WIPO Office of Legal Counsel (21 Nov 2005).

required information does not go beyond the list established for NGOs requesting permanent observer status.[41]

V. ACCREDITATION PROCEDURES

The power to accredit NGOs lies with WIPO intergovernmental bodies. It is provided in Rule 8(2) of the WIPO General Rules of Procedure that 'each body shall decide, in a general way or for any particular session or meeting, which . . . organisations shall be invited to be represented by observers'. Permanent observer status is granted by WIPO Assemblies. Ad hoc observer status admitting NGOs to meetings of particular WIPO bodies is granted by the WIPO bodies concerned.

A. Permanent Observer Status

The procedure for obtaining permanent observer status is not described on the WIPO website or in any other public source. In practice, it follows the principal steps described below.[42]

1. An NGO mails to the WIPO Director General its request for permanent observer status. In this request the NGO briefly describes its international/national character, objectives and activities, and indicates the place and date of its establishment.
2. NGO requests are forwarded to the WIPO Office of Legal Counsel for consideration. The latter informs the applicant NGO about the documents that it must provide for its application to be considered.[43]
3. The NGO submits the documents required by the Office of Legal Counsel. If the NGO fails to do this, its application remains pending for 2–3 years, with the Secretariat sending occasional reminders to the NGO, and then it is dropped from the list of applicants.
4. On the basis of the complete set of documents received from the NGO, the Office of Legal Counsel verifies whether the NGO satisfies the criteria for accreditation reviewed above. The application is rejected at this stage only if there is a 'manifest inconsistency' with one or more of the criteria. In case of an application from a national NGO, the Office of Legal Counsel does *not* consult with the Member State concerned.[44]

---

[41] ibid.
[42] The procedure is set out as described in an interview by an official from the WIPO Office of Legal Counsel (21 Nov 2005).
[43] Required documents are listed above, p 91.
[44] Interview with an official from the WIPO Office of Legal Counsel (21 Nov 2005).

5. The Office of Legal Counsel prepares a 'resumé' of the NGO, which features its date of establishment and headquarters, objectives, governance structure and membership. The NGO's name is then included in the Memorandum of the Director General for consideration of the upcoming WIPO Assemblies and the NGO's resumé is included in an annex to the said memorandum.[45] This memorandum usually lists several NGOs that have applied during the year preceding the session of the Assemblies. The Office of Legal Counsel does not make a recommendation to the Assemblies as to whether particular NGOs should or should not be accredited. NGOs are notified that their candidature has been submitted to the consideration of the WIPO Assemblies.

6. Admission of observers is one of the agenda items of the WIPO Assemblies. The Assemblies consider all listed NGOs together and unless there is an objection to a particular NGO, they are passed en bloc. In the case of objections, the matter can be decided by voting. So far, there has been no case when a government objected to the admission of a particular NGO. NGOs whose applications are being considered cannot attend the meeting, as they have yet to gain observer status.

7. The WIPO Assemblies' decisions on whether to grant permanent observer status to particular NGOs are included in the General Report.[46] The WIPO Director General sends accredited NGOs an official letter in which it confirms the grant of permanent observer status and states that, from now on, they will receive invitations to all WIPO meetings where NGO attendance is possible.

The deadline for submission of requests from NGOs is usually set in May, whereas the WIPO Assemblies are convened in late September to early October. Thus, the whole procedure takes no less than six months. There is no possibility of appeal in case the NGO request for permanent observer status is declined, but the NGO can reapply later.

B. Ad Hoc Observer Status

As is the case with the procedure for obtaining permanent observer status, the procedure applicable in requesting ad hoc observer status is not set out on the WIPO website or any publicly available document. As explained by a WIPO official, this procedure follows the basic steps of the procedure for

---

[45] See, for example, WIPO, Memorandum of the Director General, *Admission of Observers*, A/41/8 (15 August 2005), <http://www.wipo.int/meetings/en/archive.jsp>, visited 22 Nov 2005.

[46] See, for example, Assemblies of the Member States of WIPO, 40th Series of Meetings, Geneva, 27 Sept–5 Oct 2004, General Report adopted by the Assemblies, A/40/7 (5 Oct 2004) paras 180–1.

obtaining permanent observer status. However, there are two main differences:

- It is not the WIPO Office of Legal Counsel that reviews the NGO application for ad hoc accreditation. This is a task of a secretarial unit servicing a WIPO body to which the ad hoc accreditation is being requested.
- It is not the WIPO Assemblies that grant accreditation but a particular WIPO body to which the ad hoc accreditation is being requested.[47]

As with permanent observer status, so far there has not been a case where admission of ad hoc observer NGOs was blocked by a government. In case of a refusal, there is no appeal procedure but the NGO can reapply later.

There are no official and uniform deadlines for applications. They are usually set by WIPO departments that handle ad hoc accreditation to particular WIPO bodies. In practice, NGOs may sometimes request (and be granted) ad hoc observer status just several days before the meeting.

VI. MONITORING OF NGOS

WIPO does not have rules for monitoring of accredited NGOs, such as requiring them to submit annual or other reports. Also, there is no rule that would empower WIPO or prevent it from withdrawing or suspending permanent or ad hoc observer status from an NGO. So far, no such problems have arisen.[48]

As a matter of practice, NGOs are deleted from the list of permanent observers if they cease to exist as a result of dissolution or merger with another NGO. In most instances, NGOs themselves inform WIPO that they are closing down or merging. Exclusion from the list of permanent observers can also happen if the WIPO Secretariat loses contact with the NGO—in particular, when all invitations for WIPO meetings are returned to WIPO with a note that the addressee has moved out. The Office of Legal Counsel, and not the Assemblies, decides whether to remove the NGO from the list of permanent observers.[49]

---

[47] Interview with an official from the WIPO Office of Legal Counsel (21 Nov 2005).
[48] ibid.
[49] ibid.

CHAPTER 6

World Health Organization (WHO)

I. INTRODUCTION

The World Health Organization (WHO), established in 1948, is the United Nations specialized agency for health. WHO's objective, as stated in its Constitution, is the attainment by all peoples of the highest possible level of health. In support of its objective, the organization has a wide range of functions, including:

- acting as the directing and coordinating authority on international health work;
- furnishing appropriate technical assistance and, in emergencies, necessary aid upon the request or acceptance of governments;
- stimulating and advancing work on the prevention and control of epidemic, endemic and other diseases;
- establishing and stimulating the establishment of international standards for food, biological, pharmaceutical and similar products, and standardizing diagnostics procedures;
- proposing conventions, agreements and regulations, and making recommendations about international nomenclature of diseases, causes of death and public health practices.[1]

WHO has a membership of 192 Member States and two Associate Members.[2]

The work of WHO is carried out by the World Health Assembly, the Executive Board and the Secretariat.

The World Health Assembly (the 'Health Assembly') is the supreme decision-making body for WHO. The Health Assembly is composed of representatives from all WHO's Member States and Associate Members. The main tasks of the Health Assembly include the approval of WHO's budget for the following biennium and the determination of the policies of the organization. The Health Assembly also appoints the Director-General,

---

[1] See Art 2 of the WHO Constitution.

[2] According to Art 8 of the WHO Constitution, territories or groups of territories which are not responsible for the conduct of their international relations may be admitted as Associate Members by the Health Assembly upon application made on behalf of such territory or group of territories by the Member or other authority having responsibility for their international relations.

supervises the financial policies of the Organization, and considers reports of the Executive Board, which it instructs in regard to matters for which further action, study, investigation or report may be required. The Health Assembly generally meets in Geneva in May each year.[3]

The Executive Board is composed of 32 members technically qualified in the field of health, each one designated by a Member State elected to do so by the Health Assembly. Members of the Executive Board are elected for three-year terms. The main Board meeting, at which the agenda for the forthcoming Health Assembly is agreed upon and resolutions for forwarding to the Health Assembly are adopted, is held in January, with a second shorter meeting in May, immediately after the Health Assembly. The main functions of the Board are to give effect to the decisions and policies of the Health Assembly, to advise it and generally to facilitate its work.[4]

The WHO Secretariat is headed by the Director-General, who is appointed by the Health Assembly on the nomination of the Executive Board. The Secretariat works at WHO headquarters in Geneva, in the regional offices and in local offices in many Member States.

WHO Member States and Associate Members are grouped into six regions, each of which has a regional office.[5] Representatives of each Member State/Associate Member in the respective regions make up WHO Regional Committees that meet annually to formulate regional policies and supervise regional activities.

II. LEGAL FRAMEWORK

The WHO's constitutive instrument, the 1946 Constitution of the World Health Organization (WHO Constitution), contains an express legal basis for the WHO's collaboration with NGOs. Article 71 of the WHO Constitution provides:

> The Organization may, on matters within its competence, make suitable arrangements for consultation and co-operation with non-governmental international organizations and, with the consent of the government concerned, with national organizations, governmental or non-governmental.

This provision is similar to the one found in Article 71 of the UN Charter. It offers a possibility for the WHO, if it deems appropriate, to establish

---

[3] See <http://www.who.int/governance/en/>, visited 20 Oct 2005.
[4] See ibid.
[5] Africa, the Americas, South-East Asia, Europe, Eastern Mediterranean and Western Pacific.

'suitable' modalities for engagement with NGOs—primarily international ones.[6]

In 1948, the first World Health Assembly adopted a set of working principles governing admission of NGOs into official relations, amended and expanded by later Assemblies.[7] The current version of the 'Principles Governing Relations between WHO and Nongovernmental Organizations' (the 'Principles') was adopted by the Health Assembly in 1987.[8] This four-page document is the principal WHO legal instrument for relations with NGOs.

In 2001, the WHO Director-General established the Civil Society Initiative to undertake a review of official and informal relations between WHO and civil society organizations and to identify and develop propositions for more effective collaboration, information exchange and dialogue with civil society. The review process established that the current Principles are in many respects inadequate to meet the needs of WHO and the needs and aspirations of civil society.[9] Therefore, a new draft policy on WHO relations with NGOs was negotiated to replace the current Principles, but the Health Assembly has decided to postpone consideration of this new policy 'in order to provide the Director-General time to consult all interested parties'.[10] Although this study is based on the currently applicable rules and procedures, the modifications envisaged in the new draft policy will also be mentioned where appropriate.

Lastly, participation of NGOs in meetings of the Health Assembly and meetings of the Executive Board are governed (in addition to the Principles) by the Rules of Procedure of the World Health Assembly and the Rules of Procedure of the Executive Board respectively.[11] The relevant provisions will be examined in the corresponding sections below.

There are no guidelines governing operational collaboration ('working relations') between NGOs and WHO staff at headquarters or the regional and country levels.

---

[6] Additionally, two other provisions of the Constitution mention NGOs (Arts 18(h) and 33). They will be dealt with below.

[7] See the World Health Assemblies' Resolutions WHA1.130, WHA3.113, WHA11.14 and WHA21.28.

[8] See the World Health Assembly Resolution WHA40.25. See also appendix V of this book, p 263.

[9] WHO, *Policy for relations with nongovernmental organisations*, Report by the Director-General, EB111/22 (25 Nov 2002) para 14.

[10] WHO, draft *Policy for Relations with Nongovernmental Organizations*, A57/32 (1 Apr 2004), <http://www.who.int/civilsociety/documents/en/>, visited 20 Oct 2005. See also appendix V of this book, p 269; and WHO, *Decisions and list of resolutions*, A57/DIV/5 (4 June 2004), Decision WHA57(12), adopted 22 May 2004, <http://www.who.int/gb/ebwha/pdf_files/WHA57/A57_DIV5.en.pdf>, visited 20 Oct 2005.

[11] See Rules 19 and 49 of the Rules of Procedure of the World Health Assembly and Rule 4.2 of the Rules of Procedure of the Executive Board.

Within the technical departments of the WHO Secretariat, there are designated technical officers responsible for relations with particular NGOs. WHO also has a central focal point for dealing with NGOs—currently the Department for Governing Bodies and External Relations.[12] This department coordinates NGO-related activities throughout the organization and facilitates and monitors the implementation of the Principles.

III. FORMS OF NGO INVOLVEMENT

The Principles distinguish between 'working relations' and 'official relations' of WHO with NGOs. Although working relations may last for two or more years and are a mandatory pre-requisite for official relations, they are considered informal.[13] The Principles explicitly state that WHO recognizes only one category of formal relations—'official relations'.[14] The 'official relations' (OR) status is essentially similar to the 'consultative status' at ECOSOC, UNCTAD or the ILO.[15] However, a major difference with the ECOSOC system lies in the mandatory and rather complicated process leading to the admission into official relations—an NGO must first engage in working relations with WHO for at least two years.[16] In the opinion of observers, this deviation from the concept and modalities of the ECOSOC consultative status has been conscious. It stems from the difference between the two organizations. The United Nations is an organization of a parliamentary nature, where the focus of cooperation with NGOs lies in their participation in meetings and debates. WHO is, instead, an organization engaged in scientific and technical work; thus, emphasis is placed on cooperation in technical and operational activities.[17]

As stated earlier, all relations with any NGO, except for those in OR status, are considered informal. In fact, NGOs that have informal relations outnumber those in official relations. The inventory of WHO relations with NGOs (at headquarter level) revealed that in 2001, out of a total of 473 established relations, 44 per cent were with NGOs in official relations and 56 per cent were with NGOs not in official relations.[18]

---

[12] Until Dec 2005, there was a special unit of the Secretariat, the Civil Society Initiative, responsible for relations with NGOs.

[13] For more on 'working relations', see below, p 114.

[14] See WHO, *Principles Governing Relations between WHO and Nongovernmental Organizations* para 2.1, <http://www.who.int/civilsociety/relations/principles/en/index.html>, visited 28 Apr 2006.

[15] There is only one type of official relations as opposed to the three types of status at ECOSOC, UNCTAD or the ILO.

[16] For the procedure for entering into official relations, see below, p 112–116.

[17] See GL Burci and C-H Vignes, *World Health Organization* (Kluwer Law International, The Hague, 2004) 89.

[18] See WHO, *Inventory of WHO/HQ Relationships with Nongovernmental* Organizations (Feb 2002) Annex 1, <http://www.who.int/civilsociety/documents/en/>, visited 20 Oct 2005.

It would be wrong to say that as soon as an NGO is admitted into official relations it stops engaging in WHO operational activities. On the contrary, collaboration with WHO departments on technical/operational matters remains a mandatory part of WHO's engagement with such NGOs. In addition, NGOs in OR status gain an opportunity to participate in the meetings of WHO governing or other bodies, if allowed by the applicable rules of procedure.

The new draft Policy for Relations with NGOs avoids the division into working relations and official relations and establishes, instead, two other forms of WHO relations with NGOs—accreditation and collaboration. Accreditation will give NGOs access to WHO governing bodies while collaboration (for which accreditation is not required) is meant to allow for the establishment of links on the operational level. Neither of the two forms serves as a prerequisite for the other.[19] A given NGO will be able to be in both statuses at the same time or in either one of them.

The range of civil society organizations that WHO interacts with is broad. A useful illustrative list of such organizations includes:

- professional associations (such as those representing nurses);
- disease-specific NGOs (such as those dealing with malaria);
- development NGOs (such as those working on poverty reduction);
- humanitarian NGOs (such as those dealing with emergency situations);
- patient group NGOs (such as those representing diabetic patients);
- public interest NGOs (such as those representing consumers);
- scientific or academic NGOs (such as those involved in medical research);
- health-related NGOs (such as those involved in occupational health, education, technology or safety and who have health as one of their objectives); and
- non-profit organizations that represent or are closely linked with commercial interests (such as those representing the pharmaceutical industry).[20]

In their interactions with WHO, NGOs may assume different roles and carry out different functions. For example, they may act as advisors, disseminators of WHO information, service providers, data collectors and providers, risk assessors, human resources developers, fundraisers, co-

---

[19] See WHO, draft *Policy for Relations between the WHO and NGOs* (n 10), para 3.
[20] See WHO, *Review Report: WHO's Interactions with Civil Society and Nongovernmental Organizations* (2002) 11, <http://www.who.int/civilsociety/documents/en/>, visited 20 Oct 2005.

authors or peer reviewers of publications and more.[21] These roles depend on the nature, expertise and resources of particular NGOs and can be performed by NGOs in working and in official relations alike.

As of May 2005, 184 NGOs were in OR status with WHO.[22] This is compared to 26 in 1951, 68 in 1966 and 184 in 1996.[23] Some examples of NGOs in OR status include Global Health Council, World Veterinary Association, Council on Health Research for Development, International Confederation of Midwives, International Alliance of Women, Consumers International, OXFAM, International Pharmaceutical Federation, International Society of Hematology, World Blind Union, Alzheimer's Disease International, World Association of Girl Guides and Girl Scouts, and International Union of Architects.

Rights associated with the OR status are referred to in the Principles as 'privileges'. These privileges are largely limited to certain participatory rights at the governing bodies' meetings, which NGOs with only working relations do not enjoy.[24] Rights of NGOs in OR status are examined next.

A. Health Assembly

The WHO Constitution provides that one of the functions of the Health Assembly is to invite organizations, including NGOs,

> which ha[ve] *responsibilities related to those of the Organization*, to appoint representatives to *participate, without right of vote*, in its meetings or in those of the committees and conferences convened under its authority, on *conditions prescribed by the Health Assembly*; but in the case of national organizations, invitations shall be issued only with the consent of the government concerned. (Article 18(h)) (emphasis added)

The quoted article of the Constitution grants NGOs whose responsibilities are related to those of the WHO the right to participate in the meetings of

---

[21] See Burci and Vignes (n 17) 90–1.

[22] Under the draft Policy for Relations with NGOs, all NGOs currently in official relations with WHO will have to reapply for accreditation in accordance with the new rules and procedures; pending the receipt of the new accreditation, they will be deemed accredited to WHO governing bodies. See the draft resolution of the Health Assembly adopting the *Policy for Relations between WHO and NGOs*, A57/32 (1 Apr 2004) para 2, <http://www.who.int/civilsociety/documents/en/>, visited 20 Oct 2005.

[23] See Burci and Vignes (n 17) 89.

[24] See C Lanord, *A Study of WHO's Official Relations System with Nongovernmental Organizations*, prepared for Civil Society Initiative (June 2002) 8, <http://www.who.int/civilsociety/documents/en/>, visited 20 Oct 2005.

the Health Assembly but states that the latter should prescribe conditions for participation. Such conditions have been prescribed in the Rules of Procedure of the Assembly and in the Principles.

Two relevant provisions of the Health Assembly's Rules of Procedure provide:

> *Plenary meetings* of the Health Assembly will, unless the Health Assembly decides otherwise, be open to attendance by ... *invited* representatives of the United Nations and of other participating inter-governmental and *non-governmental organizations admitted into relationship with the Organization.* (Rule 19) (emphasis added)

> Representatives of non-governmental organizations with which arrangements for consultation and cooperation have been made, in accordance with Article 71 of the Constitution, may be invited to *attend plenary meetings and meetings of the main committees* of the Health Assembly and to *participate without vote* therein in accordance with those arrangements, *when invited to do* so by the President of the Health Assembly or by the chairman of a main committee, respectively. (Rule 49) (emphasis added)

Rule 19 speaks only about attendance, whereas Rule 49 entitles NGOs to attendance and participation. Both Rules provide that an invitation to attend is required. Rule 19 applies only to plenary meetings of the Health Assembly, whereas Rule 49 refers to plenary meetings and to meetings of the Assembly's main committees. The cited Rules are supplemented by the Principles which confer on accredited NGOs the right to appoint a representative to participate, without right of vote, in the WHO's meetings or in those of the committees and conferences convened under its authority.[25]

In practice, all NGOs in official relations with WHO are invited to plenary meetings and to meetings of the Assembly's main committees. Invitations and provisional agendas for each meeting are sent to NGOs in official relations two months in advance of the respective meetings.[26] Available statistics shows that on average 75 NGOs (about 40 per cent of those in OR) do in fact attend meetings of the Health Assembly.[27]

NGOs *not* in OR status may attend such meetings as part of the public but they do not have a right to participate. Representatives of non-OR

[25] See WHO, *Principles Governing Relations between WHO and Nongovernmental Organizations* (n 14) para 6.1(i).
[26] Information from a WHO source.
[27] Data for years 1998–2002. See WHO, *Analysis: NGO Participation in WHO Governing Bodies, 1998 to 2002*, prepared for Civil Society Initiative (June 2002) 3, <http://www.who.int/civilsociety/documents/en/>, visited 20 Oct 2005.

NGOs may also attend as part of the delegation of their 'umbrella' NGO, when such has OR status. Exactly for this reason, there are several NGOs whose delegations usually exceed 20 people.[28] For example, during the 55th session of the Health Assembly (2002) one delegation of such an umbrella NGO included 46 delegates.[29]

Two other NGO participatory rights envisaged in the Principles include (a) a right to make a statement, and (b) a right to submit a memorandum. In relation to the *right to make a statement*, the Principles provide:

> whenever the Health Assembly, or a committee or conference convened under WHO's authority, discusses an item in which a related NGO is particularly interested, that NGO, *at the invitation of the chairman of the meeting or on his acceding to a request from the organization*, shall be entitled *to make a statement of an expository nature*, and may, with the consent of the meeting, be *invited by the chairman* to make, in the course of the discussion of the item before the meeting, an *additional statement for purposes of clarification*. (para 6.1(i)) (emphasis added)

Accordingly, the right to make a statement is restrained by the need to receive an invitation or consent for such statement from the chairman/the meeting participants. NGO representatives may deliver their statements in person at the meetings but, in practice, the right to speak is limited to pre-submitted speeches, which makes it impossible to participate fully in the debate by reacting to unforeseen issues arising in the course of the discussion.[30] Between 15 and 25 per cent of the NGO delegations present at the Health Assembly meetings have made statements.[31]

The right to submit a memorandum in the WHO context is not quite the same as the right to circulate written statements in the context of some other institutions. The said right refers to the possibility to submit a memorandum to the Director-General, who then determines the nature and scope of its circulation.[32] In the event the Director-General considers that the memorandum may be placed on the agenda of the Health Assembly, such memorandum shall be placed before the Executive Board for possible inclusion in the agenda of the Health Assembly.[33]

No evidence has been found of memoranda being submitted pursuant to these provisions of the Principles.[34] This right is not used by NGOs,

---

[28] See ibid 4.
[30] See ibid 7.
[29] See Lanord (n 24) 6.
[31] Data for years 1998–2002. See WHO, *Analysis: NGO Participation in WHO Governing Bodies, 1998 to 2002*, 5.
[32] WHO, *Principles Governing Relations between WHO and Nongovernmental Organizations* (n 14) (n 27) para 6.1(iii).
[33] See ibid para 6.2.
[34] See Lanord (n 24) 8.

perhaps because they believe that the Secretariat will most likely disregard their submissions. In practice, therefore, the right to submit a memorandum does not appear to be an essential privilege.[35]

The new draft Policy for Relations with NGOs introduces the right 'to submit written statements pertaining to [relevant] meetings' but leaves in place a proviso that the nature and scope of distribution of these statements shall be determined by the Director-General.[36]

B. Executive Board

The Rules of Procedure of the Executive Board provide:

> Representatives of nongovernmental organizations in official relations with the Organization may participate in the deliberations of the Board as is provided for participation in the Health Assembly in the 'Principles governing relations between the World Health Organization and nongovernmental organizations'. (Rule 4)

Thus, the Rules of Procedure do not establish any substantive rules on the matter of NGO participation (aside from a statement that only NGOs in OR status may participate) but refer, instead, to the Principles. The Principles themselves do not govern NGO involvement in Executive Board meetings, but by virtue of the reference made in the Rules of Procedure, the rights granted by the Principles to NGOs in relation to Health Assembly meetings are extended to meetings of the Executive Board. These rights have been reviewed above.[37]

In practice, as is the case with the Health Assembly, all NGOs in official relations with WHO are invited to attend the sessions of the Executive Board.[38] Statistics indicate that an average of 55 NGOs (25 per cent of those in OR status) have attended January sessions of the Executive Board, while only an average of 25 NGOs (12 per cent of those in OR status) have attended May sessions.[39] About 20 per cent of NGOs in attendance have made statements.[40]

Regarding the right to make oral statements, more detailed information can be found in an information note published by the Secretariat in advance of the 117th session of the Executive Board.[41] In particular, it is established

---

[35] See ibid.
[36] See WHO, draft *Policy for Relations between the WHO and NGOs* (n 10) para 10(c).
[37] See p 102–104.
[38] Information from a WHO source.
[39] See <http://www.who/int/civilsociety/csi_statistics/en/index.html>, visited 20 Oct 2005.
[40] Data for years 1998–2002. See WHO, *Analysis: NGO Participation* (n 27), 5.
[41] See *Practical information for delegates of nongovernmental organizations (NGOs) in official relations with WHO, attending the 117th Executive Board*, CSI/NGO/EB117/1 (undated) <http://www.who.int/civilsociety/>, visited 5 Jan 2006.

that NGOs may request to speak under items of the agenda relating to technical issues only. Such requests should, in principle, be submitted by NGOs at least 24 hours before the opening of the meeting at which the agenda item of interest to the NGO is expected to be discussed. Statements should contain substantive comments directly relevant to the document prepared for the agenda item; they should take no longer than three minutes to deliver. The Chairman of the meeting decides whether a particular NGO should be allowed to make a statement.[42] According to a WHO source, NGOs' requests to speak are rarely refused.

NGOs in official relations are also allowed to display their documents/literature on tables in the proximity of the Executive Board Room.[43]

C. Other Rights

In addition to the meetings-related rights reviewed above, the Principles provide for the right of access 'to non-confidential documentation and such other documentation as the Director-General may see fit to make available through such special distribution facilities as WHO may establish'.[44]

As pointed out in the Study of WHO's Official Relations System, for NGOs, this right is more important for the saving that it represents in costs, rather than in terms of ease of access to information: WHO does not restrict information only to NGOs in OR status.[45] Since documents related to governing bodies meetings are fully available on the Internet, this OR privilege is not significant. In addition, the fact that this dissemination of information is made at the discretion of the Director-General means that this advantage for NGOs can hardly be described as a real 'privilege'.[46]

The Study of WHO's Official Relations System mentions that NGOs in OR status may also enjoy other benefits such as the purchase of medical supplies and equipment for public health programmes at reduced costs, at the discretion of the Director-General. However, these are derived from the practice and not necessarily reserved for NGOs having OR status. Deciding which organizations enjoy this benefit is left to the discretion of the Secretariat.[47]

---

[42] See ibid paras 10–13.
[43] See *Practical information for delegates of nongovernmental organizations (NGOs) in official relations with WHO, attending the 117th Executive Board* (n 41) para 16.
[44] WHO, *Principles Governing Relations between WHO and Nongovernmental Organizations* (n 14) para 6.1(ii).
[45] See Lanord (n 24) 7.
[46] See ibid.
[47] See ibid 12.

D. Regional and Country Level

Despite the acknowledged NGO significance at the country level, there is a perceived lack of guidance for regional and country offices on how to engage with NGOs and on how to assist governments in facilitating their dialogue/partnerships with NGOs. According to the WHO Review Report, country office staff are uncertain of the circumstances under which they are allowed to work with NGOs directly, or whether government endorsement is needed for all WHO collaboration with national NGOs. These uncertainties may prevent WHO from seeking NGO input to their work and reduce the WHO's ability to strengthen the capacity of NGOs.[48]

First, the Principles provide that regional or national NGOs affiliated with international NGOs in OR status are, by definition, in official relations with the WHO regional office(s). Regional offices are mandated to develop and implement programmes of collaboration with NGOs.[49] Regional offices use their lists of NGOs in official relations to invite them to participate in the Regional Committee and other regional meetings.[50] Participatory rights of NGOs in official relations at the Regional Committee level are similar to those at the Health Assembly and Executive Board.[51]

In respect of those regional and national NGOs for which there is no connected international NGO or those that are affiliated to international NGOs *not* in OR status, the Principles provide that the regional office concerned may establish *working relations* with these organizations, subject to consultation between the Regional Director and the Director-General of WHO.[52] According to the Principles, development and implementation of a programme of activities form the essential part of 'working relations'.[53]

As a matter of fact, only one out of six WHO regional offices, the Regional Office for the Americas (PAHO), has formally established modalities for cooperation with NGOs and has formally provided for participatory rights of NGOs in official working relations with it.[54] These rights are similar to the ones that are enjoyed by NGOs in OR status at the global

[48] See WHO, *Review Report: WHO's Interactions* (n 20) 16–17.
[49] See WHO, *Principles Governing Relations between WHO and Nongovernmental Organizations* (n 14) para 5.1.
[50] See WHO, *Review Report: WHO's Interactions* (n 20) 10.
[51] Information from a WHO Source.
[52] See WHO, *Principles Governing Relations between WHO and Nongovernmental Organizations* (n 14) paras 5.2 and 5.3.
[53] See ibid. These paragraphs refer to para 2.4 of the 'Principles', which will be examined below, p 114.
[54] See Pan American Health Organization (PAHO), *Principles Governing Relations between the Pan American Health Organization and Nongovernmental Organizations*, adopted by Resolution CE126.R15 (2000), <http://www.paho.org/English/DEC/part-civil.htm>, visited 20 Oct 2005.

level.[55] PAHO has admitted 17 NGOs into official working relations and many others in informal working relations. As far as the remaining WHO regional offices are concerned, their activity in this field has been minimal and kept at an informal level.[56] The practice in PAHO and in other regions is that regional/national NGOs, regardless of their relations with the WHO regional offices, only take part in regional meetings and do not participate in global meetings.[57]

Regarding the rights of NGOs in relations with a WHO regional office, the Principles provide that

> Privileges *similar* to those [granted to international NGOs in OR status] shall *normally* be accorded to national/regional NGOs having *working relations with* WHO regional offices ..., as determined by the Regional Directors in consultation with the regional committees. (para 6.3) (emphasis added)

First, this paragraph refers to national/regional NGOs having *working relations* with WHO regional offices; it does not mention NGOs in official relations with WHO regional offices.[58] Secondly, the words 'similar' and 'normally' leave room for exceptions and discretion of the Regional Directors and regional committees. Thirdly, it is not clear whether these 'similar' rights are valid for regional meetings or for both regional and global WHO meetings.

Due to these and other uncertainties of the provisions on WHO engagement with NGOs at the regional and country level, the Principles have been said to be too vague to offer clear guidance for regional (and country) offices.[59] Regrettably, the new draft Policy on Relations with NGOs does not add clarity to this issue.

IV. CRITERIA FOR OBTAINING OR STATUS

Substantive requirements that have to be satisfied by NGOs in order to gain admittance into official relations with WHO are set out in the Principles and apply to NGOs seeking OR status at the global level. Note that before an NGO can be considered for OR status it has to go through certain stages of collaboration ('first contacts' and 'working relations') described below.[60]

---

[55] See ibid 103.   [56] Information from a WHO Source.
[57] ibid.
[58] Perhaps to overcome this difficulty, PAHO, for example, refers NGOs in 'informal working relations' and in 'official working relations'. See PAHO (n 54) section 3.
[59] See Lanord (n 24) 5.
[60] See pp 112–114.

The Principles lay down a rather long list of criteria. For convenience of examination, these criteria will be divided into four groups: (1) activities, (2) nature and scope of the NGO, (3) organizational criteria, and (4) democratic legitimacy and accountability.

Activities
1. The main area of competence of the NGO must fall within the purview of WHO objectives. NGO's activities must centre on development work in health or health-related fields.[61] The main activities of WHO are set out in Article 2 of the WHO Constitution. However, this criterion requires not only that the NGO's activities are relevant to those of WHO but that health-related activities must be central to the NGO's work.[62] In light of this requirement, it seems strange to find among NGOs in OR status such names as Consumers International, International Union of Architects, OXFAM, International Federation of Business and Professional Women and other organizations whose primary field of activity is hardly health-related. This is because, in reality, it is enough for an NGO to demonstrate that at least a certain part (not necessarily its central one) of its activities is health-related. This criterion is respectively modified in the new draft Policy for Relations with NGOs.
2. NGOs' aims and activities must be in conformity with the spirit, purposes and principles of the WHO Constitution.[63] The principles on which WHO is based are found in the preamble to the WHO Constitution, and the objective of the Organization is set out in Article 1 of the Constitution, 'the attainment by all peoples of the highest possible level of health'.

Nature and scope of the NGO
3. The NGO must be free from concerns that are primarily of a commercial or profit-making nature.[64] This requirement refers to one of the fundamental features of NGOs as non-profit entities. WHO itself recognizes that in certain cases the borderline between profit and non-profit may be blurred with respect to organizations that are non-profit but are closely related to commercial enterprises, ie non-profit associations that

---

[61] See WHO, *Principles Governing Relations between WHO and Nongovernmental Organizations* (n 14) para 3.1.
[62] Burci and Vignes note that WHO has traditionally expressed reservations about expanding its network of contacts and cooperation to NGOs active in other fields—due to their lack of expertise within WHO and the risk of an undesirable shift away from the health sector. See Burci and Vignes (n 17) 91–2.
[63] See WHO, *Principles Governing Relations between WHO and Nongovernmental Organizations* (n 14) para 3.1.
[64] See ibid para 3.1.

represent business or commercial interests.[65] WHO considers such formally non-profit business and industry organizations as eligible for OR status.

4. The NGO shall generally be international in its structure and/or scope.[66] This criterion distinguishes between NGOs international in structure and NGOs international in scope. Both types are eligible. As a general rule, an NGO would be considered international if it has activities and/or members in more than one WHO region.[67] In a different paragraph, the Principles specifically name as eligible international NGOs with a federated structure (made up of national or regional groups or having individual members from different countries).[68]

5. In exceptional cases a *national* organization may be admitted into official relations in consultation with and subject to the recommendations of the WHO Regional Director and the Member State involved. Such a national organization is eligible for admission provided that: the major part of its activities and resources are directed towards international health and related work; it has developed a programme of collaborative activities with WHO; and its activities offer appropriate experience upon which WHO may wish to draw.[69] These criteria designed for national NGOs are additional and apply cumulatively with other (common) criteria (*mutatis mutandis*). The new draft Policy for Relations with NGOs excludes the possibility of accrediting national NGOs to WHO at the global level.

6. The NGO must represent a substantial proportion of the persons globally organized for the purpose of participating in the particular field of interest in which it operates.[70] This criterion is obviously aimed at ensuring the maximum representativity of organizations admitted into the OR status. It follows from this requirement that, for example, where there are several international NGOs representing one cause or one group of people (for example, nurses or diabetes patients), preference must be given to NGOs with a larger membership base. This rule does not appear to be hard and fast—for example, the currently

---

[65] See WHO, *Review Report: WHO's, Interactions* (n 20) 5.

[66] See WHO, *Principles Governing Relations between WHO and Nongovernmental Organizations* (n 14) para 3.2.

[67] See WHO, *Report of the Standing Committee on Nongovernmental Organizations*, EB113/23 (23 Jan 2004) para 12, <http://www,who.int/gb/>, visited 5 Dec 2005. The six WHO regions are listed above, footnote 5.

[68] See ibid para 3.4.

[69] See WHO, *Principles Governing Relations between WHO and Nongovernmental Organizations* (n 14) para 3.5. So far, only about five national NGOs have been admitted into official relations with WHO. Information from a WHO Source.

[70] See WHO, *Principles Governing Relations between WHO and Nongovernmental Organizations* (n 14) para 3.2.

accredited NGOs include at least three international women's organizations.[71] The Principles add that when there are several international NGOs with similar areas of interest, they may form a joint committee or other body authorized to act for the group as a whole.[72]

Organizational criteria

7. The NGO must have a constitution or similar basic document.[73] This requirement is formal—the simple existence of a constitution (or similar basic document) is sufficient; it is not required, for example, that the constitution be democratically adopted or that it provide for a democratic decision-making process. For this reason, this requirement is listed in the 'Organizational' group rather than the 'Democratic accountability and legitimacy' rubric below.

8. The NGO must have a directing or governing body and an administrative structure at various levels of action.[74] Although this requirement also resembles, at first sight, the one that requires democratic legitimacy and accountability of an organization, on closer examination, there does not seem to be any 'legitimacy/accountability' element in it. The mere presence of a governing body and an administrative structure (regardless of whether they are formed in a democratic manner or are accountable to a broader membership) is sufficient to satisfy this criterion.

9. The NGO must have an established headquarters.[75]

10. Prior to an application for admission into official relations, the NGO must normally have at least two years of successfully completed working relations with WHO.[76] The new draft Policy for Relations with NGOs, which does not use the category of 'working relations', requires instead that an NGO must have existed formally for at least three years as of the date of receipt of the application by WHO.[77]

Democratic legitimacy and accountability

11. The NGO must have authority to speak for its members through its authorized representatives.[78] Such authority can be provided for in the NGO's constitution or by-laws.

---

[71] A competent WHO source admitted that, as a matter of practice, this criterion is not taken into consideration.

[72] See WHO, *Principles Governing Relations between WHO and Nongovernmental Organizations* (n 14) para 3.2.

[73] See ibid para 3.3. [74] See ibid. [75] See ibid.

[76] ibid para 3.6. On 'working relations' see below, p 114.

[77] See WHO, draft *Policy for Relations between the WHO and NGOs*, para 5(g).

[78] See WHO, *Principles Governing Relations between WHO and Nongovernmental Organizations* (n 14) para 3.3.

12. NGO members must exercise voting rights in relation to its policies or action.[79] A voting mechanism ensures that the general direction of the organization's activities is controlled by the membership. However, mechanisms for the exercise of voting rights may differ (for example, through direct voting on policies at annual meetings, through delegating the decision-making power to the governing body, etc).

Currently WHO does not have any funding-related accreditation criteria.[80] By contrast, the new draft Policy for Relations with NGOs requires organizations to disclose their sources of financing (however, the mere disclosure is sufficient; there are no requirements as to *how* the NGO must or must not be funded).[81] Regarding the other listed accreditation criteria, the draft Policy does not make any groundbreaking changes. Despite this, all NGOs currently in OR will have to reapply for accreditation.[82] Note also that the draft Policy establishes a separate (shorter) set of criteria to select NGOs for collaboration.[83]

WHO first assesses the conformity of applicant NGOs with established criteria when NGOs apply for working relations, a mandatory stage preceding official relations. Thus, the criteria for admitting NGOs into working relations are essentially the same, although an 'imperfect' NGO may be admitted to working relation status on the understanding that in order to be granted the OR status later, it will have to make the required changes in problematic areas.[84] The final examination of NGOs against the established criteria is done when they formally apply for OR status.

V. PROCEDURE FOR OBTAINING THE OR STATUS

The procedure for entering into official relations usually takes between three and four years. It has variously been described as 'long', 'bureaucratic', 'demanding' and 'formal'.[85] The WHO Director-General herself characterized the system as 'lengthy and onerous, with drawn-out procedures ... and much administrative work for both WHO and nongovern-

[79] See ibid para 3.3.

[80] At the same time, according to a competent WHO source, WHO requires NGOs to submit their financial accounts and examines them. However, this examination is for information purposes only (to see the extent to which the organization is financed by industry or government) and does not have a bearing on the outcome of the application.

[81] See WHO, draft *Policy for Relations between the WHO and NGOs* (n 10) para 5(h).

[82] See WHO, draft resolution adopting the *Policy for Relations between WHO and NGOs*, para 2.

[83] Under the draft Policy, collaboration is a second form of relations with NGOs, alongside accreditation. See WHO, draft *Policy for Relations between the WHO and NGOs* (n 10) para 15.

[84] Information from a WHO Source.

[85] Lanord (n 24) 4.

mental organizations'.[86] With its requirement for drawing up joint work plans, the process is arguably the most demanding in the United Nations system.[87]

The establishment of relations with NGOs is an evolutionary process proceeding through a number of stages. Entry into official relations is preceded by building initial contacts, establishing work plans and joint activities, nominating focal points, assessing collaboration and finally, after a period of time, the application for admission into official relations with WHO.[88] The Principles identify the main stages of this process as:

- first contacts (informal);
- working relations (informal);
- official relations (formal).

A. First Contacts

First contacts frequently take the form of exchanges of information and reciprocal participation in technical meetings. This type of informal contacts may continue on an ad hoc basis, without time limit and without written agreement. At this stage the parties may also explore the broad objectives of collaboration and the possibility of enlarging its scope to include specific joint activities in line with the particular expertise of the NGO.[89]

In establishing contacts, NGOs may approach a WHO technical department directly or may seek the help of the Department for Governing Bodies and External Relations or its counterpart in a WHO regional office, which puts NGOs in contact with interested departments in order to explore the possibility of informal exchanges. WHO advises NGOs to provide the following documents:

- a short note on how the NGO considers its work relates to WHO priorities;
- a copy of the NGO's constitution and/or by-laws or equivalent document(s);
- membership lists, where appropriate;
- a list of elected officers or, as appropriate, members of its governing body (for example the Board);

---

[86] WHO, *Policy for relations with nongovernmental organizations, Report by the Director-General*, EB111/22 (25 Nov 2002) para 12, <http//www.who.int.gb/>, visited 28 Apr 2006.
[87] See ibid.
[88] See ibid para 5.
[89] See WHO, *Principles Governing Relations between WHO and Nongovernmental Organizations* (n 14) para 2.3.

- annual reports for the most recent three years and audited financial accounts;
- publications/media catalogue, if any;
- most recent scientific/professional journal, if any; and
- project/research evaluation reports, if any.[90]

B. Working Relations

When a number of specific joint activities have been identified, collaboration may be taken to the next stage by proceeding to a period (usually two years) of *working relations* entered into by an exchange of letters. Such letters set out the agreed basis for the collaboration, indicating details of the activities to be undertaken during the period. A joint assessment of the outcome of the collaboration is undertaken by the parties concerned at the end of the period of working relations, also including consideration of the future relationship.[91]

The joint assessment may result:

- in the continuation of the working relations for a further period;
- in an application for admission into official relations with WHO from an international NGO, for examination by the Executive Board, should there be a number of activities which might form the basis of a long-term and closer relationship with WHO; or
- in a decision that there is no scope for further contacts in the foreseeable future.[92]

Thus, official relations do not automatically follow after the first period of working relations. Working relations may be continued for a further period, or the relations between WHO and the NGO may be discontinued.[93] In any event, prior to an application for admission into official relations, the NGO must have at least two years of successfully completed working relations, concluded by a positive joint assessment of these relations by the relevant technical department of the WHO Secretariat and the NGO concerned (in writing).[94] Note that the new draft Policy for Relations with NGOs does not require NGOs to go through any preliminary stages and allows applying for accreditation directly.

---

[90] See <http://www.who.int/civilsociety/relations/en/>, visited 5 Dec 2005.
[91] See WHO, *Principles Governing Relations between WHO and Nongovernmental Organizations* (n 14) para 2.4.
[92] See ibid.
[93] However, according to a competent WHO source, this occurs quite rarely. In most instances, NGOs apply for admission into official relation straight after the first period of working relations.
[94] See WHO, *Principles Governing Relations between WHO and Nongovernmental Organizations* (n 14) para 3.6.

C. Admission into the OR Status

As mentioned above, in order for an application to be considered, an NGO must have had working relations for at least two years concluded by a positive joint assessment by WHO and the NGO. Additionally, the NGO must present a joint three-year work plan agreed to between the NGO and a technical WHO department. This plan of collaboration is based on mutually agreed upon objectives, and it outlines activities for the upcoming three-year period. It forms the basis of official relations between WHO and the NGO.[95] The three-year plans are not aligned to the WHO's own two-year work plan and their contents vary greatly in quality and depth.[96] Note that the new draft Policy for Relations with NGOs does not require a plan of collaboration in order for an NGO to be granted accreditation.

NGO applications for OR status should normally reach WHO headquarters no later than the end of July in order to be considered by the Executive Board in January of the following year. The application package includes the request to be admitted into official relations, a completed questionnaire (designed to see whether the NGO meets the established criteria), a joint assessment of the preceding period of working relations and a three-year plan of future collaboration.[97] Applications from national NGOs may be considered in consultation with, and subject to, the recommendations of the WHO Regional Director and the Member State concerned.[98]

The Executive Board is the organ responsible for deciding on the admission of NGOs into official relations with WHO.[99] The Board has a Standing Committee on Nongovernmental Organizations (NGO Committee), composed of five members, which considers applications from NGOs and makes recommendations to the Board.[100] Its deliberations are based on the presentations made by the Secretariat's designated technical officer responsible for dealing with the NGO concerned during the period of working relations. The NGO Committee may also invite NGOs to speak before it in connection with their applications. Depending on whether the NGO meets the criteria for obtaining the OR status, the NGO Committee recommends to the Board that the application in question be approved, rejected or postponed. The latter option may be used especially in cases where the NGO does not meet the criteria but, despite this, the NGO

[95] See ibid para 4.5.   [96] See Lanord (n 24) 6.
[97] Information from a WHO source.
[98] According to a WHO source, about five national NGOs have been admitted into official relations with WHO so far.
[99] See WHO, *Principles Governing Relations between WHO and Nongovernmental Organizations* (n 14) para 2.5.
[100] The term of office of the NGO Committee members is three years.

Committee considers that a continuing partnership in a framework of future collaborative activities is desirable.[101] The NGO Committee makes its decisions by consensus.[102]

The Board, after considering the recommendations of the NGO Committee, decides whether an organization is to be admitted into official relations with WHO.[103] There is no appeal procedure for NGOs whose applications are rejected. A reapplication from an NGO shall not normally be considered until two years have elapsed since the Board's decision on the original application.[104]

According to the Study of WHO's Official Relations System, in recent years the reports from the Secretariat summarizing the new applications have been approved with very few questions.[105] Typically, each year two to five NGOs are admitted into official relations.

VI. MONITORING OF NGOS

The Board, through its NGO Committee, reviews collaboration with each NGO in official relations every three years to determine the desirability of maintaining official relations. The Board's review is spread over a three-year period, one-third of the NGOs in official relations being reviewed each year.[106] The new draft Policy for Relations with NGOs requires such reports to be submitted by accredited NGOs to the Executive Board every two years, perhaps to make them correspond to the two-year work plans of WHO itself.[107]

Currently there are three grounds on which the Board may discontinue or suspend official relations:

1. The Board considers that such relations are no longer appropriate or necessary in the light of changing programmes or other circumstances;
2. The NGO no longer meets the criteria that applied at the time of the establishment of such relations; or

---

[101] See WHO, *Principles Governing Relations between WHO and Nongovernmental Organizations* (n 14) para 4.2.
[102] Information from a WHO source.
[103] On a number of occasions, the Board has disagreed with the recommendations of the NGO Committee.
[104] See WHO, *Principles Governing Relations between WHO and Nongovernmental Organizations* (n 14) paras 4.3 and 4.4.
[105] See Lanord (n 24) 6.
[106] See WHO, *Principles Governing Relations between WHO and Nongovernmental Organizations* (n 14) para 4.6.
[107] See WHO, draft *Policy for Relations between the WHO and NGOs* (n 10) para 7.

3. The NGO fails to fulfil its part in the agreed programme of collaboration.[108]

For example, in 2005 the Executive Board discontinued official relations with two NGOs because the Secretariat did not have plans to continue collaboration with them.[109] Sometimes the OR status is suspended, or the resolution of the matter is deferred, until the Board's sessions the next year in order to give the NGO concerned and the WHO Secretariat time to develop a work plan for the future.

Failure on the part of NGOs to submit their three-year report is a reason for discontinuance of official relations. Usually, the Executive Board gives NGOs that have failed to submit their report one year to remedy the situation and if this is not done OR status is withdrawn. For example, in 2005, this served as a ground to discontinue official relations with five NGOs.[110]

In general, the existing grounds for suspension/discontinuance of official relations give the Executive Board a very broad margin of discretion when considering the matter. Also, the WHO Secretariat plays a very significant role as it may unilaterally determine whether or not it would be beneficial to continue collaboration with a given NGO and thus predetermine the fate of the NGO concerned.[111]

The new draft Policy for Relations with NGOs substitutes the listed grounds for discontinuation or suspension of official relations with the following ones:

1. An NGO ceases to fulfil the accreditation criteria;
2. An NGO fails to provide its biennial report; or
3. An NGO has either directly, or through its affiliates or representatives acting on its behalf, clearly abused its status by engaging in a pattern of acts that are not consistent with the Constitution or the policies of the Organization and resolutions and decisions of the Executive Board and the Health Assembly.[112]

---

[108] See WHO, *Principles Governing Relations between WHO and Nongovernmental Organizations* (n 14) paras 4.6 and 4.7.

[109] The NGOs concerned were the International Association of Agricultural Medicine and Rural Health, and the International Council for Science. See WHO, *Report of the Standing Committee on Nongovernmental Organizations*, EB115/22 (21 Jan 2005) paras 10, 14 and 15, <http://www.who.int/gb/>, visited 28 Apr 2006.

[110] See WHO, *Report of the Standing Committee on Nongovernmental Organizations*, EB115/22 (21 Jan 2005) para 17.

[111] It has also been noted that the dependence on individual contacts between the focal point of an NGO and the designated technical officer in WHO made the system vulnerable to staff changes in both organizations. See WHO, *Policy for relations with nongovernmental organizations*, Report by the Director-General, EB111/22 (25 Nov 2002) para 12.

[112] See WHO, draft *Policy for Relations between the WHO and NGOs* (n 10) para 13.

These changes narrow down the broad discretion of the Executive Board that it enjoys under the current rules.[113]

The Principles do not provide NGOs whose OR status is being considered for suspension or discontinuance with a possibility to be heard. The new draft Policy for Relations with NGOs does provide for a written response from an NGO.[114]

---

[113] Note that under the new draft Policy, the listed grounds apply to discontinuance/suspension of *accreditation*. As far as *collaboration* is concerned, the new draft Policy provides—although the text is bracketed and thus controversial—that the Director-General shall 'suspend or discontinue collaboration if a nongovernmental organization either directly or through its affiliates or repesentatives acting on its behalf clearly abuses its status by engaging in a pattern of acts that are not consistent with the Constitution or the policies of the organization, and resolutions and decisions of the Executive Board and the Health Assembly'. See WHO, draft *Policy for Relations between the WHO and NGOs* (n 10) para 17.

[114] See WHO, draft *Policy for Relations between the WHO and NGOs* (n 10) para 13.

CHAPTER 7

United Nations Environment Programme (UNEP)

I. INTRODUCTION

The United Nations Environment Programme (UNEP), created by a UN General Assembly Resolution in 1972, serves as the focal point for the activities of the United Nations family on environmental issues.[1] Its mandate, expanded and rearticulated by the 1997 Nairobi Declaration, is

> to be the leading global environmental authority that sets the global environmental agenda, that promotes the coherent implementation of the environmental dimensions of sustainable development within the United Nations system and that serves as an authoritative advocate for the global environment.[2]

Essentially, UNEP is an international organization where governments negotiate environmental policies and adopt a programme of work in line with these policies. The Secretariat is charged with the responsibility of carrying out the Member States' decisions and works to implement UNEP programmes and projects.

As UNEP is not formally a UN specialized agency, it does not have a membership distinct from the membership of the United Nations. The UNEP organs are the Governing Council and the Committee of Permanent Representatives.

The Governing Council (GC), the supreme organ of UNEP, is composed of 58 Member States elected by the UN General Assembly for four-year terms. It functions like a 'board of directors', providing the main policy guidance and keeping both the world situation and the implementation of UNEP programmes under review. The Governing Council reports to the UN General Assembly through the Economic and Social Council.

---

[1] See Resolution of the United Nations General Assembly 2997 (XXVII) 'Institutional and financial arrangements for international environmental co-operation' (15 Dec 1972), <http://www.unep.org/resources/gov/keydocuments.asp>, visited 15 Aug 2005.

[2] Nairobi Declaration, The role and mandate of the United Nations Environment Programme, adopted by the UNEP Governing Council in 1997, para 2, <http:// www.unep.org/resources/gov/keydocuments.asp>, visited 15 Aug 2005.

The Global Ministerial Environment Forum (GMEF) was instituted in 1999 and is convened annually to review important and emerging policy issues in the field of the environment.[3] The Governing Council constitutes the Forum either in its regular sessions or special sessions. As the GC is only convened during the GMEF, UNEP normally uses the term GC/GMEF to designate a meeting of both the GC and the Ministerial Forum.

During odd years (eg 2003, 2005) UNEP convenes week-long *regular* GC/GMEF sessions at the UNEP headquarters in Nairobi, Kenya. In regular sessions the GC makes decisions on UNEP's work programme and budgetary allocation for the following two years. Since 2000 UNEP has convened once every two years in three-day *special* sessions of GC/GMEF. At these special sessions, organized in different countries, Ministers exchange and coordinate policy views on the environment.

The Committee of Permanent Representatives (CPR) is a subsidiary organ of the Governing Council composed of all the Government representatives to UNEP. The CPR's major tasks are to monitor implementation of UNEP's work programme and to draft the decisions for consideration by the Governing Council.

The Executive Director heads the UNEP Secretariat based in Nairobi. There are six UNEP regional offices, as well as field offices and collaborating centres.

II. LEGAL FRAMEWORK AND FORMS OF INVOLVEMENT

Given the unprecedented role played by NGOs in shaping the global environmental agenda, the UNEP constitutive instrument, UN General Assembly Resolution 2997 (XXVII) invited

> those non-governmental organizations that have an interest in the field of the environment to lend their full support and collaboration to the United Nations with a view to achieving the largest possible degree of cooperation.[4]

This provision constitutes an implicit legal basis for UNEP to cooperate with NGOs.

Further, Agenda 21 (a 10-year programme for sustainable development adopted at the 1992 UN Conference on Environment and Development

---

[3] See Resolution of the United Nations General Assembly 53/242, 'Report of the Secretary-General on environment and human settlements' A/RES/53/242 (10 Aug 1999) para 6, <http://www.unep.org/resources/gov/keydocuments.asp>, visited 10 Apr 2006.

[4] See Resolution of the United Nations General Assembly 2997 (XXVII), 'Institutional and financial arrangements for international environmental co-operation' (15 Dec 1972) para IV.5.

held in Rio de Janeiro) called on UNEP to raise 'general awareness and action in the area of environmental protection *through collaboration* with the general public, *non-governmental entities* and intergovernmental institutions'.[5] The same document introduced the term 'Major Groups' (now a term of art for international environmental governance) to designate key sectors of society as partners for governments and international organizations in the global environmental process. Agenda 21 included NGOs as one of these Major Groups (alongside women, children and youth, indigenous peoples, farmers, local authorities, business and industry, the scientific and technological community, workers and trade unions). Among all Major Groups, NGOs have the added importance of being the organizational form used by other categories of Major Groups.

The Rules of Procedure of the UNEP Governing Council contain a number of provisions conferring participatory rights on NGOs with respect to the sessions of the GC/GMEF.[6] However, UNEP does not have rules governing NGO participation in the implementation of UNEP's programme of work (specific projects); this area of engagement with NGOs is carried out by various UNEP divisions on an ad hoc basis.

At least in one instance, namely when setting out guidelines for making written statements by NGOs in GC/GMEF sessions, UNEP explicitly referred to ECOSOC rules on engagement with NGOs.[7] This raises questions about the applicability of relevant ECOSOC rules (in particular, ECOSOC Resolution 1996/31)[8] to UNEP's relations with NGOs. Generally, ECOSOC rules do not apply in other UN agencies and bodies, and this is the case with UNEP as well. As confirmed by an UNEP official, the Secretariat considers it appropriate to turn to the ECOSOC system (as the most elaborate and the closest to UNEP in terms of organizational kinship) only in cases where there are gaps in UNEP rules that need to be filled. An illustrative example is when a substantive right is provided for but the details of its realization are unclear, as is the case with the right of NGOs to make written statements. At the same time, such references to ECOSOC rules are references to 'good practices' and not to superior norms,

---

[5] Agenda 21, adopted by at the United Nations Conference on Environment and Development (UNCED) (14 June 1992) para 38.22(g) (emphasis added), <http://www.unep.org/Documents.multilingual/Default.asp?DocumentID=52>, visited 15 Aug 2005.

[6] See appendix VI of this book, p 277.

[7] See UNEP document, 'Modalities for Accredited International Non-Governmental Organizations to UNEP to Submit Written Inputs into the Unedited Working Documents of the UNEP's GC/GMEF and to Submit Written Statements to the GC/GMEF of UNEP' (undated), <http://www.unep.org/DPDL/civil_society/About/accreditation.asp>, visited 10 Apr 2006. See also appendix VI of this book, p 281. The reference was made to para 31 of ECOSOC Resolution 1996/31, which contains rules on NGOs' written submissions.

[8] On ECOSOC Resolution 1996/31, see above pp 22–23.

and in no way can they result in an inconsistency with the rules of UNEP.[9] Thus, ECOSOC rules remain generally inapplicable to UNEP relations, with the exception of specific cases when certain ECOSOC norms are expressly endorsed by UNEP.

The most recent impetus for the facilitation of UNEP's engagement with NGOs was given by the UNEP Governing Council Decision SS.VII/5 of 15 February 2002, which requested UNEP to further develop, review and revise as necessary the strategy for engaging civil society in UNEP's activities. In pursuance of this decision, UNEP developed a strategy paper, 'Enhancing Civil Society Engagement in the Work of the United Nations Environment Programme' (hereinafter, the Strategy Paper).[10] This paper currently serves as a basis for developing relations with NGOs. The UNEP Secretariat used the positive momentum created by the Strategy Paper to 'empower' NGOs, specifically in the area of policy development where certain previously 'dormant' procedural rights of NGOs began to be realized (see below).

Among other things, the Strategy Paper envisaged the adoption of an operational manual for CSOs, 'to increase awareness of the opportunities for working with UNEP, and build understanding of the policies and procedures for doing so'.[11] In pursuance of this mandate, the UNEP Secretariat issued a guidebook for civil society participation entitled *Natural Allies: UNEP and Civil Society* (2004), which contains a useful summary of forms and practices of UNEP's engagement with civil society, although it does not lay down any rules on civil society involvement.[12]

Within the UNEP Secretariat, the Major Groups and Stakeholders Branch manages and coordinates UNEP's engagement with NGOs.

The two major areas for the UNEP–NGO relationship are: (1) policy development, and (2) implementation of UNEP's work programme (environmental projects and programmes). These two forms of involvement will now be examined.

III. POLICY DEVELOPMENT

In its Decision SS.VII/5 of 15 February 2002 on enhancing civil society engagement in the work of UNEP, the Governing Council agreed 'to make

[9] Interview with Mr Denis Ruysschaert, UNEP Major Groups and Stakeholders Branch, 21 Oct 2005.
[10] 'Enhancing Civil Society Engagement in the Work of the United Nations Environment Programme: Strategy Paper', UNEP/GC.22/INF/13 (21 Nov 2002), <http://www.unep.org/dpdl/civil_society/PDF_docs/Enhancing_Civil_Society_Engagement_In_UNEP.pdf> visited 10 Apr 2006. See also appendix VI of this book, p 282.
[11] ibid 13.
[12] See <http://www.unep.org/Documents.Multilingual/Default.asp?DocumentID=468& ArticleID=4622&l=en>, visited 10 Apr 2006.

efforts to meaningfully consider the views of representatives of major groups and non-governmental organizations, including the private sector, giving them clear channels for providing Governments with their views, within the established rules and modalities of the United Nations system'.[13] This generally liberal attitude of the Governing Council towards civil society, including NGOs, has recently led to improvements in terms of bringing NGO views to the attention of governments and the Governing Council.

The main forms of NGO involvement in UNEP policy development are, first, through participation in sessions of the Governing Council/Global Ministerial Environmental Forum (GC/GMEF) and, secondly, through the Global Civil Society Forum (GCSF) organized immediately prior to the GC/GMEF sessions. These two forms are reviewed in turn.

A. GC/GMEF Sessions

1. Modalities of NGO participation

The Rules of Procedure of the Governing Council contain several references to NGOs as participants of the Governing Council process (in particular, in Rules 7, 9.3, 10 and 69). The core disciplines are found in Rule 69, which provides:

1. International non-governmental organizations having an interest in the field of the environment, referred to in section IV, paragraph 5, of General Assembly Resolution 2997 (XXVII), may designate representatives to sit as observers at public meetings of the Governing Council and its subsidiary organs, if any. The Governing Council shall from time to time adopt and revise when necessary a list of such organizations. Upon the invitation of the President or Chairman, as the case may be, and subject to the approval of the Governing Council or the subsidiary organ concerned, international non-governmental organizations may make oral statements on matters within the scope of their activities.

2. Written statements provided by international non-governmental organizations referred to in paragraph 1 above, related to items on the agenda of the Governing Council or of its subsidiary organs, shall be circulated by the secretariat to members of the Governing Council or of the subsidiary organ concerned in the quantities and in the languages in which the statements were made available to the secretariat for distribution.

It follows from Rule 69 that only accredited international NGOs can participate in the GC/GMEF sessions and that accreditation is permanent and not

---

[13] Governing Council Decision SS.VII/5 of 15 Feb 2002 on enhancing civil society engagement in the work of the United Nations Environment Programme, section II.1.

ad hoc for each session. However, before 2004, there was no practical difference in treatment by UNEP of accredited and non-accredited NGOs. The de facto situation was such that both categories of NGOs were admitted to GC/GMEF sessions. This changed in 2004 when UNEP started to enforce down to the letter the relevant Rules of Procedure provisions during the sessions of the GC/GMEF.

According to the Rules of Procedure, an accredited NGO has a right to:

- sit as an observer at the GC/GMEF meetings;
- make oral statements if called upon by the Chair and subject to the approval of the GC/GMEF;[14] and
- circulate written statements on the agenda of the GC/GMEF or of its subsidiary organs. UNEP's Secretariat shall circulate such statements as UNEP written information documents to the Committee of Permanent Representatives (CPR) and the governments, and post them on the official UNEP webpage for delegates.[15]

The UNEP Secretariat set the following conditions that apply to written statements of NGOs to GC/GMEF:

- The written statement should be submitted in one of the official languages (English, French, Chinese, Arabic, Russian, Spanish);
- The NGO must give due consideration to any comments that the Executive Director may make before transmitting the statement in the final form;[16] and
- The written statement should be limited to 2000 words.[17]

---

[14] For example, during the 23rd regular session of the GC/GMEF in 2005, 12 oral statements from civil society were allowed. Most of them were made on behalf of NGO groups/coalitions (as opposed to single NGOs), which increased their legitimacy, and were contributions on technical issues (as opposed to being very general or rhetorical), which increased their value for governments. Source: Interview with Mr Denis Ruysschaert, UNEP Major Groups and Stakeholders Branch (21 Oct 2005).

[15] See UNEP document, 'Modalities for Accredited International Non-Governmental Organizations' (n 7).

[16] In practice, the UNEP Secretariat only ensures that the given written submission is relevant to the agenda and does not interfere with the substance. To date, there have been no problems with this form of Secretariat control over NGO written submissions, in the sense that the submissions have always been circulated. Source: Interview with Mr Denis Ruysschaert, UNEP Major Groups and Stakeholders Branch (21 Oct 2005).

[17] During the 23rd GC/GMEF (2005) there were no written statements from civil society aside from the oral statements submitted in written form and a joint written statement at the closure of the GC/GMEF (endorsed by NGOs, trade unions, youth, women and indigenous peoples representatives). Source: Interview with Mr Denis Ruysschaert, UNEP Major Groups and Stakeholders Branch (21 Oct 2005).

Regarding the design of these conditions, the UNEP Secretariat expressly referred to ECOSOC Resolution 1996/31 and, in particular, paragraph 31.[18]

Furthermore, since 2004, in reaction to the Strategy Paper signal to facilitate NGO involvement and in the wake of the Cardoso Panel Report on UN–Civil Society Relations,[19] the UNEP Secretariat took measures to enhance NGO participatory rights by 'breathing life' into the previously 'dormant' NGO rights contained in the GC Rules of Procedure.[20] In particular, in the process leading up to the GC/GMEF it has been made possible for accredited NGOs to:

- receive (1) the provisional agenda, and (2) the unedited working documents of the UNEP GC/GMEF at the same time as the Committee of the Permanent Representatives (CPR); and
- submit written inputs into the unedited working documents of the GC/GMEF related to items on the agenda of the GC/GMEF or of its subsidiary organs. The Executive Director shall circulate such inputs to the CPR for its consideration before the government representatives meet to finalize the documents.[21]

These new opportunities provide additional incentives for NGOs to seek accreditation.

As of February 2006, 169 international NGOs were accredited as observers to the Governing Council of UNEP. More than one-third were accredited in the course of 2005—the increased interest in accreditation is apparently due to the recently enforced distinction in treatment between accredited and non-accredited NGOs and the enhanced rights of the former. Accredited NGOs include: Climate Action Network, Conservation & Management International, Forest Action Network, European Environmental Bureau, Greenpeace International, International Chamber

---

[18] ibid. On applicability of ECOSOC Resolution 1996/31 to UNEP's relations with NGOs see above, pp 121–122.

[19] Report of the Panel of Eminent Persons on United Nations-Civil Society Relations, *We the People, Civil Society, the United Nations and Global Governance* (Cardoso Report), A/58/817 (11 June 2004), <http://documents-dds-ny.un.org/doc/UNDOC/GEN/N04/376/41/pdf/N0437641.pdf?OpenElement>, visited 15 Aug 2005.

[20] Interview with Mr Denis Ruysschaert, UNEP Major Groups and Stakeholders Branch (21 Oct 2005).

[21] See UNEP document, 'Modalities for Accredited International Non-Governmental Organizations' (n 7). In the run up to the 23rd GC/GMEF (2005) only some of the larger and more organized networks (Greenpeace, European Environment Bureau and some others) took the opportunity to submit comments to the unedited working documents of the CPR. The fact that UNEP's draft decisions and background documents are quite complex, and that the NGOs did not have sufficient time may account for this fact. Source: Interview with Mr Denis Ruysschaert, UNEP Major Groups and Stakeholders Branch (21 Oct 2005).

of Commerce, International Committee of the Red Cross, International Confederation of Free Trade Unions, International Environment Law Research Centre, IUCN—The World Conservation Union, Third World Network, Water Environment Federation, Women's Environment and Development Organization, World Business Council for Sustainable Development, World Population Society, and others.[22]

2. Accreditation criteria
It follows from Rule 69 of the Rules of Procedure of the GC, that there are only three criteria for accreditation. An organization must:

(a) Be an NGO (understood as any non-profit-making entity—to separate NGOs from business entities (industry associations still qualify as NGOs)).
(b) Be international, that is, have an international scope of work.[23] The concept of an international NGO, as understood in the UNEP context, is described below in more detail.
(c) Have an interest in the field of the environment. Judging from the list of accredited NGOs, environmental protection does not have to be the primary focus of the NGO but may be just one of the many areas of its activities/interests.[24]

An NGO has to provide a file with proof that it matches these criteria. The documentation should include:

(a) proof of non-profit-making status (copy of document of incorporation);
(b) proof of being an international NGO (an account of the international scope of its activities);
(c) proof of interest in the field of the environment (such as annual reports, conference and/or seminar reports, recent press releases or media statements);
(d) a detailed account of the international scope if its activities; and
(e) a copy of its accreditation to other UN bodies and agencies, including ECOSOC, if available.[25]

---

[22] See the list of NGOs accredited to the Governing Council, <http://www.unep.org/DPDL/civil_society/Directory/index.asp>, visited 15 Aug 2005.

[23] The Strategy Paper envisaged the possibility of accrediting national NGOs but this became a contentious point on which the governments could not come to an agreement. Accordingly, accreditation has remained closed for national NGOs.

[24] See, for example, such accredited NGOs as International Chamber of Commerce, International Council of Women and many others.

[25] See UNEP document, 'Accreditation of Non-Governmental Organizations at UNEP' (see appendix VI of this book, p 278), and UNEP Secretariat, *Natural Allies: UNEP and Civil Society* (UNEP, Nairobi, 2004) 18.

Where the NGO has already obtained a consultative status with ECOSOC, it will not be required to provide proof of non-profit status.[26]

According to the information from the UNEP Secretariat, most of the problems encountered by NGOs during the accreditation process have been connected with the need to prove the international scope of their work. UNEP uses the following indicators to assure itself that the NGO's scope of work is indeed international:

- the NGO's headquarters and regional offices are located in different countries;
- the NGO's projects or programmes take place in other countries;
- the NGO's activities have international implication. For example, international water management, desertification on transboundary areas, waste management of estuaries that affect a region;
- the NGO's activities have an international scope, such as coordinating regional or international positions or work on a specific area.[27]

UNEP notes specifically that it is not sufficient for an NGO to demonstrate that it has participated in intergovernmental meetings, to have agreements with other organizations or to be a member of an international network, although these facts may be relevant in conjunction with other factors.[28]

3. Accreditation procedure
The procedure for NGO accreditation for the GC/GMEF sessions consists of the following steps.

1. The NGO has to file, with the Major Groups and Stakeholders Branch of the UNEP Secretariat, proof that it meets the accreditation criteria (see the list of documents above). The NGO also has to mention whether it has consultative status with the Economic and Social Council (where the NGO has already obtained a consultative status with ECOSOC, it will only be required to provide documentation of its interest in the field of the environment).
2. The Major Groups and Stakeholders Branch reviews the file in cooperation with the Law Branch in the Division of Policy Development and Law. If any documents required for the application are missing or need clarification, the Major Group and Stakeholders Branch will notify the NGO and request further information.

[26] See Strategy Paper (n 10) 10.
[27] See UNEP internal document, 'International scope of work', available on request from the UNEP Secretariat (Major Groups and Stakeholders Branch).
[28] See ibid.

3. When the file is complete, the Major Groups and Stakeholders Branch sends the file to the Secretariat for Governing Bodies[29] with a recommendation on whether or not to accredit the NGO.
4. The Office of the Secretariat for Governing Bodies decides to grant or to refuse the accreditation of the NGO and registers its decision in the database.
5. The Office of the Secretariat for Governing Bodies notifies the NGO about its decision.

The process can take up to six months.[30] However, if the NGO submits all required information and satisfies UNEP accreditation criteria, the process is much faster (usually completed within one month).[31]

As stated previously, there are 169 organizations on the accredited NGO list. There were about 70 NGOs that applied for UNEP accreditation but have not been accredited due to their inability to demonstrate that they satisfy the accreditation criteria (as of October 2005). The majority of these 70 NGOs have had problems with proving the international scope of their activities.[32]

This explanation of the accreditation procedure does not envisage a role for the GC and government representatives. In fact, despite its mandate, the GC does not make decisions on accrediting NGOs—the process ends at the Secretariat of the Governing Bodies.[33]

The Strategy Paper envisaged an active role for the UNEP regional offices in the accreditation process. Regional offices were supposed to undertake a preliminary assessment of all accreditation applications from their region, so that NGOs had an option to apply directly to the UNEP Secretariat, or alternatively, to apply through a regional office (or, additionally, through a national government).[34] However, only the mechanism of direct application to the UNEP Secretariat works in practice. UNEP regional offices are consulted by the UNEP Major Groups and Stakeholders Branch to obtain additional information about particular NGOs (their background, scope of work, etc), if there is a need to do so.[35]

---

[29] The Secretariat of the Governing Bodies (SGB) provides a link between UNEP and the governments as a secretariat. Being part of the UNEP Secretariat (with no government representatives in it), the SGB is the coordinating body that provides information to governments on UNEP activities, prepares and organizes the Governing Council, and assists the Committee of Permanent Representatives.

[30] See UNEP document, 'Accreditation of Non-Governmental Organizations at UNEP'; and UNEP Secretariat, *Natural Allies: UNEP and Civil Society* (n 25) 18.

[31] Interview with Mr Denis Ruysschaert, UNEP Major Groups and Stakeholders Branch (21 Oct 2005).

[32] ibid.   [33] ibid.

[34] See Strategy Paper (n 10) 10.

[35] Interview with Mrr Denis Ruysschaert, UNEP Major Groups and Stakeholders Branch (21 Oct 2005).

B. Global Civil Society Forum (GCSF)

1. The GCSF process

The Global Civil Society Forum (GCSF) is a two-day event that immediately precedes sessions of the GC/GMEF. It is jointly organized by UNEP and a Civil Society Host Committee, the latter consisting of NGOs from the region where the GCSF takes place. Agenda items for the GCSF are the same as those on the ministerial agenda (they are communicated by UNEP to the GCSF as early in advance as possible). The Strategy Paper underscores that the GCSF does not have any decision-making role in UNEP.[36] Initially, the aim of the GCSF was to produce a report and/or a statement, which would convey the views and recommendations of civil society to the GC/GMEF at the plenary of the Ministers. However, due to the fact that since then it has become easier for NGOs to deliver oral statements at the sessions of the GC/GMEF, the GCSF has changed its function—now it is more of a platform where NGOs meet, network, exchange views on policy issues, coordinate and prepare common positions in light of the upcoming session of the GC/GMEF. A joint NGO statement is now produced during the 'global drafting meeting' (see below).

More than 100 civil society representatives from 49 countries attended the 6th GCSF in 2005 (around 30 per cent from developing countries and 70 per cent from developed countries).

Prior to the GCSF, each of the six UNEP regional offices facilitates a regional CSO meeting to channel regional civil society input towards the GCSF and the GC/GMEF. The direct outcomes of each regional preparatory meeting are two-fold:

1. The elaboration of a regional statement on UNEP's programme of work and on international environment governance. Each regional preparatory statement is distributed to governments and posted on the UNEP's official website for delegates. Regional meetings often develop regional materials such as drafts of specific policy papers.
2. The election of four regional civil society representatives to participate in the GCSF.[37]

---

[36] See Strategy Paper (n 10) 10.

[37] This information relates to the regional preparatory meetings of the 5th GSCF held in March of 2004 and the 6th GCSF itself held in February 2005. This practice would seem to continue as there is no evidence to the contrary. See *Engaging civil society in the Governing Council/Global Ministerial Environment Forum*, Background document for the Regional meetings in preparation of the sixth Global Civil Society Forum (6th GCSF) (14 Oct 2004) 3, <http://www.unep.org/DPDL/civil_society>, visited 15 Aug 2005.

Starting in 2004, each of the six regional meetings additionally selects two persons from the region to represent the views of their region and participate in the 'Global drafting meeting'. The 12 participants draft a global civil society statement that is provided to the governments in preparation for the upcoming GC/GMEF session.[38] This practice was substituted for the prior practice of creating joint civil society statements during the GCSFs.

UNEP covers the costs of hosting the GCSF, including the production of background papers, translation and facilities for the meeting. UNEP also provides financial assistance for civil society representatives (to travel from their home country as well as a daily subsistence allowance) from developing countries and from countries in transition, as well as for youth representatives.[39] UNEP is committed to continuing this practice subject to its ability to raise the extra-budgetary resources required for it.[40]

2. Accreditation criteria and procedure

Usually more than 100 civil society representatives from around the world attend the GCSF. UNEP says that it is keen to have a fair representation of civil society.[41] To ensure a fair and transparent selection process, the following guidelines are used in choosing civil society representatives:

- NGOs accredited to UNEP's Governing Council are automatically invited.[42]
- Representatives of the six UNEP regions each select four regional CSOs during the regional civil society meetings organized by UNEP.
- 20–40 representatives from the hosting region are additionally selected by the Civil Society Host Committee.
- Six youth representatives, one per region, are selected by the Youth Advisory Council that advises UNEP on youth activities (and is itself elected every two years during the Tunza Youth Conference).

---

[38] See ibid 4.

[39] See ibid. In particular, UNEP funds the participation of four CSOs (one representative each) selected by each of the Regional CSO Meetings (except for the North America region where it funds none, and the Europe region where it funds two out of four (CSOs from transition economies)). UNEP also covers the costs of participation for 20–40 additional CSOs from the region where the GCSF takes place and for six youth representatives. Source: Interview with Mr Denis Ruysschaert, UNEP Major Groups and Stakeholders Branch (21 Oct 2005).

[40] Interview with Mr Denis Ruysschaert, UNEP Major Groups and Stakeholders Branch (21 Oct 2005).

[41] See UNEP Secretariat, *Natural Allies: UNEP and Civil Society* (n 25) 19.

[42] 51 out of 143 NGOs then accredited to UNEP attended the 6th GCSF in 2005. Source: Interview with Mr Denis Ruysschaert, UNEP Major Groups and Stakeholders Branch (21 Oct 2005).

- About 20 private-sector and trade unions representatives are selected by UNEP Division of Technology, Industry and the Environment (DTIE).[43]

In fact, as the GCSF is a pure 'civil society' affair for which UNEP acts only as a sponsor and facilitator, UNEP does not itself select GCSF participants. Rather, it sets approximate limits on the number of different groups of participants in order to be able to finance the event and to ensure the balanced representation at the Forum.[44] Even with respect to 20 private sector representatives, in reality the DTIE does not select them itself but, instead, 'outsources' this task to the International Chamber of Commerce (which itself is an NGO accredited with UNEP).

IV. IMPLEMENTATION OF THE UNEP'S WORK PROGRAMME

The second type of NGO engagement with UNEP is through participation in carrying out UNEP's work programme.

A. Modalities of NGO Involvement

UNEP's programme of work is based on decisions taken by the Governing Council. Most of the decisions call explicitly for active participation from civil society in their implementation. The UNEP guidebook for civil society suggests that the role of civil society is especially relevant in relation to decisions on technical topics (such as law, chemicals and atmosphere), linked to assessment (scientific, post-conflict) or implicating partnerships (Regional Seas programme, conventions).[45] Potentially, NGOs can participate in the implementation of decisions where their participation is relevant, or explicitly requested by the decision. The UNEP guidebook invites those NGOs that wish to participate in the implementation of the work programme to contact UNEP.[46]

It appears that the process can work in two ways. Either UNEP can look for expert NGO participants (for example, from the ranks of accredited

---

[43] These are the guidelines for the 6th GCSF held in Feb 2005, <http://www.unep.org/DPDL /civil_society/GCSF/index.asp> visited 15 Aug 2005. For the most part, they fall in line with the general guidelines described in UNEP Secretariet, *Natural Allies: UNEP and Civil Society* (n 25) 19–20.

[44] However, GCSF was designed as an inclusive event, and CSOs (beyond the limits identified above) who are willing to cover the costs of participation themselves can participate. Source: Interview with Mr Denis Ruysschaert, UNEP Major Groups and Stakeholders Branch (21 Oct 2005).

[45] See UNEP Secretariat, *Natural Allies: UNEP and Civil Society* (n 25) 25.

[46] See ibid.

NGOs), or interested NGOs may themselves contact UNEP and offer their expertise for particular projects (UNEP will then decide whether each particular NGO is well-suited to participate). Usually, a Memorandum of Understanding is signed between UNEP and the participating NGO and serves as a legal basis for cooperation.

The exact means of NGO participation depend on the type of activity that a certain project or programme implies. For example, activities in the area of early warning and scientific assessment aim at keeping the global environment situation under review and at reporting on it. The main activity in this area is gathering and analysing information. Since UNEP lacks the scientific resources to do it on its own, UNEP's role is to create and coordinate a network of scientific and other institutions capable of carrying out the necessary assessment/reporting activities. These assessments usually result in scientific publications (reports) that can serve as the basis for subsequent policy-making. NGOs can play an important role in these assessments, in some cases with technical or financial support from UNEP. For example, the Global Environment Outlook, an important UNEP publication, is based on a network of 37 collaborating centres, a number of which are NGOs.[47]

NGOs are frequently involved in partnerships created to implement specific policies. Partnerships are voluntary multi-stakeholder initiatives. They can include a wide range of groups who have an interest in a particular issue, and may include a range of projects or programmes.

One example of such a partnership is the Great Apes Survival Project (GRASP) Partnership launched in 2001 and managed jointly by UNEP and UNESCO. The GRASP Partnership is a multi-sectoral international initiative bringing together governmental and intergovernmental entities UN institutions, NGOs, scientific and academic foundations, local community and private sector interests. The aim of the project is to lift the threat of imminent extinction faced by great apes (gorillas, chimpanzees, bonobos and orangutans) across their ranges in equatorial Africa and South-East Asia. GRASP activities include technical missions in range States to address national policy issues through National Great Ape Survival Plan (NGASP) workshops, promotion of great ape-related issues at top political levels through visits from the Great Ape Patrons, NGO-partner project funding, fundraising, and raising public awareness. Funding of NGO-implemented projects is one type of GRASP activity. The list of NGO partners includes more than 30 organizations. They have already carried out around 10 projects within the framework of the GRASP Partnership.[48]

[47] See ibid 27.
[48] See <http://www.unep.org/grasp/>, visited 22 Oct 2005.

B. Selection Criteria and Procedures

The criteria for selection of NGOs to participate in the implementation of the UNEP's work programme have not been formalized. It is clear that for such participation an NGO does not need accreditation in the sense of Rule 69 of the GC's Rules of Procedure. The only discernable selection criterion is meeting the appropriate levels of scientific/research expertise and technical and human capacities necessary to implement a project. UNEP seems to take decisions on specific projects on the basis of the information it has regarding the knowledgeability and specializations of particular environmental NGOs. However, UNEP does not have a roster of NGOs that it can consult in order to pick candidates for particular projects. Depending on the project, the selection process is handled by various divisions and officials as they see fit. NGOs can get involved through self-nomination if they demonstrate the required expertise and capacity.

Decisions on the involvement of NGOs in particular projects are taken by the responsible UNEP divisions (when required, in consultation with the Major Groups and Stakeholders Branch). The procedures for taking such decisions have not been formalized.

V. MONITORING OF NGOS

There is no formal mechanism in place for monitoring accredited NGOs and for withdrawing accreditation from them if they cease to meet the accreditation criteria or on any other grounds. This has never been done. The UNEP Secretariat has not been entrusted with this power. At the same time, it is imaginable that, if the GC so decides, it can deny accreditation to those earlier accredited NGOs that no longer meet the criteria for accreditation. The GC's mandate to adopt/revise a list of accredited NGOs could serve as a legal basis for such action.

In 2004 the UNEP started the process of checking whether the accredited NGOs still exist. In case an NGO cannot be contacted (non-functioning postal/email addresses, telephone), it is kept on the list for another four years. If during these four years the contact still cannot be established, the NGO is deleted from the list. This process started in 2004, and the first NGOs will be removed in 2008. As of October 2005, 28 NGOs are being considered for exclusion.[49]

---

[49] Interview with Denis Mr Ruysschaert, UNEP Major Groups and Stakeholders Branch (21 Oct 2005).

CHAPTER 8

United Nations Development Programme (UNDP)

I. INTRODUCTION

The United Nations Development Programme (UNDP) was established in 1965 by the UN General Assembly Resolution 2029 (XX) 'Consolidation of the Special Fund and the Expanded Programme of Technical Assistance in a United Nations Development Programme'.[1] Nominally, UNDP is an organ of the United Nations linked to the General Assembly through the Economic and Social Council but, in fact, it functions more like a UN specialized agency. It has a mandate to provide and coordinate policy advice and grant funding for development cooperation. UNDP is one of the world's largest multilateral sources of grant funding for economic and social development, deriving its funds from the voluntary contributions of UN Member States and affiliated agencies as well as from other funding arrangements, including cost-sharing. UNDP works to build developing countries' capacity for sustainable human development by promoting and supporting efforts to alleviate poverty, manage natural resources to benefit both people and the environment, improve governance and create opportunities for people to improve their lives. The UNDP main focus areas are:

- democratic governance;
- poverty reduction;
- crisis prevention and recovery;
- energy and environment; and
- HIV/AIDS.[2]

The UNDP's main organ, the Executive Board, is made up of representatives from 36 donor and programme countries from around the world, who serve on a rotating basis.[3] Through its Bureau, consisting of representatives from five regional groups, the Board oversees and supports the activities of

---

[1] Available at <http://www.un.org/documents/resga.htm>, visited 12 Oct 2005.
[2] See <http://www.undp.org/about/>, visited 12 Oct 2005.
[3] The Executive Board superseded the 48-member Governing Council in 1994, which was the main UNDP organ before that time. The Executive Board also guides the work of the United Nations Populations Fund (UNFPA).

UNDP. The Board usually meets three times a year, once for its annual session and twice for regular sessions. Decisions of the Board are traditionally adopted by consensus.

The Administrator of the UNDP is the organization's chief executive officer. He is appointed by the UN Secretary-General and confirmed by the UN General Assembly for a term of four years. The UNDP Administrator also chairs the United Nations Development Group (UNDG), a committee of the heads of all United Nations funds, programmes and departments that carry out operational activities for development.

UNDP has headquarter departments for five regions: Africa, the Arab States, Asia and the Pacific, Europe and the CIS, and Latin America and the Caribbean. Each of these is responsible for the country offices in the relevant regions. Being a largely decentralized organization, UNDP has a presence in nearly every developing country in the world, with 166 field offices. Country offices are headed by UNDP Resident Representatives.

II. LEGAL FRAMEWORK

UN General Assembly Resolution 2029 (XX), by which UNDP was established, does not contain a provision on cooperation with NGOs. According to the information published on the UNDP website, UNDP derives its mandate to work with civil society from the United Nations Charter.[4] It will be recalled that Article 71 of the UN Charter enables the UN Economic and Social Council (ECOSOC) to 'make suitable arrangements for consultation with non-governmental organizations which are concerned with matters within its competence'.[5]

The cited provision of the UN Charter empowered only ECOSOC (not other UN organs or bodies) to make arrangements with NGOs. UNDP uses Article 71 as the legal basis, probably because UNDP is formally a UN organ that reports to ECOSOC. It would be logical to assume then that UNDP would link its system of engagement with NGOs to that of ECOSOC and, in particular, that it would recognize NGOs in consultative status with ECOSOC and their participatory rights, as well as accreditation criteria and procedures applied by ECOSOC.[6] However, this is not the case.[7] The UNDP does not apply, even as a supplementary source, any rules contained in ECOSOC Resolution 1996/31 governing ECOSOC–NGO

---

[4] See <http://www.undp.org/cso/>, visited 10 Oct 2005.
[5] For the details, see above, pp 19–20.
[6] For a detailed discussion of the ECOSOC system see above, pp 19–44.
[7] With the exception that the UNDP Executive Body may invite, if it wishes to do so, particular NGOs in consultative status with ECOSOC to participate in its session(s). However, this is rarely the case. See below, p 143.

relations.[8] Thus, the UNDP position on this matter appears somewhat inconsistent. At the same time, as demonstrated by other international organizations, an express mandate for engagement with NGOs in the organization's constitutive instrument is not a necessary prerequisite for such engagement.[9]

Similarly to several other international institutions, UNDP treats NGOs as part of a broader category of civil society organizations (CSOs), defined by UNDP as non-State actors whose aims are neither to generate profits nor to seek governing power; CSOs unite people to advance shared goals and principles and comprise the full range of formal and informal organizations within civil society.[10]

The first UNDP strategy paper that provided a framework for UNDP collaboration with CSOs was adopted in 1993.[11] Another policy document on cooperation with CSOs was created in 1997. These documents were updated in 2001, drawing upon past interaction between UNDP and CSOs and following the further growth of NGO significance in the international arena. Changes were also due to institutional reform within the organization and adoption of its other new policies. The revised document is called *UNDP and Civil Society Organizations: A Policy Note on Engagement.*[12]

As far as NGO involvement in implementation of UNDP projects is concerned, the UNDP has adopted specific procedures for project execution by NGOs that form part of the UNDP Programming Manual.[13] The procedures provide a set of requirements applicable to NGOs in charge of the execution of UNDP-supported projects. They outline policies and principles guiding execution as well as the necessary administrative and reporting requirements.[14] Further, when an NGO is contracted for the provision of goods or services for a specific project (without being in charge of the project), the UNDP Procurement Manual applies.

---

[8] On ECOSOC Resolution 1996/31, see above, pp 22–23.

[9] See, for example, the chapters on the World Bank and the International Monetary Fund.

[10] See UNDP, *UNDP and Civil Society Organizations: A Toolkit for Strengthening Partnerships* (UNDP, 2006) 3, <http://www.undp.org/cso/>, visited 16 Apr 2006. Among CSOs, UNDP lists NGOs, community-based organizations (CBOs), indigenous peoples' organizations (IPOs), academia, journalist organizations, faith-based organizations, trade-unions and trade associations.

[11] See UNDP, *UNDP and Organizations of Civil Society: Building Sustainable Partnerships* (1993).

[12] See UNDP, *UNDP and Civil Society Organizations: A Policy Note on Engagement* (2001), 5 <http://www.undp.org/cso/policies.html>, visited 10 Oct 2005. See also appendix VII of this book, p 297.

[13] See UNDP, *UNDP Programming Manual* (Dec 2000) chapter 6: Operations of Programmes and Projects, <http://www.undp.org/cso/policies.html>, visited 12 Oct 2005. See also appendix VII of this book, p 318.

[14] On NGO participation in execution of UNDP projects see below, pp 143–150.

One other source of information on UNDP–CSO relations is the UNDP publication entitled *UNDP and Civil Society Organizations: A Toolkit for Strengthening Partnerships* (2006). Without setting binding rules, the *Toolkit* 'seeks to equip UNDP country offices with the essential tools, instruments and information to build substantive partnerships with CSOs [and]… provides examples of successful and innovative initiatives of UNDP engagement with CSOs at the programme and policy levels'.[15] This *Toolkit* substituted the *Sourcebook on Building Partnerships with Civil Society Organizations* (2002);[16] in contrast to the *Sourcebook*, the new *Toolkit* is precise in its language, and reader-friendly.

At the headquarter level, UNDP CSO Division is responsible for strengthening UNDP policies and procedural methods to collaborate more effectively and systematically with CSOs. This includes, inter alia, providing programme support and guidance to country offices to strengthen their capacity to work with CSOs, which is an important challenge given the diverse country environments.

III. FORMS OF NGO INVOLVEMENT

In the early years of engagement, UNDP partnerships with CSOs were primarily for implementation of projects and delivery of services where governments or markets were unable or unwilling to provide them. With the 1990 launch of the Human Development Report, CSOs have also increasingly participated in the policy-making and advocacy work, through means such as research, analysis and evaluation of development projects and promotion of long-term policy changes. The Millennium Development Goals process—in which UNDP has a mandate as manager and score-keeper—has further raised the policy role of CSOs. According to UNDP, CSOs have a critical role to play in realizing the Millennium Development Goals by mobilizing public opinion, monitoring progress, stimulating public debate and policy options, and creating bottom-up demand that holds leaders accountable for the achievement of the goals.[17]

An important UNDP tool for stimulating policy debate is the Human Development Report (HDR) issued by UNDP every year. CSOs have contributed to the analysis in the global and country reports and have also used them for advocacy with governments. In particular, CSOs have been generating local debates on findings from HDRs, translating the report into

---

[15] UNDP, *A Toolkit for Strengthening Partnerships* (n 10) iv.
[16] See UNDP, *Sourcebook on Building Partnerships with Civil Society Organizations* (UNDP, 2002), <http://www.undp.org/poverty/docs-civilsociety/sourcebook.pdf>, visited 27 Apr 2006.
[17] See UNDP, *A Policy Note on Engagement* (n 12) para 37.

advocacy strategies and campaigns for effecting policy changes and bringing about policy studies, poverty assessments and regional and national qualitative indices for monitoring poverty.[18]

According to UNDP, it is important to have CSOs present at the 'policy table'. But this must not detract from collaboration with CSOs in downstream work. This implies a CSO approach and practice that actively builds links between macro-level policy and pro-poor micro initiatives.[19]

Aside from its own engagement with CSOs, much of UNDP's efforts 'on the ground' are aimed at creating the so-called 'multi-stakeholder partnerships' (involving, in addition to UNDP and CSOs, the government, the business sector, aid agencies and other actors) that help to increase the visibility and participation of CSOs in country-level policy-making. In other words, UNDP contributes to bringing civil society into the mainstream of national public affairs.[20] In a given country, relevant UNDP activities may include promoting an enabling legal/regulatory environment and political space for civil society to express its views and influence policy dialogue and key legislative processes; supporting the societal watchdog function of CSOs within the existing structure of governance; and capacity-building activities through the small grants programme and other activities. Since these UNDP activities do not involve CSOs in the policy-making or project implementation of the UNDP itself, they are not covered in this study.[21]

UNDP does not have a permanent accreditation scheme for CSOs and does not involve CSOs in policy deliberations of its organs directly through participation in their meetings. The three main forms of UNDP engagement with NGOs are the following:

1. UNDP has an institutional framework that serves to feed input from civil society into the UNDP policy-making framework—the CSO Advisory Committee at the global level and similar committees at several country offices.
2. NGOs are admitted as observers to meetings of the UNDP Executive Board.
3. NGOs may be involved in execution of UNDP projects.

This section reviews in turn these three forms of NGO involvement in the activities of UNDP.

---

[18] See ibid.   [19] See ibid para 16.
[20] See UNDP, *Sourcebook on Building Partnerships with Civil Society Organizations* (n 16) 16.
[21] For more information on this subject, see ibid chs 3 and 4, pp 16–29. On the small grants programme, see UNDP, *A Toolkit for Strengthening Partnerships* (n 10) 17–18.

A. UNDP CSO Advisory Committee to the Administrator

1. Role and functioning of the Advisory Committee

The UNDP CSO Advisory Committee to the Administrator, created in 2000, is an institutionalized forum for dialogue and debate, as well as for providing advice on UNDP policy direction. The Committee is currently comprised of 15 CSO representatives with one-third of its membership rotating annually. CSO members of the Committee act in their personal capacity and do not represent the views of their respective organizations.[22] The primary functions of the Committee are:

- to provide advice and strategic guidance to the Administrator and senior management of UNDP (with special emphasis on the issue of enhancement of UNDP engagement with civil society);
- to support and monitor the implementation of key information policy and advocacy efforts; and
- to pilot strategic CSO/UNDP initiatives and activities.[23]

The agreed areas of mutual concern on substantive issues were identified in a series of consultations between the UNDP management and the Advisory Committee. They include:

(a) poverty reduction and sustainable debt;
(b) inclusive globalization: democratizing trade and finance;
(c) conflict prevention and peace-building;
(d) human rights and human development; and
(e) private-sector engagement.

The Committee does not make formal decisions; it has only advisory and consultative functions that serve as a conduit for the views and ideas of civil society. In particular, to date, the Advisory Committee has advised UNDP on:

- policies of engagement with CSOs and the business sector, indigenous peoples, and the public information and disclosure policy;
- human Development Reports: through the involvement in readers' groups; and
- the 2003 UNDP report, *Making Global Trade Work for the People*, through contributions to, and drafting of, background papers.[24]

---

[22] This format was chosen by the Committee members themselves, possibly to minimize the need to consult governing bodies and constituencies of their respective organizations.

[23] See UNDP, *Concept Paper on the Establishment of a CSO Advisory Committee to UNDP* (Apr 2000) 1, <http://www.undp.org/cso/partnerships.html>, visited 12 Oct 2005. See also appendix VII of this book, p 315.

[24] For more activities of the Advisory Committee, see UNDP, *A Toolkit for Strengthening Partnerships* (n 10) 31–2.

The Committee meets once a year for three and a half days. It holds meetings with the UNDP Administrator and senior management including regional directors. The agenda for these meetings is set jointly by members of the Committee and UNDP management. The Committee has a small secretariat responsible for assisting with the coordination of activities, including: establishing agendas, (co-) chairing meetings, monitoring funds and disseminating information.[25]

2. Criteria and procedures for selection of CSOs

The initial Committee members were selected by UNDP (through consultations with regional and central UNDP bureaux and with approval of the Administrator). As mentioned above, the Committee has a rotating membership (one-third of the membership rotates on an annual basis).[26] New members are proposed by the CSO Committee itself. However, these candidatures are subject to review by the UNDP management and approval by the Administrator.[27] There is no formal application procedure for NGOs that would like to be represented at the Committee.

With respect to the selection criteria, UNDP states, in its Policy Note on Engagement with CSOs, that it collaborates with CSOs whose goals, values and development philosophy correspond to its own.[28] This requirement applies to all CSOs that UNDP cooperates with, including members of the Advisory Committee. This does not imply that there cannot be any divergence of opinion between CSOs and UNDP. The requirement of shared goals, values and development philosophy is of the most general nature and is, perhaps, similar to the requirement of compliance with the 'spirit, purposes and principles' of the UN Charter in the ECOSOC context.[29] In particular, UNDP engages with civil society actors that work towards:

- inclusive globalization that allows countries to enter markets on terms that take into account the human development concerns of people;
- promoting accountability, transparency, and inclusiveness in governance structures; and
- developing capacities of civil society actors to increase political participation and collective action.[30]

---

[25] See UNDP, *Concept Paper on the Establishment of a CSO Advisory Committee to UNDP* (n 23) 3.

[26] The list of the current Committee members is available at <http://www.undp.org/cso/partnerships.html>, visited 20 Jan 2006.

[27] See UNDP, *Concept Paper on the Establishment of a CSO Advisory Committee to UNDP* (n 23) 3.

[28] See UNDP, *A Policy Note on Engagement* (n 12) para 6.

[29] See above, p 31.

[30] See <http://www.undp.org/cso/>, visited 12 Oct 2005.

The 2000 Concept Paper on the establishment of the Advisory Committee spelled out further criteria for selection of members for the Committee. The Committee members should:

- have necessary expertise to advise and guide UNDP on substantive policy issues (governance, debt, trade, human rights, poverty reduction, conflict prevention, environment and gender);
- represent, in their majority, developing countries or regions (reflecting UNDP programme country focus);
- represent a range of CSOs with which UNDP engages, including (but not limited to) policy-focused CSOs, advocacy and rights-based organizations, indigenous peoples' organizations, peoples' movements, community-based organizations and trade unions;
- represent different levels of CSO activity (local, national, regional and global), with a balanced regional representation; and
- be balanced in gender.[31]

The Concept Paper states that ECOSOC status is considered an asset but not a requirement for Committee members.[32]

The listed criteria are quite basic and broad; they allow a relatively large number of eligible CSOs. The choice of the Committee members is largely done in the process of informal consultations inside the Committee and with the UNDP management.

3. CSO Advisory Committees at the country level

As part of its *CSO Champions* initiative aimed at the development of UNDP–CSO relationships at a country level, UNDP encourages the creation of local CSO advisory committees. In its Policy Note on Engagement with CSOs, UNDP stated that it was committed to making local and regional CSO advisory committees a regular feature of its partnership of engagement with CSOs at the country and, where appropriate, regional levels.[33] A number of such local committees have been created. For example, in 2003 the first such committee was established in Botswana with an objective to contribute to 'policy development and thinking' within UNDP in Botswana and to advise the Resident Representative on various policy issues. Members are appointed by the Resident Representative (membership is to be gender balanced and to cover a broad diversity of interests and backgrounds) and serve for a period of two to three years (in their individual capacity and not as representatives of their respective orga-

---

[31] See UNDP, *Concept Paper on the Establishment of a CSO Advisory Committee to UNDP* (n 23) 3.
[32] See ibid.
[33] See UNDP, *A Policy Note on Engagement* (n 12) para 30.

nizations). The committee meets at least three times a year—each meeting focusing on one or two thematic issues, with senior management participating. With approximately the same objectives and in approximately the same operational format, a civil society advisory committee was created in Brazil. Colombia, Kenya, Liberia and Sri Lanka have established committees that focus on sectoral issues.[34]

B. UNDP Executive Board

The Executive Board does not formally recognize participation of CSOs in Board sessions; accordingly, there is no system of permanent CSO accreditation to UNDP for the purpose of such participation. The Rules of Procedure of the Executive Board provide that the Board may, when it considers it appropriate, invite NGOs that are in consultative status with the Economic and Social Council to participate in its deliberations on questions that relate to their activities.[35]

In practice, according to the UNDP Executive Board Secretariat, Board meetings are open, so anyone who wishes may attend.[36] NGOs may also request an invitation to a particular Board session by contacting the Director of the Executive Board Secretariat. Invited NGOs are permitted to have copies of their written statements made available to delegates in the conference room, and have a right to make oral statements from the floor upon conclusion of Board members' interventions.[37] There is no formal set of criteria that NGOs must fulfil in order to participate; the only condition is that they must be in consultative status with ECOSOC. NGOs without ECOSOC consultative status attending an Executive Board session do not enjoy participatory rights.[38]

CSOs are not involved in pre-session informal meetings that are held two weeks in advance of each session in order to set the agenda and review the documentation for that session. These informal consultations are designed primarily to assist members of the Executive Board to prepare for the upcoming session and are attended by members of the Executive Board only.

C. Project Execution

Execution of UNDP projects is governed by the UNDP Programming

---

[34] For more information regarding CSO advisory committees at the country level, see UNDP, *A Toolkit for Strengthening Partnerships* (n 10) 33–44.
[35] See Rule 16.3 of the Rules of Procedure of the Executive Board.
[36] Information from the UNDP Executive Board Secretariat.
[37] ibid.
[38] ibid.

Manual (the 'Manual').[39] The Manual envisages four ways of project execution depending on the type of entity managing the project (implementing partner or executing agency). One of these ways refers to execution by NGOs—it is a management arrangement whereby an NGO assumes responsibility for the management of a UNDP-supported project.[40] When an NGO is designated as an implementing partner for UNDP activities, management responsibility for the entire project, including achieving the project objectives, lies with the NGO. This arrangement is particularly useful if one NGO can provide the bulk of project materials and services or can undertake the project activities and has the necessary administrative/accounting capacity to manage the project and track and report expenditures. The NGO has full control over project operations, and can use its own supply channels for recruitment and procurement, provided that the process is in line with UNDP standard requirements and is based on 'best value for money'.[41]

The designated NGO generally carries out the project activities directly but, if necessary, it may also contract other entities, including other NGOs, to undertake specific activities. Also, in cases where a project is executed not by an NGO but, for example, by a governmental agency or an international financial institution, NGOs may be involved in the project as contractors. The UNDP Procurement Manual normally applies in such situations.[42]

UNDP considers that management by an NGO is appropriate in the case of a project that:

(a) involves close interaction with target groups such as the poor and vulnerable;
(b) would benefit from established contacts with grass-roots associations; or
(c) calls for expertise in the use of participatory methods.[43]

Usually, it is a relevant UNDP country office that decides which entity would be the most suitable implementing partner. Over the years there has been a marked increase in the involvement of NGOs in the management of

---

[39] See UNDP, *UNDP Programming Manual*, Chapter 6: Operations of Programmes and Projects (Dec 2000), <http://www.undp.org/cso/policies.html>, visited 12 Oct 2005. See also appendix VII of this book, p 318.

[40] The remaining three ways are: national execution (by a governmental entity) which is the norm; execution by the UN agency or a multilateral bank; and direct execution by UNDP itself.

[41] See UNDP, *A Toolkit for Strengthening Partnerships* (n 10) 13.

[42] On NGOs as contractors see below, pp 149–150.

[43] See UNDP, *A Toolkit for Strengthening Partnerships* (n 10) 14.

UNDP projects.[44] Available statistics show that in 2001, NGO-implemented projects accounted for 10 per cent of the UNDP programming budget.[45] Projects with NGO participation may include post-crisis and post-conflict recovery, supplying certain health, education and other services, and introducing new sources of energy (like solar power systems). UNDP acknowledges that many NGOs demonstrate high-quality management capacity, technical specialization, operational depth, and better overall performance compared to other UNDP partners (ownership and compliance with plans, high-quality work, less staff turnover and more efficient use of resources).[46] Among other advantages of NGOs, UNDP points out that NGOs are quick to respond, mobile, and well-positioned to reach communities at the grass-roots level. Further, NGOs share the UNDP goals for programme impact and institutional empowerment; collaboration with NGOs enables UNDP to promote positive relations between government and civil society.[47]

Designated NGOs may be national or international.[48] The Manual sets out basic criteria that NGOs must meet in order to be selected for project execution as an implementing partner. An NGO must:

- have the legal status to operate in accordance with the laws governing NGOs in the programme country;[49]
- be apolitical and non-profit-making;[50]
- have adequate staff and reasonably sound financial status;
- have experience in working with external organizations or donors; and
- have the necessary capacities within their fields of expertise to carry out activities and achieve results on behalf of UNDP.[51]

The most important of these criteria appear to be the requirement for an NGO to have the necessary capacity (including adequate staff) to implement the project. The Manual sets out guidelines for UNDP country offices

---

[44] See UNDP, *Simplification of NGO Execution for Crisis and Post Conflict Situations* (UNDP Aug 2004) 1, <http://www.undp.org/cso/policies.html>, visited 27 Apr 2006. See also appendix VII of this book, p 331.
[45] Interview with a UNDP CSO Division officer (20 Jan 2006).
[46] See UNDP, *Simplification of NGO Execution for Crisis and Post Conflict Situations* (n 44) 2.
[47] See ibid.
[48] An international NGO is defined as an NGO operating in a programme country but legally registered in another country. See UNDP, *UNDP Programming Manual* (n 39) section 6.2.4, para 4.
[49] See ibid s 6.2.4, para 4.
[50] See ibid Annex 6E: 'Standard Project Cooperation Agreement between UNDP and a Non-Governmental Organization', Recital 3.
[51] See ibid s 6.2.4, para 1.

to assess the capacity of the NGO to carry out the project.[52] Taking into account the particularities of a given project, the major elements to be assessed include:

- technical capacity (ability to monitor the technical aspects of the project);
- managerial capacity (ability to plan, monitor and coordinate activities);
- administrative capacity (ability to procure goods, services and works on a transparent and competitive basis; to prepare, authorize and adjust commitments and expenditures; to manage and maintain equipment; to recruit and manage the best-qualified personnel on a transparent and competitive basis); and
- financial capacity (ability to produce a project budget; to ensure physical security of advances, cash and records; to disburse funds in a timely and effective manner; to ensure financial recording and reporting).[53]

The Manual also describes, in a separate table, where to find information on the capacities of NGOs when NGO execution is considered. Some of the relevant documents listed in this table include:

- charter documents;
- legal incorporation documents;
- annual reports;
- policy documents;
- copies of rules and procedures;
- an NGO organizational chart;
- reports on the annual meetings of the governing body;
- minutes of management or decision-making meetings;
- evaluation and monitoring reports and newsletters;
- audited finances;
- bank statements; and
- balance sheets.[54]

These documents may be requested by a UNDP country office to make an assessment of whether an NGO complies with the requirements relating to technical, managerial, administrative and financial capacities. The list of

---

[52] See ibid Annex 6A: 'Capacity for Programme and Project Management: Key Considerations'.
[53] See ibid.
[54] For the full table, see ibid.

documents is exemplary and not exhaustive, thus other pertinent information may be requested as well.

In addition to the criteria enshrined in the Manual, the CSO Division has developed the so-called 'CSO Capacity Assessment Tool' (2006). This Tool identifies selection criteria to offer UNDP country offices a 'broad framework to assess capacity when selecting a CSO partner', primarily for project execution.[55]

The Tool consists of two parts. Part I is aimed at assessing CSO commitment to the UNDP principles of participatory human development and democratic governance. It includes the following sections:

- legal status and history of a CSO;
- its mandate, policies and governance; and
- constituency and external support.

Part II aims at assessing CSO capacity for project management. It comprises the following sections:

- technical capacity;
- managerial capacity;
- administrative capacity; and
- financial capacity.[56]

Each section is divided into subsections that include two to five questions each. Some of these questions are specific ('Who makes up the governing body and what is it charged with?'). Others may be quite vague ('Is there a long-term community vision?'). Many questions require answers that depend on the needs of a particular project ('Does the CSO have the technical skills required?' 'Does the CSO have the knowledge needed?' 'Does the CSO have useful contacts and networks?'). For each subsection, the Tool helpfully identifies relevant sources of information that can be used by UNDP officials to search for answers to the questions.

There is no indication as to how the criteria in the Tool relate to the criteria in the Manual; they overlap to a large extent. In an interview, a UNDP official suggested that the two sets of criteria complement each other and may be applied concurrently.[57] It is emphasized that the Tool provides guidance

[55] UNDP, *A Toolkit for Strengthening Partnerships* (n 10) 22–27. See also appendix VII of this book p 325.

[56] A separate tool is used to assess financial capacity. See UNDP, *Framework for Cash Transfers to Implementing Partners*, Annex III (Sept 2005), <http://www.undg.org/documents/6642-Framework_for_Cash_Transfers_to_Implementing_Partners.doc>, visited 15 Feb 2006.

[57] Interview with a UNDP CSO Division officer (20 Jan 2006).

for selection and should not be seen as a one-size-fits-all approach to selection, nor as a scorecard for CSOs. These guidelines may have to be adjusted to reflect national and local capacities.

With regard to the procedures for selection of an NGO, the Manual states that a competitive process should normally be employed.[58] The word 'normally' leaves room for exceptions at the discretion of responsible UNDP officials. Where the competitive process takes place, the proposal to designate an NGO is reviewed and its competitiveness verified—on the basis of criteria and documents listed above—by the Local Programme Advisory Committee (LPAC).[59] According to the Manual, a considered NGO will be designated as an implementing partner when one specific NGO is clearly the most suitable to manage the project or when no other NGOs are available or interested. The LPAC minutes must describe the outcome of the review, the alternatives considered and the reasons why the proposed NGO was selected.[60]

According to the Toolkit for UNDP–CSO relations, in the past, country offices have limited their partners to well-known and established NGOs, overlooking the potential of other civil society actors.[61] To rectify this, UNDP now encourages its country offices to undertake a 'CSO *mapping*' of the country and create, as a result, a roster of CSOs with an accompanying assessment of their expertise and capacity to manage a project.[62] The CSOs selected for the roster have to be agreed upon by a Selection Committee that should be composed of both the Government and UNDP officials. The criteria for the review of NGOs must include the area of expertise of each NGO, as well as its level of management capacity. Under this approach, all NGOs approved by the Selection Committee are deemed qualified as potential execution agencies for projects in their area of expertise and up to the size commensurate with their management capacity, as determined by the Selection Committee.[63] Thus, when there is a need to designate an executing agency quickly (for example, in crisis and post-conflict situations), these rosters of pre-approved NGOs can be helpful.

After the selection of the designated NGO is made, both parties sign a standard Project Cooperation Agreement, which serves as the basic legal

---

[58] See UNDP, *UNDP Programming Manual* (n 39) s 6.2.4, para 6.
[59] The LPAC is established by the Resident Representative to assist in appraising the quality of UNDP programme activities. In addition to persons charged with the immediate programme preparation process, the LPAC may include technical specialists, government officials, representatives of NGOs, UN agencies and donor organisations. See UNDP, *UNDP Programming Manual* (n 39) s 2.5.2.
[60] See ibid s 6.2.4, para 6.
[61] See UNDP, *A Toolkit for Strengthening Partnerships* (n 10) 8.
[62] See UNDP, *Simplification of NGO Execution for Crisis and Post Conflict Situations* (n 44) 2.
[63] See ibid.

agreement between UNDP and the NGO and sets forth the general terms and conditions of the cooperation between the parties.[64] The NGO must provide UNDP and the government coordinating authority with periodic reports on the progress, activities, achievements and results of the projects, including quarterly financial reports and an annual progress report.[65]

As mentioned above, NGOs may also be involved in UNDP projects as *contractors*. The intention of a contract with an NGO is to provide project input or to conduct a specific project activity through an NGO that is the best supplier for the service or goods. While a contracted NGO can be tasked to take over a certain degree of project management, the overall responsibility, especially regarding budget control and reporting, rests with the implementing partner (a national institution, a UN agency, an NGO or UNDP country office). Within the framework of a contract, the implementing partner and the NGO can freely agree on the scale and scope of the service, the timetable, the reporting requirements/frequency and the payment schedule.[66]

The Manual does not lay down criteria that NGOs must satisfy in order to become contractors because the overall responsibility for the project (including the contracted parts) rests with the project-executing agency. However, the Manual requires that NGOs be chosen according to the same process that would apply to a private company.[67] The selection process must be built upon the principles of:

- *Competitiveness*. The designated institution must undertake a wide search for the most qualified candidates or suppliers. It must recruit the best-suited individual or accept the best offer for the task identified in the job description. A key consideration in all cases is cost-effectiveness. The procurement and acquisition of services and goods must be done according to the 'Common guidelines for procurement by organizations of the United Nations system'.
- *Transparency*. The selection process must be transparent and open, giving full and equal information to all candidates or suppliers, with clear selection criteria and with several persons participating in the decision-making process. Proper records must be kept.
- *Multilateralism*. The selection of goods and services must be made without regard to country of origin. Procurement and recruitment must be undertaken on a wide geographical basis. However, procure-

---

[64] For the text of the Standard Project Cooperation Agreement between UNDP and a Non-Governmental Organization, see UNDP, *UNDP Programming Manual* (n 39) Annex 6E.
[65] See Art X of the Standard Project Cooperation Agreement.
[66] See UNDP, *A Toolkit for Strengthening Partnerships* (n 10) 16.
[67] See UNDP, *UNDP Programming Manual* (n 39) s 6.4.3, para 5.

ment within the country (local procurement) is also encouraged, because of its benefits to the national economy.[68]

The Manual provides that the designated (project-executing) institution may follow its own procurement procedures provided they conform to international competitive-bidding practices. The institution may alternatively apply relevant UNDP procedures (the UNDP Procurement Manual).[69]

Lastly, UNDP may enter with CSOs (as well as with other actors, for example, private companies) into Long-Term Agreements (LTAs) for the provision of specific services. The main advantage of LTAs is that, when there arises a need for the services concerned, UNDP does not have to go through a regular protracted and expensive process to award a particular contract but, instead, can use an LTA contractor (vendor). This kind of arrangement is particularly useful in crisis or post-crisis environments. Thus, LTAs constitute a mechanism for the procurement of services that is both cost-effective and efficient. All LTAs are concluded for an initial period of two years and may be subsequently extended for one more year, depending on the vendor's performance. CSOs may enter into LTAs with the UNDP Headquarters or UNDP country offices. The user guidelines for LTAs provide information on contracting, areas of work, pricing and roles and responsibilities.[70]

[68] See ibid s 6.4.1, para 3.
[69] See ibid para 5. See also the UNDP Procurement Manual (UNDP, May 2003), <http://www.undp.org/procurement/PROCUREMENT%20MANUAL.May.2003.pdf>, visited 12 Oct 2005.
[70] See UNDP, User Guidelines, *Long Term Agreements for Professional and/or Consultancy Services*, available on request from UNDP Headquarters.

CHAPTER 9

World Bank

I. INTRODUCTION

The World Bank group consists of five closely associated institutions.[1] However, in this study, the name 'World Bank' is used to refer only to one of these institutions, the International Bank for Reconstruction and Development, to which the information in this chapter is confined.[2] Created in 1944, it is an international financial institution whose mission is to provide loans to developing countries for projects that alleviate poverty and promote social and economic development. Deriving its loan capital from subscriptions of its member countries and from borrowing on the international capital markets, the World Bank engages in public-sector lending, providing loans in more than a dozen financial, social and infrastructure areas, such as economic management, public-sector governance, education, health, rural development, environmental protection, transportation and energy. The Bank also provides analytical and advisory services. It has 184 member governments.

The World Bank is owned and governed by national governments, which become members by subscribing to capital stock. Each member appoints a governor (usually the minister of finance) whose voting power depends on its respective government's shares of the World Bank capital. The Board of Governors is responsible for core institutional decisions, such as admitting or suspending members, increasing or decreasing the authorized capital stock, determining the distribution of net income, reviewing financial statements and budgets and exercising other powers that have not been delegated to the Executive Directors. The Board of Governors meets once a year at the Bank's Annual Meeting, together with the Board of Governors of the International Monetary Fund (IMF). Each spring, the joint Bank–IMF Development Committee and the IMF's International Monetary and

---

[1] They are: International Bank for Reconstruction and Development, International Development Association, International Finance Corporation, Multilateral Investment Guarantee Agency and International Center for Settlement of Investment Disputes.

[2] This chapter is also relevant for the International Development Association (IDA), created in 1960 under its own 'Articles of Agreement' to provide interest-free loans and grants to the poorest countries. The International Bank for Reconstruction and Development and IDA share the same staff and governing bodies but draw on different resources for their lending. 165 countries are IDA members.

Financial Committee hold meetings to discuss progress on the work of the Bank and the Fund ('Spring Meetings').[3]

The major part of the Bank's decision-making is done by the Board of Executive Directors. The Governors have delegated to the executive directors all the powers that are not expressly reserved to the Governors under the Bank's Articles of Agreement. In particular, the Board decides on major policies that guide the Bank's operations and approves all projects financed by the Bank. The Board has 24 members. The five largest shareholders (France, Germany, Japan, the UK and the USA) appoint one executive director each. Other countries are grouped into constituencies, each represented on the Board by one executive director. Voting power is determined by the percentage of shares possessed by each State, the largest shareholder being the United States, which has control over approximately 17 per cent of the vote. The Board also appoints the President of the Bank (by tradition a US national), who serves as the Board's Chairman. The executive directors normally meet twice a week and decisions are usually made by consensus.

The World Bank operates day to day under the direction of the President. The Bank has 26 vice presidents who manage six geographic regions, seven thematic networks, and 13 financial, programmatic and administrative units. Vice presidents are the principal managers at the World Bank.[4]

II. LEGAL BASIS AND FORMS OF INVOLVEMENT

The constituent instrument of the Bank, the 1944 Articles of Agreement, does not provide for engagement with NGOs. Article V, Section 2(v) of the Articles of Agreement refers to cooperation with 'other international organizations', which are deemed to include only intergovernmental institutions. However, the Bank does maintain relations with NGOs. According to the Bank, its engagement with civil society is entirely permissible under the Bank's Articles of Agreement, so long as the general provisions of the Articles are observed.[5]

The Bank's relations with NGOs are part of its relations with civil society organizations (CSOs)—a term used to refer to a wide array of non-

---

[3] See <http://web.worldbank.org/WBSITE/EXTERNAL/EXTABOUTUS/0,,contentMDK: 20040580~menuPK:1696997~pagePK:51123644~piPK:329829~theSitePK:29708,00.html>, visited 25 Sept 2005.

[4] See ibid; and World Bank, *Working Together: World Bank–Civil Society Relations* (The International Bank for Reconstruction and Development / The World Bank, 2003) 7, <www.worldbank.org/civilsociety/publications>, visited 27 Apr 2006.

[5] See World Bank, *Issues and Options for Improving Engagement between the World Bank and Civil Society Organizations* (The International Bank for Reconstruction and Development / The World Bank, 2005) 7, <www.worldbank.org/civilsociety>, visited 25 Sep 2005.

governmental and non-profit organizations which have a presence in public life, expressing the interests and values of their members or others.[6] In addition to NGOs,[7] CSOs include trade unions, community-based organizations, social movements, faith-based institutions, disabled persons organizations, charitable organizations, indigenous peoples' organizations, non-profit media, research centres, foundations, student organizations, professional associations and others.[8]

The main Bank policy document that contains guidelines for engagement with NGOs is the World Bank Operational Manual, *Involving Nongovernmental Organizations in Bank-Supported Activities*.[9] It applies to Bank-supported activities, including economic and sectoral work, and all stages of project processing—identification, design, implementation, monitoring and evaluation—and thus is mostly relevant to the project-related work.[10] This document belongs to the 'Good Practices' category, meaning it is advisory, but non-binding. It 'contains information that World Bank staff may find useful in carrying out the Bank's policies and procedures'.[11] The Manual is currently being reviewed, and a newly revised edition is expected.

To provide additional assistance for World Bank staff, civil society consultation guidelines have been developed.[12] These guidelines are aimed at facilitating consultations with CSOs on projects, policy, and investment lending. The guidelines are also non-mandatory; they reflect advice and good practices distilled from experience.[13] The Civil Society Consultation Sourcebook, which expands the guidelines with additional materials, tools and techniques, serves essentially the same purpose.[14]

---

[6] See ibid 3.

[7] In the World Bank context, NGOs are understood in the narrow sense as 'professional, intermediary and non-profit organizations which advocate and/or provide services in the areas of economic and social development, human rights, welfare and emergency relief'. See ibid.

[8] World Bank, *Issues and Options for Improving Engagement* (n 5) 3. The diversity of CSOs that wish to engage with the Bank is sometimes referred to as one of the obstacles to designing meaningful modalities for Bank–CSO interactions.

[9] World Bank Operational Manual: Good Practices, 'Involving Nongovernmental Organizations in Bank-Supported Activities', <http://wbln0018.world-bank.org/Institutional/Manuals/OpManual.nsf/0/1DFB2471DE05BF9A8525672C007D0950?OpenDocument>, visited 25 Sept 2005. See also appendix VIII of this book, p 335. Provisions of the Manual are reviewed in more detail below.

[10] See ibid para 1.   [11] ibid, preamble.

[12] See World Bank, *Consultations with Civil Society Organizations: General Guidelines for World Bank Staff* (The International Bank for Reconstruction and Development / The World Bank, 2000), <http://web.worldbank.org/WBSITE/EXTERNAL/TOPICS/CSO/0,,content MDK:20098396~menuPK:220449~pagePK:220503~piPK:220476~theSitePK:228717,00. html>, visited 25 Sept 2005.

[13] See ibid 3.

[14] See World Bank, 'Consultations with Civil Society: A Sourcebook', World Bank working document (May 2004), <http://siteresources.worldbank.org/CSO/Resources/Consultations-SOURCEBOOK-May-2004.pdf>, visited 25 Sept 2005.

Further, there are a number of Bank operational policies and procedures on specific issues (like involuntary resettlement, environmental assessments or indigenous peoples) that provide for CSO involvement, primarily in the form of consultations. These so-called 'safeguard policies' (they seek to safeguard Bank projects from the undesirable side-effects of environmental, social or other nature) envisage CSO participation only in relation to specific Bank-financed projects, as opposed to dialogue on general policies.

In sum, the World Bank has very few (binding) rules for engagement with NGOs. The Bank's constitutive instrument does not contain an explicit authorization for cooperation with NGOs. The Bank's secondary rules governing NGO participation largely consist of non-binding norms and guidelines. The only binding norms are found in the Bank's 'safeguard policies' relating to specific issues (environmental, etc), which provide for a certain role for civil society in Bank-financed projects. The scarcity of legal rules deprives NGOs of stability and predictability with regard to the possibilities to become involved in the Bank's activities. However, a Bank official noted in an interview that in many situations this lack of rules is to the advantage of civil society. Given the current political reality, it is hardly imaginable that governments sitting on the Board of Directors could agree on a set of binding rules governing NGO involvement that would be far-reaching enough and satisfactory for NGOs. In this situation, the absence of hard and fast rules gives Bank staff a certain freedom of action, which they frequently use to engage with NGOs in greater depth than they otherwise could.[15] Also, according to this Bank official, it would be very difficult for an institution like the World Bank, which implements such a variety of projects in different political and cultural settings, to devise a code that would fit every particular situation, so a certain degree of flexibility is warranted.[16]

At present, as a matter of practice, the Bank does consult with CSOs on policies, programmes, studies and projects. Dialogue occurs in many forms and venues, and at the local, national or transnational levels, on both specific projects and more general policies. The Bank acknowledges that CSOs have become significant players in global development finance and that they are increasingly influencing the shape of global and national public policy.[17] According to the Bank, since the 1990s it has placed a high priority on strengthening engagement with CSOs. Allegedly, civic engagement is now an integral part of the Bank's strategy to strengthen the investment climate and promote empowerment in developing countries, and is

[15] Interview with Ms Carolyn Reynolds, World Bank Global Civil Society Team (26 Jan 2006).
[16] ibid.
[17] See World Bank, *Issues and Options for Improving Engagement* (n 5) x.

part of the Bank's business model.[18] By contrast, many CSOs still find that the Bank remains insufficiently transparent, lacking in its accountablity and not fully responsive to public concerns. They object that too often, the Bank has failed to consider adequately their most important concerns or incorporate their recommendations into policy or project decision-making. The actual influence of civil society on Bank policy and Bank-supported projects remains very limited and uneven.[19] Some CSOs are therefore wary of engaging with the Bank because they find it cumbersome to do so, or they do not believe it will yield much benefit.[20]

Having accepted many of the civil society criticisms, the Bank is currently reviewing the framework for its relations with CSOs. The general direction and principal elements of future reforms have been outlined in the Bank paper entitled 'Issues and Options for Improving Engagement between the World Bank and Civil Society Organizations'.[21] CSOs were consulted on this paper and contributed to its development. The purpose of the paper is 'to assess the World Bank's recent relations with CSOs, and to propose options for promoting more effective civic engagement in Bank-supported activities'.[22] The text shows that the basic structure of the Bank's engagement with civil society will not become subject to radical changes. For example, it does not envisage a system whereby accredited CSOs would be granted permanent observer status with the organs of the Bank and does not envisage more participatory rights for NGOs in the Bank's decision-making processes.

It is the Bank management and Bank staff—as opposed to the Bank's intergovernmental organs—who engage with stakeholders from civil society, although some directors may regularly meet with CSOs in their personal capacity. Bank management gives CSOs the opportunity to express their views and concerns regarding the Bank's strategies, policies, and programmes. The Bank staff, especially at country level, involve civil society in specific lending projects.[23] However, CSOs have few opportunities to influence important policy decisions made by the Board of Executive Directors.

Currently more than 120 civil society engagement staff (the Civil Society Team) work throughout the institution and provide institutional coordination for relations with CSOs by formulating Bank-wide strategy, providing

---

[18] See ibid ix.
[19] See World Bank, 'A Call for Participatory Decision Making: Discussion Paper on World Bank–Civil Society Engagement', Draft for public comment (14 Apr 2005) 3, 6–7, <http://web.worldbank.org/WBSITE/EXTERNAL/TOPICS/CSO/0,,contentMDK:20327929~pagePK:220503~piPK:220476~theSitePK:228717,00.html>, visited 25 Sept 2005.
[20] See World Bank, *Issues and Options for Improving Engagement* (n 5) x.
[21] See ibid.   [22] See ibid 1.
[23] Interview with Ms Carolyn Reynolds, World Bank Global Civil Society Team (26 Jan 2006).

advice to senior management, and reaching out to CSOs at the global level. The Civil Society Group (about 40 staff members) brings together civil society specialists who work at Bank headquarters in Washington, DC in various regional departments, different thematic networks and with a variety of constituencies, such as labour unions, indigenous peoples and foundations. At the country level, there are Civil Society country staff working in approximately 70 offices worldwide. While their specific work programmes vary according to the country, they generally carry out social analysis, liaise with civil society, manage outreach programmes and work to involve CSOs in Bank-financed projects.[24] The Bank Civil Society Team is decentralized; there are no direct reporting lines within its parts—this may sometimes lead to situations when similar matters may be handled differently by different staff members.

The main functions of the Civil Society Team are set out in the Operational Manual, 'Involving Nongovernmental Organizations in Bank-Supported Activities'.[25] They are:

- to develop and coordinate the Bank's overall relationship with NGOs;
- to provide advice and operational assistance to Bank staff on working with NGOs;
- to promote within the Bank practices and procedures that facilitate collaboration with NGOs;
- to monitor NGO involvement in Bank-financed activities;
- to disseminate good practice in working with NGOs;
- to coordinate training for staff;
- to assist Bank staff in organizing policy consultations with NGOs;
- to conduct research on NGO-related issues;
- to maintain an electronic database on NGOs; and
- to respond to NGO requests for information or to direct NGO requests to the appropriate Bank staff.[26]

Many country offices have appointed CSO specialists or CSO liaison officers to act as points of contact and communication with civil society. These specialists play a lead role in establishing and maintaining effective relations among the Bank, the borrower and CSOs at the country level—for example, gathering information about CSOs, responding to requests from and disseminating information to CSOs, assisting staff in identifying and assess-

[24] See World Bank, *Working Together: World Bank–Civil Society Relations* (n 4) 30–1.
[25] The Operational Manual refers to the NGO/Civil Society Unit, whose functions were subsequently taken over by the Civil Society Team. See World Bank Operational Manual 'Involving Nongovernmental Organizations in Bank-Supported Activities' (n 9).
[26] See ibid para 31.

ing CSO partners, organizing systematic consultations with CSOs on country strategy and operational and policy matters and advising the government on fostering an enabling environment for CSOs.[27]

The three major types of the Bank's engagement with CSOs are (1) dialogue on general policy issues; (2) involvement of CSOs in the planning, implementation and evaluation of projects financed by the Bank; and (3) involvement of CSOs in the Bank's quasi-dispute settlement mechanism (the Inspection Panel procedure). These three types of engagement are reviewed in turn.

III. INVOLVEMENT IN BANK POLICY DEVELOPMENT

A. *Introduction*

As mentioned above, the only binding rules that provide for NGO participation within the Bank address the operational or technical level of implementation of specific Bank projects—'safeguard policies'. Existing consultation procedures on general issues (like structural adjustment, information disclosure, rural development, forest management, etc) are not based on binding rules. According to commentators, it does not currently seem realistic to ask for such rules for NGO participation in World Bank policy-making or official NGO observer privileges in, for example, meetings of the Board of Executive Directors or the negotiations between the Bank management and governments.[28]

Despite the lack of binding rules governing the Bank's consultations with NGOs on policy issues, such substantive discussions occur in numerous forms and on different levels. Generally, the World Bank has made consultations the norm rather than the exception. 'Consultation' has become an obligatory feature in collecting information and opinions on policy issues. Almost no public document is prepared without some form of public consultation.[29]

Consultations are advisory and non-binding. The Bank gives civil society the opportunity to comment on projects, strategies and policies before they are submitted for approval to its decision-making organ. Consultation in

---

[27] See ibid para 30.

[28] See 'Participation of Non-Governmental Organisations in International Environmental Governance: Legal Basis and Practical Experience', on behalf of the Umweltbundesamt (German Federal Environment Agency) Final Report, June 2002, prepared by Ecologic and FIELD, p 202, <http://www.ecologic.de/download/projekte/1850-1899/1890/report_ngos_en.pdf>, visited 15 Aug 2005.

[29] See P Nelson, 'Access and Influence: Tensions and Ambiguities in the World Bank's Expanding Relationship with Civil Society Organizations', prepared for the project *Voices: The Rise of Nongovernmental Voices in Multilateral Institutions* (Apr 2002) 9, <http://www.nsi-ins.ca/english/pdf/access_influence.pdf>, visited on 5 Oct 2005.

this context does not mean negotiation and it does not imply acceptance of the views of the consulted party or a mandatory influence (in whatever form) on the decisions taken by the Bank.[30] Rather, consultation implies 'receiving adequate information [from civil society representatives], listening to them with an open mind and readiness to take their views into account before the Bank reaches its own conclusion'.[31] According to the Bank, its dialogue with civil society is not necessarily expected to result in specific, short-term outcomes, but it can lead to greater development and effectiveness over time by improving understanding of issues and encouraging cooperation.[32]

Some more prominent recent examples of consultative processes on policy issues include CSO participation in the review process of the Bank's 'safeguard policies'; in the Extractive Industries Review; in the formulation of national Poverty Reduction Strategy Papers (PRSPs) and of Country Assistance Strategies (CAS); in the Comprehensive Development Framework (CDF); in the World Commission on Dams; in the Structural Adjustment Participatory Review Initiative (SAPRI); in the World Development Report process; in the Strategic Policy Workshops on trade, rural livelihoods, HIV/AIDS and others. Some of these interactions have taken place on the global level, others on a country level; some have been fully 'Bank-owned' processes, others (such as the RPSP or CAS) have been conducted under the responsibility of national governments. Such consultations can be carried out through various modalities including face-to-face meetings, video conferences and web-discussions.[33]

The Bank acknowledges that there is no consistent institutional approach to dialogue and consultations, particularly at the global level.[34] This continues to pose problems for the Bank regarding civil society relations:

[30] As an exception to this general rule, the recently revised Bank policy on indigenous peoples provides that for all projects affecting indigenous peoples, the Bank provides financing 'only where free, prior, and informed consultation results in broad community support to the project by the affected Indigenous Peoples'. See World Bank Operational Manual: Operational Policy, 'Indigenous Peoples', OP 4.10 (Jan 2005) paras 1 and 11, <http://wbln0018.worldbank.org/Institutional/Manuals/OpManual.nsf/B52929624EB2A353 8525672E00775F66/0F7D6F3F04DD70398525672C007D08ED?OpenDocument#This%20 policy%20should%20be%20read%20togeth>, visited 27 Jan 2006.
[31] See S Schlemmer-Schulte, 'International Law Weekend Proceedings: The Impact of Civil Society on the World Bank, the International Monetary Fund and the World Trade Organization: The Case of the World Bank' (2001) 7 International Law Students Association J Intl & Comp L 399, 406.
[32] See World Bank, *Issues and Options for Improving Engagement* (n 5) 10.
[33] See World Bank, *World Bank–Civil Society Engagement: Review of Fiscal Years 2002–2004* (The International Bank for Reconstruction and Development/The World Bank, 2005) 4. This publication also gives a fuller description of several recent examples of consultations with CSOs, including consultations on adjustment lending, extractive industries, the World Development Reports and others. See ibid 4–8.
[34] See ibid 6.

While consultation with CSOs occurs widely across the Bank today, Bank staff and civil society representatives alike report that their breadth and quality vary considerably. CSOs report that these consultations are often unsatisfactory in terms of preparation, logistics, and methodology. Further, timely and useful feedback has not always been provided to those CSOs consulted, leaving them uncertain whether their inputs were considered and/or incorporated by the Bank. These and other problems have contributed to what is being referred to as 'consultation fatigue' within development circles.[35]

Because the Bank does not have clear and mandatory protocols for designing consultative processes, it creates them on an ad hoc basis. This fact complicates the comprehensive review of arrangements for the Bank's dialogues/consultations with civil society and compels limiting such review to the more institutionalized forms of NGO/CSO involvement.

The next section will give a short account of the history of World Bank–NGO relations, focusing on its institutional side. Following will be a review of the more permanent arrangements for NGO involvement (Annual and Spring Meetings) and a description of the World Bank–Civil Society Global Policy Forum held in 2005.

B. History

The World Bank first began to interact with civil society in the 1970s through dialogue with NGOs on environmental issues. In 1981, the Bank's Board of Directors approved the first operational policy note on relations with NGOs. In 1982, leading international NGOs and the Bank established the NGO–World Bank Committee, which was the most significant forum for policy dialogue between the Bank and CSOs during the 1980s and 1990s. This Committee was composed of senior Bank managers and 15 NGOs from around the world; it held regular meetings to discuss Bank policies, programmes and projects in areas such as environment, debt and structural adjustment.

When in the late 1990s an ever larger number and range of civil society actors not involved in the Committee (such as labour unions, social movements, or faith-based groups) sought to engage with the Bank and, at the same time, a variety of global, regional and national venues for engagement emerged around issues such as education, HIV/AIDS, and the Poverty Reduction Strategy Papers (PRSPs), it became clear that the dialogue between the Bank and CSOs had to be broadened to make it more inclusive. Thus, the World Bank–NGO Committee was phased out in late 2000,

---

[35] ibid.

and an interim and informal Joint Facilitation Committee (JFC) was formed in 2001 with the task to produce new mechanisms for Bank–civil society engagement on the global level.[36] The JFC was created as a time-finite transitional body to facilitate dialogue and engagement between the Bank and civil society.

By the end of 2005, the JFC had ceased to exist, and has not been substituted by any other institutional arrangement. The JFC process has not led to any specific and lasting outcomes, as JFC members did not reach consensus on matters before it. The few tangible results of the JFC work include a discussion paper on World Bank–civil society engagement entitled 'A Call for Participatory Decision Making',[37] which analyses relations between the Bank and civil society, identifies problems and recommends certain measures to overcome them. The JFC also prepared the first Bank–Civil Society Global Policy Forum (April 2005), although this has not grown into an annual event.[38] As a result of the JFC process phase-out, the Bank currently has no institutional arrangement for engagement with CSOs.

C. Annual and Spring Meetings[39]

Annual and Spring Meetings have developed into the primary biannual communication point between the Bretton Woods institutions and the NGOs concerned with them.[40]

To recall, each autumn the World Bank, together with the IMF, hold Annual Meetings of their Boards of Governors to discuss a range of issues falling within the mandates of the two institutions and to assess their work programme. The week of Annual Meetings includes two days of plenary sessions, during which the Boards of Governors take decisions on how current policy issues should be addressed and approve corresponding resolutions. The Annual Meetings are preceded by meetings of the IMF's International

---

[36] The JFC was composed of staff and senior managers of the Bank and of 14 regional and international civil society organizations (primarily networks with global reach) representing a broad cross-section of civil society including trade unions, indigenous groups, faith-based organizations, NGOs and foundations. Organizations involved in the JFC were drawn from a diverse group of civil society sectors and geographical regions on the basis of the pre-established selection criteria. See *Joint Resolution between the World Bank and the NGO Working Group* (6 Dec 2000), <http://www.staff.city.ac.uk/p.willetts/NGOWG/JNT-RES.HTM>, visited 25 Sept 2005.

[37] See World Bank, 'A Call for Participatory Decision Making: Discussion Paper on World Bank-Civil Society Engagement' (n 19).

[38] On the Annual World Bank–Civil Society Forum, see below, p 164.

[39] The information in this section relates to the Annual and Spring Meetings held in 2005. There are no standing Bank/IMF regulations governing CSO participation in the Annual and Spring Meetings, therefore relevant procedures may be easily changed in the years to come.

[40] See RE Kelly, 'A Micro-View of Global Governance: The Spring and Annual Meetings of the Bretton Woods Institutions' (2003) 55 Transnational Associations 203.

Monetary and Financial Committee (IMFC), the joint Bank–IMF Development Committee and of various groups of countries. Additionally, each spring the IMFC and the Development Committee hold meetings to discuss progress of the Bank's and the Fund's work, the 'Spring Meetings'.

In order to attend the Meetings, CSOs must be accredited. Accreditation criteria and procedures for Annual and Spring Meetings have been streamlined and do not differ in any substantial way. Nonetheless, accreditation remains ad hoc—a particular CSO representative has to request accreditation for each particular set of Meetings.

Accreditation to the Meetings does not entitle participants to attend meetings of the IMFC, nor the meetings of the Development Committee. Only member-country delegates have access to these meetings. A practice has evolved, when immediately prior to the Annual and Spring Meetings, the heads of the World Bank and the IMF, and the chairs of the IMFC and the Development Committee hold a joint meeting with CSOs to inform them of recent developments and to listen to their concerns.[41] Aside from that, NGOs may only attend the concluding plenary session of the Boards of Governors during the Annual Meetings. However, at this session, CSOs do not enjoy any further participatory rights—they cannot make oral statements or submit written statements, comment on draft documents and so on. Therefore, most CSOs find little use in attending these sessions; they benefit more from participating in the activities running parallel, and in connection with, the Annual and Spring Meetings. As described below, these programmes include Dialogues with Civil Society, the Program of Seminars sessions and press events. CSOs use these opportunities to network, meet World Bank and IMF staff and publicize their activities by reaching out to wider audiences through the mass media.

In connection with both the Annual and the Spring Meetings, the World Bank and the IMF organize Dialogues with Civil Society. The Dialogues serve as a forum for discussion of topical issues by the Bank/IMF officials, government representatives and civil society. For example, the 2005 Spring Dialogues addressed such topics as debt sustainability analysis, transparency in extractive industries, the World Development Report 2006, health financing and IMF conditionality, among others. As one commentator observed, these meetings provide a place for the many attendees to share information, forge personal relationships, follow up previous information distribution and return monitoring reports and anecdotal narratives 'from the ground'.[42] Formally, for participation in the Dialogues, no accreditation

---

[41] For details of participation in such meetings, CSOs should contact the External Affairs Department of the Bank (civilsociety@worldbank.org) or the External Relations Department of the Fund (ngoliaison@imf.org). Source: Interview with Ms Carolyn Reynolds, World Bank Global Civil Society Team (26 Jan 2006).

[42] See RE Kelly, 'A Micro-View of Global Governance' (n 40) 205.

is required on days prior to when the official Meetings begin and security measures are increased, but CSOs benefit from accreditation as this allows them to have easier access to the IMF and the World Bank buildings.[43]

During the week of the Annual Meetings, accredited CSOs can additionally attend—also free of charge—the Program of Seminars sessions. The Program includes roundtable discussions, seminars, and regional briefings with the participation of senior Bank and IMF officials, private sector representatives, government delegates and representatives of civil society. The topics of the thematic sessions reflect the current issues that are making headlines and are affecting the lives of people throughout the world.

CSO representatives accredited to the Meetings are usually allocated a meeting space in both the IMF and Bank buildings. Both spaces are equipped with computers, printers, copiers and phones, and the IMF room is additionally equipped with a live feed from the press conference room and the Board of Governors sessions during the Annual Meetings. Among other things, they can use the IMF room to hold meetings with journalists and to organize CSO press conferences. A limited number of CSOs (on a first-come, first-served basis) are also allowed to attend press conferences held in the regular press room by government representatives or IMF/Bank staff, albeit without the right to ask questions.[44]

Accreditation criteria and procedures applied by the Bank and the IMF have not been legally established but exist rather as a matter of practice for both institutions. According to the Bank website, to be accredited, NGOs have to engage with the Bank and the Fund on a broad range of development operations and in policy dialogue at the local, national and global level.[45] As a matter of practice, the Bank and the IMF do not require that CSOs *engage* with either of the institutions but only satisfy themselves that the CSOs' activities concern development policy or other issues relevant to either of the two institutions.[46] There are no requirements concerning the organizational or governance structure of CSOs, their decision-making processes, funding, length of existence or other criteria applied by other international organizations. These lax requirements of the Bank and IMF are probably due to the fact that NGOs are not able to influence the course of the Meetings as they do not enjoy any important participatory rights.

---

[43] Interview with Ms Simonetta Nardin and Ms Jennifer Bisping, IMF External Relations Department (24 Jan 2006).

[44] ibid.

[45] See <http://web.worldbank.org/WBSITE/EXTERNAL/TOPICS/CSO/0,,contentMDK: 20094168~pagePK:220503~piPK:220476~theSitePK:228717,00.html>, visited 25 Sept 2005.

[46] Interview with Ms Simonetta Nardin and Ms Jennifer Bisping, IMF External Relations Department (24 Jan 2006).

Since 2005, requests for accreditation have been submitted online. NGOs may also check the status of their applications through the Bank's website. All requests are reviewed by the External Affairs Department of the Bank (EXT) and the External Relations Department of the Fund (EXR). Working collaboratively, these two departments make an assessment of whether applying CSOs are bona fide (not fictitious) and whether they meet the accreditation criterion. As no documents are required from NGOs for accreditation, this assessment is made on the basis of previous contacts and knowledge about the organization and the individuals concerned; in case of doubt, Bank/Fund officials may conduct Internet searches, contact the Bank's relevant country office or contact the organization directly. EXR/EXT automatically recommends accreditation for those CSO representatives that were accredited to previous Annual or Spring Meetings.[47] Accreditation is denied for individuals/organizations whom EXT/EXR is unable to identify and/or contact and to those who do not meet the accreditation criterion.

EXT/EXR makes a joint decision on each of the applicants and emails, on a weekly basis, the names of organizations and individuals who have applied to the Executive Director's office that represents the country from which the request originated,[48] with the proposed action (clearance or denial) on each particular application. In the absence of any objection from the Executive Director, the decision is deemed approved on a lapse-of-time basis after eight working days. If the Executive Director objects to the accreditation of a particular CSO he/she is expected to give reasons for his/her opinion. This opinion is not subject to review or appeal, although it may be subject to negotiations.

For the 2005 Annual Meetings, the number of accredited CSOs equalled 274 (1 refusal), out of which 180 representatives actually attended. For the 2004 Annual Meetings, 328 CSOs were accredited (5 refusals), out of which only 151 CSO representatives were present. Spring Meetings attract less attention, with only 80 CSOs being accredited for the 2005 Spring Meetings (no refusals).[49]

[47] ibid.

[48] Recall that the five executive directors represent the five largest shareholder nations and the remaining 19 each represent a constituency of countries. Respective governments determine which director (that on the IMF Executive Board or on the Bank Board of Executive Directors) will be reviewing applications for accreditation. Usually, this power is given to the Director sitting on the Bank's Board of Executive Directors. Source: Interview with Ms Simonetta Nardin and Ms Jennifer Bisping, IMF External Relations Department (24 Jan 2006).

[49] Statistics obtained from Ms Simonetta Nardin and Ms Jennifer Bisping, IMF External Relations Department, 24 Jan 2006.

D. *World Bank–Civil Society Forum*

Annual Bank–civil society forums were envisaged in the 2000 Joint Resolution, which conceptualized the forum as a key space for dialogue between the Bank and civil society on specific issues.[50] According to the Joint Resolution, the forum was meant to be

> as inclusive as possible and, depending on the issues discussed, it will convene representatives of NGOs, trade unions, community organizations, religious groups, women['s] organizations and other organized expressions of civil society with relevant expertise in issues identified as the annual focus of the forum.[51]

The Joint Facilitation Committee, as described above, was established by the Resolution to facilitate the organization of the annual forum.

The first World Bank–Civil Society Global Policy Forum was organized in April 2005, a few days after the Spring Meetings. This two-day event brought together some 200 civil society leaders, government officials, parliamentarians, donor-agency representatives, IMF staff, and Bank managers. There were CSOs present from over 50 countries, the majority from developing countries, representing a broad array of NGOs, labour unions, faith-based groups, foundations, and community-based organizations.[52] The two main topics of the Forum were the assessment of implementation and development impact of the Poverty Reduction Strategy process at the country level and the Bank–civil society engagement at the global level. On both items, CSOs addressed to the Bank their communiqués.

Although the Forum was envisaged as a lasting arrangement, so far there has not been enough momentum or CSO pressure for it to continue on an annual basis. The Forum did not take place in 2006, although it may revive in the future should there be strong demand from civil society.[53]

IV. PARTICIPATION IN BANK-FINANCED PROJECTS

A. *Legal Framework and Forms of Involvement*

According to the World Bank, the participation of CSOs in Bank-financed

---

[50] See Joint Resolution between the World Bank and the NGO Working Group (6 Dec 2000) <http://www.staff.city.ac.uk/p.willetts/NGOWG/JNT-RES.HTM>, visited 25 Sept 2005.

[51] See ibid, operative part, para. 1.

[52] See <http://web.worldbank.org/WBSITE/EXTERNAL/TOPICS/CSO/0,,contentMDK: 20327929~pagePK:220503~piPK:220476~theSitePK:228717,00.html>, visited 25 Sept 2005.

[53] Interview with Ms Carolyn Reynolds, World Bank Global Civil Society Team (26 Jan 2006).

projects can enhance operational performance and sustainability by contributing local knowledge, technical expertise, and social legitimacy.[54] The Bank's portfolio has been undergoing a significant shift toward financing in the social sectors and conservation programmes—areas in which many NGOs have clear strengths—a fact that warrants even wider NGO participation.[55] At the same time, the Bank's project lending has often been a source of contention with civil society. CSOs have long accused the Bank of financing socially and environmentally harmful projects despite concerted local opposition; they claim that too often the Bank has failed to adequately consider CSOs' most important concerns or incorporate their recommendations into project decision-making.[56]

Loans are the main type of Bank-funded projects. Each type of loan follows a similar project cycle that contains seven distinct, yet overlapping, stages: identification, appraisal, preparation, negotiation, implementation, monitoring and evaluation. For each of the loans it considers funding, the Bank assigns task managers who assemble multidisciplinary project teams. The Bank and government teams work closely throughout the project cycle.[57]

The Bank's statistics indicate that civil society involvement in World Bank loan projects has risen steadily from 21.5 per cent of the total number of projects in the fiscal year 1990 to 74 per cent in the fiscal year 2004.[58] To classify CSO involvement, the Bank uses four broadly defined 'levels of participation': information-sharing (one-way communication), consultation (two-way communication), collaboration (shared control over decisions and resources), and empowerment (transfer of control over decisions and resources).[59] According to the Bank, although CSO participation may occur throughout the project cycle, from the design and planning stages through implementation and monitoring,[60] it is generally more likely to take place in the initial stages of the participation process (information-sharing and consultation) than in the later stages (collaboration and empowerment).[61] CSOs consider that their actual influence on bank-supported projects remains very limited and uneven and that much of the increased participa-

---

[54] See World Bank, *Working Together: World Bank–Civil Society Relations* (n 4) 33.
[55] See World Bank Operational Manual, 'Involving Nongovernmental Organizations in Bank-Supported Activities' (n 9) para 4.
[56] See World Bank, 'A Call for Participatory Decision Making: Discussion Paper on World Bank–Civil Society Engagement' (n 19) 4, 45.
[57] See World Bank, *Working Together: World Bank–Civil Society Relations* (n 4) 11.
[58] See World Bank, *Review of Fiscal Years 2002–2004* (n 33) 18. The figures presented report on *actual* civil society participation activities undertaken during the identification, preparation, and appraisal stages of the project cycle, but on *intended* involvement during the subsequent implementation, monitoring, and evaluation phases See ibid.
[59] See ibid 19.
[60] See World Bank, *Working Together: World Bank–Civil Society Relations* (n 4) 33.
[61] See World Bank, *Review of Fiscal Years 2002–2004* (n 33) 19.

tion has been narrow in scope, rushed, superficial, or otherwise ineffective.[62]

The Bank's engagement with NGOs in relation to specific projects is guided by the World Bank Operational Manual entitled 'Involving Nongovernmental Organizations in Bank-Supported Activities'.[63] It applies to Bank-supported activities, including economic and sectoral work and all stages of project processing—identification, design, implementation, monitoring and evaluation.[64] As mentioned above, this document belongs to the 'Good Practices' category, ie is non-binding but advisory.

The general attitude of the Manual is that NGO involvement in Bank-supported activities should be encouraged.[65] For the most part, however, engagement is left to the discretion of project staff. Consultations are only required (by the Bank's 'safeguard policies') where projects will have significant adverse environmental impacts,[66] affect indigenous peoples,[67] or resettle people involuntarily.[68] In all other cases, decisions concerning NGO involvement in lending operations are the responsibility of the borrower country (project documentation describing intended NGO involvement is agreed with the borrower). [69] However, Bank staff generally encourage and facilitate the involvement of NGOs throughout the project cycle.

The Manual envisages several ways in which NGOs may be involved in Bank-supported activities—for example, as informal advisers, consultants, implementing agencies, construction managers, or co-financiers.[70] In practice, NGOs most frequently become involved either as advisers/consultants or implementing agencies for a component of the project. The Manual does not spell out specific rights and obligations associated with any of these roles; this is determined individually for each specific project by relevant Bank and government officials. Where consultations are held with CSOs,

---

[62] See World Bank, 'A Call for Participatory Decision Making: Discussion Paper on World Bank–Civil Society Engagement' (n 19). For an account of problems related to CSO involvement in Bank-supported projects, see ibid 47–53.

[63] See World Bank Operational Manual: Good Practices, 'Involving Nongovernmental Organizations in Bank-Supported Activities,' (n 9).

[64] See ibid para 1.

[65] See ibid.

[66] See World Bank Operational Manual: Operational Policy, 'Environmental Assessment', OP 4.01 (1999).

[67] See World Bank Operational Manual: Operational Policy, 'Indigenous Peoples', OP 4.10 (2005).

[68] See World Bank Operational Mannual: Operational Policy, 'Involuntary Resettlement', OP 4.12 (2001). This policy is currently being revised. For all safeguard policies, see <http://lnweb18.worldbank.org/ESSD/sdvext.nsf/52ByDocName/SafeguardPolicies>, visited 25 Sept 2005.

[69] See World Bank Operational Manual: Good Practices, 'Involving Nongovernmental Organizations in Bank-Supported Activities' (n 9) paras 13 and 17.

[70] See ibid para 13.

Bank guidelines for its staff for consultations with civil society are relevant.[71]

Just like other types of organizations, NGOs can compete to provide goods and services in connection with Bank-funded activities. CSOs may contract with government agencies to deliver social services—for example, work on AIDS prevention, manage village water systems, run day care centres, advance micro- and small-enterprise development, participate in environmental park management.[72] Increasing numbers of NGOs are contracted by government agencies and World Bank offices at country level to provide training and technical assistance within Bank-financed projects in such areas as capacity-building, institutional planning, leadership training, curriculum design and project design.[73] CSOs are also being invited to assist with monitoring and evaluating core projects by participating in project supervision missions, carrying out social impact analysis, and attending project review workshops. When competing for contracts for Bank-funded projects, NGOs have to follow regular Bank contracting and procurement policies and procedures.[74]

The Manual provides that when NGOs participate in Bank-financed projects, Bank staff should describe anticipated and actual NGO involvement in the project documentation and should set out in the legal documents any arrangements agreed with the borrower.[75]

B. Selection Criteria and Procedures

The Manual states that NGO partners should be selected according to the specific skills and expertise required for the task at hand as it relates to the development goals being pursued.[76] Thus, the most general requirement is the availability of relevant expertise. Further, the Manual says that the Bank concentrates on establishing links with those NGOs that have extensive grass-roots experience and can facilitate reaching and involving the poor. The Bank also aims to maintain open dialogue with NGOs that have significant influence on public opinion or governments in terms of development policy and programmes.[77] Consequently, the requirements of relevant

---

[71] See World Bank, *Consultations with Civil Society Organizations: General Guidelines for World Bank Staff* (n 12).
[72] See World Bank, *Review of Fiscal Years 2002–2004* (n 33) 17. For specific examples of CSO involvement see ibid 17–18.
[73] See <http://web.worldbank.org/WBSITE/EXTERNAL/TOPICS/CSO/0,,contentMDK: 20094613~menuPK:220448~pagePK:220503~piPK:220476~theSitePK:228717,00.html>, visited 25 Sept 2005.
[74] See ibid.
[75] The World Bank Operational Manual: Good Practices, 'Involving Nongovernmental Organizations in Bank-Supported Activities' (n 9) para 13.
[76] See ibid para 15.   [77] See ibid para 5.

expertise, grass-roots links and the ability to influence public opinion are considered to be the most essential in selecting partner NGOs.

In addition to these main criteria, the Manual sets out a list of more specific NGO qualities that should perhaps be read as an elaboration of the above-mentioned general criteria:

(a) credibility: acceptability to both stakeholders and government;
(b) competence: relevant skills and experience, proven track record;
(c) local knowledge;
(d) representation: community ties, accountability to members/beneficiaries, gender sensitivity;
(e) governance: sound internal management, transparency, financial accountability, efficiency;
(f) legal status; and
(g) institutional capacity: sufficient scale of operations, facilities, and equipment.[78]

This is not an invariable set of criteria that have to be satisfied by any NGO participating in any Bank project. The specific set of required qualities may depend on the nature and purpose of a particular task. Thus, the NGO selection criteria are subject to discretion.

The Manual does not explain how Bank officers or government officials should assess whether a particular NGO complies with the set criteria. There is no list of documents and information that interested NGOs should submit and to whom. The Manual only gives guidance as to where to obtain information about NGOs:

- Civil Society Thematic Team staff;
- NGO/civil society specialists in Bank country and technical departments;
- previous project and sector reports;
- NGO networks;
- directories and databases prepared by governments and multilateral, bilateral, and other donors; and
- informed people in the country.[79]

The Manual also mentions that Bank staff can benefit from working closely with NGO networks that are formed at the national, regional and international levels. It suggests that such networks can be a valuable source of information about, and contacts within, the NGO community.[80]

---

[78] See ibid para 15.   [79] See ibid para 14.   [80] See ibid para 8.

The Manual distinguishes between two types of NGOs that the Bank principally interacts with: (a) operational NGOs, whose primary purpose is to fund, design or implement development-related programmes or projects, and (b) advocacy NGOs, whose primary purpose is to defend or promote a specific development cause and which seek to influence the development policies and practices of the Bank, governments and other bodies.[81] It is stated, however, that the difference between these two groups is not rigid and that the majority of NGOs fall somewhere in between the two extremes.[82] The Manual does not give explicit preference to either of the two types and states that although operational NGOs usually have more field-level experience that is relevant to the Bank, advocacy groups may also be able to offer valuable grass-roots insights and challenge conventional development thinking.[83]

The Manual does not establish a formal procedure for selecting NGOs for specific Bank-supported activities. In practice, when CSOs are selected for implementing Bank projects, this is done through a competitive process, in line with Bank's rules on procurement. These rules apply to both CSO and non-CSO bidders.[84]

Usually, the Bank's country staff, together with additional headquarters staff assigned to particular projects, is responsible for an effective liaison between the Bank and NGOs. The Manual assigns the following specific tasks to the Bank's country offices:

- gather and maintain information about local NGOs and NGO activities in their country;
- inform visiting Bank missions about NGOs and NGO activities relevant to their work;
- organize meetings between local NGOs and visiting mission staff;
- as appropriate, organize consultations with NGOs and government representatives on policy and sectoral issues;
- respond to NGO requests for information; and
- work with the government to promote an enabling environment for NGOs.[85]

There are no statistics on the share of Bank projects implemented by CSOs but in some programmes this share may be significant. For example, the Bank's HIV/AIDS programme (totalling US$1 billion) requires that 40 per cent of funds be channelled through CSOs.[86]

[81] See ibid para 7.   [82] See ibid.   [83] See ibid.
[84] For details, see the Bank's web-pages on procurement, <http://web.worldbank.org/WBSITE/EXTERNAL/PROJECTS/PROCUREMENT/0,,pagePK:84271~theSitePK:84266,00.html>, visited 27 Jan 2006.   [85] See ibid para 30.
[86] Interview with Ms Carolyn Reynolds, World Bank Global Civil Society Team (26 Jan 2006).

V. ROLE IN DISPUTE SETTLEMENT (BANK ACCOUNTABILITY MECHANISM)

A. Introduction

The World Bank Inspection Panel procedure provides the most formal and most fully institutionalized mechanism for NGO involvement. The Inspection Panel is the key component of the Bank's quasi-dispute settlement and accountability mechanism. The Panel was created in 1993 to hold the Bank accountable for violations of its policies and procedures connected to specific Bank projects. The Bank's various operational policies and procedures have rules that help to minimize adverse impacts of Bank-financed projects, such as displacement of local communities, disruption of indigenous peoples, and the destruction or degradation of the environment. The Panel serves as a guarantee that these rules will not be disregarded. It provides a formal mechanism for people directly affected by Bank-financed projects to bring complaints before it on grounds of the Bank's failure to abide by its own policies and procedures in the design, appraisal and implementation of the projects it finances.

The Panel's task is to determine whether, in a particular project, the Bank was acting in compliance with its policies and procedures. Note that only mandatory policies and procedures fall within the purview of the Panel while policies and procedures in the form of Good Practices do not.[87] Relevant mandatory 'safeguard policies' include, inter alia, Involuntary Resettlement, Environmental Assessments, Disclosure of Operational Information and Energy and Integrated Pest Management.

The Panel is composed of three members nominated by the President of the Bank and approved by the Board of Executive Directors. The members of the Panel serve for five-year terms. The Panel has its own secretariat that is institutionally separate from the World Bank.

Two documents—Bank Resolution 93-10 and the Inspection Panel Operating Procedures—lay down the basic procedures for the Panel. They define the composition of the Panel, the criteria for eligibility and the necessary components of a claim, and govern the Panel procedure. The Resolution was approved by the Board of Executive Directors.[88] The Procedures were developed by the original Panel.

B. Procedure

A request for an inspection can be filed when the Bank allegedly violates its operational policies or procedures during the design, appraisal and/or

---

[87] Thus, the World Bank Operational Manual 'Involving Nongovernmental Organizations in Bank-Supported Activities' is not within the competence of the Panel.

[88] It was also clarified by the Board of Executive Directors in 1996 and in 1999.

implementation of a Bank-financed project and when two or more persons are adversely affected or are likely to be harmed by the project. The Panel is supposed to be the last resort of objection for those negatively affected by projects and should only be contacted if the World Bank staff have not reacted to the concerns that were brought forward. Before submitting a request, steps must have been taken (or efforts made) to bring the matter to the attention of the Bank management with a result unsatisfactory to the requester.[89]

A request can only be filed where the project is under consideration or has been approved by the Bank but the loan has not yet been substantially disbursed. Claims are barred after 95 per cent or more of the funds have been disbursed.[90]

When the Panel decides to conduct an investigation, it first presents its recommendation to carry out such an investigation to the Board of Directors, which has a certain objection period during which any Executive Director can register its objection to the Panel's Recommendation. Once the objection period has passed, the Panel investigation can include meetings with the requester, affected individuals, Bank staff, government officials and NGOs. During the investigation, it is also possible to hold public meetings, visit project sites, hire independent consultants or use any other research method that seems reasonable, including researching Bank files.[91]

Once an investigation is completed, the Panel sends its findings and recommendations to the Board of Directors and the Bank management. Within six weeks, the management prepares its response to the Panel's findings on how to solve problems observed, and presents it to the Board. Based on the final recommendations by the Panel and the management, during a formal meeting at the Board with the Panel and management, the Board agrees on the management-developed action plan for resolving the policy violations, or asks management to make amendments to the action plan.

C. *NGO Involvement*

NGOs consider the Panel an instrument with which they can influence decisions with regard to particular Bank-funded projects by initiating inspections that create public awareness and mobilize public support for their claims.[92]

---

[89] See World Bank, 'Operating Procedures of the Inspection Panel', paras 1, 5(e), 12(a) and 12(b), <http://www.inspectionpanel.org>, visited 27 Apr 2006.
[90] See ibid para 2(c).   [91] See ibid para 45.
[92] 'Participation of Non-Governmental Organisations in International Environmental Governance: Legal Basis and Practical Experience', on behalf of the Umweltbundesamt (German Federal Environment Agency), Final Report, June 2002, prepared by Ecologic and FIELD, p 193, <http://www.ecologic.de/download/projekte/1850-1899/1890/report_ngos_en.pdf>, visited 15 Aug 2005.

A local NGO may act as a claimant requesting the Panel procedure provided that, as one option, it has among its members two or more people 'who believe that as a result of the Bank's violation their rights or interests have been, or are likely to be adversely affected in a direct and material way'.[93]

Alternatively, the adversely affected people may authorize an NGO, of which they are not members, to represent their interests and to file the request on their behalf. Normally, this would have to be a local NGO, but, in exceptional cases, the NGO can be foreign or international. This last possibility is open when 'there is no adequate or appropriate representation in the country where the project is located'.[94] This would be the case, for example, when the political regime in the country concerned does not allow NGOs independent from the government, where there is a risk of retaliation, or where the local NGOs lack the capacity necessary to effectively represent the adversely affected people. Evidence of these or other relevant circumstances will have to be produced.

If the claim is filed by an NGO as a representative, that NGO must demonstrate that it has explicit authorization to act as the agent of the adversely affected people. The affected people must sign either the claim itself or a written authorization designating their representative. In several cases, NGOs (both local and non-local) represented interests of affected residents.[95]

Thus, for an NGO to be eligible to participate in the procedure as a requester, either the project has to directly affect members of the NGO, or the NGO must be authorized to file a request by the local peoples directly affected. This, and the requirement concerning local/non-local NGOs mentioned above, form the only eligibility criteria for particular NGOs to act as claimants. There are no requirements relating, for example, to the NGO's internal governance, decision-making procedures, membership, funding, etc.

NGO requesters will, and other NGOs may, be involved in the Panel's investigation. As stated above, there does not exist a strictly prescribed set of investigatory methods. According to the Panel's Operating Procedures, they may include, inter alia (only NGO-relevant methods are listed here):

- meetings with the requester and with local and international NGOs;
- holding public meetings in the project area (which can include NGO participants);

---

[93] ibid para 4(a).
[94] ibid paras 4 and 11.
[95] For example, in the Yacyretá case, Singrauli case, China Western Poverty Reduction Project and others.

- requesting written or oral submissions on specific issues from the requester and from local or international NGOs; and/or
- hiring independent consultants to research specific issues relating to the request (NGOs possessing relevant expertise may be hired as such consultants).[96]

Thus, the Operating Procedures provide opportunities for NGO participation even if a particular NGO is not the claimant. It must be remembered, however, that all these methods are not mandatory and will be employed only if the Panel considers them necessary or helpful for its mission.

The Operating Procedures additionally give the requester the right to provide the Panel, during the course of investigation, with supplementary information relevant to evaluating the request. Also, to facilitate understanding of specific points, the Panel may (although is not obliged to) discuss its preliminary findings of fact with the requester.[97]

* * *

The Panel, by its nature, is not an enforcement or judicial mechanism; it has certain investigative and reporting duties. The final outcome depends on the Bank's Board of Directors. In many cases, the Panel has facilitated increased public input and consultation in problem projects. In several situations, it was only after the requests were filed that the complaints of affected people were taken seriously. Increased public participation and consultation as a result of the Panel process and access to information also have the impact of empowering local communities and NGOs. Thus, the Panel process constitutes an important tool for NGOs to influence Bank's activities.

VI. CONCLUSION

It has been established that the Bank has few binding rules on engagement with NGOs. Involvement of civil society in a variety of Bank activities is more a de facto part of the Bank's operational policy framework.[98]

As stated in the 2005 Discussion Paper on Bank–Civil Society Engagement, there is an overriding contradiction at the centre of the Bank's approach to public participation. On the one hand, Bank literature and policy statements are replete with testimonials about the importance of participation and empowerment in achieving good development outcomes. However, on the other hand, the Bank has no *required* procedures for developing policy, and no clear minimum standards for soliciting or incorporating public inputs

---

[96] See World Bank, 'Operating Procedures of the Inspection Panel' (n 89) para 45.
[97] See ibid paras 47 and 49.
[98] World Bank, *Issues and Options for Improving Engagement* (n 5) 8.

in its lending operations. Moreover, its internal incentive structures tend to subordinate participation to other considerations. As a result, public participation is usually ad hoc and discretionary, and the Bank generally only formalizes or requires it when forced to do so under external pressure.[99]

The Bank itself has admitted the lack of clarity, fragmentation, and the ad hoc nature of the existing operational guidelines for staff. It confirmed that although existing good practices encourage staff to consult or otherwise engage CSOs, it is optional for staff to avail themselves of best practices, advice or training in this area, and incentives to do so are often weak.[100] While consultation with CSOs is sometimes required and is employed widely across the Bank today, the quality of these consultations remains uneven. Consultation guidelines are not widely followed; consultations often occur in an arbitrary fashion with very short notice and/or very late in the process, rather than as a systematic opportunity to learn and help shape policies and programmes before they are finalized.[101]

Civil society has consistently called on the Bank to review its norms and mechanisms for engagement; to further mainstream participation in Bank-supported research and analysis, policy dialogue and operations; and to encourage member governments to open space for civic engagement in development policy-making and programming.

The mentioned Discussion Paper suggests that the Bank develop two sets of mandatory process-based participation standards. First, it should articulate a fixed administrative procedure for developing and revising Bank operational policies and strategies. Secondly, it should develop a set of minimum requirements for public involvement in different types of lending operations.[102]

In 2005, a 10-point action plan for improving Bank–civil society relations was adopted by the Bank's Board of Executive Directors.[103] This plan defines principal elements for improving the Bank's engagement with civil society. The action plan includes the following points:

1. Establish new global mechanisms for Bank–CSO engagement to help promote mutual understanding and cooperation.
2. Establish a Bank-wide advisory service/focal point for consultations and an institutional framework for consultation management and feedback.

---

[99] See World Bank, 'A Call for Participatory Decision Making: Discussion Paper on World Bank–Civil Society Engagement' (n 19) 9–10.

[100] See World Bank, *Issues and Options for Improving Engagement* (n 5) 7.

[101] See ibid 14

[102] See ibid 10

[103] This action plan can be found in World Bank, *Issues and Options for Improving Engagement* (n 5) xii.

3. Pilot a new Bank-wide monitoring and evaluation system for civic engagement.

4. Conduct a review of Bank funds available for civil society engagement in operations and policy dialogue, and explore possible realignment or restructuring.

5. Review the Bank's procurement framework with a view toward facilitating collaboration with CSOs.

6. Institute an integrated learning programme for Bank staff and member governments on how to engage CSOs more effectively, as well as capacity-building for CSOs on how to work effectively with the Bank and its member governments.

7. Hold regular meetings of senior management, and periodically with the Board, to review Bank–civil society relations.

8. Develop and issue new guidelines for Bank staff on the institution's approach, best practices, and a framework for engagement with CSOs.

9. Emphasize the importance of civil society engagement in the guidance to Bank staff on the preparation of the Country Assistance Strategies (CAS) as well as in CAS monitoring and evaluation.

10. Develop tools for analytical mapping of civil society to assist country and task teams in determining the relevant CSOs to engage on a given issue, project or strategy.

A close reading of these points leads to the conclusion that they aim primarily at enhancing the current practices of the Bank rather than at developing binding obligations on staff to take NGO views into consideration. In sum, the action plan urges greater availability of information and increased use of consultation with civil society rather than providing for mandatory participation or strengthening the legal basis for NGO involvement. However, if fully implemented, the plan will still be a step forward in the enhancement of NGO involvement in the activities of the World Bank.

CHAPTER 10

International Monetary Fund (IMF)

I. INTRODUCTION

The International Monetary Fund (IMF, or Fund), created together with the World Bank in 1944, is concerned with international monetary cooperation, exchange rate stability, and orderly exchange arrangements. It provides temporary financial assistance to countries to help ease balance-of-payments adjustment as well as advice and technical assistance to design and implement effective macro-economic and structural policies.[1] The IMF has 184 member countries.

The supreme IMF organ is the Board of Governors, which consists of one Governor (usually the minister of finance or the governor of the central bank) from each of the IMF member countries. In practice, the Board of Governors retains responsibility only for major decisions concerning the institution itself, such as changes to the Fund's structure, and accepting new members; all other powers rest with the Executive Board. The Board of Governors meets once each year at the IMF–World Bank Annual Meetings.

The Executive Board manages the day-to-day work of the IMF. It reviews Article IV surveillance reports,[2] approves and monitors stabilization and structural adjustment programmes, mandates technical assistance activities and discusses issues related to the overall global financial architecture. The Board is composed of 24 directors, who are appointed by member countries or by groups of countries. The five largest shareholders of the IMF—US, Japan, Germany, France and the UK—appoint one director each. Other countries are grouped into constituencies. In some constituencies the appointment of the executive director is rotated amongst the country members. In others, the country with the largest number of votes appoints the director. The Board usually meets several times each week. By tradition, most decisions are taken by consensus rather than majority vote.

Two other important organs are the International Monetary and Finance Committee (IMFC) and the Development Committee. Each consists of 24 members determined in accordance with the same constituency system as

---

[1] See <http://www.imf.org/external/about.htm>, visited 1 Apr 2005.
[2] Pursuant to Art IV of the IMF Articles of Agreement, in the annual process of monitoring and consultation usually referred to as 'surveillance', the Fund conducts appraisals of each member country's exchange rate policy as well as of the general economic situation and policy strategy.

the Executive Board. The IMFC has the responsibility of advising, and reporting to, the Board of Governors on matters primarily relating to supervising the management and adaptation of the international monetary and financial system. The Development Committee, a joint committee of the IMF and the World Bank, advises the Boards of Governors of the IMF and World Bank on critical development issues and on the financial resources required to promote economic development in developing countries. Its mandate also includes trade and global environmental issues.[3]

The Managing Director is head of the IMF staff and Chairman of the Executive Board. He is assisted by three Deputy Managing Directors. Staff departments undertake the detailed work of policy formulation, implementation and review of the Fund. Each of the five geographic area departments contain several divisions that cover several countries. The eight functional departments address policy realms such as fiscal affairs, legal issues and monetary concerns.[4]

II. LEGAL BASIS AND FORMS OF NGO INVOLVEMENT

A. Legal Basis

The constituent instrument of the IMF, the 1944 Articles of Agreement of the International Monetary Fund, does not provide for cooperation with NGOs. Article X of the IMF Articles of Agreement, entitled 'Relations with other International Organizations', only refers to 'general' and 'public' international organizations. It does not refer to non-governmental organizations.[5] While relations with NGOs are not explicitly provided for in its constituent instrument, the IMF does maintain relations with NGOs.

Although the Fund does not have binding secondary rules on engagement with CSOs, there is a relevant non-binding policy document in place, the 'Guide for Staff Relations with Civil Society Organizations',[6] which offers a general framework of good practices. The Guide is not mandatory and does not apply in all situations; it is intended to 'supplement, not replace, sound judgment and experience' of IMF staff.[7]

---

[3] See <http://www.imf.org/external/about.htm>, visited 1 Apr 2005.

[4] For more details, see J Scholte, 'Civil Society Voices and the International Monetary Fund', prepared for the project *Voices: The Rise of Nongovernmental Voices in Multilateral Institutions* (May 2002) 6, <http://www.nsi-ins.ca/english/pdf/Int_Mon_Fund.pdf>, visited 5 Oct 2005.

[5] In the late 1990s, suggestions were made to amend the Articles of Agreement in order to legalize the Fund's exchanges with civil society, but this proposal has not gone further. See Scholte, 'Civil Society Voices and the International Monetary Fund' (n 4) 21.

[6] IMF, 'Guide for Staff Relations with Civil Society Organizations' (10 Oct 2003), <http://www.imf.org/external/np/cso/eng/2003/101003.htm>, visited 5 Oct 2005. See also appendix IX of this book, p 345.   [7] ibid para I.2.

According to the Guide, the Fund views NGOs as part of 'civil society', which is understood as an arena where voluntary associations of citizens seek to shape governance structures and policies.[8] In addition to NGOs, civil society organizations (CSOs) include business forums, faith-based associations, labour movements, local community groups, philanthropic foundations and think tanks. Civil society does not include parliamentarians, political parties, sub-national authorities, individual businesses or the mass media.[9]

B. Opportunities for NGO Involvement

The IMF began engagement with civil society in the 1980s in response to advocacy at the global level by groups concerned with economic and social justice. Such engagement remains central in IMF–NGO relations.[10] However, until the mid-1990s, the IMF attracted only limited and sporadic attention from NGOs, most prominently in countries implementing adjustment policies with IMF support. The civil society opposition to the Fund intensified in the latter half of the 1990s, particularly in the context of structural adjustment policies, multilateral debt problems and financial market crises in Asia, Latin America and Russia.[11] Still, the overall extent of IMF engagement with civil society remains modest today, much less developed than, for example, in the World Bank.[12]

Generally, the IMF's position is that it is accountable primarily to the governments of its member countries (as opposed to society at large). For this reason, as explained in the Guide, the IMF sees its member governments as primarily responsible for dialogue with CSOs. IMF contacts with CSOs are deemed a supplement to, and not a substitute for, government dialogue with citizen groups.[13]

The IMF does not have a permanent institutional arrangement for consultations with NGOs similar to the UNDP Civil Society Advisory Committee. Nor does the Fund have any permanent accreditation schemes for NGOs/CSOs as many other international organizations do. Fund staff are not under an obligation to consult CSOs in relation to their specific lending operations. All interactions with CSOs occur on an ad hoc basis.

---

[8] See ibid para II.2.

[9] See ibid paras I.5 and II.3.

[10] See IMF, 'The IMF and Civil Society Organizations: A Factsheet' (Sept 2005), <http://www.imf.org/external/np/exr/facts/civ.htm>, visited 5 Oct 2005.

[11] See T Dawson and G Bhatt, 'The IMF and Civil Society Organizations: Striking a Balance', IMF policy discussion paper, PDP/01/2 (Sept 2001) 2, <http://www.imf.org/ external/pubs/ft/pdp/2001/pdp02.pdf>, visited 5 Oct 2005; and Scholte (n 4) 8.

[12] Scholte (n 4), 21, 48.

[13] See IMF, 'Guide for Staff Relations with Civil Society Organizations (n 6), section V.A.

This entails a considerable difference in practices across countries, departments, and policy settings.[14]

The IMF asserts that it seeks to engage with CSOs through information sharing, dialogue and consultation at both global and national levels.[15] The majority of contacts take place at the IMF headquarters in Washington, DC, thus Washington-based organizations find themselves in a privileged position.[16] According to the Guide, the IMF engages with civil society because such engagement can correct misunderstandings, improve policy content and enhance the political viability of IMF advice.[17] Specifically, contacts with CSOs are ascribed the following main aims and benefits:

- Such contacts can help the IMF to be transparent about its work, explain itself to people whom it affects and dispel public misconceptions regarding the Fund and its activities.
- CSOs can highlight important issues for the formulation, implementation and review of Fund policies and programmes and improve its policy advice.
- CSOs can give the IMF helpful information to supplement official data and insights that may differ from perspectives in official circles.
- Discussions with CSOs can help to measure support for, or resistance against, IMF policies in a given context.
- Dialogue with citizens complements the IMF's primary accountability to its member countries.[18]

The IMF acknowledges that although the dialogue with CSOs has gradually improved, there remains dissatisfaction on both sides, possibly even a degree of mutual mistrust.[19] Some CSOs tend to think that the Fund preaches, does not listen and does not integrate CSO input from the dialogue into its policy-making.[20] As reported in 2001, CSOs have frequently characterized the IMF as an unapproachable, secretive and undemocratic organization that is resistant to public opinion and participa-

---

[14] See IMF staff paper, 'A Review of the Fund's External Communication strategy', prepared by the External Relations Department Annex III, p 97 (13 Feb 2003), <http://www.imf.org/external/np/exe/docs/2003/021303. htm>, visited 5 Oct 2005.

[15] See IMF, 'The IMF and Civil Society Organizations: A Factsheet' For the results of the IMF-conducted survey on country-level outreach to civil society, see IMF staff paper, 'A Review of the Fund's External Communication strategy', Annex II.

[16] Interview with Ms Simonetta Nardin and Ms Jennifer Bisping, IMF External Relations Department (24 Jan 2006).

[17] See IMF, 'Guide for Staff Relations with Civil Society Organizations' (n 6) para V.G.3.

[18] See IMF, 'Guide for Staff Relations with Civil Society Organizations' (n 6) section III.

[19] See IMF staff paper, 'A Review of the Fund's External Communication strategy (n 14) Annex III, p 96.

[20] See ibid.

tion.[21] At the same time, some Fund staff may perceive CSOs as generally being interested mainly in pushing their own agendas, often imprecisely defined, and believe that CSOs often lack broad support, legitimacy and accountability.[22]

Principal organs of the Fund are closed to civil society participation. NGOs are not allowed to attend the meetings of the Executive Board, the International Monetary and Finance Committee (IMFC) or the joint IMF–World Bank Development Committee. Only the Board of Governors is a little more open to civil society—ad hoc accredited CSOs can at least attend and observe (without further participatory rights) certain plenary sessions (see below).

The Fund meets/consults with CSOs on the following occasions:

- during Annual and Spring Meetings;
- at ad hoc meetings, conferences, seminars, briefings and workshops;
- during various Fund missions: Article IV missions, Use of Fund Resources (UFR) missions (especially as they concern longer-term programmes of structural reform), External Relations missions, Financial Sector Assessment Program (FSAP) missions, and some technical assistance missions;
- upon invitations extended by the IMF to contribute to reviews of its policies, by attending seminars or by providing comments to papers posted on its website; and
- the Resident Representative, an IMF staff member based in the member country, can consult with CSOs ahead of a mission and feed their information and views into the mission's preparation.[23]

Reportedly, contacts between the IMF and CSOs have become more frequent and the discussions more substantive.[24] In 2001–2005, the overall number of meetings with CSOs ranged between 45 and 75 a year, with an average of 330 CSOs involved in these meetings annually.[25] A substantial part of Fund interactions with CSOs occur during the Annual and Spring Meetings—they account for around 20 per cent of all meetings with CSOs and involve many CSOs. Most of remaining interactions take the form of

---

[21] See T Dawson and G Bhatt (n 11) 3.

[22] See IMF staff paper, 'A Review of the Fund's External Communication strategy' (n 14) Annex III, p 96.

[23] As of 30 July 2004, there were approximately 90 member countries with a Resident Representative.

[24] See T Dawson and G Bhatt (n 11) 21.

[25] Data obtained from Ms Simonetta Nardin and Ms Jennifer Bisping, IMF External Relations Department (24 Jan 2006). These data reflect only those meetings that the IMF External relation Department (EXR) was aware of, or involved in. Other meetings between IMF officials and civil society representatives might occur without EXR's knowledge.

(typically bilateral) meetings organized upon the requests of CSOs with relevant IMF headquarters staff and, far less frequently, with Resident Representatives.[26] The Guide instructs IMF staff to reply promptly to such requests but, at the same time, states that, in practice, IMF staff cannot meet all CSOs that have an interest in IMF activities.[27]

Regarding the content of IMF–CSO contacts, they may address broad questions of IMF policy or concern country-specific IMF advice.[28] The more prominent issues include:

- IMF policy advice, especially to low-income countries (related, for example, to macro-economic targets, adjustments of taxes and subsidies, civil service reform, changes to labour legislation, etc), including, in the context of 'Article IV' consultation missions;[29]
- the social and environmental implications of IMF advice;
- debt relief—in particular, the Heavily Indebted Poor Countries (HIPC) initiative;
- programme conditionalities;
- poverty reduction strategies—specifically, Poverty Reduction Strategy Paper (PRSP) consultations;
- governance and transparency; and
- the voice and representation of developing countries in the IMF and World Bank.[30]

Naturally, subjects of meetings depend on the IMF activities at a particular period of time. In this sense, a Work Programme, adopted by the Executive Board each year, can serve as a good basis for both relevant IMF staff and NGOs to see what issues are worth discussing.

As for the type of CSOs that the Fund mostly engages with, on the whole the Fund has maintained the greatest number and intensity of direct civil society contacts with economic research bodies. Next to university departments, think tanks and consultants in the area of economics, the IMF has pursued its most substantial contacts in civil society with business associations.[31] The number of involved public interest NGOs has remained quite

---

[26] ibid.
[27] See IMF, 'Guide for Staff Relations with Civil Society Organizations' (n 6) para IV.C.2 and Annex para A.2.
[28] For a brief discussion of main disagreements between the Fund and NGOs, see F Larsen, 'The IMF's Dialogue with the NGOs' (2000) 52 Transnational Associations 278.
[29] On Article IV appraisals, see above, footnote 2. To gather information for the appraisal, IMF economists visit the member country and hold discussions with government and central bank officials and other relevant stakeholders, which may include CSOs.
[30] See IMF, 'Guide for Staff Relations with Civil Society Organizations' (n 6) section IV.F; and IMF, 'The IMF and Civil Society Organizations: A Factsheet'.
[31] See Scholte (n 4) 22.

small. The activity has mainly come from a handful of specialized bureaux, the debt campaigns and certain development and environmental NGOs.[32]

General coordination of IMF relations with CSOs occurs through the External Relations Department (EXR). Contacts with CSOs concerning general lines of IMF policy are normally handled through the relevant functional and service departments of the Fund, with backing from EXR, as other departments do not have specialized CSO liaison officers. Contacts with CSOs concerning the IMF's country-specific surveillance and financial and technical assistance are normally handled through the relevant geographic area department, especially the mission chief and, where one exists, the Resident Representative for the country, with backing from EXR.[33] The Fund has not copied the practice started in the mid-1990s by the World Bank and the United Nations Development Programme (UNDP) of adding an official specifically designated for civil society liaison to many of their resident missions.[34]

EXR gathers information relating to IMF activities and summarizes events, papers and discussions relevant to CSOs in a quarterly newsletter, which is sent (by email and mail) to subscribers and published on the IMF website.[35]

C. Format of Participation

Annual Meetings of the World Bank and IMF Boards of Governors are held each autumn. Immediately preceding these meetings, the International Monetary and Finance Committee (IMFC) and the joint IMF–World Bank Development Committee hold their sessions. The Spring Meetings host another round of sessions of the IMFC and the Development Committee. In conjunction with both the Annual and Spring Meetings (usually during the week preceding the meetings) the World Bank and the IMF organize numerous events with the participation of civil society and Bank/IMF management and staff (dialogues, workshops, seminars, etc).

Arrangements for civil society participation in the Annual and Spring Meetings, and in associated activities, are described in the chapter on the World Bank.[36] The general conclusion is that although it is not difficult to receive accreditation to the Meetings, the means to influence the decision-making process are almost non-existent. This is because CSOs have no

---

[32] See ibid 16. Some examples include the Fifty Years is Enough coalition, the Bretton Woods Project, the European Network on Debt and Development (EURODAD), Oxfam, Friends of the Earth, and the World Economy, Environment and Development (WEED). See ibid 14–16.

[33] See IMF, 'Guide for Staff Relations with Civil Society Organizations' (n 6) section IV.B.

[34] See Scholte, (n 4) 21.

[35] See <http://www.imf.org/external/np/exr/cs/eng/index.asp>, visited 5 Oct 2005.

[36] See above, pp 160–3.

participatory rights at the high-level meetings to which most of the time they are not even admitted. NGOs can genuinely participate only in parallel activities. At the same time, a possibility to attend formal meetings of the IMFC, the Development Committee or the Board of the Governors would not enhance opportunities for NGOs to influence decision-making because, as a matter of fact, decisions of respective organs are negotiated in advance of the formal meetings. This is why some NGOs have adopted the practice of coming to Washington in advance of formal meetings in order to attempt informal lobbying through Executive Directors.

The information concerning CSO participation in other types of meetings is very scarce. There are no format requirements for such meetings; they are organized and held on an ad hoc basis at the discretion of relevant Fund officials. Most of these meetings are organized following requests from NGOs. In the course of such—usually bilateral—consultations, NGOs seek to obtain up-to-date information about IMF activities (for example, regarding particular countries or loans, or possible general policy changes) as well as channel their views and concerns on relevant issues.

An Annex to the Guide for Staff Relations with CSOs contains some general recommendations on preparations, proceedings and the follow-up to such meetings—for example, it recommends responding promptly to requests for consultations with NGOs, agreeing to a precise agenda in advance of the meetings, distributing relevant documentation before the meeting, allowing both sides to have a say in what is discussed, and creating and publishing follow-up notes of meetings.[37]

The Guide also warns both CSOs and Fund staff that they should not have unrealistic expectations of such meetings. In particular, it is made clear that the possibility of CSOs actually to influence IMF policy is rather limited, 'given the depth and complexity of many economic issues, as well as the complexities of decision making at ... the IMF'.[38]

III. ACCREDITATION/SELECTION CRITERIA AND PROCEDURES

With respect to the Annual and Spring Meetings, accreditation criteria and procedures are described in the chapter on the World Bank.[39]

With respect to other IMF meetings with civil society, the rules on CSO selection criteria and relevant procedures remain to a large degree not formalized.

---

[37] See IMF, 'Guide for Staff Relations with Civil Society Organizations' (n 6) Annex.
[38] See ibid section V.E.
[39] See above, pp 162–3.

The Fund's broad policy as to which CSOs to engage with is built around the following points:

(a) Engage with different sectors of civil society.
(b) Aim to alternate the Fund's contacts between different CSOs, rather than always and only meeting the same organizations.
(c) Contact locally based associations as well as the local offices of transnational CSOs (in particular, staff should not rely on North-based groups to speak on behalf of South-based stakeholders).
(d) Meet with CSOs across the political spectrum (include critics as well as supporters of the IMF and/or of the current government of a country).
(e) Reach out beyond civil society circles that look familiar.[40]

These points do not serve as criteria for determining which CSOs can be consulted and which cannot. Rather, they help to divide the multitude of civil society actors into groups which should be represented and given a voice in the IMF's outreach to civil society. To engage with the IMF, CSOs can be international, regional, national or local. As mentioned above, CSOs with offices in Washington find themselves in a privileged position.

Additionally, the Guide for Staff Relations with CSOs sets out another set of (non-binding) guidelines for selection of CSOs for cooperation. The offered criteria are designed to ensure that selected CSOs have the necessary legitimacy. The Guide suggests considering the following features of CSOs:

(a) Legality—ie whether they are officially recognized and registered.
(b) Morality—ie whether they pursue a noble and right cause.
(c) Efficacy—ie whether they perform competently.
(d) Membership base.
(e) Governance—ie whether they operate in a participatory, tolerant, transparent, and accountable manner.[41]

According to competent IMF officials, they do not check whether NGOs that apply for meetings with the Fund staff satisfy each of these criteria. The criteria serve as very general guidelines, rather than as a mandatory check-list applied in every situation. Relevant Fund officials already know most of the NGOs that have an interest in Fund activities, so these do not require any additional verification.[42] Additionally, most of these criteria are quite

---

[40] See IMF, 'Guide for Staff Relations with Civil Society Organizations' (n 6) para IV.C.2.
[41] See IMF, 'Guide for Staff Relations with Civil Society Organizations' (n 6) paras V.F.1 and 2; and section 'Legitimacy Concerns' of the Summary.
[42] Interview with Ms Simonetta Nardin and Ms Jennifer Bisping, IMF External Relations Department (24 January 2006). Note that this familiarity with relevant NGOs has not taken form of an official IMF database of NGOs, so institutional memory can be short in this sense.

imprecise and leave it to relevant IMF officials to determine, for example, which cause is 'right and noble', whether the CSO membership base is sufficiently broad, or whether the CSO performs competently enough. This does not necessarily mean, however, that Fund officials use their discretion to limit the number of NGOs that they interact with, or to close access to NGOs considered 'undesirable'. On the contrary, according to Fund officials, the flexibility of the selection criteria allows the IMF to avoid the long and cumbersome bureaucratic accreditation/selection procedures that exist in some other international organizations, and to maintain an 'open door policy' in relation to NGOs.[43] However, the negative side of the loose legal regulation and the broad discretion is that they may one day lead to an easy substitution of the 'open door policy' by a 'closed door policy'. Possibly to prevent this, the Guide suggests that, in general, the IMF should seek to apply an inclusive approach to CSO involvement and should only deny a CSO access with good reason (for example, if the organization has malicious intent or presents a seriously distorted account of itself).[44] However, this provision can hardly be an effective safeguard because of the non-binding nature of the Guide.

The Guide does not enumerate documents or information that CSOs are required to submit to demonstrate that they meet the set requirements (for example, proof of registration, statutes, by-laws, annual reports, etc). It only names the sources that could be consulted in order to assess whether a particular CSO meets the set standards. These sources include:

- the IMF's own records of civil society contacts;
- government officials;
- bilateral donor agencies;
- embassies;
- local staff in IMF Resident Representative offices;
- staff of the World Bank and other multilateral institutions (especially their civil society specialists where these exist);
- apex civil society bodies;
- relevant academic specialists; and
- other professional consultants.[45]

To request a meeting, NGOs may contact the IMF External Relations Department (EXR), a relevant geographic area or functional department or the IMF Resident Representative in a particular country. Although a relevant geographic area/functional department does not need authorization

---

[43] ibid.

[44] See IMF, 'Guide for Staff Relations with Civil Society Organizations' (n 6) Annex para A. 3.

[45] See ibid paras V.F.3 and 5.

from the EXR to hold meetings with CSOs, in most cases, it is the EXR that will be involved in organizing a meeting, at least as far as logistics is concerned.[46]

The Guide also makes clear that the IMF should be sensitive to the opinions of national governments in relation to particular CSOs. It provides that if a government raises objections to the Fund's relations with certain, or all, CSOs, staff should first try to explain the rationale for such contacts. If the difference of views persists, staff should refrain from the contacts and refer the disagreement to headquarters for possible follow-up with the government concerned.[47] In practice, at least at the headquarter level, governments (represented by Executive Directors) do not exercise any control over meetings held by IMF staff with CSOs.[48]

In sum, the (non-binding) rules concerning the criteria and procedures for selection of CSOs that are common to all interactions with CSOs leave a large number of matters unsettled—for example, which organ makes a decision on CSO selection, which documents/information it can request from CSOs, whether it considers CSOs aside from the one that has shown interest in a particular meeting, what are the time-limits, what are possible grounds for refusal, etc. Thus, the relevant rules and practices cannot be uniform and consistent; they vary across the institution and depend on the context of particular situations.

[46] Interview with Ms Simonetta Nardin and Ms Jennifer Bisping, IMF External Relations Department (24 Jan 2006).

[47] See IMF, 'Guide for Staff Relations with Civil Society Organizations' (n 6) para V. B.3

[48] Except for the Annual and Spring Meetings, when all CSOs (as well as all other 'visitors') wishing to obtain accreditation require approval of the Executive Director concerned.

CHAPTER 11

World Trade Organization (WTO)[1]

I. INTRODUCTION

The World Trade Organization (WTO), which was created by the Marrakesh Agreement Establishing the World Trade Organization (WTO Agreement) and came into being in 1995, is the key international organization concerned with trade relations among countries. It is not part of the United Nations family. The WTO facilitates the implementation of 20 international agreements on trade, provides the forum for negotiation of new multilateral trade agreements, reviews the national trade policies of its 150 member countries and settles international trade disputes between them.

The institutional structure of the WTO includes: at the highest level, the Ministerial Conference; at a second level, the General Council, the Dispute Settlement Body and the Trade Policy Review Body; and, at lower levels, specialized councils, committees and working parties. Its structure also includes quasi-judicial bodies and the WTO Secretariat. There are, at present, a total of around 70 WTO bodies, of which more than 30 are standing bodies.

The Ministerial Conference is the 'supreme' body of the WTO. It is composed of representatives from all Members and has decision-making powers on all matters under any of the multilateral WTO agreements. Specific powers of the Ministerial Conference include adopting authoritative interpretations of the WTO agreements, granting waivers of obligations under the agreements, adopting amendments, taking decisions on accession, appointing the Director-General and adopting staff regulations. The Ministerial Conference normally meets once every two years.

The General Council is responsible for the 'day-to-day' management of the WTO and its many activities. In between sessions of the Ministerial Conference, the General Council exercises the full powers of the Ministerial Conference. In addition, the General Council also carries out some functions specifically assigned to it, such as adopting the annual budget and the financial regulations and making appropriate arrangements for effective cooperation with international organizations and NGOs. The General Council is composed of ambassador-level diplomats from all WTO Members and normally meets once every two months.

---

[1] This section draws upon P Van den Bossche, *The Law and Policy of the World Trade Organization: Text, Cases and Materials* (CUP, Cambridge, 2005) 76–306.

The functions specifically assigned to the General Council also cover dispute settlement and trade policy review. The General Council, the Dispute Settlement Body (DSB) and the Trade Policy Review Body (TPRB) are, in fact, the same body. When the General Council administers the WTO dispute settlement system, it convenes and acts as the DSB. When the General Council administers the WTO trade policy review mechanism, it convenes and acts as the TPRB. Both the DSB and the TPRB have at least one meeting a month.

The three specialized councils (the Council for Trade in Goods, the Council for Trade in Services and the Council for Trade-Related Aspects of Intellectual Property Rights) oversee the functioning of the respective multilateral WTO agreements. These specialized councils are open to all WTO Members. In addition to the three specialized councils, there are a number of committees and working parties that assist the Ministerial Conference and the General Council in carrying out their functions.

The WTO structure also includes the quasi-judicial bodies, including the ad hoc dispute settlement panels and the standing Appellate Body. Their function is to conduct dispute settlement procedures with a view to resolve disputes arising between the WTO Members concerned.

The Director-General, appointed by the Ministerial Conference, heads the WTO Secretariat. Neither the Director-General nor the WTO Secretariat have any decision-making powers. They act as a 'facilitator' of the decision-making processes within the WTO primarily by providing technical, professional and administrative support to WTO bodies.

II. LEGAL BASIS

The WTO Agreement explicitly empowers the WTO to engage with NGOs. Its Article V:2 provides: 'The General Council may make appropriate arrangements for consultations and cooperation with non-governmental organizations concerned with matters related to those of the WTO'.[2] In practice, the General Council has done little to give full effect to this provision. Although it has undertaken certain steps to improve the WTO's engagement with NGOs, the latter remain outside formal WTO processes.

---

[2] It is interesting to note that the 1948 Havana Charter on the International Trade Organization (ITO) already contained a similarly worded provision (see Art 87(2) of the Havana Charter). The ITO, however, never became operational and the 1947 General Agreement on Tariffs and Trade (GATT) filled the gap left by the ITO for almost 50 years. The GATT, by contrast, did not have any provision on cooperation with NGOs. Under the GATT, informal and ad hoc contacts existed with NGOs. However, NGOs were denied access to meetings and conferences. That was also the case for the Marrakesh Conference at which the WTO Agreement was signed. NGOs as such were not invited to Marrakesh; those NGOs present were registered as members of the press.

Pursuant to Article V:2 of the WTO Agreement, in 1996 the General Council adopted the Guidelines regarding the relations of the WTO with non-governmental organizations (the 1996 Guidelines).[3] In this one-page document Members recognized that NGOs can play a role 'to increase the awareness of the public in respect of WTO activities', and that NGOs are a 'valuable resource' that can 'contribute to the accuracy and richness of the public debate'.[4] In the 1996 Guidelines it was agreed that interaction with NGOs should be developed through:

- organization of symposia for NGOs on specific WTO-related issues;
- informal arrangements to receive the information NGOs may wish to make available for consultation by interested delegations;
- the WTO Secretariat responding to requests for general information and briefings about the WTO; and
- participation of chairpersons of WTO councils and committees (in their personal capacity) in discussions and meetings with NGOs.[5]

The 1996 Guidelines also made the limits of NGO involvement clear. In the concluding paragraph, the General Council referred to the special character of the WTO, which is both a legally-binding intergovernmental treaty of rights and obligations among its Members and a forum for negotiations. The General Council then concluded:

As a result of extensive discussions, there is currently a broadly held view that it would not be possible for NGOs to be directly involved in the work of the WTO or its meetings. Closer consultation and cooperation with NGOs can also be met constructively through appropriate processes at the national level where lies primary responsibility for taking into account the different elements of public interest which are brought to bear on trade policy-making.[6]

Thus, not in full consistency with Article V:2 of the WTO Agreement, the General Council transferred the main responsibility for engaging with civil society to the national level. As far as the WTO itself is concerned, the General Council instructed the Secretariat to engage with NGOs and effectively barred them from participation in the work of WTO intergovernmental bodies.

---

[3] See Decision by the General Council, *Guidelines for arrangements on relations with Non-Governmental Organizations*, WT/L/162 (23 July 1996). See appendix X of this book p 361.
[4] ibid paras II and IV.
[5] ibid paras IV and V.
[6] ibid para VI.

The subject of NGO involvement in WTO activities was discussed in the 2005 Report by the Consultative Board to the Director-General, *The Future of the World Trade Organization: Addressing Institutional Challenges in the New Millennium* (the Sutherland Report).[7] While generally supporting NGO involvement ('[t]oday, the issue is no longer whether, but how to partner and collaborate effectively'), the Sutherland Report concluded that within the limited bounds of an institution, such as the WTO, founded on contractual commitments negotiated among governments, there are limits to how much further the WTO can go in involving NGOs in its deliberations and processes.[8] At the same time, the Report called upon the WTO membership to develop a new set of clearer guidelines for the relations of the WTO Secretariat with NGOs as well as to scale up the administrative capacity and financial resources of the WTO Secretariat.[9] The findings of the Report are reviewed in more detail below.[10]

Within the WTO Secretariat, the External Relations Division, consisting of five staff members, is the focal point for WTO interactions with NGOs. Alongside developing relationships with civil society groups, the Division is charged with liaising with international intergovernmental organizations and national legislative representatives.

III. FORMS OF INVOLVEMENT

While the degree of the WTO's outreach to NGOs has increased in recent years, to date the WTO has not developed modalities to bring NGOs into its processes. It is not on a par with most other international institutions with regard to having arrangements for engagement with NGOs. The WTO has not yet taken contacts with civil society actors far beyond public relations exercises.[11]

In particular, the WTO does not have a system for the permanent accreditation of NGOs that would grant to accredited NGOs consultative, observer or similar status, and corresponding participatory rights. To repeat, the 1996 Guidelines explicitly stated that 'it would not be possible for NGOs to be directly involved in the work of the WTO or its meetings'.[12] NGOs are not allowed to attend meetings of any WTO bodies

---

[7] Report by the Consultative Board to the Director-General Supachai Panitchpakdi, *The Future of the WTO: Addressing Institutional Challenges in the New Millennium* (Sutherland Report) (Jan 2005), <http://www.wto.org/english/thewto_e/10anniv_e/10anniv_e.htm#future>, visited 7 June 2005.

[8] See ibid paras 179 and 206.   [9] See ibid para 212.

[10] See below, pp 199–200.

[11] See JA Scholte, 'The WTO and Civil Society', in S McGuire and B Hocking (eds), *Trade Politics* (2nd edn, Routledge, London, 2004) 155.

[12] Decision by the General Council, *Guidelines for arrangements on relations with Non-Governmental Organizations* (n 3) para VI.

except for the formal plenary meetings of the Ministerial Conference that take place once every two years. Most WTO Members are of the opinion that trade negotiations require confidentiality and that the dialogue with civil society is first and foremost the responsibility of Member governments.

Neither does the WTO have a permanent body through which a formal 'dialogue' between the WTO Members and civil society, including NGOs, could take place. Suggestions to establish such consultative bodies have received little support from WTO Members. However, in 2003 the then WTO Director-General, Dr Supachai Panitchpakdi, took a personal initiative to establish the Informal NGO Advisory Body and the Informal Business Advisory Body. Both advisory bodies were established as informal because, under the 1996 Guidelines, the Director-General does not have a mandate to formally institutionalize relations with NGOs in such a manner.

The Informal NGO Advisory Body, made up of 10 high-level representatives from NGOs, was designed to provide a platform for dialogue between the Director-General (not WTO Members) and NGOs from around the world. The role of the Informal Business Advisory Body, comprising business representatives, was to provide a platform for dialogue with international business organizations and leading companies from around the world.

To form the Informal NGO Advisory Body, the Director-General selected—on a discretionary basis—those NGOs that he considered influential and broadly representative, seeking, where possible, to maintain regional balance and balance between NGOs from developed and developing countries.[13] The main function of the Informal NGO Advisory Body is to advise the WTO Director-General on WTO-related matters and to express the positions and concerns of civil society on international trade. Although the Director-General is not a party to WTO negotiations, he is the Chairman of the Trade Negotiations Committee and thus can serve as an intermediary between NGOs and the WTO membership. So far, the Informal NGO Advisory Body has been meeting once a year and during these meetings has mainly discussed the state of play in the ongoing trade

---

[13] Interestingly, Friends of the Earth International and Oxfam International have rejected the invitation to become a member, supposedly because of fears of criticism from their peers and potential bad publicity. Perhaps for the same reason, the NGOs that had agreed to participate asked the Director-General to abstain from publicizing the existence of the Advisory Body. This is why the WTO website does not include any information on it. Members of the informal NGO Advisory Body include Consumers International, Consumer Unity and Trust Society, the International Federation of Agricultural Producers, World Wide Fund for Nature (WWF) International, Third World Network, Christian Aid, the International Confederation of Free Trade Unions, Public Services International, the International Center for Trade and Sustainable Development, and the International Institute for Sustainable Development. See WTO Reporter, 17 June 2003.

negotiations, with participants exchanging their views and identifying issues of concern. Participants have also discussed with the Director-General ways to improve WTO relations with civil society. These meetings have not resulted in any specific outcomes, such as official meeting reports or NGO statements that would be communicated to the WTO membership, for example.[14]

The principal forms of the WTO's engagement with NGOs are:

- admission of NGOs to formal plenary meetings of WTO Ministerial Conference;
- organization of public symposia or forums on WTO-related issues;
- arrangements for improved access to WTO information and opportunities for information exchange; and
- occasional informal meetings of chairpersons of WTO bodies and of WTO Secretariat officials with NGOs.

These forms of WTO–NGO interaction are reviewed below. Subsequently, in a separate section, NGO involvement in WTO dispute settlement is discussed.

A. *Attendance of the Ministerial Conference Sessions*

There is no standing legal arrangement for NGOs to participate in sesssions of the Ministerial Conference. Before each session, the General Council agrees on NGO attendance and procedures for NGO accreditation.[15] Thus far, these General Council decisions have not shown any substantial differences.

The number of NGOs attending the Sessions of the WTO Ministerial Conference has increased from 108 (Singapore 1996) to 836 (Hong Kong 2005). The number of accredited NGOs reached 1065 for the Hong Kong Session. NGO representatives can only attend the formal plenary meetings where heads of governments and trade ministers read out short prepared statements. Access to all other meetings, including negotiating sessions, is denied. At plenary meetings, NGOs are not allowed to make oral statements or circulate written statements, nor do they have any other participatory rights. During sessions of the Ministerial Conference, NGOs are usually provided with an NGO centre, equipped with office and media facilities, and are briefed about the conference developments by WTO Secretariat officials.

[14] Interview with Mr Bernard Kuiten, WTO External Relations Division (17 Nov 2005).
[15] For the latest of these decisions, see WTO Ministerial Conference, *Procedures Regarding Registration and Attendance of Non-Governmental Organizations at the Sixth Session of the Ministerial Conference*, WT/MIN(05)/INF/6 (1 June 2005).

Table 4: Trends in NGO Representation at Ministerial Conference Sessions[16]

	Number of accredited NGOs	NGOs attended
Singapore 1996	159	108
Geneva 1998	153	128
Seattle 1999	776	686
Doha 2001	651	370
Cancún 2003	961	795
Hong Kong 2005	1065	836

As far as the criteria for NGO accreditation to Ministerial Conferences are concerned, their only source is Article V:2 of the WTO Agreement, which provides for consultation and cooperation with NGOs 'concerned with matters related to those of the WTO'. The 1996 Guidelines did not establish any further accreditation criteria. Therefore, the WTO Secretariat accredits all NGOs that can point to activities related to those of the WTO. The representative nature, democratic legitimacy, the national/international scope or other features of NGOs are not examined. The only additional accreditation criterion applied is the non-profit character of the NGO. Strictly speaking, the non-profit character is not a criterion for selection among NGOs but rather a characteristic of all NGOs that distinguishes them from other types of organizations. On this basis, the WTO Secretariat has refused accreditation to private companies and law firms. To prove their non-profit status, NGOs are required to produce registration documents or a charter pointing to the aims of the organization. If these are not available, the WTO requires as a minimum the production of documents legally proving the existence of the organization. The accreditation procedure is waived for those NGOs that were duly registered for at least two previous sessions of the Ministerial Conference.[17]

Despite these rather lax criteria for accreditation, only 1,065 NGOs out of roughly 1,630 applicants were accredited for the 2005 Hong Kong Ministerial meeting. Of those *not* accredited, about 220 requests for accreditation were not processed because of lack of further response or information from the NGOs. The remaining requests were refused due to

---

[16] See <http://www.wto.org/enlgish/news_e/news03_e/ngo_minconf_6oct03_e.htm>, visited 8 Feb 2004 and <http://www.wto.org/english/thewto_e/minist_e/min05_e/list_ngo_hk05_e.pdf>, visited 12 Oct 2006.

[17] WTO Ministerial Conference, *Procedures Regarding Registration and Attendance of Non-Governmental Organizations at the Sixth Session of the Ministerial Conference* (n 15).

insufficient evidence of WTO-related activities or of NGO status.[18] Given the high number of requests for registration for the Hong Kong Conference, the WTO has become stricter in sieving applications for accreditation as compared to the 1990s. For example, applications from pure research institutions or student associations, which do not have any advocacy functions or similar features typical of NGOs, were refused.[19]

The actual accreditation process is fully handled by the WTO Secretariat; WTO intergovernmental bodies are only involved in deciding the accreditation procedure. This can be explained by the fact that the rights of NGOs are minimal, so that even if particular accredited NGOs are hostile towards the WTO or certain governments, they cannot interfere with the negotiating and decision-making processes, and therefore, governments are not very concerned with who will be accredited. After the end of the accreditation procedure, the list of eligible NGOs is circulated to all WTO Members for information.[20] Although, potentially, the General Council can at any time address any issue concerning accreditation, the practice has evolved that accreditation is fully in the hands of the WTO Secretariat; WTO membership has tacitly agreed not to interfere in this process.

B. *Public Symposia or Forums*

Pursuant to the 1996 Guidelines, in the second half of the 1990s, a number of symposia for NGOs and delegations of Members on specific issues have been organized by the WTO Secretariat (including three on trade and the environment, one on trade and development and one on trade facilitation).[21] These first symposia were organized in the form of plenary sessions with hundreds of participants gathered in one room. This format was criticized as ineffective because it resulted in poorly focused discussions and overly general conclusions.[22]

In reaction to this criticism, in 2000 the WTO changed the format of the symposia and has turned them into annual two- or three-day events featuring many separate workshops and seminars where panellists and interested participants discuss a broad range of topical WTO-related issues. These annual symposia or forums, as they have been called since 2006, are fully financed from extra-budgetary sources, such as voluntary government contributions.

---

[18] Interview with Mr Bernard Kuiten, WTO External Relations Division (17 Nov 2005).
[19] ibid.
[20] See WTO Ministerial Conference, *Procedures Regarding Registration and Attendance of Non-Governmental Organizations at the Sixth Session of the Ministerial Conference* (n 15).
[21] See <http://www.wto.org/english/forums_e/ngo_e/intro_e.htm>, visited 1 Nov 2005.
[22] See S Charnovitz, 'Opening the WTO to Non-Governmental Interests' (2000) 24 Fordham Intl L J 173, 191, 214; and G Marceau and P Pedersen, 'The World Trade Organization and Civil Society' (1999) 33 J of World Trade 5, 18.

Since 2005, the WTO has not exercised control over the issues discussed at the symposia or forums, or over the speakers, panellists or other participants. Its role is confined to arranging for rooms, interpretation, financial support to speakers from developing countries, etc. Themes of seminars and workshops that constitute the symposium or forum are suggested by NGOs themselves (alongside other organizations, such as academic institutions). Any NGO may approach the WTO Secretariat with a suggestion to organize a workshop on a particular issue. The NGO itself then determines the speaker(s) and the panellists. The WTO does not interfere with this process. Up to five or six workshops can take place simultaneously, which creates a competitive atmosphere between NGOs (and other organizers) who have to fight for the attention of participants.[23]

At the WTO Public Symposium of May 2004 on 'Multilateralism at the Crossroads', there were almost 1,200 registered participants and 150 speakers. This three-day event featured a total of 29 workshops organized by NGOs,[24] WTO Members, international organizations, academic institutions and the WTO Secretariat.[25] About one-fifth of the sessions dealt with various aspects of agricultural negotiations; a second fifth addressed perspectives and prospects of developing countries post-Cancún and a third fifth of the sessions attempted to tackle the question of how to translate trade liberalization into sustainable development. The remaining sessions dealt with the environment and biodiversity, WTO scope, reform and future prospects, South-South cooperation in the multilateral trading system and the challenges and benefits presented by regional trade agreements.[26]

In April 2005, the topic of the WTO Public Symposium was 'WTO After 10 Years: Global Problems and Multilateral Solutions'. Most of the discussions focused on the Doha Round negotiations, with much attention devoted to agriculture and other current issues. Some 23 workshops were held on a wide variety of themes, with between five and six concurrent sessions held each morning or afternoon. The 2007 Public Forum will be held on 4 and 5 October, and will focus on the question 'How can the WTO help harness globalization?'

Symposia and forums are open to the public. Participants are comprised mainly of academics, NGO representatives, students, press, WTO Secretariat officials and representatives of WTO Members, although attendance of

---

[23] Interview with Mr Bernard Kuiten, WTO External Relations Division (17 Nov 2005).

[24] Including, for example, the International Centre for Trade and Sustainable Development, International Farmers Coalition for Fair and Equitable Agricultural Trade Rules at the WTO, Third World Network, Oxfam, Geneva Women for International Trade and others.

[25] See <www.wto.org/english/tratop_e/dda_e/sym_devagenda_prog_04_e.htm>, visited 31 May 2004.

[26] See A Lofthouse and F Jubany, Report for International Trade Canada on WTO Public Symposium 'Multilateralism at the Crossroads' (June 2004), <http://www.dfait-maeci.gc.ca/tna-nac/WTO-NGO-en.asp>, visited 1 Nov 2005.

governmental officials is not high. To participate, one must register by submitting his/her name, organization affiliation and contact details. No pre-approval is required for participation.[27]

WTO public symposia or forums do not lead to any specific outcomes, such as civil society statements to WTO bodies. Essentially, they serve as a forum for participants to exchange views and perspectives in a frank and open way, to argue their positions, to network and establish contacts.

C. Improved Access to WTO Information and Opportunities for Information Exchange

In the absence of a right to attend meetings of WTO bodies, the right of access to documents produced in the course of, and in relation to, these meetings becomes essential for NGOs that wish to keep WTO activities under scrutiny. In parallel with the 1996 Guidelines, the General Council adopted procedures for the circulation and de-restriction of WTO documents, establishing the basic principle that most documents would be immediately circulated as unrestricted. However, this principle was, at the time, still subject to important exceptions. In particular, working documents, minutes of WTO meetings, WTO Secretariat background papers and Ministerial Conference summary records were only de-restricted, and thus made available to the public, after eight to nine months. In 2002, after years of discussion, the General Council reached a decision to accelerate de-restriction of official WTO documents, cutting the time period in which most documents are made publicly available to 6–12 weeks, and also reducing significantly the list of exceptions.[28]

Therefore, today, most WTO documents are immediately available to the public and those documents that are initially restricted are de-restricted much faster. All unrestricted WTO documents are available online, in all three official WTO languages (English, French and Spanish).

Further, since 1998, the WTO External Relations Division has been organizing briefings for NGOs on meetings of WTO bodies. Normally, NGO briefings are held after meetings of the General Council and of the Trade Negotiations Committee. Usually between 20 and 30 NGOs—mostly those with offices in Geneva—attend them.[29] If there are other NGOs that would like to attend, they have to send a request to the External Relations Division. Having satisfied itself that the applicant is indeed an NGO, the External Relations Division includes it in the list of participants.[30]

---

[27] Interview with Mr Bernard Kuiten, WTO External Relations Division (17 Nov 2005).
[28] See Decision of the General Council, *Procedures for the Circulation and Derestriction of WTO Documents*, WT/L/452 (16 May 2002).
[29] The WTO informs Geneva-based NGOs about the briefings by email.
[30] Interview with Mr Bernard Kuiten, WTO External Relations Division (17 Nov 2005).

Lastly, since 1998, a special 'NGO Room' on the WTO website has been in place.[31] It holds specific information for civil society, in particular records and statistics from past NGO events organized by the WTO Secretariat and announcements of registration procedures for sessions of the Ministerial Conference and the annual public forums. In addition, the NGO Room features NGO position papers received by the Secretariat.

D. Informal Meetings with NGOs

The 1996 Guidelines envisaged the possibility for chairpersons of WTO councils and committees to meet with NGOs. There are no written procedures that govern such meetings. They usually take place at the initiative of Geneva-based NGOs, which use them as yet another opportunity to keep up to date with the developments in WTO negotiations. Sometimes meetings are held upon the suggestion of the relevant chairperson or of the WTO Secretariat, but in most cases, the WTO Secretariat is not involved in the organization. The information about upcoming meetings is rarely published; it is circulated within NGO networks informally. There is no NGO selection; participation is naturally confined to those NGOs that know about the meeting. Usually during these meetings NGOs and chairs of relevant councils/committees exchange information and views, mostly in relation to ongoing negotiations. Due to the informal nature of these meetings, with few exceptions, no reports are issued.

Similar informal meetings take place between NGOs and WTO Secretariat staff from various divisions. These may be devoted to negotiations or cover technical issues of interest to NGOs. There is no schedule for these meetings; they are organized on an ad hoc basis, but normally some WTO–NGO interaction of this nature occurs almost every week.

Additionally, three to four times a year, the WTO Secretariat organizes presentations of NGO studies or publications where representatives of all WTO Members and observers are invited. These often technical presentations arouse limited interest among government officials.[32]

E. Prospects

The 2005 Sutherland Report, *The Future of the WTO*, raised the question of whether in view of the big strides in increasing transparency and civil society engagement in recent years, there was a case for more civil society engagement in the WTO. The Report confirmed the view that the primary responsibility for engaging civil society in trade policy matters rested with

---

[31] See <http://www.wto.org/english/forums_e/ngo_e/ngo_e.htm>, visited 1 Nov 2005.
[32] Interview with Mr Bernard Kuiten, WTO External Relations Division (17 Nov 2005).

the WTO Members themselves. It also noted that while all international organizations shared common objectives in the pursuit of transparency, each organization's peculiar mandate and structure might call for specific objectives, forms of involvement and the choice of civil society organizations with whom to collaborate.[33]

The authors of the Sutherland Report were sceptical about the possibility of introducing a formal system of accreditation in the WTO. While they recognized that such a system might have 'attractions' (for example, ensuring that responsible NGOs get the advantage of a closer relationship with the WTO), in their view, it would impose a continuing bureaucratic burden to receive, sieve and make judgments about candidate NGOs.[34] The Sutherland Report also said that it was unclear what the purpose of the accreditation might be: '[a]part from attendance at the plenary sessions of Ministerial meetings every two years, it is unlikely that accreditation would mean the right to observe WTO meetings first hand.'[35] It expressed doubts as to whether a formal system of accreditation was 'a worthy investment for a small organization with a limited budget'.[36]

The Sutherland Report drew a distinction between having a formal system of accreditation and the Secretariat's need to make decisions about the NGOs with which it will have regular or ad hoc relationships.[37] As far as the latter is concerned, the Report said that 'the 1996 Guidelines... should be further developed so as to guide the WTO Secretariat staff in their consultations and dialogue with civil society and the public'.[38] In particular, the Report suggested establishing a set of clear objectives for the Secretariat's relations with civil society and formalizing the 'criteria to be employed in selecting those civil society organisations with which the Secretariat might develop more systematic and in-depth relations'.[39] At the same time, the Report was silent about the types of activities that such 'systematic and in-depth relations' could comprise.[40]

In sum, the Sutherland Report did not offer any substantial improvements in the degree of the WTO's engagement with NGOs. Rather, it called for streamlining and further developing the existing forms of engagement, with an emphasis on the Secretariat's (as opposed to WTO membership's) relations with NGOs.

---

[33] See Sutherland Report (n 7) para 186 and 212.
[34] ibid para 207.
[35] ibid.
[36] ibid para 208.
[37] See ibid.
[38] ibid para 212.
[39] ibid.
[40] Such activities could include, for example, joint WTO Secretariat–NGO research projects and NGO involvement in WTO training and technical assistance programmes. Interview with Mr Bernard Kuiten, WTO External Relations Division (17 Nov 2005).

IV. NGO INVOLVEMENT IN DISPUTE SETTLEMENT

Settlement of trade disputes between WTO Members is one of the most important functions of the WTO. States make active use of the WTO dispute settlement system. Described briefly, the procedure looks as follows. It begins with mandatory consultations between the parties to the dispute with a view to resolve the dispute amicably. If that is not possible, the complainant can refer the dispute to a panel for adjudication. The panel proceedings will result in a panel report. This report can be appealed to the Appellate Body. The appellate review proceedings will result in an Appellate Body report upholding, modifying or reversing the panel report. The panel report, or in the case of an appeal, the Appellate Body report and the panel report, will be adopted by the Dispute Settlement Body (DSB). After the adoption of the reports, the respondent, if found to be in breach of WTO law, will have to implement the recommendations and rulings adopted by the DSB. The process is governed by the WTO Dispute Settlement Understanding (DSU).[41]

The panel and appellate review proceedings are in many respects similar to a conventional judicial process and include written submissions and oral pleadings, examination of evidence, and may involve participation of experts, etc. The difference lies in the fact that the panel and Appellate Body reports do not have legal force per se, but must be endorsed by the DSB to become binding;[42] that is why the system is frequently referred to as quasi-judicial.

The following sections cover three relevant issues:

- attendance of dispute settlement proceedings by NGOs;
- submission of *amicus curiae* briefs by NGOs; and
- participation of NGO representatives as experts and legal counsel.

A. Attendance of Proceedings

WTO proceedings are closed to the public. Consultations, panel proceedings and appellate review proceedings are all confidential. The meetings of the DSB also take place behind closed doors. Thus, NGOs cannot attend the proceedings and DSB meetings.[43]

---

[41] See *Understanding on Rules and Procedures Governing the Settlement of Disputes*, Annex 2 to the WTO Agreement.

[42] Note, however, that such endorsement is, in fact, automatic because the DSB adopts the panel and Appellate Body reports by reverse consensus (see Article 16 and 17 of the DSU).

[43] Also, all written submissions to a panel or to the Appellate Body by the parties and third parties to a dispute are confidential. Parties may make their own submissions available to the public, but most parties choose to keep their submissions confidential.

In September 2005, for the first time in its history, a WTO panel opened up its hearings to the public. The proceedings in the long-standing *EC–Hormones* dispute among the European Union, the United States and Canada were broadcast through closed-circuit television at the WTO headquarters to an audience consisting mainly of trade negotiators, NGO representatives, media and academics. Up to 400 people could observe the meeting.[44] Such practice is only possible if no party to a particular case objects to it. In the mentioned case the Panel accepted the parties' joint request to open up the hearing.

B. Amicus Curiae *Briefs*

Only WTO Members can be parties and third parties to a case—NGOs have no direct access to the WTO dispute settlement system. They cannot bring claims of violation of WTO rights or obligations. Under the current rules, they do not have the right to be heard or to participate in the proceedings. However, under Appellate Body case law, panels and the Appellate Body have the authority to accept and consider written briefs submitted by NGOs (as well as by individuals or companies). In a number of disputes, environmental and human rights NGOs, labour unions and industry associations have attempted to make themselves heard and to influence the outcome of disputes by submitting such unsolicited written briefs. NGO briefs can be attached to parties' submissions or be submitted independently. They can serve at least three different functions: (1) providing legal analysis and interpretation; (2) providing factual analysis as well as evidence; and (3) placing the trade dispute into a broader political and social context.[45] NGOs can advance arguments WTO Members fear using because they are concerned that later, in other disputes, those arguments may be used against them.[46]

As of 2003, more than 70 NGOs have submitted *amicus curiae* briefs either to panels or the Appellate Body.[47] The acceptance by panels and the Appellate Body of these *amicus curiae* briefs has been controversial and criticized by most WTO Members.

In *US–Shrimp*, the Appellate Body came to the conclusion that panels

---

[44] See BRIDGES Weekly Trade News Digest (14 Sept 2005) 9(30).

[45] See L Johnson and E Tuerk, 'CIEL's Experience in WTO Dispute Settlement: Challenges and Complexities from a Practical Point of View' in T Treves, M Frigessi di Rattalma, A Tanzi, A Fodella, C Pitea and C Ragni (eds), *Civil Society, International Courts and Compliance Bodies* (TMC Asser Press, The Hague, 2005) 249.

[46] See S Charnovitz, 'Participation of Non-Governmental Organizations in the World Trade Organization' (1996) 17 University of Pennsylvania J of Intl Economic L 331, 353.

[47] M Jeffords, 'Turning the Protester into a Partner for Development: The Need for Effective Consultation Between The WTO and NGOs' (2003) 28 Brooklyn J of Intl L 937, 961.

have the authority to accept and consider *amicus curiae* briefs.[48] A few panels in later disputes did, on the basis of this ruling of the Appellate Body, accept and consider *amicus curiae* briefs. In many other disputes, however, panels refused to do so.

In *US–Lead and Bismuth II*, the Appellate Body ruled with respect to its own authority to accept and consider *amicus curiae* briefs submitted in appellate review proceedings. It concluded that it had the legal authority to decide whether or not to accept and consider any information that it believed to be pertinent and useful. However, in this particular case, the Appellate Body did not find it necessary to take the two *amicus curiae* briefs filed into account in rendering its decision.[49]

In October 2000, the Appellate Body Division, hearing the appeal in *EC–Asbestos*, adopted an Additional Procedure to deal with *amicus curiae* briefs which the Appellate Body expected to receive in great numbers in that dispute.[50] The procedure required applicants to file for leave to submit a brief. The application had to respond to a set of questions, among them information on the objectives and financing of the applicant and how the proposed brief would make a contribution that is not likely to be repetitive of what the governments have already said. In drafting the Additional Procedure, the Appellate Body stated that it was acting to promote the 'interests of fairness and orderly procedure'.[51]

Many WTO Members were infuriated by the Appellate Body's adoption of the Additional Procedure and its apparent willingness to accept and consider *amicus curiae* briefs where certain requirements are fulfilled. A special meeting of the General Council was convened to discuss this issue. Most delegations expressed the opinion that since there was no specific provision regarding *amicus* briefs, they should not be accepted. There was only one delegation (the United States) who believed that there was both a legal and a substantive reason to use *amicus* briefs. No agreement was reached on this point.[52] In his observations at the end of this tumultuous meeting, the Chairman of the General Council stated, however, that 'in light of the views expressed and in the absence of clear rules, he believed that the

---

[48] See Appellate Body Report, *United States–Import Prohibition of Certain Shrimp and Shrimp Products* ('*US–Shrimp*'), WT/DS58/AB/R, adopted 6 Nov 1998, paras 104, 105 and 106.

[49] Appellate Body Report, *United States–Imposition of Countervailing Duties on Certain Hot-Rolled Lead and Bismuth Carbon Steel Products Originating in the United Kingdom* ('*US–Lead and Bismuth II*'), WT/DS138/AB/R, adopted 7 June 2000, paras 39 and 42.

[50] See Appellate Body Report, *European Communities–Measures Affecting Asbestos and Asbestos-Containing Products* ('*EC–Asbestos*'), WT/DS135/AB/R, adopted 5 Apr 2001, paras 51–2.

[51] ibid.

[52] See Minutes of the General Council Meeting of 22 Nov 2000, WT/GC/M/60, dated 23 Jan 2001, paras 114–15, 118, and 120.

Appellate Body should exercise extreme caution in future cases until members had considered what rules are needed'.[53]

Note that even before the special meeting of the General Council, the Appellate Body summarily rejected all 17 applications for leave to submit a brief in the *EC–Asbestos* appeal. In response to the form-letter rejections, several NGOs issued a critical press statement. The statement complained that the Appellate Body gave no reason for the rejections. Among the signatories to the statement were the WWF and Greenpeace International.[54]

To date, WTO Members have been unable to adopt any clear rules on *amicus curiae* briefs. The Appellate Body has repeatedly confirmed its case law on the authority of panels and the Appellate Body to accept and consider these briefs. In no appellate proceedings thus far has the Appellate Body deemed it useful in deciding on an appeal to accept and consider *amicus curiae* briefs submitted to it.

C. Experts and Legal Counsel

Potentially, NGO representatives may act as experts in panel proceedings.[55] Article 13 of the DSU gives panels the authority to seek information and technical advice from any individual or body that it deems appropriate. Panels may consult experts to obtain their opinion on certain aspects of the matter under consideration. As many NGOs possess specialized knowledge, potentially, their representatives could be chosen as experts. To date, panels have consulted experts in disputes involving complex scientific issues.[56] In these cases, the panels typically selected the experts in consultation with the parties; presented the experts with a list of questions to which each expert individually responded in writing; and finally, called a special meeting with the experts where these and other questions were discussed with the panellists and the parties. The panel report usually contained both the written responses of the experts to the panel's questions as well as a transcript of the discussions at the meeting with the panel. So far, panels have never selected experts from the ranks of NGOs.

Furthermore, theoretically, there seem to be no obstacles for a disputing party or third party to retain an NGO representative as its counsel; particularly, this might be imaginable for low-income countries that do not have

[53] ibid 120.

[54] See Charnovitz (n 22) 189.

[55] This is not possible at the appellate stage as the Appellate Body does not have a fact-finding role.

[56] For example, *EC–Measures Concerning Meat and Meat Products (Hormones)* ('*EC–Hormones*'); *Australia–Measures Affecting Importation of Salmon* ('*Australia–Salmon*'); *Japan–Measures Affecting Agricultural Products* ('*Japan–Agricultural Products II*'); *EC–Asbestos*; and *Japan–Measures Affecting the Importation of Apples* ('*Japan–Apples*').

sufficiently prepared State officials and are unable or unwilling to pay high fees to a private lawyer. NGOs such as International Lawyers and Economists Against Poverty or the Geneva-based International Commission of Jurists that could, in principle, provide specialists of the required competence. The DSU does not explicitly address the issue of representation of the parties before panels or the Appellate Body. In *EC–Bananas III*, the issue arose whether private counsel, not employed by government, may represent a party or third party (Saint Lucia, in that case) before the Appellate Body. In its ruling, the Appellate Body noted that nothing in the WTO Agreement, the DSU, customary international law or the prevailing practice of international tribunals, prevented a WTO Member from determining the composition of its own delegation in WTO dispute settlement proceedings.[57] A party can, therefore, decide that private counsel forms part of its delegation and will represent it in WTO dispute settlement proceedings.[58] This reasoning would appear to allow NGO representatives to be members of WTO Members' delegations.

[57] See Appellate Body Report, *European Communities–Regime for the Importation, Sale and Distribution of Bananas* ('*EC–Bananas III*'), WT/DS27/AB/R, adopted 25 Sept 1997, para 10. This reasoning was later confirmed for panel proceedings.

[58] The parties and third parties are responsible for all members of their delegations and must ensure that all members of the delegation, private counsel included, act in accordance with the rules of the DSU and the Working Procedures of the panel, particularly with respect to the confidentiality of the proceedings. See in this respect Appellate Body Report, *Thailand–Anti-Dumping Duties on Angles, Shapes and Sections of Iron or Non-Alloy Steel and H-Beams from Poland* ('*Thailand–H-Beams*'), WT/DS122/AB/R, adopted 5 Apr 2001, paras 62–78.

CHAPTER 12

Comparative Analysis

As pointed out at the outset of this study, the rise of the global civil society has led to the aspiration of many NGOs to influence the outcomes of international policy-deliberation, decision-making, policy-implementation and other processes 'from the inside', that is, through involvement in the work of international organizations. The study has shown that, while not always wholeheartedly, international organizations have responded positively to the call of NGOs for involvement and currently allow—to different extents and in different ways—NGOs to participate in their activities.[1]

On the basis of the preceding findings, this concluding chapter compares the rules and practices employed by different international organizations to 'accommodate' NGOs. Following the structure of the previous chapters, the analysis focuses on:

I.   Legal basis for engagement with NGOs.
II. Forms of NGO involvement and their participatory rights.
III. NGO accreditation criteria.
IV. NGO accreditation procedures.
V.   Arrangements for monitoring accredited NGOs.

While the analysis in this chapter is limited to the 10 international organizations covered in this study, it nevertheless gives a good picture of the rich variety of types, degrees and mechanisms of engagement of international organizations with NGOs.

I. LEGAL BASIS

Most international organizations have a general legal basis for engagement with NGOs in their *constituent instruments* (eg UN Charter, Agreement Establishing the World Trade Organization, Constitution of the International Labour Organisation, Convention Establishing the World Intellectual Property Organization, etc). In most cases, such legal basis is unspecific. It merely authorizes the organization concerned to make '(suitable) arrangements for consultation and cooperation' with NGOs (eg UN,

---

[1] Only two international organizations (WTO and IMF) have expressly taken a position that engagement with civil society is primarily the task of national governments.

ILO, WHO, WIPO, WTO).[2] In the case of the United Nations, its constituent instrument—the UN Charter—limits NGO involvement to only one of its organs, the Economic and Social Council. Constituent instruments of three examined international organizations—the World Bank, the IMF and UNDP—do not provide for the involvement of NGOs.[3]

Further rules on relations with NGOs governing particular forms of NGO involvement, their participatory rights, rules on accreditation or selection of NGOs, and monitoring of NGOs are typically set out in *secondary regulations*, ie documents adopted by the governing body or bodies of the organization concerned (UN/ECOSOC, UNCTAD, ILO, WHO, etc).[4]

Interestingly, there appears to be no necessary or direct link between the fact that the engagement with NGOs is envisaged in the organization's constituent instrument, and the intensity of such engagement. The mandate found in the constituent instrument can be fleshed out by secondary regulations in different ways. For example, Article V:2 of the WTO Agreement and Article 71 of the UN Charter both empower—in very similar wording—the respective organizations to engage with NGOs, but there is a world of difference in what they have done with this mandate. The WTO General Council has used that legal basis in a restrictive way, leaving the main responsibility for engaging with civil society to the individual WTO Members, ie at the national rather than international level. Moreover, the WTO General Council has effectively barred NGOs from participation in the policy-deliberation and decision-making activities of WTO bodies.[5] Unlike the WTO, the UN ECOSOC and other international organizations with similarly worded clauses on cooperation with NGOs in their constituent instruments have provided for a much higher degree of NGO involvement and have granted them more participatory rights.[6] Despite the fact that constituent instruments of the World Bank, the IMF and UNDP do not provide for involvement of NGOs, all three organizations interact with NGOs and have secondary rules that govern, or guide, such interaction.[7] The World Bank, for example, engages with NGOs more actively than the WTO.

That being said, it still appears important to include an explicit legal basis for engagement with NGOs in the constituent instrument as it accords increased legitimacy to NGO participation in the work of the international

---

[2] See above, pp 19–20 (UN ECOSOC), p 69 (ILO), p 98 (WHO), p 85 (WIPO) and p 190 (WTO).

[3] See above, p 152 (World Bank), p 178 (IMF) and p 136 (UNDP).

[4] See above, p 22 (UN ECOSOC), p 52 (UNCTAD), p 69 (ILO) and p 99 (WHO).

[5] See above, p 192 (WTO).

[6] Even the least privileged category of NGOs accredited with the UN ECOSOC (NGOs on the 'Roster') has more participatory rights than NGOs within the WTO.

[7] See above, p 153 (World Bank), p 178 (IMF) and p 137 (UNDP).

organization concerned. The constituent instrument is agreed by all Member States of the organization and is a document of superior authority.

Secondary rules may be formulated as *mandatory* or as *non-binding*.[8] The ECOSOC Resolution 1996/31 on the 'Consultative Relationship between the United Nations and Non-Governmental Organizations' is an example of a detailed set of rules cast in mandatory language.[9] Non-binding norms on cooperation with NGOs may take the form of guidelines, good practices, strategy papers and policy papers (IMF, World Bank, UNEP, UNDP).[10] Generally, non-binding norms appear to be more convenient for the international organizations because they afford more flexibility to Member States and organization officials and allow them to adjust more easily to different, and ever evolving, situations. In some circumstances, the absence of binding rules may also be to the benefit of NGOs, particularly in organizations where far-reaching rules on NGO involvement are not politically feasible. In such organizations the absence of hard and fast rules gives secretariats a certain freedom of action, which means that they can engage with NGOs in greater depth than they otherwise could have done. However, generally, non-binding norms on cooperation are disadvantageous for civil society, as they do not provide certainty and predictability with regard to the status and rights of NGOs and make them dependent on the discretion of officials. The absence of (binding) rules on NGO involvement may also lead to considerable differences in practice across regional and country offices, departments and policy settings of one and the same organization (eg IMF, World Bank).

The level of detail of secondary rules may also vary considerably, ranging from very detailed (eg, UN ECOSOC) to minimalist (eg, WTO or WIPO).[11] In fact, most international organizations have a mix of *formal* and *informal* mechanisms for NGO involvement. Formal involvement means that involvement is allowed and is governed by legal rules; informal engagement is a matter of practice rather than regulation. The analysis has shown that typically, there is more regulation of arrangements for NGO involvement in the policy-making processes of the organization's governing bodies than in the organization's operational activities. Although organizations such as ILO, UNCTAD, WHO or UNEP all engage in operational activities of some sort, formal regulation of NGO involvement in these activities is absent or minimal.[12] Generally, formalization of NGO involvement is beneficial for

---

[8] In a number of cases, secretariats of international organisations also compile existing experience and practice of cooperation with NGOs in publications of a descriptive nature (eg World Bank, UNEP, UNDP).
[9] See above, p 22 (UN ECOSOC).
[10] See above, p 178 (IMF), p 153 (World Bank), p 122 (UNEP) and p 137 (UNDP).
[11] See above, p 22 (UN ECOSOC), p 191 (WTO) and p 85 (WIPO).
[12] See above, p 70 (ILO), p 53 (UNCTAD), p 100 (WHO) and p 131 (UNEP).

NGOs because it accords legitimacy to such involvement, provides legal certainty and predictability, narrows down discretion of relevant officials and decreases arbitrariness in the treatment of NGOs.

As far as policy-deliberation and decision-making processes are concerned, in most cases, there is no separate document comprehensively governing the status of NGOs in the organization's decision-making body or bodies (UNCTAD, WIPO, World Bank, IMF, WTO, UNEP, UNDP). The only separate and comprehensive set of rules, both substantive and procedural, can be found in the UN ECOSOC Resolution 1996/31. In a number of cases, regulation is carried out through insertion of special provisions on NGO participation into the documents of general application like the rules of procedure of the intergovernmental body concerned (WIPO, UNEP).[13] The ILO, WHO and UNCTAD combine the two approaches: these organizations set out relevant provisions both in the general rules of procedure and in separate documents specifically dedicated to the subject of NGO involvement in their activities.[14]

To deal with NGO-related matters, a number of organizations have created special units within their secretariats (eg, NGO Section of the Department of Economic and Social Affairs at the UN, Civil Society Outreach at UNCTAD).[15] Other secretariats do not have a special unit but one or more designated officers within a department that deals with broader external relations issues (eg, External Relations Division at the WTO, External Relation Department at the IMF).[16] Still other organizations have officers to deal with NGOs in different departments within the organization with an additional focal point (eg, ILO, WHO, World Bank) or without such a focal point (WIPO).[17] The different types of institutional structures generally reflect the different forms of NGO involvement and different levels of intensity of cooperation with NGOs.

II. FORMS OF NGO INVOLVEMENT AND PARTICIPATORY RIGHTS

Forms of NGO involvement depend on the type of activities undertaken by particular international organizations. The main types of activities include:

- policy deliberations and decision-making;
- planning, implementation and monitoring of projects (operational activities); and
- dispute settlement.

---

[13] See above, p 85, (WIPO) and p 121 (UNEP).
[14] See above, p 69 (ILO), p 99 (WHO) and p 52 (UNCTAD).
[15] See above, p 22 (UN ECOSOC) and p 53 (UNCTAD).
[16] See above, p 192 (WTO) and p 183 (IMF).
[17] See above, p 69 (ILO), p 100 (WHO), pp 155–6 (World Bank) and p 86 (WIPO).

Some organizations, like the UN, serve almost exclusively as forums for intergovernmental meetings and policy deliberations. Other organizations focus on operational activities, ie policy implementation, usually through carrying out projects in individual countries and regions of the world (eg, UNDP, World Bank). Dispute settlement is relevant in the context of only two of the examined organizations (WTO and World Bank).

Formal regulation of NGO involvement has traditionally focused on policy-deliberation and decision-making processes of international organizations, ie NGO participation in meetings of governing bodies of the organizations concerned. Organizations grant NGOs participatory rights with a view to, on the one hand, securing expert information or advice from NGOs with special competence in the relevant subjects, and on the other hand, enabling NGOs that represent important elements of public opinion to express their views.[18] Formally regulated NGO participation is also typical for dispute settlement procedures (WTO, World Bank), given the quasi-judicial nature of this type of activity.[19]

Informal mechanisms are more characteristic of NGO participation in operational activities, especially where the activities are only supplementary in the work of the organization whose main focus is on policy-making (eg technical cooperation and capacity-building activities of UNCTAD or WIPO). Organizations with a primary focus on project implementation, such as the World Bank or UNDP, have formal rules governing NGO involvement in their projects and programmes.[20]

By definition, informal NGO involvement is *sine legem*, ie without a legal basis. The practice of NGO involvement can also be *ultra legem* where it goes beyond what is provided in the relevant rules. While in some organizations NGO involvement seems to remain within the limits set by the relevant rules, in others it does not. For example, in the UN context, in addition to what is provided in the UN Charter and secondary rules, in practice NGOs may become involved in the work of the special sessions of the UN General Assembly.[21] At the same time, the analysis in the previous chapters has not revealed any forms of NGO involvement in direct contradiction with existing rules (involvement *contra legem*).

Instances of informal NGO involvement are very difficult to examine. Additionally, these practices can easily be changed. This study has mainly focused on formal mechanisms for engagement with NGOs, although, where possible, an attempt has been made to discern informal ways of interaction.

---

[18] These objectives are recorded in UN ECOSOC Resolution 1996/31, para 20.
[19] See above, pp 201–5 (WTO) and pp 170–3 (World Bank).
[20] See above, pp 53, 164–9 (World Bank) and pp 143–50 (UNDP).
[21] See above, p 20, note 4 (UN ECOSOC).

One can distinguish between NGO involvement in the activities of an organization's *intergovernmental body* or bodies that exercise policy-making powers, and cooperation with that organization's *secretariat*, which mainly performs administrative and support functions. Cooperation between NGOs and the secretariats may be a very important form of NGO involvement. Secretariats of international organizations, because of their technical expertise, often play an important role in managing policy implementation. This is particularly so in organizations with an emphasis on operational activities like UNDP, the World Bank and the IMF. In the World Bank and the IMF, cooperation with the secretariats of these organizations is the predominant form of NGO involvement because NGOs lack access to the intergovernmental bodies of these organizations.[22] This is also the case for the WTO, even though this organization does not focus on operational activities.[23] Interaction with secretariats is often ad hoc and informal (eg ILO, WTO, UNCTAD, IMF). However, for some organizations NGO interaction with their secretariats is explicitly authorized (eg UN ECOSOC, UNDP),[24] or even required (World Bank).[25]

One *institutionalized form* of cooperation between NGOs and secretariats is through a body formed by representatives of NGOs and (high-level) officials of the international organization concerned. Such a body can serve as an additional, or as an exclusive, means of channeling the views of NGOs to the organization concerned. However, this mechanism is not very common among the organizations examined in this study. Only UNDP has such permanent and formal institutional arrangements for consultations with NGOs—the CSO Advisory Committee to the Administrator and similar committees at several of its country offices.[26] The WTO has an Informal NGO Advisory Body but its effectiveness is unclear.[27] The World Bank had such a body in the past but it was phased out because it was considered not to be sufficiently inclusive.[28]

One can further distinguish between cooperation with NGOs at *headquarter level* and at *regional* or *country levels*. Some organizations, like the WTO, WIPO or UNCTAD, do not have regional or country offices. For them, this distinction is not relevant. Other organizations, like UNDP, the World Bank, the IMF or the WHO, have regional and/or country offices and may have arrangements for engagement with NGOs at those levels. Research has shown that interactions with NGOs follow the distribution of

---

[22] See above, p 157 (World Bank) and p 181 (IMF).
[23] See above, pp 192–4 (WTO).
[24] See above, p 28 (UN ECOSOC) and p 140 (UNDP).
[25] See above, p 166 (World Bank).
[26] See above, pp 140–3 (UNDP).
[27] See above, p 193 (WTO).
[28] See above, pp 159–60 (World Bank).

competence within the organization concerned. With regard to general policy deliberations and decision-making, most interactions with NGOs occur at the headquarter level where the relevant processes tend to take place, while with regard to operational activities undertaken by local or regional offices, interactions with NGOs 'descend' to that level (eg UNDP, World Bank).[29]

Interaction with NGOs may take more *permanent/regular* forms or may be carried out on an *ad hoc* basis. The former are introduced by putting in place permanent NGO accreditation schemes, holding regular civil society events or introducing institutional arrangements of the UNDP CSO Advisory Committee type. Permanent/regular forms make cooperation with NGOs more predictable and inclusive. Ad hoc forms lack those benefits and become frequently limited to NGOs that know about a particular event where NGOs are allowed to participate and/or are based in the same city as the international organization concerned (eg, NGO meetings with WTO or IMF staff).[30]

One form of interaction with NGOs which has been adopted by several international organizations is convening regular *large civil society events* (forums), often alongside (ie simultaneously with, or prior to) the meetings of the supreme decision-making body of the organization (eg civil society forums and hearings at UNCTAD, Global Civil Society Forum at UNEP, WTO symposia and forums, civil society events held in conjunction with the Annual and Spring meetings of the World Bank and the IMF).[31] The purpose of such events is networking, raising awareness, disseminating information, exchanging views on relevant issues, and sometimes the formulation of common civil society positions in order to speak to the organization concerned with a 'single voice'. The organizations themselves tend to 'dissociate' themselves from these civil society events, but frequently lend logistical and/or financial support in order to make them possible (eg UNEP, WTO, UNCTAD, World Bank, IMF).[32]

The majority of examined organizations have permanent NGO *accreditation schemes*, whereby NGOs that meet certain criteria can become permanently accredited with the organization concerned and enjoy associated participatory rights that non-accredited NGOs do not have. This appears to be a feature of the UN-family organizations (UN ECOSOC, UNCTAD, ILO, WHO, WIPO, UNEP).[33] UNDP, which does not have a

---

[29] See above, p 144 (UNDP) and p 169 (World Bank).
[30] See above, p 199 (WTO) and p 180, 184 (IMF).
[31] See above, pp 57–9 (UNCTAD) , pp 129–31 (UNEP), pp 196–8 (WTO), and pp 160–3 (World Bank and IMF).
[32] See ibid.
[33] See above, p 24 (UN ECOSOC), p 54 (UNCTAD), p 70 (ILO), p 100 (WHO), p 87 (WIPO) and pp 123–4 (UNEP).

separate accreditation scheme, is an exception in this respect.[34] Although formally the World Bank and the IMF are part of the UN family, these organizations are traditionally more independent and less influenced by UN rules and practices. They do not have accreditation schemes similar to the ones existing in other UN organizations. Neither does the WTO. Instead, the WTO, the World Bank and the IMF all apply a system of ad hoc accreditation for *single* events.[35] Such a system is probably better referred to as a system of 'NGO registration', rather than a system of 'NGO accreditation'. The ILO and UNCTAD combine the two systems: they have permanent accreditation schemes and at the same time provide non-accredited NGOs with an opportunity to apply for accreditation to particular meetings that are of interest to these NGOs.[36]

Permanent accreditation schemes typically distinguish between different categories of NGOs. For example, the accreditation scheme of ECOSOC distinguishes between NGOs with general consultative status, NGOs with special consultative status and NGOs included on the roster.[37] Other accreditation schemes make similar distinctions.[38] NGOs are placed into one of these categories at the time of accreditation. Typically, permanent accreditation entitles all accredited NGOs to attend meetings of the organization's decision-making bodies. However, participatory rights may differ depending on the category of the NGO. Another option is that all accredited NGOs have the same participatory rights, regardless of their particular status; the difference lies in the range of meetings to which they have admission (ILO, WIPO and partly UNCTAD).[39]

As regards NGO participation in meetings, *participatory rights* granted to NGOs may potentially include the following:

- to attend/observe the meetings;
- to make oral statements;
- to circulate written statements;
- to propose agenda items; and
- to receive (and comment on) pre-meeting working documents.

In a number of organizations, NGOs still lack the very basic right of attendance of most meetings (WTO, World Bank, IMF).[40] However, in most

---

[34] Note that in practice, UNDP makes (limited) use of UN ECOSOC's accreditation facility. See p 143.
[35] See above, pp 194–6 (WTO), pp 160–3 (World Bank) and (IMF).
[36] See above, p 78 (ILO) and p 64 (UNCTAD).
[37] See above, pp 24–8 (UN ECOSOC).
[38] See above, pp 54–5 (UNCTAD), pp 70–3 (ILO) and pp 87–8 (WIPO).
[39] See above, p 73 (ILO), p 89 (WIPO) and p 57 (UNCTAD).
[40] See above, pp 142–3 (WTO), p 157 (World Bank) and p 181 (IMF).

organizations with permanent accreditation schemes, accredited NGOs are allowed to attend all, or most, meetings of the organization's bodies, although there may be exceptions. For example, accredited NGOs may not attend the meetings of the Coordination Committee of WIPO.[41] Normally, if an NGO is allowed to attend the meetings (and participate in the work) of a certain body, it is allowed to attend the meetings (and participate in the work) of its subsidiary bodies as well. However, the reverse is not true.

There is a tendency, especially in less NGO-friendly organizations, to allow NGOs to attend the (rarely convened) formal meetings of supreme organs of the organization concerned (eg the biannual sessions of the Ministerial Conference of the WTO, annual meetings of the Board of Governors of the World Bank and the IMF, or the Assemblies of WIPO) but deny their participation in the meetings of intergovernmental organs guiding the day-to-day functioning of these organizations (respectively, the General Council of the WTO, Boards of Executive Directors of the World Bank and the IMF, the Coordination Committee of WIPO).[42] The effectiveness of this mode of NGO involvement is questionable, as in most cases meetings of the supreme organs have a *pro forma* character, their decisions being negotiated in advance of formal meetings. This tendency does not hold true for UNEP, UN ECOSOC, WHO and UNCTAD, where NGOs are allowed to participate at both levels.

In all organizations where NGOs are entitled to deliver *oral statements*, this right is subject to the discretion of the meeting's chairperson or the meeting itself (UN ECOSOC, ILO, UNEP, UNCTAD, WHO, WIPO).[43] By imposing restrictions on the right to deliver oral statements, international organizations understandably seek to prevent turning the meetings into civil society forums and 'talking shops' that could paralyse the decision-making process.

Where NGOs are allowed to circulate *written statements*, this right may be restricted by requiring that the statements be relevant to the meeting's agenda items and by limiting the length of written statements. In some organizations, written statements are circulated (and thus, 'pre-read') by the secretariats (eg UN ECOSOC, UNCTAD, UNEP).[44] In other organizations NGOs take care of the circulation themselves (eg WIPO).[45] A formal right to *propose items for the agenda* or to comment on pre-meeting working

---

[41] See above, pp 88–9 (WIPO).
[42] See above, pp 192–3 (WTO), pp 157–61 (World Bank), p 181 (IMF) and pp 88–9 (WIPO).
[43] See above, p 29 (UN ECOSOC), p 71 (ILO), p 124 (UNEP), p 56 (UNCTAD), p 104 (WHO) and p 89 (WIPO).
[44] See above, pp 24–7 (UN ECOSOC), p 56 (UNCTAD) and pp 123–4 (UNEP).
[45] See above, p 89 (WIPO).

documents is rare—it exists only in the UN ECOSOC (only for NGOs in the general consultative status) and in UNEP.[46]

Listed rights, if granted, can be exercised in *formal* meetings of the bodies concerned and usually do not extend to informal/preparatory meetings of those bodies, where such meetings are held. Also, in none of the international organizations examined in this study—except the ILO with its very particular tripartite system[47]—does NGO participation mean negotiations with NGOs or granting voting rights to them. Participatory rights of NGOs 'merely' enable them to make themselves heard and to promote their views so that these views are (at best) taken into account before the intergovernmental body concerned comes to its conclusions and takes a decision on a particular issue.

Note that apart from participatory rights relevant in the context of intergovernmental meetings, NGOs may have other rights, such as the right of access to documents or the right to meet with or be briefed by officials of an organization.[48]

III. ACCREDITATION CRITERIA

Understandably, international organizations want to keep the number of NGOs involved in their activities 'manageable' and avoid involvement of NGOs that could potentially harm them in their efforts to achieve the organization's objectives. Therefore, they need to select among the NGOs that seek to engage with them. This is the raison d'être of the NGO accreditation systems existing in many international organizations. Rules on NGO accreditation are supposed to ensure that only those NGOs which 'add value' to the organization's activities enjoy specific forms of involvement and associated rights.

As mentioned above, out of the 10 examined international organizations, six have permanent NGO accreditation schemes (ECOSOC, UNCTAD, ILO, WHO, WIPO, UNEP).[49] Three other organizations (WTO, World Bank, IMF) have ad hoc, rather than permanent, NGO accreditation/registration schemes in that they regularly accredit/register NGOs for particular events on an ad hoc basis.[50] UNDP is the only organization (out of those examined) that does not have either a permanent or an ad hoc accreditation scheme for NGOs, although in practice UNDP allows participation of ECOSOC-accredited NGOs in the meetings of the

---

[46] See above, pp 24, 29 (UN ECOSOC) and p 125 (UNEP).
[47] See above, pp 67–8 (ILO).
[48] Eg, p 28 (UN ECOSOC) and pp 198–9 (WTO).
[49] See above, p 214.
[50] See ibid.

UNDP Executive Board, ie UNDP makes use of the ECOSOC accreditation facility.[51]

Rules on accreditation consist of:

- *substantive rules* setting out the requirements that an NGO must meet to be accredited; and
- *procedural rules* that govern the accreditation procedure as well as subsequent monitoring of accredited NGOs.[52]

Accreditation criteria are typically established in secondary regulations governing relations with NGOs, although constituent instruments may also imply existence of certain requirements—for example, that NGOs activities must be relevant to those of the organization concerned (eg UN ECOSOC, WTO, UNCTAD, UNEP).[53] The case of WIPO, where accreditation criteria for international NGOs are unwritten but established and applied as a matter of practice, is exceptional.[54]

The number of applicable criteria in international organizations with permanent accreditation schemes may differ from one organization to another (from three in UNEP to 10 or more in UN ECOSOC, UNCTAD and WHO).[55] In organizations with ad hoc accreditation/registration schemes, criteria are less numerous and less strict (WTO, World Bank, IMF).[56] The difference in approaches is primarily explained by the difference in participatory rights granted to NGOs. The more rights afforded, the more 'hurdles' (in the form of accreditation criteria and relevant procedures) are introduced in order to sieve applicant NGOs. The fact that the WTO, the World Bank and the IMF do not grant substantial rights to NGOs explains the absence of elaborate accreditation rules.

The main or basic criteria applied in organizations with *permanent* accreditation schemes are:

- the relevance of the NGO to the activities of the international organization concerned;
- the non-profit nature of the NGO;
- the non-governmental character of the NGO (including financial independence from governments); and
- the international structure/scope of the NGO.

---

[51] See above, p 143 (UNDP).
[52] Accreditation procedures are examined in the following section.
[53] See above, p 19 (UN ECOSOC), p 190 (WTO), p 52 (UNCTAD) and p 120 (UNEP).
[54] See above, p 90 (WIPO).
[55] See above, p 188 (UNEP), pp 31–3 (UN ECOSOC), pp 59–61 (UNCTAD) and pp 108–12 (WHO).
[56] See above, p 195 (WTO), p 162 (World Bank and IMF).

Other common criteria include the ones according to which the NGO must:

- be of recognized standing;
- have a certain (minimum) membership base;
- have a certain (minimum) geographical coverage;
- have aims and purposes that are in conformity with the spirit/ purposes/principles of the accrediting organization;
- have an established headquarters and an executive officer;
- have a constitution or similar basic document;
- have a conference, congress or other representative body;
- have authority to speak for its members through its authorized representatives; and
- attest that it has been in existence for a certain (minimum) period of time.

Common accreditation criteria can be classified in several groups:

(1) Nature of the organization (non-governmental character, non-profit status);
(2) Activities (relevance, conformity with general principles of the accrediting organization);
(3) Geographical scope (international/regional/national/local);
(4) Standing (recognition, membership base, participation in other NGO networks);
(5) Democratic legitimacy and accountability (constitution/charter, authority to speak for members, voting rights of members, accountability of executives to the NGO's representative body); and
(6) Formal requirements (registration/official status in a country of registration, established headquarters, executive/liaison officers, minimum period of existence).

In several cases, the criteria relating to the nature of an organization as an NGO—non-governmental character and non-profit status—have not been made explicit. However, in these cases, the two mentioned criteria are applied implicitly as inherent in the notion of an 'NGO' (eg ILO, UNCTAD).[57]

Frequently, accreditation criteria are quite imprecise, lending themselves to subjective interpretations. For example, when reviewing NGOs' applications, the ILO takes into account the 'length of existence of the NGO' (without specifying what is an acceptable minimum period of existence), 'membership and geographical coverage' (without specifying how broad

---

[57] See below, p 76 (ILO) and pp 61–2 (UNCTAD).

those must be), or 'practical achievements of the NGO' (without explaining what can qualify as such achievements).[58]

Despite the existence of numerous criteria, an accrediting organ usually does not assess applicant NGOs very strictly against each and every one of these criteria. As follows from interviews with officials dealing with accreditation in various organizations, the criteria most thoroughly examined are:

- the relevance of the NGO to the activities of the organization concerned, as evidenced by verifiable proof;
- the international nature of the NGO (although some organizations also give access to national NGOs—eg UNCTAD, UN ECOSOC, WIPO);[59]
- the non-governmental character of the NGO;
- the non-profit nature (which does not preclude accreditation of industry associations); and
- the formal legal status in the country of residence, existence of headquarters and executive/liaison officers.

Although there is a degree of consistency in the meaning ascribed to particular accreditation criteria in different organizations, it may also be that the same criterion has different meanings in different organizations. For example, the criterion of the international nature of an NGO may mean that an NGOs must be: (1) international in structure (the NGO must have offices in different countries or have member organizations from different countries), or (2) international in the scope of its activities (the NGO must carry out activities in several countries without necessarily any institutional presence or link there). Some international organizations employ both meanings of the criterion of the international nature simultaneously.[60] Furthermore, for some organizations, a two-country coverage is sufficient; in other cases broader coverage encompassing two or more regions of the world is required.

In organizations where accredited NGOs are grouped into different status categories (eg UNCTAD's General Category, Special Category and the Roster), there are further criteria that guide the placement of applicant NGOs in a particular category.[61] The definitive criterion in this respect is commonly the content of the NGO's mandate—the closer it relates to the one of the international organizations concerned, the higher the status that will be granted (UN ECOSOC, UNCTAD).[62] Geographical coverage may

[58] See above, eg, p 76 (ILO).
[59] See above, p 54 (UNCTAD), pp 27, 33 (UN ECOSOC) and p 87 (WIPO).
[60] See, for instance, pp 126–7 (UNEP).
[61] See above, p 62 (UNCTAD).
[62] See above, pp 34–5 (UN ECOSOC) and p 62 (UNCTAD).

also play a role—for example, the ILO has categories of *general* and of *regional* consultative status, with the difference being the geographical reach of relevant NGOs.[63]

Somewhat different from accreditation criteria are *selection criteria* for NGO participation in operational activities/projects/programmes of the international organizations. These criteria are usually either unwritten/ customary or of recommendatory nature and subject to the discretion of relevant officials of the organization (eg UNEP).[64] Even if formalized, they are usually non-binding and serve as general guidelines for relevant staff of the organization concerned (World Bank).[65] Permanent accreditation is normally not required for NGOs that wish to participate in operational activities of the organization (UNCTAD, ILO, WHO, WIPO, UNEP). The fact that a particular NGO has such status may be taken into account but it is not a prerequisite.

IV. ACCREDITATION PROCEDURES

Procedural rules on NGO accreditation ensure the uniformity, transparency and fairness of the process. In organizations with permanent NGO accreditation schemes (UN ECOSOC, UNCTAD, ILO, WHO, WIPO, UNEP), accreditation procedure typically consists of the following steps:

1. An NGO requests accreditation and submits to the international organization concerned the required documents (that allow verification of whether the NGO meets the accreditation criteria) and/or a completed questionnaire.[66]
2. The relevant unit of the secretariat of the organization concerned assesses the application on a technical level. If the secretariat does not find manifest inconsistencies with accreditation criteria, it transmits the application—usually in the form an information note summarizing the data on the NGO concerned—to the organization's accrediting (intergovernmental) organ.
3. The accrediting organ assesses the application and takes a decision on granting a particular status. At this stage, deliberations tend to be less technical and more political, compared to the secretariat stage.

As an exception, the full procedure, including the final decision, may be completed by the organization's secretariat without any involvement of an

---

[63] See above, pp 70–2 (ILO).
[64] See above, p 133 (UNEP).
[65] See above, pp 167–9 (World Bank).
[66] Exceptionally, the WHO requires a minimum of two years of operational collaboration before an application (this practice is soon to be phased out). See above, pp 112–14 (WHO).

intergovernmental organ. For example, in UNEP, the power to accredit NGOs formally lies with the Governing Council. However, in practice, the latter is not involved in the process. The final decision is made by the secretariat.[67] In organizations that have ad hoc, as opposed to permanent, accreditation/registration schemes (WTO, World Bank, IMF), accreditation is also typically carried out by the secretariats. Their intergovernmental organs do not play a role.[68] The ILO and UNCTAD combine the two approaches. In the ILO, the more important general or regional consultative status is granted by the Governing Body, while the Director-General has the power to include NGOs into the Special List, a less privileged type of status.[69] UNCTAD has a similar system.[70]

In a number of organizations, there is a smaller intergovernmental body between the secretariat and the principal organ formally authorized to accredit NGOs (such as the NGO Committee of the UN ECOSOC; the NGO Committee of WHO; the Bureau of the Trade and Development Board of UNCTAD).[71] This smaller body reviews NGOs' applications (initially processed by the secretariat) and takes decisions on accreditation, while the principal organ simply 'rubberstamps' these decisions. Such practice may be explained by the reluctance of principal intergovernmental organs to 'waste time' deliberating these issues. They prefer to outsource the job to a smaller, although still intergovernmental, body created for this purpose.

In most organizations, the accreditation procedure takes between six months and one year from the date of application to the date of granting (or refusal to grant) of the relevant status, provided that the NGO submits all required documents and information. At WHO, the procedure takes three or even four years due to the mandatory requirement of a minimum two-year operational collaboration before granting the 'official relations' status, but this is exceptional. Besides, the mentioned WHO system is being reformed in order to simplify the process.[72]

NGOs are rarely given an opportunity to speak, or even to be present, at the deliberations concerning the matter of their accreditation. The contrary practice of the NGO Committee of the UN ECOSOC is exceptional.[73] Also, there is no right of appeal in case of a negative decision. However, nothing precludes rejected NGOs to reapply subsequently, although sometimes a minimum period of time must elapse between applications (eg WHO).[74]

---

[67] See above, p 128 (UNEP).
[68] See above, p 196 (WTO), p 163 (World Bank and IMF).
[69] See above, pp 75–8 (ILO).
[70] See above, p 64 (UNCTAD).
[71] See above, pp 21, 36–9 (UN ECOSOC), pp 115–16 (WHO) and p 64 (UNCTAD).
[72] See above, pp 112–16 (WHO).
[73] See above, p 38 (UN ECOSOC).
[74] See above, p 116 (WHO).

V. MONITORING NGOS

The issue of monitoring NGOs arises because international organizations need, first, to ensure that accredited NGOs continue to satisfy relevant accreditation criteria, and, secondly, to prevent abuses of NGOs' preferential status. The methods to achieve these purposes are two-fold:

- checking the relevant parameters of accredited NGOs by requiring NGOs to report periodically to the organization; and
- suspending or withdrawing accreditation of the NGO in case of abuse.

Most international organizations have not put relevant mechanisms in place. This may be because preventing abuse and ensuring continued conformity with the accreditation requirements is not perceived as important and/or feasible in view of the resource constraints confronting the international organizations concerned. For obvious reasons, organizations, which have a system of ad hoc accreditation/registration, instead of permanent accreditation schemes (WTO, World Bank, IMF), do not need to monitor NGOs with the help of the mentioned instruments. Of the organizations that have permanent NGO accreditation schemes, only UN ECOSOC and WHO have formal rules that provide for monitoring of NGOs.[75] Both UN ECOSOC and WHO require NGOs to submit periodic reports: every four years in the case of UN ECOSOC and every three years in the case of WHO.

ECOSOC and WHO are also the only organizations (of those examined) that have established formal grounds for withdrawal and suspension of the NGO preferential status. The research demonstrated that no NGO has been deprived of its status because of the information submitted in its report, and, moreover, that the information in the reports is hardly ever verified. Rare cases of suspension and withdrawal of status have occurred due to incidents involving NGOs and on the basis of complaints of individual governments alleging, for example, that certain NGOs are involved in illegal activities. At the same time, a *failure* to submit a report may serve as a ground to withdraw accreditation. Generally, however, although a reporting requirement may be the most cost-effective way for international organizations to ensure continued conformity with accreditation criteria, it is probably not the most efficient way.

The four other international organizations with permanent NGO accreditation schemes (UNCTAD, ILO, WIPO, UNEP) do not have rules on reporting or on withdrawal/suspension of accreditation. However, the ILO, for example, requires all NGOs on its Special List to submit each year a

---

[75] See above, pp 40–4 (UN ECOSOC) and pp 116–18 (WHO).

copy of their annual reports.[76] Although these reports are not examined, those NGOs which do not fulfil this obligation are considered for exclusion from the Special List as not being active in the relevant field any longer.

As far as withdrawal/suspension of accreditation is concerned, some consider that even in the absence of explicit legal rules, the power to withdraw/suspend accreditation is an implied power of the accrediting organ (UNCTAD, UNEP).[77] This understanding stems from the fact that only those NGOs that at all times satisfy the accreditation criteria can have the status of an accredited NGO. If a particular NGO ceases to conform to one or more criteria, the accreditation may be withdrawn or suspended. At the same time, aside from UN ECOSOC and WHO, where the power to disaccredit is explicitly provided for, the present study has not revealed any cases where an international organization has deprived a previously accredited NGO of its status for the reason of its non-conformity with the accreditation criteria.

All six organizations with permanent NGO accreditation schemes monitor accredited NGOs to see whether the latter are still active. In most organizations, the practice is to exclude NGOs from relevant accreditation lists if contact with them has been lost for a number of years (usually, three to four years) and there is no indication that the NGO is still in existence.[78]

VI. CONCLUDING REMARKS

The inquiry into the rules on, and practices of, NGO involvement in the activities of international organizations has shown that the relevant arrangements differ considerably from organization to organization. The differences concern the content, binding nature and the degree of detail of the relevant rules, the extent to which practice conforms to the rules, and further, the forms and intensity of NGO involvement, participatory rights granted to NGOs, applicable accreditation criteria and procedures, as well as the rules on monitoring NGOs. Many of these differences are explained by the specific characteristics of the international organizations concerned, and in particular their respective objectives and activities as well as their 'corporate/organizational cultures' with respect to openness, inclusiveness and transparency of their processes. However, in addition to many differences, the present study has also identified trends and features with regard to NGO involvement that all or, in any case, many of the examined international organizations share.

[76] See above, p 82 (ILO).
[77] See above, p 66 (UNCTAD) and p 133 (UNEP).
[78] See above, eg, p 66 (UNCTAD) and p 95 (WIPO).

While a harmonization of legal arrangements for NGO involvement may be inappropriate in view of differing needs, international organizations would generally benefit from a further 'legalization' of NGO involvement. Providing for explicit rules on engagement with NGOs would contribute to the predictability and legitimacy of this engagement and prevent arbitrariness. International organizations should learn from each other's legal arrangements relating to NGO involvement in order to build the kind of relationship with NGOs that maximizes the benefits and minimizes the drawbacks of NGO involvement, discussed in chapter 1 of this study.[79] The differences and similarities in the relevant legal arrangements of the international organizations examined in this study may serve as a source of inspiration for the international community when it pursues a further 'legalization' of the involvement of NGOs in global governance.

---

[79] See above, p 11–13.

Appendix I

UN ECOSOC

CHARTER OF THE UNITED NATIONS

> **Signed on 26 June 1945**
> Source: 892 UNTS 119

[excerpt]
Chapter X
Economic and Social Council

Article 71
The Economic and Social Council may make suitable arrangements for consultation with non-governmental organizations which are concerned with matters within its competence. Such arrangements may be made with international organizations and, where appropriate, with national organizations after consultation with the Member of the United Nations concerned.

RESOLUTION 1996/31 ON CONSULTATIVE RELATIONSHIP BETWEEN THE UNITED NATIONS AND NON-GOVERNMENTAL ORGANIZATIONS

> **Adopted by UN Economic and Social Council**
> **5 July 1996**
> **Document number: ECOSOC Resolution 1996/31**
> Source: <http://www.un.org/documents/ecosoc/res/1996/eres 1996-31.htm>

The Economic and Social Council,
Recalling Article 71 of the Charter of the United Nations,
Recalling also its resolution 1993/80 of 30 July 1993, in which it requested a general review of arrangements for consultation with non-governmental organizations, with a view to updating, if necessary, Council resolution 1296 (XLIV) of 23 May 1968, as well as introducing coherence in the rules governing the participation of non-governmental organizations in international conferences convened by the United Nations, and also an examination of ways and means of improving practical arrangements for the work

of the Committee on Non-Governmental Organizations and the Non-Governmental Organizations Section of the Secretariat,

Recalling further its decision 1995/304 of 26 July 1995,

Confirming the need to take into account the full diversity of the non-governmental organizations at the national, regional and international levels,

Acknowledging the breadth of non-governmental organizations' expertise and the capacity of non-governmental organizations to support the work of the United Nations,

Taking into account the changes in the non-governmental sector, including the emergence of a large number of national and regional organizations,

Calling upon the governing bodies of the relevant organizations, bodies and specialized agencies of the United Nations system to examine the principles and practices relating to their consultations with non-governmental organizations and to take action, as appropriate, to promote coherence in the light of the provisions of the present resolution,

Approves the following update of the arrangements set out in its resolution 1296 (XLIV) of 23 May 1968:

ARRANGEMENTS FOR CONSULTATION WITH NON-GOVERNMENTAL ORGANIZATIONS

Part I
Principles to be Applied to the Establishment of Consultative Relations
The following principles shall be applied in establishing consultative relations with non-governmental organizations:

1. The organization shall be concerned with matters falling within the competence of the Economic and Social Council and its subsidiary bodies.
2. The aims and purposes of the organization shall be in conformity with the spirit, purposes and principles of the Charter of the United Nations.
3. The organization shall undertake to support the work of the United Nations and to promote knowledge of its principles and activities, in accordance with its own aims and purposes and the nature and scope of its competence and activities.
4. Except where expressly stated otherwise, the term 'organization' shall refer to non-governmental organizations at the national, subregional, regional or international levels.
5. Consultative relationships may be established with international, regional, subregional and national organizations, in conformity with the Charter of the United Nations and the principles and criteria estab-

lished under the present resolution. The Committee, in considering applications for consultative status, should ensure, to the extent possible, participation of non-governmental organizations from all regions, and particularly from developing countries, in order to help achieve a just, balanced, effective and genuine involvement of non-governmental organizations from all regions and areas of the world. The Committee shall also pay particular attention to non-governmental organizations that have special expertise or experience upon which the Council may wish to draw.

6. Greater participation of non-governmental organizations from developing countries in international conferences convened by the United Nations should be encouraged.

7. Greater involvement of non-governmental organizations from countries with economies in transition should be encouraged.

8. Regional, subregional and national organizations, including those affiliated to an international organization already in status, may be admitted provided that they can demonstrate that their programme of work is of direct relevance to the aims and purposes of the United Nations and, in the case of national organizations, after consultation with the Member State concerned. The views expressed by the Member State, if any, shall be communicated to the non-governmental organization concerned, which shall have the opportunity to respond to those views through the Committee on Non-Governmental Organizations.

9. The organization shall be of recognized standing within the particular field of its competence or of a representative character. Where there exist a number of organizations with similar objectives, interests and basic views in a given field, they may, for the purposes of consultation with the Council, form a joint committee or other body authorized to carry on such consultation for the group as a whole.

10. The organization shall have an established headquarters, with an executive officer. It shall have a democratically adopted constitution, a copy of which shall be deposited with the Secretary-General of the United Nations, and which shall provide for the determination of policy by a conference, congress or other representative body, and for an executive organ responsible to the policy-making body.

11. The organization shall have authority to speak for its members through its authorized representatives. Evidence of this authority shall be presented, if requested.

12. The organization shall have a representative structure and possess appropriate mechanisms of accountability to its members, who shall exercise effective control over its policies and actions through the exercise of voting rights or other appropriate democratic and transparent decision-making processes. Any such organization that is not established by a

governmental entity or intergovernmental agreement shall be considered a non-governmental organization for the purpose of these arrangements, including organizations that accept members designated by governmental authorities, provided that such membership does not interfere with the free expression of views of the organization.

13. The basic resources of the organization shall be derived in the main part from contributions of the national affiliates or other components or from individual members. Where voluntary contributions have been received, their amounts and donors shall be faithfully revealed to the Council Committee on Non-Governmental Organizations. Where, however, the above criterion is not fulfilled and an organization is financed from other sources, it must explain to the satisfaction of the Committee its reasons for not meeting the requirements laid down in this paragraph. Any financial contribution or other support, direct or indirect, from a Government to the organization shall be openly declared to the Committee through the Secretary-General and fully recorded in the financial and other records of the organization and shall be devoted to purposes in accordance with the aims of the United Nations.

14. In considering the establishment of consultative relations with a non-governmental organization, the Council will take into account whether the field of activity of the organization is wholly or mainly within the field of a specialized agency, and whether or not it could be admitted when it has, or may have, a consultative arrangement with a specialized agency.

15. The granting, suspension and withdrawal of consultative status, as well as the interpretation of norms and decisions relating to this matter, are the prerogative of Member States exercised through the Economic and Social Council and its Committee on Non-Governmental Organizations. A non-governmental organization applying for general or special consultative status or a listing on the Roster shall have the opportunity to respond to any objections being raised in the Committee before the Committee takes its decision.

16. The provisions of the present resolution shall apply to the United Nations regional commissions and their subsidiary bodies *mutatis mutandis*.

17. In recognizing the evolving relationship between the United Nations and non-governmental organizations, the Economic and Social Council, in consultation with the Committee on Non-Governmental Organizations, will consider reviewing the consultative arrangements as and when necessary to facilitate, in the most effective manner possible, the contributions of non-governmental organizations to the work of the United Nations.

Part II

Principles Governing the Nature of the Consultative Arrangements

18. A clear distinction is drawn in the Charter of the United Nations between participation without vote in the deliberations of the Council and the arrangements for consultation. Under Articles 69 and 70, participation is provided for only in the case of States not members of the Council, and of specialized agencies. Article 71, applying to non-governmental organizations, provides for suitable arrangements for consultation. This distinction, deliberately made in the Charter, is fundamental and the arrangements for consultation should not be such as to accord to non-governmental organizations the same rights of participation as are accorded to States not members of the Council and to the specialized agencies brought into relationship with the United Nations.

19. The arrangements should not be such as to overburden the Council or transform it from a body for coordination of policy and action, as contemplated in the Charter, into a general forum for discussion.

20. Decisions on arrangements for consultation should be guided by the principle that consultative arrangements are to be made, on the one hand, for the purpose of enabling the Council or one of its bodies to secure expert information or advice from organizations having special competence in the subjects for which consultative arrangements are made, and, on the other hand, to enable international, regional, sub-regional and national organizations that represent important elements of public opinion to express their views. Therefore, the arrangements for consultation made with each organization should relate to the subjects for which that organization has a special competence or in which it has a special interest. The organizations given consultative status should be limited to those whose activities in fields set out in paragraph 1 above qualify them to make a significant contribution to the work of the Council and should, in sum, as far as possible reflect in a balanced way the major viewpoints or interests in these fields in all areas and regions of the world.

Part III

Establishment of Consultative Relationships

21. In establishing consultative relationships with each organization, regard shall be had to the nature and scope of its activities and to the assistance it may be expected to give to the Council or its subsidiary bodies in carrying out the functions set out in Chapters IX and X of the Charter of the United Nations.

22. Organizations that are concerned with most of the activities of the Council and its subsidiary bodies and can demonstrate to the satisfaction

of the Council that they have substantive and sustained contributions to make to the achievement of the objectives of the United Nations in fields set out in paragraph 1 above, and are closely involved with the economic and social life of the peoples of the areas they represent and whose membership, which should be considerable, is broadly representative of major segments of society in a large number of countries in different regions of the world shall be known as organizations in general consultative status.

23. Organizations that have a special competence in, and are concerned specifically with, only a few of the fields of activity covered by the Council and its subsidiary bodies, and that are known within the fields for which they have or seek consultative status shall be known as organizations in special consultative status.

24. Other organizations that do not have general or special consultative status but that the Council, or the Secretary-General of the United Nations in consultation with the Council or its Committee on Non-Governmental Organizations, considers can make occasional and useful contributions to the work of the Council or its subsidiary bodies or other United Nations bodies within their competence shall be included in a list (to be known as the Roster). This list may also include organizations in consultative status or a similar relationship with a specialized agency or a United Nations body. These organizations shall be available for consultation at the request of the Council or its subsidiary bodies. The fact that an organization is on the Roster shall not in itself be regarded as a qualification for general or special consultative status should an organization seek such status.

25. Organizations to be accorded special consultative status because of their interest in the field of human rights should pursue the goals of promotion and protection of human rights in accordance with the spirit of the Charter of the United Nations, the Universal Declaration of Human Rights and the Vienna Declaration and Programme of Action.

26. Major organizations one of whose primary purposes is to promote the aims, objectives and purposes of the United Nations and a furtherance of the understanding of its work may be accorded consultative status.

Part IV
Consultation with the Council
Provisional agenda

27. The provisional agenda of the Council shall be communicated to organizations in general consultative status and special consultative status and to those on the Roster.

28. Organizations in general consultative status may propose to the

Council Committee on Non-Governmental Organizations that the Committee request the Secretary-General to place items of special interest to the organizations in the provisional agenda of the Council.

Attendance at meetings

29. Organizations in general consultative status and special consultative status may designate authorized representatives to sit as observers at public meetings of the Council and its subsidiary bodies. Those on the Roster may have representatives present at such meetings concerned with matters within their field of competence. These attendance arrangements may be supplemented to include other modalities of participation.

Written statements

30. Written statements relevant to the work of the Council may be submitted by organizations in general consultative status and special consultative status on subjects in which these organizations have a special competence. Such statements shall be circulated by the Secretary-General of the United Nations to the members of the Council, except those statements that have become obsolete, for example, those dealing with matters already disposed of and those that had already been circulated in some other form.

31. The following conditions shall be observed regarding the submission and circulation of such statements:

(a) The written statement shall be submitted in one of the official languages;

(b) It shall be submitted in sufficient time for appropriate consultation to take place between the Secretary-General and the organization before circulation;

(c) The organization shall give due consideration to any comments that the Secretary-General may make in the course of such consultation before transmitting the statement in final form;

(c) A written statement submitted by an organization in general consultative status will be circulated in full if it does not exceed 2,000 words. Where a statement is in excess of 2,000 words, the organizations shall submit a summary which will be circulated or shall supply sufficient copies of the full text in the working languages for distribution. A statement will also be circulated in full, however, upon a specific request of the Council or its Committee on Non-Governmental Organizations;

(e) A written statement submitted by an organization in special consultative status or on the Roster will be circulated in full if it does not exceed 500 words. Where a statement is in excess of 500 words, the organization shall submit a summary which will be circulated; such statements will be circulated in full, however, upon a specific request of the Council or its Committee on Non-Governmental Organizations;

(f) The Secretary-General, in consultation with the President of the Council, or the Council or its Committee on Non-Governmental Organizations, may invite organizations on the Roster to submit written statements. The provisions of subparagraphs (a), (b), (c) and (e) above shall apply to such statements;

(g) A written statement or summary, as the case may be, will be circulated by the Secretary-General in the working languages, and, upon the request of a member of the Council, in any of the official languages.

Oral presentations during meetings

32. (a) The Council Committee on Non-Governmental Organizations shall make recommendations to the Council as to which organizations in general consultative status should make an oral presentation to the Council and on which items they should be heard. Such organizations shall be entitled to make one statement to the Council, subject to the approval of the Council. In the absence of a subsidiary body of the Council with jurisdiction in a major field of interest to the Council and to organizations in special consultative status, the Committee may recommend that organizations in special consultative status be heard by the Council on the subject in its field of interest;

(b) Whenever the Council discusses the substance of an item proposed by a non-governmental organization in general consultative status and included in the agenda of the Council, such an organization shall be entitled to present orally to the Council, as appropriate, an introductory statement of an expository nature. Such an organization may be invited by the President of the Council, with the consent of the relevant body, to make, in the course of the discussion of the item before the Council, an additional statement for purposes of clarification.

Part V
Consultation with Commissions and Other Subsidiary Organs of the Council
Provisional agenda

33. The provisional agenda of sessions of commissions and other subsidiary organs of the Council shall be communicated to organizations in general consultative status and special consultative status and those on the Roster.

34. Organizations in general consultative status may propose items for the provisional agenda of commissions, subject to the following conditions:

    (a) An organization that intends to propose such an item shall inform the Secretary-General of the United Nations at least 63 days before the commencement of the session and before formally proposing an item shall give due consideration to any comments the Secretary-General may make;

    (b) The proposal shall be formally submitted with the relevant basic documentation not later than 49 days before the commencement of the session. The item shall be included in the agenda of the commission if it is adopted by a two-thirds majority of those present and voting.

Attendance at meetings

35. Organizations in general consultative status and special consultative status may designate authorized representatives to sit as observers at public meetings of the commissions and other subsidiary organs of the Council. Organizations on the Roster may have representatives present at such meetings that are concerned with matters within their field of competence. These attendance arrangements may be supplemented to include other modalities of participation.

Written statements

36. Written statements relevant to the work of the commissions or other subsidiary organs may be submitted by organizations in general consultative status and special consultative status on subjects for which these organizations have a special competence. Such statements shall be circulated by the Secretary-General to members of the commission or other subsidiary organs, except those statements that have become obsolete, for example, those dealing with matters already disposed of and those that have already been circulated in some other form to members of the commission or other subsidiary organs.

37. The following conditions shall be observed regarding the submission and circulation of such written statements:

    (a) The written statement shall be submitted in one of the official languages;

    (b) It shall be submitted in sufficient time for appropriate consultation to take place between the Secretary-General and the organization before circulation;

    (c) The organization shall give due consideration to any comments that the Secretary-General may make in the course of such consultation before transmitting the statement in final form;

(d) A written statement submitted by an organization in general consultative status will be circulated in full if it does not exceed 2,000 words. Where a statement is in excess of 2,000 words, the organization shall submit a summary, which will be circulated, or shall supply sufficient copies of the full text in the working languages for distribution. A statement will also be circulated in full, however, upon the specific request of the commission or other subsidiary organs;

(e) A written statement submitted by an organization in special consultative status will be circulated in full if it does not exceed 1,500 words. Where a statement is in excess of 1,500 words, the organization shall submit a summary, which will be circulated, or shall supply sufficient copies of the full text in the working languages for distribution. A statement will also be circulated in full, however, upon the specific request of the commission or other subsidiary organs;

(f) The Secretary-General, in consultation with the chairman of the relevant commission or other subsidiary organ, or the commission or other subsidiary organ itself, may invite organizations on the Roster to submit written statements. The provisions in subparagraphs (a), (b), (c) and (e) above shall apply to such statements;

(g) A written statement or summary, as the case may be, will be circulated by the Secretary-General in the working languages and, upon the request of a member of the commission or other subsidiary organ, in any of the official languages.

Oral presentations during meetings

38. (a) The commission or other subsidiary organs may consult with organizations in general consultative status and special consultative status either directly or through a committee or committees established for the purpose. In all cases, such consultations may be arranged upon the request of the organization;

(b) On the recommendation of the Secretary-General and at the request of the commission or other subsidiary organs, organizations on the Roster may also be heard by the commission or other subsidiary organs.

Special studies

39. Subject to the relevant rules of procedure on financial implications, a commission or other subsidiary organ may recommend that an organization that has special competence in a particular field should undertake specific studies or investigations or prepare specific papers for the commission. The limitations of paragraphs 37 (d) and (e) above shall not apply in this case.

Part VI

Consultations with Ad Hoc Committees of the Council

40. The arrangements for consultation between ad hoc committees of the Council authorized to meet between sessions of the Council and organizations in general consultative status and special consultative status and on the Roster shall follow those approved for commissions of the Council, unless the Council or the committee decides otherwise.

Part VII

Participation of Non-Governmental Organizations in International Conferences Convened by the United Nations and their Preparatory Process

41. Where non-governmental organizations have been invited to participate in an international conference convened by the United Nations, their accreditation is the prerogative of Member States, exercised through the respective preparatory committee. Such accreditation should be preceded by an appropriate process to determine their eligibility.

42. Non-governmental organizations in general consultative status, special consultative status and on the Roster, that express their wish to attend the relevant international conferences convened by the United Nations and the meetings of the preparatory bodies of the said conferences shall as a rule be accredited for participation. Other non-governmental organizations wishing to be accredited may apply to the secretariat of the conference for this purpose in accordance with the following requirements.

43. The secretariat of the conference shall be responsible for the receipt and preliminary evaluation of requests from non-governmental organizations for accreditation to the conference and its preparatory process. In the discharge of its functions, the secretariat of the conference shall work in close cooperation and coordination with the Non-Governmental Organizations Section of the Secretariat, and shall be guided by the relevant provisions of Council resolution 1296 (XLIV) as updated.

44. All such applications must be accompanied by information on the competence of the organization and the relevance of its activities to the work of the conference and its preparatory committee, with an indication of the particular areas of the conference agenda and preparations to which such competence and relevance pertain, and should include, inter alia, the following information:

(a) The purpose of the organization;

(b) Information as to the programmes and activities of the organization in areas relevant to the conference and its preparatory process and the country or countries in which they are carried out. Non-governmental organizations seeking accreditation shall be asked to confirm their interest in the goals and objectives of the conference;

(c) Confirmation of the activities of the organization at the national, regional or international level;

(d) Copies of the annual or other reports of the organization with financial statements, and a list of financial sources and contributions, including governmental contributions;

(e) A list of members of the governing body of the organization and their countries of nationality;

(f) A description of the membership of the organization, indicating the total number of members, the names of organizations that are members and their geographical distribution;

(g) A copy of the constitution and/or by-laws of the organization.

45. In the evaluation of the relevance of applications of non-governmental organizations for accreditation to the conference and its preparatory process, it is agreed that a determination shall be made based on their background and involvement in the subject areas of the conference.

46. The secretariat shall publish and disseminate to Member States on a periodic basis the updated list of applications received. Member States may submit comments on any of the applications on the list 14 days from receipt of the above-mentioned list by Member States. The comments of Member States shall be communicated to the non-governmental organization concerned, which shall have the opportunity to respond.

47. In cases where the secretariat believes, on the basis of the information provided in accordance with the present resolution, that the organization has established its competence and the relevance of its activities to the work of the preparatory committee, it shall recommend to the preparatory committee that the organization be accredited. In cases where the secretariat does not recommend the granting of accreditation, it shall make available to the preparatory committee its reasons for not doing so. The secretariat should ensure that its recommendations are available to members of the preparatory committee at least one week prior to the start of each session. The secretariat must notify such applicants of the reasons for non-recommendation and provide an opportunity to respond to objections and furnish additional information as may be required.

48. The preparatory committee shall decide on all recommendations for accreditation within 24 hours after the recommendations of the secretariat have been taken up by the preparatory committee in plenary meeting. In the event of a decision not being taken within this period, interim accreditation shall be accorded until such time as a decision is taken.

49. A non-governmental organization that has been granted accreditation

to attend a session of the preparatory committee, including related preparatory meetings of regional commissions, may attend all its future sessions, as well as the conference itself.

50. In recognition of the intergovernmental nature of the conference and its preparatory process, active participation of non-governmental organizations therein, while welcome, does not entail a negotiating role.

51. The non-governmental organizations accredited to the international conference may be given, in accordance with established United Nations practice and at the discretion of the chairperson and the consent of the body concerned, an opportunity to briefly address the preparatory committee and the conference in plenary meetings and their subsidiary bodies.

52. Non-governmental organizations accredited to the conference may make written presentations during the preparatory process in the official languages of the United Nations as they deem appropriate. Those written presentations shall not be issued as official documents except in accordance with United Nations rules of procedure.

53. Non-governmental organizations without consultative status that participate in international conferences and wish to obtain consultative status later on should apply through the normal procedures established under Council resolution 1296 (XLIV) as updated. Recognizing the importance of the participation of non-governmental organizations that attend a conference in the follow-up process, the Committee on Non-Governmental Organizations, in considering their application, shall draw upon the documents already submitted by that organization for accreditation to the conference and any additional information submitted by the non-governmental organization supporting its interest, relevance and capacity to contribute to the implementation phase. The Committee shall review such applications as expeditiously as possible so as to allow participation of the respective organization in the implementation phase of the conference. In the interim, the Economic and Social Council shall decide on the participation of non-governmental organizations accredited to an international conference in the work of the relevant functional commission on the follow-up to and implementation of that conference.

54. The suspension and withdrawal of the accreditation of non-governmental organizations to United Nations international conferences at all stages shall be guided by the relevant provisions of the present resolution.

Part VIII
Suspension and Withdrawal of Consultative Status

55. Organizations granted consultative status by the Council and those on the Roster shall conform at all times to the principles governing the

establishment and nature of their consultative relations with the Council. In periodically reviewing the activities of non-governmental organizations on the basis of the reports submitted under paragraph 61 (c) below and other relevant information, the Council Committee on Non-Governmental Organizations shall determine the extent to which the organizations have complied with the principles governing consultative status and have contributed to the work of the Council, and may recommend to the Council suspension of or exclusion from consultative status of organizations that have not met the requirements for consultative status as set forth in the present resolution.

56. In cases where the Committee on Non-Governmental Organizations has decided to recommend that the general or special consultative status of a non-governmental organization or its listing on the Roster be suspended or withdrawn, the non-governmental organization concerned shall be given written reasons for that decision and shall have an opportunity to present its response for appropriate consideration by the Committee as expeditiously as possible.

57. The consultative status of non-governmental organizations with the Economic and Social Council and the listing of those on the Roster shall be suspended [for] up to three years or withdrawn in the following cases:

   (a) If an organization, either directly or through its affiliates or representatives acting on its behalf, clearly abuses its status by engaging in a pattern of acts contrary to the purposes and principles of the Charter of the United Nations including unsubstantiated or politically motivated acts against Member States of the United Nations incompatible with those purposes and principles;

   (b) If there exists substantiated evidence of influence from proceeds resulting from internationally recognized criminal activities such as the illicit drugs trade, money-laundering or the illegal arms trade;

   (c) If, within the preceding three years, an organization did not make any positive or effective contribution to the work of the United Nations and, in particular, of the Council or its commissions or other subsidiary organs.

58. The consultative status of organizations in general consultative status and special consultative status and the listing of those on the Roster shall be suspended or withdrawn by the decision of the Economic and Social Council on the recommendation of its Committee on Non-Governmental Organizations.

59. An organization whose consultative status or whose listing on the Roster is withdrawn may be entitled to reapply for consultative status or for inclusion on the Roster not sooner than three years after the effective date of such withdrawal.

Part IX
Council Committee on Non-Governmental Organizations
60. The members of the Committee on Non-Governmental Organizations shall be elected by the Council on the basis of equitable geographical representation, in accordance with the relevant Council resolutions and decision (1/) and rules of procedure of the Council (2/). The Committee shall elect its Chairman and other officers as necessary.
61. The functions of the Committee shall include the following:
   (a)   The Committee shall be responsible for regular monitoring of the evolving relationship between non-governmental organizations and the United Nations. With a view to fulfilling this responsibility, the Committee shall hold, before each of its sessions, and at other times as necessary, consultations with organizations in consultative status to discuss questions of interest to the Committee or to the organizations relating to the relationship between the non-governmental organizations and the United Nations. A report on such consultations shall be transmitted to the Council for appropriate action;
   (b)   The Committee shall hold its regular session before the substantive session of the Council each year and preferably before the sessions of functional commissions of the Council to consider applications for general consultative status and special consultative status and for listing on the Roster made by non-governmental organizations and requests for changes in status, and to make recommendations thereon to the Council. Upon approval by the Council, the Committee may hold other meetings as required to fulfil its mandated responsibilities. Organizations shall give due consideration to any comments on technical matters that the Secretary-General of the United Nations may make in receiving such applications for the Committee. The Committee shall consider at each such session applications received by the Secretary-General not later than 1 June of the preceding year, on which sufficient data have been distributed to the members of the Committee not later than six weeks before the applications are to be considered. Transitional arrangements, if possible, may be made during the current year only. Reapplication by an organization for status, or a request for a change in status, shall be considered by the Committee at the earliest at its first session in the second year following the session at which the substance of the previous application or request was considered, unless at the time of such consideration it was decided otherwise;
   (c)   Organizations in general consultative status and special consultative status shall submit to the Council Committee on Non-

Governmental Organizations through the Secretary-General every fourth year a brief report of their activities, specifically as regards the support they have given to the work of the United Nations. Based on findings of the Committee's examination of the report and other relevant information, the Committee may recommend to the Council any reclassification in status of the organization concerned as it deems appropriate. However, under exceptional circumstances, the Committee may ask for such a report from an individual organization in general consultative status or special consultative status or on the Roster, between the regular reporting dates;

(d) The Committee may consult, in connection with sessions of the Council or at such other times as it may decide, with organizations in general consultative status and special consultative status on matters within their competence, other than items in the agenda of the Council, on which the Council or the Committee or the organization requests consultation. The Committee shall report to the Council on such consultations;

(e) The Committee may consult, in connection with any particular session of the Council, with organizations in general consultative status and special consultative status on matters within the competence of the organizations concerning specific items already in the provisional agenda of the Council on which the Council or the Committee or the organization requests consultation, and shall make recommendations as to which organizations, subject to the provisions of paragraph 32 (a) above, should be heard by the Council or the appropriate committee and regarding which subjects should be heard. The Committee shall report to the Council on such consultations;

(f) The Committee shall consider matters concerning non-governmental organizations that may be referred to it by the Council or by commissions;

(g) The Committee shall consult with the Secretary-General, as appropriate, on matters affecting the consultative arrangements under Article 71 of the Charter, and arising therefrom;

(h) An organization that applies for consultative status should attest that it has been in existence for at least two years as at the date of receipt of the application by the Secretariat. Evidence of such existence shall be furnished to the Secretariat.

62. The Committee, in considering a request from a non-governmental organization in general consultative status that an item be placed in the agenda of the Council, shall take into account, among other things:

(a)   The adequacy of the documentation submitted by the organization;
(b)   The extent to which it is considered that the item lends itself to early and constructive action by the Council;
(c)   The possibility that the item might be more appropriately dealt with elsewhere than in the Council.

63. Any decision by the Council Committee on Non-Governmental Organizations not to grant a request submitted by a non-governmental organization in general consultative status that an item be placed in the provisional agenda of the Council shall be considered final unless the Council decides otherwise.

Part X
Consultation with the Secretariat

64. The Secretariat should be so organized as to enable it to carry out the duties assigned to it concerning the consultative arrangements and the accreditation of non-governmental organizations to United Nations international conferences as set forth in the present resolution.

65. All organizations in consultative relationship shall be able to consult with officers of the appropriate sections of the Secretariat on matters in which there is a mutual interest or a mutual concern. Such consultation shall be upon the request of the non-governmental organization or upon the request of the Secretary-General of the United Nations.

66. The Secretary-General may request organizations in general consultative status and special consultative status and those on the Roster to carry out specific studies or prepare specific papers, subject to the relevant financial regulations.

67. The Secretary-General shall be authorized, within the means at his disposal, to offer to non-governmental organizations in consultative relationship facilities that include:
(a)   Prompt and efficient distribution of such documents of the Council and its subsidiary bodies as shall in the judgement of the Secretary-General be appropriate;
(b)   Access to the press documentation services provided by the United Nations;
(c)   Arrangement of informal discussions on matters of special interest to groups or organizations;
(d)   Use of the libraries of the United Nations;
(e)   Provision of accommodation for conferences or smaller meetings of consultative organizations on the work of the Economic and Social Council;
(f)   Appropriate seating arrangements and facilities for obtaining documents during public meetings of the General Assembly dealing with matters in the economic, social and related fields.

Part XI
Secretariat Support

68. Adequate Secretariat support shall be required for fulfilment of the mandate defined for the Committee on Non-Governmental Organizations with respect to carrying out the wider range of activities in which the enhanced involvement of non-governmental organizations is envisaged. The Secretary-General is requested to provide the necessary resources for this purpose and to take steps for improving the coordination within the Secretariat of units dealing with non-governmental organizations.

69. The Secretary-General is requested to make every effort to enhance and streamline as appropriate Secretariat support arrangements, and to improve practical arrangements on such matters as greater use of modern information and communication technology, establishment of an integrated database of non-governmental organizations, wide and timely dissemination of information on meetings, distribution of documentation, provision of access and transparent, simple and streamlined procedures for the attendance of non-governmental organizations in United Nations meetings, and to facilitate their broad-based participation.

70. The Secretary-General is requested to make the present resolution widely known, through proper channels, to facilitate the involvement of non-governmental organizations from all regions and areas of the world.

Notes

1/ Council resolutions 1099 (XL) and 1981/50 and Council decision 1995/304.

2/ Rule 80 of the rules of procedure of the Council.

Appendix II

UNCTAD

RESOLUTION OF THE UNITED NATIONS GENERAL ASSEMBLY
1995 (XIX), 'ESTABLISHMENT OF THE UNITED NATIONS
CONFERENCE ON TRADE AND DEVELOPMENT AS AN ORGAN
OF THE GENERAL ASSEMBLY'

> **Adopted by the UN General Assembly**
> **30 December 1964**
> **Document number: A/RES/1995 (XIX)**
> Source: <http://daccessdds.un.org/doc/RESOLUTION/GEN/NR0/
> 210/ 89/IMG/NR021089.pdf?OpenElement>

[excerpt]

11. The [Trade and Development] Board may make arrangements for representatives of inter governmental bodies ... to participate, without vote, in its deliberations and in those of the subsidiary bodies and working groups established by it. Such participation may also be offered to non-governmental organizations concerned with matters of trade and of trade as related to development.

RULES OF PROCEDURE OF THE TRADE AND DEVELOPMENT
BOARD

> **Adopted by the Trade and Development Board of UNCTAD**
> **27 April 1965**
> **Document number: TD/B/16/Rev.4**

[excerpt]
(xv) Observers for non-governmental organizations

Rule 77
1. Non-governmental organizations concerned with matters of trade and of trade as related to development, referred to in paragraph 11 of General Assembly resolution 1995 (XIX), may designate representatives to sit as observers at public meetings of the Board, its sessional commit-

tees and subsidiary organs. The Secretary-General of the Conference, in consultation with the Bureau of the Board, shall from time to time prepare a list of such organizations for the approval of the Board. Upon the invitation of the President or Chairman, as the case may be, and subject to the approval of the Board or of the subsidiary organ concerned, non-governmental organizations may make oral statements on matters within the scope of their activities.

2. Written statements provided by non-governmental bodies referred to in paragraph 1 above, related to items on the agenda of the Board or of its subsidiary organs, shall be circulated by the secretariat to the members of the Board or the subsidiary organ concerned.

RULES OF PROCEDURE OF THE CONFERENCE

> **Adopted by the Quadrennial Conference of UNCTAD**
> **1 February 1968**
> **Document number: TD/63/Rev.2**

[excerpt]

Rule 81 'Observers from Non-Governmental Organizations'

1. Non-governmental organizations concerned with matters of trade and of trade as related to development, referred to in paragraph 11 of General Assembly resolution 1995 (XIX) and included in the list referred to in the *Arrangements for the participation of non-governmental organizations in the activities of the UNCTAD*, may designate representatives to sit as observers at public meetings of the Conference, its main committees and other sessional bodies. Upon the invitation of the President of the Conference or the Chairman of the main committee or of the sessional body, as the case may be, and subject to the approval of the conference or of the sessional body concerned, non-governmental organizations may make oral statements on matters within the scope of their activities.

2. Written statements provided by non-governmental bodies referred to in paragraph 1 above, related to items on the agenda of the Conference shall be circulated by the secretariat to the members of the Conference.

RULES OF PROCEDURE OF THE MAIN COMMITTEES OF THE
TRADE AND DEVELOPMENT BOARD

Adopted by Trade and Development Board of UNCTAD 8 September 1978 Document number: TD/B/740

[excerpt]

Rule 75
1. Non-governmental organizations concerned with matters of trade and of trade as related to development, referred to in paragraph 11 of General Assembly resolution 1995 (XIX) and included in the list referred to in rule [77] of the rules of procedure of the Board, may designate representatives to sit as observers at public meetings of the Committee, its sessional committees and subsidiary bodies. Upon the invitation of the Chairman, and subject to the approval of the body concerned, non-governmental organizations may make oral statements on matters within the scope of their activities.
2. Written statements provided by non-governmental organizations referred to in paragraph 1 of this rule, related to items on the agenda of the Committee or of its subsidiary bodies, shall be circulated by the secretariat to the members of the Committee or the subsidiary body concerned.

ARRANGEMENTS FOR THE PARTICIPATION OF NON-
GOVERNMENTAL ORGANIZATIONS IN THE ACTIVITIES OF THE
UNITED NATIONS CONFERENCE ON TRADE AND
DEVELOPMENT

Adopted by the Trade and Development Board of UNCTAD 20 September 1968[1] Document number: Board Decision 43 (VII)

I. Criteria to be Applied in the Establishment of the List of Non-Governmental Organizations Provided for in Rule 79[2] of the Rules of Procedure of the Trade and Development Board
1. The organization shall be concerned with matters of trade and of trade as related to development. In this connection the organization shall provide the necessary evidence that it is concerned with matters falling

---

[1] Replacing Board decision 14 (II) of 7 September 1965.
[2] As of March 1989, replace Rule 79 of the Board by Rule 77 (TD/B/16/Rev.4).

within the terms of the functions which devolve upon the United Nations Conference on Trade and Development (UNCTAD) under General Assembly resolution 1995 (XIX) of 30 December 1964.

2. In considering an application from a non-governmental organization under rule 79 of the rules of procedure the Secretary-General of the Conference and the Bureau of the Board shall be guided by the principle that relationship arrangements are to be made, on the one hand, for the purpose of enabling the Board and/or its subsidiary bodies to secure information or advice from organizations having special competence in the subjects for which relationship arrangements are made, and, on the other hand, to enable organizations which represent important elements of public opinion to express their views. Therefore, the participation of each organization in the activities of UNCTAD should involve only the subjects for which that organization has a special competence or in which it has special interest.

3. The aims and purposes of the organization shall be in conformity with the spirit, purposes and principles of the Charter of the United Nations.

4. The organization shall undertake to support the work of UNCTAD and to promote knowledge of its principles and activities, in accordance with its own aims and purposes and the nature and scope of its competence and activities.

5. The organization shall be of recognized standing and shall represent a substantial proportion of the organized persons within the particular field in which it operates. To meet this requirement, a group of organizations may be represented by a joint committee or other body authorized to carry on consultations for the group as a whole. It is understood that when a minority opinion develops on a particular point within such a liaison committee, it will be presented to UNCTAD along with the opinion of the majority.

6. The organization shall have an established headquarters with an executive officer. It shall have a conference, convention or other policy-making body. In submitting its application under rule 79, the organization shall indicate the name of the executive officer, or of its authorized representative who shall be in charge of maintaining liaison with the Secretary-General of UNCTAD.

7. The organization shall have authority to speak for its members through its authorized representatives. Evidence of this authority shall be presented, if requested.

8. The organization shall be international in its structure, with members who exercise voting rights in relation to the policies or action of the international organizations. Any international organization which is not established by intergovernmental agreement shall be considered as a non-governmental organization for the purposes of rule 79.

9. An international organization which is a member of a committee or of a group composed of international organizations which has already been included in the list provided for in rule 79 shall not normally be included in the list.

10. In considering the inclusion of a non-governmental organization in the list provided for under rule 79, the Secretary-General of UNCTAD and the Bureau of the Board will take into account whether or not the field of activity of the organization is wholly or mainly within the field of a specialized agency or an intergovernmental organization of those referred to in paragraph 18 of General Assembly resolution 1995 (XIX).

11. In including a non-governmental organization in the list provided for in rule 79 regard shall be had to the nature and scope of its activities and to the assistance that may be expected by UNCTAD in carrying out the functions set out in General Assembly resolution 1995 (XIX).

12. In establishing the list provided for in rule 79, the Board shall distinguish between:
   (a) Organizations which exercise functions, and have a basic interest, in most of the activities of the Board and which would, therefore, be entitled to the rights provided for in rule 79 of the Board at meetings of the Board, and under rule 78 of the Committees at meetings of all the Committees (to be known as organizations in the General Category); and
   (b) Organizations which have a special competence in, and are concerned with, specific matters falling within the terms of reference of one or two Committees or of the Board itself and which would, therefore, be entitled to the rights provided for in rule 78 of the rules of procedure of the Committees concerned, and, when the Board has these specific matters under consideration, the rights provided under rule 79 of the Board (to be known as organizations in the Special Category)

II. Procedures to be Applied by the Bureau in Discharging its Functions Under Rule 79 of the Rules of Procedure of the Board

1. The Bureau shall meet upon the recommendation of the Secretary-General of UNCTAD whenever matters falling within the terms of rule 79 must be considered. Whenever possible, the Secretary-General of UNCTAD shall also consult the members of the Bureau by mail.

2. The Bureau shall consider the applications which have been submitted to the Secretary-General of UNCTAD by non-governmental organizations as well as the explanatory memoranda and other documentation that the organizations may have attached to their applications. In this connection, due account shall be taken of the recommendations and

explanatory notes submitted by the Secretary-General regarding each application.

3. Upon the basis of the documentation submitted under paragraph 2 above and of the criteria for the establishment of relationship arrangements with non-governmental organizations, the Bureau shall then give advice to the Secretary-General of UNCTAD as to which non-governmental organizations should be included in the list provided for in rule 79. If required, the matter shall be put to the vote and decided by majority vote of the members of the Bureau present and voting. Any recommendation of the Bureau against the inclusion of a non-governmental organization in the list shall be considered as final.

III. Arrangements for the Association of National Non-Governmental Organizations with the Activities of UNCTAD (the Register)

National non-governmental organizations of recognized standing which are deemed to have a significant contribution to make to the work of UNCTAD may be entered by the Secretary-General of UNCTAD in a Register established for that purpose. Entry in the Register of a national organization shall be subject to prior consultation with the member State concerned.

IV. Secretariat Relations with Non-Governmental Organizations

The Secretary-General of UNCTAD shall be authorized, within the means at his disposal, to offer to non-governmental organizations which are included in the list provided for in rule 79 (ie non-governmental organizations in the General and Special Categories) and to non-governmental organizations entered in the Register referred to in part III above, the following facilities:

1. Distribution of such documents of the Board and its subsidiary organs as shall in the judgement of the Secretary-General of UNCTAD be appropriate.
2. Access to the press documentation of UNCTAD, and, periodically, to such other public information material relating to the activities of UNCTAD as may be considered appropriate.
3. Arrangements for informal discussions of matters of special interest to groups or organizations.

V. Application of Rule 79 of the Board and Rule 78 of the Committees of the Board

For the purposes of applying rule 79 of the Board and rule 78 of the Committees of the Board only non-governmental organizations admitted to either the General or the Special Category provided for in part I, paragraph 12, above, shall be deemed to be included in the list referred to in those rules and, consequently, to be entitled to the rights set out therein.

172nd Plenary Meeting,
20 September 1968

Appendix III

ILO

CONSTITUTION OF THE INTERNATIONAL LABOUR
ORGANIZATION

Adopted by the Versailles Peace Conference in April 1919

[excerpt]

Chapter I

Organization

Article 12
3. The International Labour Organization may make suitable arrangements for such consultation as it may think desirable with recognized non-governmental international organizations, including international organizations of employers, workers, agriculturists and co-operators.

REPORT OF THE COMMITTEE ON LEGAL ISSUES AND
INTERNATIONAL LABOUR STANDARDS

Adopted by the Governing Body of the ILO November 2005 Document number: GB.294/9(Rev) Source: <http://www.ilo.org/public/english/standards/relm/gb/docs/ gb294/ pdf/gb-9.pdf>

[Annex V 'Representation of non-governmental international organizations at ILO meetings' (pp.81-89), reproduced below, compiles a number of earlier ILO documents governing the status of NGOs.]

Representation of non-governmental international organizations at ILO meetings
Introductory note
The International Labour Organization distinguishes between several different types of non-governmental international organization:
  – organizations which enjoy general consultative status under article 12(3) of the Constitution of the ILO;

- organizations which enjoy regional consultative status, established by the Governing Body at its 160th Session (November 1964);
- organizations included in the 'Special List' of non-governmental international organizations, established by the Governing Body at its 132nd Session (June 1956);
- employers' or workers' organizations other than those enjoying general or regional consultative status;
- other organizations.

A number of texts define the relations between the ILO and non-governmental international organizations, as well as the privileges conferred on them by their respective statutes.
[Source: GB.245/SC/2/1, paras 3–4.]

Rules applicable to non-governmental international organizations enjoying general consultative status
Resolution adopted by the Governing Body at its 105th Session (14 June 1948)
Whereas paragraph 3 of article 12 of the Constitution of the International Labour Organization provides that:

> The International Labour Organization may make suitable arrangements for such consultation as it may think desirable with recognized non-governmental international organizations of employers, workers, agriculturists and cooperators.

And whereas, in order to promote effective coordination of international action in the economic and social field, the Governing Body considers it desirable to make arrangements for such consultation with a view to facilitating the reference to the International Labour Organization by non-governmental organizations of proposals which such organizations may desire to make for official international action upon matters primarily within the competence of the International Labour Organization:

1. The Governing Body decides that representatives of non-governmental international organizations with an important interest in a wide range of ILO activities with which it has decided to establish consultative relationships may attend ILO meetings in accordance with the provisions of the following paragraphs.
2. Such representatives may be invited by the Governing Body to attend a specified meeting of the Governing Body or of one of its committees during the consideration of matters of interest to them. The Chairman may in agreement with the Vice-Chairmen, permit such representatives to make statements for the information of the meeting upon matters

included in its agenda. If such agreement cannot be secured, the question is submitted to the meeting for decision without any discussion. These arrangements do not apply to meetings dealing with administrative or financial matters.

3. Such representatives may attend the meetings of regional conferences, industrial committees and advisory committees appointed by the Governing Body. The Chairman may, in agreement with the Vice-Chairmen, permit such representatives to make statements for the information of the meeting upon matters included in its agenda. If such agreement cannot be secured, the question is submitted to the meeting for decision without any discussion.

4. Any organization applying to the Governing Body for the establishment of consultative relationships shall communicate to the Director-General with its application for the information of the Governing Body the following information: a copy of its constitution; the names and addresses of its officers; particulars of its composition and of the membership of the national organizations affiliated thereto; a copy of its latest annual report.

5. The Governing Body may at any time revoke a decision to establish consultative relationships.

6. The Governing Body recommends the Conference to decide that non-governmental international organizations with which consultative relationships have been established in pursuance of paragraph 1 may be represented at meetings of the Conference and its committees and that the President of the Conference or the Chairman of the committee may, in agreement with the Vice-Presidents or Vice-Chairmen, invite the representatives of such organizations to make statements for the information of the Conference or the committee upon matters under discussion by them. If such agreement cannot be secured, the question is submitted to the meeting for decision without any discussion. These arrangements would not apply to meetings dealing with administrative or financial matters or meetings of the Selection Committee, the Credentials Committee and the Drafting Committee.

7. The Director-General of the International Labour Office will make the necessary arrangements for the regular communication of documents to organizations with which standing arrangements have been made.

8. The Governing Body may, from time to time, invite non-governmental international organizations which have a special interest in some particular sector of the work of the ILO to be represented at specified meetings of the Governing Body, regional conferences, industrial committees or at committees appointed by the Governing Body during the consideration of matters of interest to them; the Governing Body draws the attention of the Conference to the possibility of making

similar arrangements in appropriate cases; the Director-General will make the necessary arrangements for the communication to such organizations of documents of interest to them.

[Source: GB.105 (June 1948) (fourth item on the agenda) (with editorial changes)].

Regional consultative status for non-governmental organizations
Adopted by the Governing Body at its 160th Session (20 November 1964):

1. The Governing Body, on the recommendation of its Officers, may grant regional consultative status to regional organizations of employers and workers which fulfil the following conditions:
   (a) the applicant organization must be broadly representative of interests concerned with a wide range of ILO activities in the region concerned and active there;
   (b) the applicant organization must communicate to the Director-General with its application, for the information of the Governing Body, the following information: a copy of its constitution; the names and addresses of its officers; particulars of its composition and of the membership of the national organizations affiliated to it; and a copy of its latest annual report.
2. Non-governmental organizations granted regional consultative status should be permitted:
   (a) to attend ILO regional meetings and ILO tripartite meetings of a regional nature in their respective regions;
   (b) to attend regional advisory committees—eg the Asian Advisory Committee, the African Advisory Committee or the Inter-American Advisory Committee—appointed by the Governing Body for the regions for which they had been accorded consultative status;
   (c) at any of the above meetings, to make or circulate, with the permission of the President or Chairman in agreement with the Vice-Presidents or Vice-Chairmen, statements upon matters (other than administrative or financial matters) included in the agenda;
   (d) to receive ILO documents regularly.

[Source: (January 1965) 48(1) Official Bulletin 29.]

Note concerning arrangements applicable to non-governmental international organizations included in the Special List
Note based on the decision of the Governing Body at its 132nd Session (2 June 1956) and the amendments made at its 245th Session (1 March 1990)

Introductory note
In June 1956 the Governing Body of the International Labour Office

approved the establishment by the Director-General of a Special List of Non-Governmental International Organizations (NGOs).

Apart from the eight non-governmental international organizations which have already been granted full consultative status and the 16 which have regional consultative status, and apart from the employers' and workers' international organizations which, although not enjoying consultative status, play, under the Constitution, an essential part in the work of the International Labour Organization, there are non-governmental international organizations whose aims and activities are of interest to the International Labour Organization and which are in a position to afford it valuable cooperation. The purpose of the establishment of the Special List was to place the ILO's relations with these organizations on a systematic footing.

I. Criteria and procedure for admission to the Special List

1. Only non-governmental international organizations which meet certain conditions are eligible for admission to the Special List.
2. The aims and objectives of organizations requesting admission to the Special List should be in harmony with the spirit, aims and principles of the ILO Constitution and the Declaration of Philadelphia. Length of existence, membership, the geographical coverage of the organization, its practical achievements and the international nature of its activities constitute the main criteria for such admission. A further requirement is that the organization in question should have, by reason of the aims it pursues, an evident interest in at least one of the fields of activity of the ILO. The fact that an organization has already been granted official status with the Economic and Social Council or a specialized agency of the United Nations is relevant, but does not necessarily imply inclusion in the Special List of the ILO.
3. Any non-governmental international organization wishing to be admitted to the Special List is required to forward to the Director-General in one of the working languages of the Organization a copy of its statutes, a list of the names and addresses of its officers, information regarding its composition and the aggregate membership of the national organizations affiliated to it, and a copy of its latest annual report or detailed and verifiable information about its activities.
4. In each case the Director-General decides, on behalf of the Governing Body, whether the organization supplying the information listed above should be admitted to the Special List. The Director-General communicates to the Governing Body at specific intervals the names of the organizations admitted to the Special List. The Director-General reviews the Special List from time to time and makes any necessary recommendations to the Governing Body with a view to the revision of the List.

II. Privileges of organizations admitted to the Special List
Participation in ILO meetings

5. The mere fact of inclusion in the Special List does not of itself confer on any organization the right to participate in ILO meetings. It does, however, facilitate consideration of the advisability of inviting the organization to a particular meeting, as full information regarding it is deemed to have been made available at the time of its admission to the Special List.

International Labour Conference
Criteria

6. Non-governmental international organizations wishing to be invited to be represented at the International Labour Conference should take careful note of the following revised criteria and procedure, which came into force in June 1990, for the issuance of such invitations by the Governing Body.

7. An organization on the Special List wishing to be invited to be represented at the Conference should satisfy the following criteria. It:
   (a) should have formally expressed an interest—clearly defined and supported by its Statutes and by explicit reference to its own activities—in at least one of the items on the agenda of the Conference session to which it requests to be invited; these details should be supplied with the request for an invitation; and;
   (b) should have made its request for an invitation in accordance with the procedure set out in the Standing Orders of the Conference.

Procedure

8. The procedure to be followed by NGOs for requesting invitations to the International Labour Conference is contained in article 2(4) of the Standing Orders of the Conference. It reads as follows: Requests from non-governmental international organizations for an invitation to be represented at the Conference shall be made in writing to the Director-General of the International Labour Office and shall reach him at least one month before the opening of the session of the Conference. Such requests shall be referred to the Governing Body for decision in accordance with criteria established by the Governing Body.

9. The special attention of NGOs is drawn to the fact that, under the new procedure, the Selection Committee of the Conference will no longer deal, as in the past, with requests for invitations to be represented at the Conference which are submitted late. However, requests to be represented on the committees of the Conference (other than those dealing with the agenda item, 'Programme and budget proposals and

other financial questions') which are to consider the agenda items in which such international non-governmental organizations have expressed interest will continue to be examined by the Selection Committee of the Conference, once the invitation to the organizations in question to be represented at the Conference has been duly issued by the Governing Body in conformity with the new procedure.

Governing Body

10. Admission to the Special List does not change the present situation in respect of meetings of the Governing Body, to which only the non-governmental international organizations with full consultative status are invited.

Regional Meetings

11. Organizations on the Special List with a special interest in the work of a Regional Meeting may be invited to be represented at the meeting in conformity with article 1, paragraph 6, of the Rules for Regional Meetings. Applications must be received not later than one month before the session of the Governing Body preceding the Regional Meeting in question.

Industrial and joint committees and tripartite technical meetings

12. Upon receipt of duly substantiated requests from organizations on the Special List to participate in meetings of industrial and joint committees and tripartite technical meetings, the Director-General submits to the Governing Body proposals to invite the organizations to be represented by observers at those meetings to which they are in a position to make a significant contribution on account of their special competence. The supporting material accompanying the request from the applicant organization should relate to its interest not only in the subjects to be discussed at the meeting but also in the industry or the branch of economic activity in question. Applications must be received not later than one month before the session of the Governing Body preceding the meeting in respect of which a request is made. The provisions of the Standing Orders for such meetings apply to organizations invited to send observers.

Committee of experts

13. Organizations on the Special List are not invited to attend meetings of committees of experts (or other meetings that are not tripartite). They may, however, forward to the Director-General documents of a technical nature on agenda items. The Director-General decides whether to place such documents at the experts' disposal.

Circulation of statements by international non-governmental organizations
14. Any organization authorized to circulate a statement under the applicable Standing Orders is responsible for the translation and reproduction of the statement.

Technical information
15. In addition to the above rules concerning participation in ILO meetings by organizations on the Special List, the Office is ready at any time to take into account information and suggestions of a technical character provided by such an organization if the Director-General considers the information of real value.

Documentation for meetings
16. Organizations on the Special List regularly receive a list of ILO meetings giving the date, place and agenda for the meetings. Documents for the meetings at which they are invited to be represented are also forwarded to them.

III. Obligations of organizations on the Special List
17. Organizations on the Special List are expected to cooperate with the International Labour Organization and to further its activities within the nature and scope of their competence.
18. The organizations are requested to transmit to the ILO the agendas of their meetings, congresses, conferences, etc, other than meetings of a purely private or business nature, together with the background reports or documents published for such meetings and the final reports or minutes thereof.
19. Such organizations are also required to send to the ILO either annual reports on their work or documents from which it is possible to obtain detailed information on their activities during each year.
[Source: Governing Body, 132nd Session, sixth item on the agenda. Establishment of a Special List of Non-Governmental International Organizations, modified at its 245th Session (1 March 1990).]

Note concerning arrangements applicable to non-governmental international organizations other than those enjoying general or regional consultative status or those included on the Special List
Adopted by the Governing Body at its 245th Session (1 March 1990)

1. An NGO wishing to be invited to be represented at a session of the International Labour Conference:
   (a) should demonstrate the international nature of its composition and activities; in this connection, it should be represented or have affiliates in a considerable number of countries; and

(b) should have aims and objectives that are in harmony with the spirit, aims and principles of the Constitution of the ILO and the Declaration of Philadelphia; and

(c) should have formally expressed an interest—clearly defined and supported by its statutes and by explicit reference to its own activities—in at least one of the items on the agenda of the Conference session to which it requests to be invited; these details should be supplied with the request for an invitation; and

(d) should have made its request for an invitation in accordance with the procedure set out in the Standing Orders of the Conference.

International non-governmental organizations enjoying general or regional consultative status and international non-governmental organizations on the Special List would already be deemed to have satisfied criteria (a) and (b), which would have been verified when they were admitted to these categories, as would organizations enjoying consultative status with ECOSOC in their categories I and II.
[Source: GB.245/8/19, paras 43, 44 and 50].

Appendix IV

WIPO

CONVENTION ESTABLISHING THE WORLD INTELLECTUAL
PROPERTY ORGANIZATION

Signed on 14 July 1967

[excerpt]

Article 13
Relations with Other Organizations
(2) The Organization may, on matters within its competence, make suitable arrangements for consultation and cooperation with international non-governmental organizations and, with the consent of the Governments concerned, with national organizations, governmental or non-governmental. Such arrangements shall be made by the Director General after approval by the Coordination Committee.

ADMISSION OF OBSERVERS

Memorandum of the WIPO Director General
August 15, 2005
Document number: A/41/8
Source: <http://www.wipo.int/edocs/mdocs/govbody/en/a_41/a_41_8.pdf>

[excerpt]

III. Admission of International Non-Governmental Organizations as Observers

1. At their previous sessions, the Assemblies adopted a set of principles to be applied in extending invitations to international non-governmental organizations to attend, as observers, the meetings of the Assemblies concerned (AB/X/32, paragraph 17, and AB/X/17, Annex V; TRT/A/I/2 and 4, paragraph 5; BP/A/I/2 and 5, paragraph 5; V/A/I/1, paragraphs 25 to 29, and V/A/I/2, paragraph 7; and FRT/A/I/3 and 9, paragraph 10).

2. The international non-governmental organizations admitted to attend, as observers, the meetings of the Assemblies, and which have been invited to attend the Fortyfirst series of meetings of the Assemblies and the Unions administered by WIPO, are listed in the Annex to document A/41/INF/1 Rev 1.

3. Once an international non-governmental organization is admitted to attend, as an observer, the meetings of the Assemblies of the Member States of WIPO, it is also invited to attend, as an observer, meetings of committees, working groups, or other bodies subsidiary to the Assemblies, if their subject matter seems to be of direct interest to that organization.

4. Since the fortieth series of meetings of the Assemblies, from September 27 to October 5, 2004, when decisions were last taken concerning the admission of international nongovernmental organizations to attend, as observers, the meetings of certain Assemblies of Member States of WIPO (A/40/5, paragraphs 8 to 13, and A/40/7, paragraph 180), the Director General has received requests, with the necessary information, from each of the following international non-governmental organizations for admission to attend, as an observer, the meetings of the Assemblies of the Member States of WIPO concerned:

(i)   African Intellectual Property Association (AIPA);
(ii)   Alfa Redi;
(iii)   Business Software Alliance (BSA);
(iv)   Computer & Communication Industry Association (CCIA);
(v)   Computer Professionals for Social Responsibility (CPSR);
(vi)   Consumers International (CI);
(vii)   Creative Commons International (CCI);
(viii)   Electronic Information for Libraries (eIFL.net);
(ix)   European Consumers' Organization (BEUC);
(x)   European Digital Media Association (EDIMA);
(xi)   European Digital Rights (EDRI);
(xii)   European Law Students' Association (ELSA International);
(xiii)   Hipatia;
(xiv)   International Center for Trade and Sustainable Development (ICTSD);
(xv)   International Environmental Law Research Center (IELRC);
(xvi)   International Organization of Performing Artists (GIART);
(xvii)   International Policy Network (IPN);
(xviii) IP Justice;
(xix)   Public Interest Intellectual Property Advisors (PIIPA);
(xx)   The Royal Society for Encouragement of Arts, Manufacturers and Commerce (RSA);
(xxi)   Third World Network Berhad (TWN);
(xxii)   Union for the Public Domain (UPD).

5. A brief statement about each of the organizations mentioned in paragraph 13, above—its objectives, structure and membership—appears in Annex III of this document. It is proposed that, as concerns each of the organizations mentioned in paragraph 13, above, the Assemblies of the Member States include the said organizations in the category of international nongovernmental organizations.

6. The Assemblies of the Member States of WIPO are invited, each in so far as it is concerned, to take a decision on the proposal appearing in paragraph 14, above.

IV. Admission of National Non-Governmental Organizations as Observers

7. At the Thirty-seventh series of meetings of the Assemblies, from September 23 to October 1, 2002, the Assemblies of the Member States of WIPO, each in so far as it was concerned, agreed to adopt the following proposals as principles applicable in extending invitations to national non-governmental organizations (NGOs), as observers (A/37/14, paragraph 316):

(a) The organization shall be essentially concerned with intellectual property matters falling within the competence of WIPO and shall, in the view of the Director General, be able to offer constructive, substantive contributions to the deliberations of the Assemblies of WIPO;

(b) The aims and purposes of the organization shall be in conformity with the spirit, purposes and principles of WIPO and of the United Nations;

(c) The organization shall have an established headquarters. It shall have democratically adopted statutes, adopted in conformity with the legislation of the Member State from which the NGO originates. One copy of the statutes shall be submitted to WIPO;

(d) The organization shall have authority to speak for its members through its authorized representatives and in accordance with the rules governing observer status; and

(e) The admission of national NGOs to observer status shall be the subject of prior consultations between Member States and the Secretariat.

8. Since the fortieth session of meetings of the Assemblies, from September 27 to October 5, 2004, when decisions were last taken concerning the admission of national non-governmental organizations to attend, as observers, the meetings of certain Assemblies of Member States of WIPO (A/40/5, paragraphs 14 to 17 and A/40/7, paragraph 181), the Director General has received requests, with the necessary information, from each of the following national non-governmental organizations for admission to attend, as an observer, the meetings of the Assemblies of the Member States of WIPO concerned:

(i)   Brazilian Center for International Relations (CEBRI);
(ii)   Center for Information Society and Intellectual Property (CISIP/CIOS);
(iii)   Center for Performers' Rights Administration (CPRA) of GEIDANKYO;
(iv)   Chamber of Patent Attorneys (PAK);
(v)   Fundaçao Getulio Vargas (FGV);
(vi)   Generic Pharmaceutical Association (GPhA);
(vii)   German Association for Industrial Property and Copyright Law (GRUR);
(viii)   Healthcheck;
(ix)   Innovation Business Club (Intelcom);
(x)   Institute for Policy Innovation (IPI);
(xi)   Intellectual Property Left (IPLeft);
(xii)   International Trade Law Institute (IDCID);
(xiii)   Korean Progressive Network (JINBONET);
(xiv)   Library Copyright Alliance (LCA);
(xv)   Mexican National Association of Pharmaceutical Manufacturers (ANAFAM);
(xvi)   Open Knowledge Foundation (OKF);
(xv)   Public Knowledge, Inc.;
(xvii)   United States Telecom Association (USTA).

9. A brief statement about each of the organizations mentioned in paragraph 17,—its objectives, structure and membership—appears in Annex IV of this document. It is proposed that, as concerns each of the organizations mentioned in paragraph 17, above, the Assemblies of the Member States decide, in accordance with the principles set out in paragraph 16, above, whether to include the said organizations in the category of national nongovernmental organizations.

10. The Assemblies of the Member States of WIPO are invited, each in so far as it is concerned, to take a decision on the proposal appearing in paragraph 18, above.

Appendix V

WHO

CONSTITUTION OF THE WORLD HEALTH ORGANIZATION

> **Signed on 22 July 1946**

[excerpt]

Chapter XVI
Relations with Other Organizations

Article 71
The Organization may, on matters within its competence, make suitable arrangements for consultation and co-operation with non-governmental international organizations and, with the consent of the Government concerned, with national organizations, governmental or non-governmental.

PRINCIPLES GOVERNING RELATIONS BETWEEN WHO AND NON-GOVERNMENTAL ORGANIZATIONS

> **Adopted by the World Health Assembly of WHO**
> **Document number: WHA40.25**
> Source: <http://policy.who.int/cgibin/om_isapi.dll?infobase=
> Basicdoc&softpage=Browse_Frame_Pg42>

The Fortieth World Health Assembly,

Recalling Article 71 of the Constitution whereby WHO may make suitable arrangements for consultation and cooperation with nongovernmental organizations in carrying out its international health work;

Recalling that the Working Principles Governing the Admission of Nongovernmental Organizations into Official Relations with WHO were adopted by the First World Health Assembly and amended by the Third, Eleventh and Twenty-first World Health Assemblies (resolutions WHA1.130, WHA3.113, WHA11.14 and WHA21.28);

Recognizing the important role of nongovernmental organizations, as emphasized by the Thirty-eighth World Health Assembly in resolution

WHA38.31, and the complementarity of the resources they represent in the network of governments, peoples and WHO striving for health development;

Emphasizing the need to mobilize national and international nongovernmental organizations for accelerated implementation of health-for-all strategies;

Taking into account the usefulness of a broad framework dealing with the development of informal relations with nongovernmental organizations as well as with their admission into official relations with WHO;

DECIDES to adopt the revised Principles Governing Relations between the World Health organization and Nongovernmental Organizations.

Hbk Res, Vol III (1st ed.), 7.2.1 (Twelfth plenary meeting, 15 May 1987—Committee B, second report)

1. Introduction

1.1 As stated in Article 2 of the Constitution, one of the main functions of the World Health Organization (WHO) is to act as the directing and coordinating authority on international health work. In support of this function, and in accordance with Article 71 of the Constitution, WHO may make suitable arrangements for consultation and cooperation with nongovernmental organizations (NGOs) in carrying out its international health work.

1.2 WHO should, in relation to NGOs, act in conformity with any relevant resolutions of the General Assembly or Economic and Social Council of the United Nations.

1.3 The objectives of WHO's collaboration with NGOs are to promote the policies, strategies and programmes derived from the decisions of the Organization's governing bodies; to collaborate with regard to various WHO programmes in jointly agreed activities to implement these strategies; and to play an appropriate role in ensuring the harmonizing of intersectoral interests among the various sectoral bodies concerned in a country, regional or global setting.

2. Types of relations at the global level and their development

2.1 WHO recognizes only one category of formal relations, known as official relations, with those NGOs which meet the criteria described in these Principles. All other contacts, including working relations, are considered to be of an informal character.

2.2 The establishment of relations with NGOs shall be an evolving process proceeding through a number of separate stages as described in the following paragraphs.

2.3 First contacts with an NGO in order to create mutual understanding and assist in developing mutual interests frequently take the form of exchanges of information and reciprocal participation in technical meetings. This type of informal contact may continue on an ad hoc basis, without time limit and without written agreement. However, the definition of the broad objectives of collaboration and the possibility of enlarging its scope to include specific joint activities in line with the particular expertise of the nongovernmental organization are also explored at this stage.

2.4 When a number of specific joint activities have been identified, collaboration may be taken a stage further by proceeding to a period (usually two years) of working relations entered into by an exchange of letters. Such letters set out the agreed basis for the collaboration, indicating details of the activities to be undertaken during the period, providing an estimate of the resources to be supplied by WHO and the NGO, and naming focal points in the NGO and in WHO (designated technical officer). A joint assessment of the outcome of the collaboration thus planned is undertaken at the end of the period of working relations by the parties concerned, including also consideration of the future relationship. This may result: in the continuation of the working relations for a further period; in an application for admission into official relations with WHO from an international NGO, for examination by the Executive Board, should there be a number of activities which might form the basis of a long-term and closer relationship with WHO; or in a decision that there is no scope for further contacts in the foreseeable future. This arrangement for consultation and cooperation with NGOs is considered as informal.

2.5 The Executive Board shall be responsible for deciding on the admission of NGOs into official relations with WHO.

3. Criteria for the admission of NGOs into official relations with WHO

3.1 The main area of competence of the NGO shall fall within the purview of WHO. Its aims and activities shall be in conformity with the spirit, purposes and principles of the Constitution of WHO, shall centre on development work in health or health-related fields, and shall be free from concerns which are primarily of a commercial or profit-making nature. The major part of its activities shall be relevant to and have a bearing on the implementation of the health-for-all strategies as envisaged in the Global Strategy for Health for All by the Year 2000 and the

3.2 The NGO shall normally be international in its structure and/or scope, and shall represent a substantial proportion of the persons globally organized for the purpose of participating in the particular field of interest in which it operates. When there are several international NGOs with similar areas of interest, they may form a joint committee or other body authorized to act for the group as a whole.

3.3 The NGO shall have a constitution or similar basic document, an established headquarters, a directing or governing body, an administrative structure at various levels of action, and authority to speak for its members through its authorized representatives. Its members shall exercise voting rights in relation to its policies or action.

3.4 Thus, organizations eligible for admission into official relations with WHO include various types of international NGOs with a federated structure (made up of national or regional groups or having individual members from different countries), foundations that raise resources for health development activities in different parts of the world, and similar bodies promoting international health.

3.5 In exceptional cases a national organization, whether or not affiliated to an international NGO, may be considered for admission into official relations, in consultation with and subject to the recommendations of the WHO Regional Director and the Member State involved. Such a national organization [or a number of national organizations working under a federated (umbrella) structure] shall be eligible for admission provided that: the major part of its activities and resources are directed towards international health and related work; it has developed a programme of collaborative activities with WHO as indicated in paragraph 2.4; and its activities offer appropriate experience upon which WHO may wish to draw.

3.6 There shall normally have been at least two years of successfully completed working relations, as described in paragraph 2.4, prior to an application for admission into official relations.

4. Procedure for admitting NGOs into official relations with WHO

4.1 Applications should normally reach WHO headquarters not later than the end of the month of July in order to be considered by the Executive Board in January of the following year. They shall specify a structured plan for collaborative activities agreed upon by the organization and WHO. Applications from national organizations shall contain the endorsements of the WHO Regional Director and the government of the Member State concerned. Applications should normally be transmitted to Board members by the Secretariat two months in advance of the session at which they will be considered.

4.2 During its January session the Board's Standing Committee on Nongovernmental Organizations, composed of five members, shall consider applications submitted by NGOs, voluntarily or by invitation, and shall make recommendations to the Board; it may invite any such organization to speak before it in connection with the organization's application. Should the applicant organization be considered not to meet the established criteria, and bearing in mind the desirability of ensuring a valuable continuing partnership based on defined objectives and evidenced by a record of successful past collaboration and a framework for future collaborative activities, the Standing Committee may recommend postponement of consideration or rejection of an application.

4.3 The Board, after considering the recommendations of the Standing Committee, shall decide whether an organization is to be admitted into official relations with WHO. A re-application from an NGO shall not normally be considered until two years have elapsed since the Board's decision on the original application.

4.4 The Director-General shall inform each organization of the Board's decision on its application. He shall maintain a list of the organizations admitted into official relations, and this list and any amendments thereto shall be circulated to the Members of WHO.

4.5 A plan for collaboration based on mutually agreed objectives and outlining activities for the coming three-year period shall form the basis of official relations between WHO and the NGO. This plan shall be transmitted also to the WHO regional offices to encourage closer collaboration at regional level as appropriate.

4.6 The Board, through its Standing Committee on Nongovernmental Organizations, shall review collaboration with each NGO every three years and shall determine the desirability of maintaining official relations. The Board's review shall be spread over a three-year period, one-third of the NGOs in official relations being reviewed each year.

4.7 The Board may discontinue official relations if it considers that such relations are no longer appropriate or necessary in the light of changing programmes or other circumstances. Similarly, the Board may suspend or discontinue official relations if an organization no longer meets the criteria that applied at the time of the establishment of such relations, or fails to fulfil its part in the agreed programme of collaboration.

5. Relations with NGOs at the regional and national levels

5.1 Regional or national NGOs affiliated to international NGOs in official relations with WHO

These NGOs are, by definition, in official relations with the WHO Regional Office(s). They shall develop and implement a programme of collaboration with the regional and national levels of WHO to ensure implementation of health-for-all strategies at the country level.

5.2 Regional and national NGOs for which there is no international NGO

The regional office concerned may establish working relations with these organizations, subject to consultation between the Regional Director and the Director-General of WHO. A programme of activities developed and implemented as described in paragraph 2.4 would be essential.

5.3 Regional or national NGOs affiliated to international NGOs not in official relations with WHO
In order that WHO may promote and support the formation of strong international NGOs in the various technical fields, the regional office concerned may establish working relations with the above-mentioned regional or national organizations, subject to consultation between the Regional Director and the Director-General of WHO. Such working relations shall be based on a programme of activities developed and implemented as described in paragraph 2.4.

6. Privileges conferred on NGOs by relationship with WHO
6.1 The privileges conferred by official relationship shall include:
  (i) the right to appoint a representative to participate, without right of vote, in WHO's meetings or in those of the committees and conferences convened under its authority, on the following conditions: whenever the Health Assembly, or a committee or conference convened under WHO's authority, discusses an item in which a related NGO is particularly interested, that NGO, at the invitation of the chairman of the meeting or on his acceding to a request from the organization, shall be entitled to make a statement of an expository nature, and may, with the consent of the meeting, be invited by the chairman to make, in the course of the discussion of the item before the meeting, an additional statement for purposes of clarification;
  (ii) access to non-confidential documentation and such other documentation as the Director-General may see fit to make available through such special distribution facilities as WHO may establish;
  (iii) the right to submit a memorandum to the Director-General, who would determine the nature and scope of the circulation.
6.2 In the event of a memorandum being submitted which the Director-General considers might be placed on the agenda of the Health Assembly, such memorandum shall be placed before the Executive Board for possible inclusion in the agenda of the Assembly.
6.3 Privileges similar to those stated above shall normally be accorded to national/regional NGOs having working relations with WHO regional offices, in accordance with section 5, as determined by the Regional Directors in consultation with the regional committees.
6.4 A national organization which is affiliated to an international NGO covering the same subject on an international basis shall normally present its views through its government or through the international

NGO to which it is affiliated, unless other arrangements are made in view of its particular relationship with WHO

7. Responsibilities of NGOs in their relationship with WHO

7.1 NGOs shall be responsible for implementing the mutually agreed programme of collaboration and shall inform WHO as soon as possible if for any reason they are unable to fulfil their part of the agreement.

7.2 NGOs shall utilize the opportunities available to them through their normal work to disseminate information on WHO policies and programmes.

7.3 NGOs shall collaborate individually or collectively in WHO programmes to further health-for-all goals.

7.4 NGOs shall individually or collectively collaborate with the Member States where their activities are based in the implementation of the national/regional/global health-for-all strategies.

POLICY FOR RELATIONS WITH NONGOVERNMENTAL
ORGANIZATIONS
[DRAFT]

> Note by the Director-General of WHO
> 1 April 2004
> Document number: A57/32
> Source: <http://www.who.int/gb/ebwha/pdf_files/WHA57/A57_32-en.pdf>

1. At its 113th session, and in accordance with the request of the Health Assembly in its decision WHA56(10), the Executive Board reconsidered a proposal for a policy for relations with nongovernmental organizations.[1] The Board requested the Director-General to hold additional consultations to enable Member States to discuss the matter further, and to report to the Fifty-seventh World Health Assembly on the outcome of those consultations.

2. Accordingly, the Director-General invited all Member States to participate in consultations held in Geneva. Three consultations took place over the course of three days in February 2004. The resulting text of the draft resolution and policy reflects the consensus achieved on a number of suggested amendments. As discussions were not completed on all proposals, some bracketed text remains in paragraph 5 of the draft resolution and in paragraphs 9, 14, 17 and 18 of the draft policy.

---

[1]   See document EB113/2004/REC/2, summary record of the tenth meeting, section 5.

Action by the Health Assembly

3. The Health Assembly is invited to consider the draft resolution set out below and the draft policy contained in the Annex.

The Fifty-seventh World Health Assembly,

Having considered the policy for relations between the World Health Organization and nongovernmental organizations,

Emphasizing the important role that the Principles Governing Relations between the World Health Organization and Non-governmental Organizations have played since its adoption;

Recognizing the importance of civil society and its contributions to public health, and the growth in the numbers and influence of nongovernmental organizations active in health at global, regional and national levels;

Recognizing that, in accordance with Article 2 of the Constitution, one of the main functions of the World Health Organization is to act as the directing and coordinating authority on international health work and that, in accordance with Article 71, the Organization may make suitable arrangements for consultation and cooperation with nongovernmental organizations in carrying out its international health work;

Noting that the existing Principles Governing Relations between the World Health Organization and Nongovernmental Organizations adopted by the Fortieth World Health Assembly in 1987 (resolution WHA40.25) have been reviewed;

Noting the need to improve existing collaboration and dialogue with nongovernmental organizations, and to encourage new cooperative activities with such bodies,

1. DECIDES to adopt the policy for relations between the World Health Organization and nongovernmental organizations annexed hereto, which replaces the current Principles Governing Relations between the World Health Organization and Nongovernmental Organizations;

2. DECIDES that, as a transitional measure, all nongovernmental organizations in official relations with WHO as of the date of this resolution will be advised of the new policy and invited to submit an application for accreditation, and that, pending receipt of the duly completed application for accreditation and decision by the Executive Board on the application, they will be deemed to be accredited to WHO governing bodies;

3. REQUESTS the Director-General to establish suitable measures to implement the policy, including guidelines on the accreditation of, and collaboration with, nongovernmental organizations, which include clear and specific guidelines on avoiding conflict of interest and

submit those measures and guidelines to the Executive Board for approval at its 115th session;

4. REQUESTS the Director-General to review mechanisms to enhance representation and substantive participation of nongovernmental organizations from developing countries and countries with economies in transition, so that WHO can benefit from the specific technical expertise and perspectives that these entities can bring.

5. REQUESTS the Director-General to institute [an external, independent review of] mechanisms to safeguard WHO's integrity and independence, including the WHO Guidelines for Interactions with Commercial Enterprises.[2]

Annex
Policy for Relations between the World Health Organization and Non-Governmental Organizations

Introduction

1. Article 2 of the Constitution of the World Health Organization (WHO) states that one of the Organization's main functions is to act as the directing and coordinating authority on international health work. In support of this function, and in accordance with Article 71 of the Constitution, WHO may, on matters within its competence, make suitable arrangements for consultation and cooperation with nongovernmental organizations. In addition, Article 18(h) makes a similar reference in authorizing the Health Assembly to invite nongovernmental organizations to participate in its meetings or in those of committees and conferences convened under its authority.

2. WHO should, in relation to nongovernmental organizations, where appropriate, act in conformity with any relevant resolutions of the General Assembly or Economic and Social Council of the United Nations.

3. The objectives of relations between WHO and nongovernmental organizations are to strengthen mutually beneficial relations at global, regional and national levels in ways that improve health outcomes, strengthen health actions and place health issues on the development agenda. The policy for achieving these objectives comprises two elements: accreditation and collaboration.

4. An organization that is not established by a governmental entity or intergovernmental agreement shall be considered a nongovernmental organization, including organizations that accept members designated by governmental authorities, provided that such membership does not

---

[2] Document EB107/20.

interfere with the free expression of views of the organization.[3] For the purpose of this policy, nongovernmental organizations include a wide range of organizations, such as groups that represent consumers and patients, associations with humanitarian, developmental, scientific and/or professional goals and not-for-profit organizations that represent or are closely linked with commercial interests.

Accreditation Policy
  5. To be eligible for accreditation to the Health Assembly, Executive Board and committees and conferences convened under their authority, a nongovernmental organization shall:
  (a) have aims and purposes consistent with WHO's Constitution and in conformity with the policies of the Organization as well as resolutions and decisions adopted by the Executive Board and the World Health Assembly;
  (b) demonstrate competence in a field of activity related to the work of WHO;
  (c) have membership and/or activities that are international in scope;
  (d) be non-profit in nature;
  (e) have an established structure, a constitutive act, and accountability mechanisms;
  (f) for a membership organization, have the authority to speak for its members and have a representative structure;
  (g) have existed formally for at least three years as of date of receipt of the application by WHO;
  (h) disclose information on its objectives, structure, membership of executive body, field of activities and source of financing, and, where applicable, its status with other entities of the United Nations system;
  (i) agree to provide WHO regularly with updated information as well as to inform WHO of any changes with respect to criteria (a)–(h) as soon as they take place.
  6. Completed applications should reach WHO headquarters by the beginning of June in order to be considered by the Executive Board in January of the following year. Applications should be transmitted to Member States by the Secretariat two months in advance of the session at which they will be considered. A re-application from a nongovernmental organization shall not be considered until two years have elapsed since the Board's decision on the original application.

---

[3] United Nations Economic and Social Council, resolution 1996/31. 'Consultative relationship between the United Nations and non-governmental organizations', paragraph 12.

7. Once a nongovernmental organization is accredited, information gathered on its objectives, structure, membership of executive body, field of activities and source of funding, including updated information, shall be made publicly available. A report on accredited nongovernmental organizations shall be submitted every two years to the Executive Board.

8. Regional committees may invite representatives of accredited nongovernmental organizations to participate in their meetings, consistent with arrangements set out in this policy.

9. Regional committees shall be responsible for decisions regarding the accreditation to them of [national or regional] nongovernmental organizations [having membership and/or activities that are [national or] regional in scope, [in accordance with Article 71 of the WHO Constitution and] [consistent] with arrangements set out in this policy].

10. For a nongovernmental organization, accreditation shall confer the following privileges:
    (a) to appoint a representative to participate, without a right of vote, in Executive Board sessions and Health Assemblies, and in committees and conferences convened under their authority;
    (b) to make a statement of an expository nature at such meetings on agenda items of relevance to the nongovernmental organization, at the invitation of the Chairman; and
    (c) to submit written statements pertaining to such meetings, the nature and scope of distribution of which shall be determined by the Director-General.

11. For a nongovernmental organization, accreditation shall confer the following responsibilities:
    (a) it shall follow the rules of procedure of the Executive Board and Health Assembly as they apply to nongovernmental organizations;
    (b) it shall utilize available opportunities to disseminate information on WHO policies and programmes.

12. The Executive Board shall be responsible for deciding on the accreditation of a nongovernmental organization and its discontinuation or suspension. The Executive Board shall be advised by its Standing Committee on Nongovernmental Organizations, composed of five members, which shall meet during the Board's January session. The Standing Committee shall make recommendations on matters relevant to paragraphs 5, 6, 7 and 13 of this policy.

13. Decisions on discontinuation or suspension of accreditation shall take into consideration whether the nongovernmental organization has fulfilled the criteria listed in paragraph 5(a)–(i) above and a written response from the nongovernmental organization concerned to the recommendation of the Standing Committee. The non-provision of

information for the biennial report shall be grounds for a decision that the nongovernmental organization has not fulfilled the criteria. The accreditation of a nongovernmental organization shall also be suspended or discontinued if the Executive Board determines that the organization has, either directly or through its affiliates or representatives acting on its behalf, clearly abused its status by engaging in a pattern of acts that are not consistent with the Constitution or the policies of the Organization and resolutions and decisions of the Executive Board and the Health Assembly.

Collaboration Policy
14. The objectives of this policy are to encourage and facilitate cooperative activities with nongovernmental organizations and to establish coherent methods of work between WHO and nongovernmental organizations [, be they national, regional or international in scope [in accordance with Article 71 of the Constitution.] OR—[In the case of national nongovernmental organizations, collaboration shall be conducted only with the consent of the Government concerned.] OR [footnote[4]] collaboration with WHO shall not depend on a nongovernmental organization being accredited to WHO governing bodies.

15. Collaboration between nongovernmental organizations and WHO shall be guided by the following principles:
   (a) collaboration shall advance the objectives of WHO and be in conformity with the policies of the Organization as well as resolutions and decisions adopted by the Executive Board and the Health Assembly;
   (b) collaboration shall be with a nongovernmental organization that has a demonstrated competence in a field of activity related to the work of WHO;
   (c) collaboration shall be based on adequate knowledge of relevant characteristics of the nongovernmental organization such as its objectives, structure, membership of executive body, field of activities and source of financing, so as to enable the Director-General or officials designated by the Director-General to assess the suitability of collaboration;
   (d) collaboration shall not compromise the independence and objectivity of WHO and shall be designed to avoid any conflicts of interests.

[4] Before collaboration is established between WHO and a national nongovernmental organization, appropriate measures will be taken to consult the government concerned in accordance with Article 71 of the WHO Constitution.

16. The Director-General shall keep under review collaboration arrangements with nongovernmental organizations to ensure that such collaboration continues to be guided by the principles set out in paragraph 15. If it is determined that collaboration with the nongovernmental organizations is no longer in accordance with those principles, measures shall be taken to suspend or discontinue collaboration arrangements, as appropriate.

17. [The Director-General shall also suspend or discontinue collaboration if a nongovernmental organization either directly or through its affiliates or representatives acting on its behalf clearly abuses its status by engaging in a pattern of acts that are not consistent with the Constitution or the policies of the Organization, and resolutions and decisions of the Executive Board and the Health Assembly.]

18. [The Director-General shall [periodically]—OR—[biennially] keep the Executive Board informed on the implementation of this collaboration policy.] [The Executive Board may request the Director- General to report, as appropriate, on the implementation of this collaboration policy.]—OR—[The Director-General shall provide the Executive Board biennially with a summary report on the general outlines of the implementation of this collaboration policy.]

Appendix VI

UNEP

RESOLUTION OF THE UNITED NATIONS GENERAL ASSEMBLY
2997 (XXVII) 'INSTITUTIONAL AND FINANCIAL ARRANGEMENTS
FOR INTERNATIONAL ENVIRONMENTAL CO-OPERATION'

> **Adopted by the UN General Assembly**
> **15 December 1972**
> **Document number: 2997(XXVII)**
> Source: <http://daccessdds.un.org/doc/RESOLUTION/GEN/NR0/
> 270/27/IMG/NR027027.pdf?OpenElement>

[excerpt]

IV
Environment Co-ordination Board
5. Also invites other intergovernmental and those non-governmental organizations that have an interest in the field of the environment to lend
their full support and collaboration to the United Nations with a view to
achieving the largest possible degree of co-operation and co-ordination.

RULES OF PROCEDURE OF THE GOVERNING COUNCIL OF THE
UNEP

> **Adopted by the Governing Council of the UNEP**
> **11 March 1974**
> **Document number: UNEP/GC/3/Rev.1**
> Source: <http://www.unep.org/download_file.multilingual.asp?
> FileID=11>

[excerpt]

Chapter XIV—Observers of International Non-Governmental Organizations

Rule 69
1. International non-governmental organizations having an interest in the
field of the environment, referred to in section IV, paragraph 5, of

General Assembly resolution 2997 (XXVII), may designate representatives to sit as observers at public meetings of the Governing Council and its subsidiary organs, if any. The Governing Council shall from time to time adopt and revise when necessary a list of such organizations. Upon the invitation of the President or Chairman, as the case may be, and subject to the approval of the Governing Council or the subsidiary organ concerned, international nongovernmental organizations may make oral statements on matters within the scope of their activities.

2. Written statements provided by international non-governmental organizations referred to in paragraph 1 above, related to items on the agenda of the Governing Council or of its subsidiary organs, shall be circulated by the secretariat to members of the Governing Council or of the subsidiary organ concerned in the quantities and in the languages in which the statements were made available to the secretariat for distribution.

ACCREDITATION OF NON-GOVERNMENTAL ORGANIZATIONS AT UNEP

> **Adopted by UNEP**
> Source: <http://www.unep.org/civil_society/PDF_docs/accreditation_modalities_english_july06.pdf>

UNEP's interest in accreditation for non-governmental organizations
UNEP owes a lot to non-governmental organizations. Its creation in 1972 during the Stockholm Conference can largely be attributed to the pressure and commitment of civil society (all the major groups as defined by the Rio Summit in 1992). Most of the well-known multilateral environment agreements (Basel Convention, Montreal Protocol, Kyoto Protocol, Cartagena Protocol,...) exist because of the hard work of your organization. As you know, the priority today is on the concrete implementation of intergovernmental agreements, bearing in mind the need and the right of the developing countries to have a significantly larger share in the distribution of the world's wealth.

But why should non-governmental organizations be interested to engage themselves more proactively in UNEP's policy design and, as a consequence, strengthen UNEP itself? Because UNEP recognises that there is an imbalance of power in the international governance in disfavour of the environmental concerns, which needs to be rectified. Whatever the future of the intergovernmental institutional architecture will be after the UN reform, the sooner we work to correct these imbalances, the better it will be for the collective human well-being.

In order to achieve this goal, a renewed and strengthened cooperation between UNEP and NGOs at the 'governance level' is needed. To address environmental concerns in an adequate manner, NGO participation is required especially in the intergovernmental decision making-process, during which UNEP develops its operational policies and work programme. The re-launch of this productive cooperation is fully in line with the decision SS.VII/5 of UNEP's Governing Council, inviting 'the Executive Director to consider the best way to include the views of civil society in the proceedings of the Governing Council/Global Ministerial Environmental Forum'.

We encourage you strongly to apply for accreditation at the UNEP Governing Council/Global Ministerial Environment Forum (GC/GMEF). Accreditation will grant your organization consultative status at UNEP, within the rules of procedure of UNEP GC/GMEF. We will implement our goal of closer cooperation with NGOs on an incremental basis, considering that UNEP is an intergovernmental organization in which the Member States have the final decision making role.

There are immediate advantages to be accredited. In the process leading up to the GC/GMEF the accredited NGOs have the possibility to:
1. Receive unedited working documents of the UNEP GC/GMEF at the same time as the Committee of the Permanent Representatives (CPR).
2. Submit written inputs into the unedited working documents of the UNEP GC/GMEF, for the consideration by the CPR.
3. Submit written statements on the working documents of the UNEP GC/GMEF, for consideration by the Governments.

During the GC/GMEF, the accredited NGOs have the opportunity to:
1. Attend the Plenary, the Committee of the Whole and the Government Discussions, as an observer.
2. Make oral statements during the GC/GMEF discussions at the invitation of the chair.
3. Based on our common experience and your suggestions, further steps will be considered after the GC/GMEF in February 2005.

Accreditation process

The NGO seeking accreditation has to send the following documents to the UNEP Major Groups and Stakeholders Branch:
A. A letter requesting accreditation.
B. Proof of non-profit making status (copy of document of incorporation).
C. Proof of interest in the environment (such as annual reports; conference and/or seminar reports; recent press releases and copies of media statements; newsletters and other periodicals).

D. A detailed account of the international scope of its activities.
E. In addition, NGOs can send a copy of its accreditation to other UN bodies and agencies, including ECOSOC. This is not mandatory, but it helps to speed up the process.

> Major Groups and Stakeholders Branch
> Division of Policy Development and Law
> United Nations Environment Programme
> P.O. Box 30552 Nairobi, Kenya
> Email: civil.society@unep.org

The documents can be sent in hard copies or electronic version.

The accreditation process consists of the following steps:
A. The Major Groups and Stakeholders Branch will review the file in cooperation with the Law Branch in the Division of Policy Development and Law. If any documents required for the application are missing or need clarification, the Major Group and Stakeholders Branch will notify the NGO and request further information.
B. When the file is completed, the Major Groups and Stakeholders Branch sends the file to the Secretariat for Governing Bodies with a recommendation on whether to accredit it or not. The Office of the Secretariat for Governing Bodies decides to grant or to refuse the accreditation of the NGO and registers its decision in the database. The Office of the Secretariat for Governing Bodies notifies the NGOs about its decision.

> Office of the Secretariat for Governing Bodies
> United Nations Environment Programme
> P.O. Box 30552
> Nairobi, Kenya
> Fax (00 254 20) 623 748/929

NB: To speed up the process, the non-governmental organizations are advised to submit only a complete accreditation request with all the required documentation.

MODALITIES FOR ACCREDITED INTERNATIONAL NON-
GOVERNMENTAL ORGANIZATIONS TO UNEP TO SUBMIT
WRITTEN INPUTS INTO THE UNEDITED WORKING DOCUMENTS
OF THE UNEP'S GC/GMEF AND TO SUBMIT WRITTEN
STATEMENTS TO THE GC/GMEF OF UNEP

Adopted by UNEP
Source: <http://www.unep.org/civil_society/PDF_docs/accreditation_
%20modalities.pdf>

A. Written inputs into the unedited working documents of UNEP's GC/GMEF

1. In keeping with rule 9.3 of the rules of procedure of the Governing Council the provisional agenda, and the unedited working documents of UNEP's Governing Council/Global Ministerial Environment Forum shall be communicated to accredited international non-governmental organizations at the same time as to the Committee of Permanent Representatives (CPR).

2. Accredited international non-governmental organizations may submit written inputs into the unedited working documents of the UNEP's Governing Council/Global Ministerial Environment Forum on subjects in which these organizations have a special competence and related to items on the agenda of the Governing Council/Global Ministerial Environment Forum or of its subsidiary organs. In keeping with decision SS.VII 15 of 15 February 2002, the Executive Ditector shall circulate such inputs to the CPR, for its consideration.

B. Written statements for submission to UNEP's GC/GMEF

1. In keeping with rule 69.2 of the rules of procedure of the Governing Council, accredited international non-governmental organizations may submit written statements to the work of UNEP's Governing Council/Global Ministerial Environment Forum on subjects in which these organizations and groups have a special competence and related to items on the agenda of the Governing Council/Global Ministerial Environment Forum or of its subsidiary organs. UNEP's Secretariat shall circulate such statements as UNEP written information documents to the Committee of Permanent Representatives (CPR), the Governments and post them on the official UNEP web page for delegates.

2. The following conditions should apply regarding the submission and circulation of written statements. These conditions are based on ECOSOC resolution 1996/31 on the consultative relationship between the United Nations and Non-Governmental Organizations.

(a)   The written statement should be submitted in one of the official languages (English, French, Chinese, Arabic, Russian, Spanish).

(b)   The accredited international non-governmental organization, shall give due consideration to any comments that the Executive Director may make before transmitting the statement in the final form;

(c)   The written statement should be limited to 2000 words.

The following modalities are implemented

(a)   The NGOs send their proposal of written statements by e-mail to UNEP's Secretariat at olivier.deleuze@unep.org

(b)   UNEP's Secretariat may decide:

b. (1) To distribute the statement.

b. (2) To provide comments about the statement to the accredited NGO.

(c)   As far as the distribution is concerned, for the upcoming ninth special session of the GC/GMNEF of 7 to 9 February 2005:

   – If the written statement has been accepted before 28 January 2006, it will be sent by e-mail to the governments and the accredited NGOs.

   – If the written statement has been accepted after the 28 January 2006, the statement will be copied in adequate quantities and distributed as written information document.

ENHANCING CIVIL SOCIETY ENGAGEMENT IN THE WORK OF THE UNITED NATIONS ENVIRONMENT PROGRAMME IMPLEMENTATION OF GCSS.VII/5

> **Revised Strategy Paper**
> **Issued by the Governing Council of the UNEP**
> **21 November 2002**
> **Document number: UNEP/GC.22/INF/13**
> Source: <http://www.unep.org/civil_society/PDF_docs/Enhancing_Civil_Society_Engagement_In_UNEP.pdf>

Definitions

Civil Society Organizations (CSOs): For the purpose of this strategy, UNEP uses the definition as set out in decision GCSS.VII/5 of the seventh special session of the Governing Council/Global Ministers of the Environment Forum. Civil society encompasses major groups, namely farmers, women, the scientific and technological community, children and youth, indigenous people and their communities, workers and trade unions, business and industry, non-governmental organizations as well as local authorities. The strategy focuses on engagement with the organizations established by each of these major groups in so far as they engage in public interest activities. **Public Policy Networks** (PPNs): Multi-stakeholder processes established to build consensus around specific public policy issues. PPNs bring together representatives from different major groups, as well as government and inter-governmental bodies, who may initially have opposing views on the issue being addressed. The World Commission on Dams is often cited as a prime example of a PPN.

1. Introduction & Background

In decision GCSS.VII/5 of the seventh special session of the Governing Council/Global Ministers of the Environment Forum (GC/GMEF) of the United Nations Environment Programme the Executive Director was requested 'to further develop, and review and revise as necessary the strategy for engaging civil society in the programme of activities of the United Nations Environment Programme, in consultation with Governments and civil society. The strategy should provide clear direction to the secretariat to ensure that all programmes take into account opportunities for multi-stakeholder participation in design, implementation, monitoring of activities, and dissemination of outputs'.

This decision was a reflection of the strong interest expressed by the member states of UNEP to see the organization playing a stronger role in catalysing effective action to protect the environment through enhanced collaboration with the multitude of civil society actors who share the same purpose and values around the world. In accordance with this request, the Executive Director has developed the following strategy to enhance UNEP's engagement with civil society, including the private sector, in its programmes and activities.

The strategy proposed in this paper has been derived from consultations and communication over the past year and a half with many representatives of civil society constituencies, as well as with UNEP programmes and the Governing Council and its Committee of Permanent Representatives (CPR).

(a) Overview & Definitions

The United Nations Environment Programme (UNEP) owes much to civil society for its establishment. In 1972 the global community for the first time met to discuss global environmental issues, and their Stockholm Declaration recognised the important role civil society has to play. Thus UNEP, at its creation, was encouraged to work together with civil society.

Civil society is a natural ally of UNEP—an ally in working with peoples, governments, and non-state organizations. The role of civil society organizations—including representatives of the private sector—in the design, implementation and monitoring of a range of projects and programmes is widely recognised. Over the past 30 years UNEP has established a strong linkage with civil society. Through its support to civil society participation in preparations for UNCED, and during the negotiations for the 'Rio Conventions', as well as by recognition of the importance of partnerships with civil society organizations (CSOs) in the Nairobi and Malmö Declarations, these linkages have been clearly established.

Engaging stakeholders as partners is important for the following reasons:
- External stakeholders have many different perspectives to be taken into account in order to foster long-term, broad-based support for UNEP's work.
- Engaging a wide range of stakeholders in addressing environmental issues expands the reach and impact of strategies far beyond the capability of UNEP's own limited financial and human resources.
- Active involvement of stakeholders at the national level, where many environmental problems need to be addressed, and where many of UNEP's programme partners are located, complements UNEP's operational presence at the regional and global levels.

For the purpose of this strategy, civil society encompasses major groups, that is farmers, women, the scientific and technological community, children and youth, indigenous people and their communities, workers and trade unions, business and industry, non-governmental organizations as well as local authorities. The strategy focuses on engagement with the organizations established by each of these major groups in so far as they are involved in public interest activities.

(b) Background on UNEP's historical engagement with civil society, private sector and other major groups
The Stockholm Conference on the Human Environment in 1972 and the accompanying NGO Forum marked a breakthrough in the way major groups related to and sought to influence an intergovernmental decision making process. From its inception, UNEP promoted a policy to invite wide NGO input and collaboration. An NGO Section was set up in 1973. This office was charged with coordinating UNEP's programmatic activities with parallel efforts of NGOs. In 1974 an independent coalition of environmental NGOs was established as the Environment Liaison Centre to connect groups around the world with the work of UNEP.

The 1980s saw UNEP forging new links with a wide variety of major groups. These included: women's groups (1985 World Conference on Women in Nairobi); religious groups (1984 launching of 'UNEP Environmental Sabbath'); business and industry (1984 'World Industry Conference on Environmental Management'); children and youth (Global Youth Forums and a network of youth advisors for various regions). In 1985 a strategy to set up UNEP national committees began. The UN

Conference on Environment and Development (UNCED) in 1992 is often recognized as the point at which civil society truly became a full player in the global decision-making arena. Civil society had, by then, built up its capacity and legitimacy and had grown to become a prominent voice in policy discussions. Agenda 21 calls on UNEP to raise 'general awareness and action in the area of environmental protection through collaboration with the general public, non-governmental entities and intergovernmental institutions' (Chapter 28).

In 1995, the Governing Council called upon UNEP to develop a framework for working more closely with NGOs. Consequently, UNEP agreed to support NGO and Major Group input into project design, implementation and evaluation, UNEP policy development as well as environmental governance. These decisions were formalized in UNEP's Project Manual.

c) Overview of current practice
At the operational level, there are many examples of successful engagement with civil society by UNEP programmes. These include:
- Expanding and enhancing regular communication and consultation with CSOs through the establishment in 2000 of the NGO/civil society Unit in the Division of Policy Development and Law (DPDL),
- promoting mechanisms for engagement with CSOs in information-sharing and assessment activities, such as with the Global Environmental Outlook (GEO), UNEP.Net and Infoterra,
- identifying and collaborating with CSOs in the design and implementation of GEF medium sized projects, including work with indigenous peoples and biodiversity,
- fostering strong CSO constituencies by convention secretariats and regional and out-posted offices,
- implementing special initiatives jointly with civil society actors, such as the Coral Reef Initiative.
- The Communication and Public Information Division implements several projects in partnership with civil society and private sector groups, and has spearheaded UNEP's outreach to youth organizations. UNEP also undertakes extensive work with educational organizations on environmental education.

Representing business and industry, associations from various sectors and all regions participate in the annual consultative meeting of UNEP with industry and trade associations, where they have the opportunity to advise UNEP DTIE on the execution of its work programme.

UNEP has engaged with industry and business associations to promote cleaner production, management of industrial pollution, and voluntary environmental initiatives. A major aspect of this role has been to establish partnerships with the private sector, to launch corresponding outreach activities, to disseminate information and implement activities in the regions. UNEP also collects information regarding the relevant needs of the countries and private sector groups.

Key examples of voluntary initiatives promoted by UNEP include:
- The Financial Institutions Initiative
- The Insurance Industry Initiative
- The Tour Operators Initiative for Sustainable Tourism Development
- A Telecommunications Initiative
- The Global Reporting Initiative (GRI)
- The Global Compact initiative of the United Nations Secretary-General

d) Recent Developments in Enhancing Engagement with Civil Society
In the spirit of the Nairobi and Malmö Declarations, the UNEP Governing Council, in early 2001, called on the Executive Director 'to further the consultative process, including at the regional level, with Governments, the civil society, private sector and other major groups on ways and means to enhance the active engagement and participation of civil society in the work of the United Nations Environment Programme'.

Subsequently, the seventh special session of the GC/GMEF, in February 2002, requested the Executive Director, inter alia, 'to further develop, and review and revise as necessary the strategy for engaging civil society in the programme of activities of the United Nations Environment Programme', and 'to consider the best way to include the views of civil society in the proceedings of the Governing Council/Global Ministerial Environment Forum'.

As a result of these decisions, the past year has witnessed an acceleration of consultations and collaborative thinking on how UNEP should be working with civil society and the private sector in order to enhance commitment and effectiveness in addressing the environmental and sustainable development challenges of the 21st century. Global and regional meetings have been convened with civil society representatives to gather their views on engagement with UNEP, and electronic consultations have also been conducted. In this endeavour it is clear that the way forward is to build stronger bonds among the multitude of constituencies and major groups engaged with UNEP.

2. Strategic Framework for Enhancing Engagement
It is clear from the above that UNEP already engages with civil society in a wide variety of ways and at numerous levels. So the issue is not so much how to increase engagement, but how to make it more effective in supporting UNEP's mandate and objectives. This is necessary in order to respond to the evolving context of international governance as it relates to the

formulation and implementation of environmental and sustainable development policy.

There are two principal focuses for engagement with civil society. One is at the level of governance and policy formulation, the other is at the level of programme operations. As these two focuses are quite distinct, they are treated as two of three pillars in the new UNEP strategy for engaging civil society. What they have in common is a need for an institutional environment with good information and communication mechanisms in order to ensure qualitative exchange between UNEP and its partners at both the policy and the programmatic levels. This institutional environment forms the third pillar, although it will be addressed first since it underpins the strategies for addressing the other two.

The strategy will emphasize an incremental approach, building on current mechanisms and practices, and envisioning activities and innovations to strengthen civil society engagement over three to four years, after which the strategy should be reviewed. The fact that it would be unrealistic to propose new activities that will require mobilization of substantial financial resources that patently are not available, argues for such an approach. In addition, any strategy that aims to enhance the quality of inter-institutional relationships must take into account that attitudes towards and practices of 'working together' cannot be made to change overnight. It takes time to build trust and harmonious relations.

This does not mean that UNEP will in any way delay implementation of the strategy. On the contrary, demands for a stronger role in engaging civil society in addressing the global environmental agenda, particularly in the follow-up to the WSSD, require that the organization move forward expediently in this area. To this end the Secretariat will commence implementation of the strategy before the end of 2002, concentrating on components that will provide the foundation for other changes. These will include strengthening of information/communication systems, developing regional strategies for enhanced engagement, and preparing for a CSO forum to coincide with the 22nd session of the GC/GMEF in February 2003.

3. Strategy Pillar I: Strengthening institutional relations and information management on Civil Society—mechanisms for coordination:

(a) Introduction

In decision GCSS.VII/5 in Cartagena, the GC/GMEF further requested the Executive Director to review the practices of civil society engagement in other United Nations agencies, as well as precise modalities of civil society engagement, including involvement of the private sector in the work of the United Nations Environment Programme to achieve constructive partnership with the business community. This involvement should be further discussed, developed, and formulated in consultation with the representatives of civil society and under the guidance of the Committee of Permanent Representatives.

Frequent concerns expressed in consultations relate to information management about and for CSOs. Concerns include: lack of information about who is doing what with which CSOs; how to find appropriate CSOs to engage with; questions of the legitimacy of organizations as representatives at international forums; how CSOs can interact with each other to have more effective input to UNEP, etc. There are many ways that CSOs interact with UNEP, and all divisions have some level of engagement with civil society, but coordination has been weak. Until 2000 there was no programme dedicated solely to civil society matters—although matters have been somewhat different with respect to the private sector, where the Division of Technology, Industry and Economics is dedicated to address this sector. Apart from the outreach programme run under the former Information and Public Affairs Branch, the rest of the major groups have not had a comparable and consistent access. Another inhibiting factor has been the lack of a national level presence for UNEP, where much civil society activity takes place.

The first pillar of the strategy to strengthen engagement of civil society must therefore address such issues of institutional and information-communication support mechanisms. Special focus will be given in this area to addressing the needs of CSOs from developing countries.

(b) Roles of regional and outposted offices

Regional and outposted offices will be the 'front line' in implementation of the CS engagement strategy. Regional Offices need to be proactive in strengthening and working with national and regional CSO networks, and these should have a link with global forums. Funding sources will need to be found to support the Regional Offices in this activity, particularly for identifying appropriate CSO partners and convening periodic consultations with them in order to foster regional networking structures. Regional Offices, as the primary contact point with CSOs, will play a lead role in fostering programmatic engagement. Regional Offices will help delivering UNEP outreach to business and industry, and will have primary responsibility for database management (see below).

(c) Databases and other information management mechanisms

A new civil society (CS) database is under development by the CS Unit, which will oversee its long-term maintenance in collaboration with the Division of Early Warning and Assessment (DEWA). It will be linked to the Environmental Directory. It will be the job of the CS focal point in each regional office, however, to ensure the accuracy and regular updating of the database for their respective region. The database will hold qualitative data on UNEP-CS engagement history, areas of expertise and basic contact information. It will also be the mechanism for managing information to be used for accreditation and programme partnership identification purposes.

Better quality information management systems will support the strengthening of accreditation procedures. By viewing accreditation and assessment procedures as a facility in the engagement process beyond mere participation in governance activities, it takes on a much broader role as, in a sense, a gateway to engagement. Well-formulated assessment criteria can assist UNEP to identify CSOs with capacity and areas of technical expertise that can be valuable for programme implementation.

UNEP will improve its support to business and industry in the areas of capacity building and technology through its databases such as:

- **MaESTro** information system of UNEP IETC, providing a database on environmentally sound technology products and contacts.
- **Sustainable Alternatives Network (SANet)**, and web portal system to disseminate information and advance a network of partnerships to replicate win-win solutions in the field of technology transfer.

(d) Internet and other information/communication media
UNEP.Net can be a prototype for modalities to guarantee independent voice and participation by civil society, as well as an opportunity for capacity-building and fostering national and regional networking.UNEP.Net is the global environmental information portal being developed by UNEP in cooperation with a diverse range of partner institutions world-wide, and CSOs have a key role to play in this implementation process.

UNEP.Net will provide national CSOs with a practical mechanism to promote their activities and joint cooperation with UNEP, making use of a CSO section of the country profile, which can evolve into a comprehensive NGO bulletin board. This will facilitate two-way information exchange between UNEP and CSOs at the national level as recommended in the UN Secretary-General's Task Force on Environment and Human Settlements.

Some of the most dynamic civil society activity over the past decade has been built on internet-based communication systems. List-serves, on-line conferences, and other such mechanisms have supported information sharing and technical advice, consensus-building around specific issues, early warning of emerging environmental threats, joint advocacy for policy change, etc. In fact, there is so much activity of this nature that it is often difficult to find the information channels most relevant to an organization's needs. It should be noted, however, that the predominant users of these technologies are in the developed countries. An important role that can be played by UNEP.net is to provide a service to link CSOs at the local and national level with related internet-based activity. This will focus especially on increasing the participation in such activity by CSOs from developing countries and countries with economies in transition.

There need to be put in place mechanisms for strengthening communication with UNEP's civil society constituency. When it is fully operational UNEP.Net and the CS database will provide the primary contact base for such communication. The CS Unit will be responsible for providing regular communication to this contact base on matters of interest to the constituency. There are numerous communication tools that can be utilised to strengthen the engagement of civil society, and the CS Unit in consultation with the interdivisional working group (see below) will design a comprehensive strategy to fulfil its outreach potential.

The communication strategy will aim to ensure that UNEP's outreach to civil society becomes more than simply an information dissemination process, but rather a mechanism of engagement through which organizations interact in dialogue with UNEP and with each other, share information and identify emerging issues.

With specific reference to business and industry, UNEP will continue to prepare and update technical publications and electronic information systems on cleaner and safer production, environmental technologies and sustainable consumption. This will be done through:

- sector specific websites related to its voluntary initiatives with industry sectors and its work on chemicals, ozone, energy and trade;
- improved electronic information systems for information exchange and promoting dialogues on key issues and policies, including its: Mineral Resources Forum, Offshore Oil and Gas Environment Forum, and Sustainable Agri-food Production and Consumption Forum.

(e) Inter-divisional Coordination

Every UNEP division—as well as regional and out-posted offices—will have a focal point for CSO issues. The Civil Society Unit in isolation cannot achieve the mainstreaming of CSO engagement. Integration will require a focused effort by all parts of UNEP. The CS Unit will therefore coordinate with the different programmes to identify CSO focal points, and establish a working group that will meet on a monthly basis to address common issues related to CSO engagement, advise the Unit, and support the implementation and evaluation of the civil society engagment strategy.

The working group will also examine possibilities for a more coordinated approach to working with the various major groups. At present groups such as women/gender, youth, NGOs and the private sector are all dealt with by separate programme divisions, as are UNEP National Committees, which cross over several major groups. This diversity of approaches calls for a more systematic framework, which the inter-divisional working group will be naturally placed to address.

4. Strategy Pillar II: Modalities of Civil Society input at policy level:

In decision GCSS.VII/5 in Cartagena, the GC/GMEF requested 'the Executive Director to continue the current practice of convening a civil society forum that is regionally balanced and representative in conjunction with the meetings of the Governing Council/Global Ministerial Environment Forum in close consultation with civil society'. It further invited 'the Executive Director to consider the best way to include the views of civil society in the proceedings of the Governing Council/Global Ministerial Environment Forum'.

Several mechanisms are planned to implement these decisions of the Governing Council.

(a) Civil Society Forum

Decision GCSS.VII/5 has to a certain extent institutionalized the convening of global CS forums to coincide with GC/GMEF meetings. The challenge now is to develop mechanisms that will strengthen the quality of input from these forums to the GC/GMEF, both in terms of the competence of the participating CSOs, and how they are facilitated to bring relevant, helpful, consensus views to the GC/GMEF. The regional networking will be the main strategy to support this.This multi-stakeholder body will meet prior to the GC/GMEF meetings, to reflect on issues of major concern to UNEP and the Governing Council, and to make recommendations on these matters arising from their meetings. Such a body shall not have any decision-making role in UNEP. It is proposed as well that multi-stakeholder 'dialogue sessions' be organized at future GC/GMEF sessions, where representatives of major groups participating in the CS forum will engage with government delegations in discussions on the issues being addressed in the GC/GMEF session.

In consideration of the need to ensure that such stakeholder contributions reflect a balanced representation from all regions, as well as reflecting as much as possible the views of local and national level stakeholders, Regional Offices will play a key role in facilitating participation. To this end, the strategy envisions increased support for the convening of sub-regional and regional multi-stakeholder forums, on the model of the World Summit on Sustainable Development (WSSD) preparatory process. These regional processes would nominate representatives to the global forum. Extra resources will need to be allocated to ensure the participation of CSOs from developing countries and countries with economies in transition.

In order to identify relevant participants for the sub-regional and regional forums, UNEP's Regional Offices will work in consultation with national level umbrella groups or networks of major groups, or with National Councils for Sustainable Development (NCSDs), UNEP National Committees, or other appropriate civil society entities. Where such bodies do not exist, governments can be requested to convene multi-stakeholder meetings that can select representatives to regional meetings, as well as deliberate and provide recommendations on substantive issues. In either case, an important part of the function of Regional Offices in this process will aim to strengthen capacity of national bodies in building consensus around environmental issues. The Civil Society Unit will work closely with the Regional Offices to design and implement this component of the strategy.

(b) CSO advisory group to ED
A mechanism will be established (possibly as a standing committee) for providing ongoing advice to the Executive Director. They will meet as required by the Executive Director, but will form a nucleus of civil society partners who as individuals can provide qualitative input to policy and programme strategy formulation (see also under Pillar III). Members of this committee will be selected by UNEP on the basis of their experience and expertise in environmental and sustainable development issues, and will, as much as possible, be members of existing CSO networks focused on the multi-lateral environmental agreements or other international environment and sustainable development processes.

(c) CSO Liaison with the Committee of Permanent Representatives
The Committee of Permanent Representatives (CPR) is responsible for much of the intersessional work of the GC/GMEF. It would be useful for the CPR in pursing its function to benefit from the views of civil society on the matters under its consideration. To this end the Secretariat will develop mechanisms for improved information exchange between the CPR and CSOs, in consultation with the CSO Advisory Group to the Executive Director.

(d) Institutional support to Public Policy Networks
The regional networks and information system should assist the identification of participants in PPNs. UNEP should build in-house capacity to support PPNs as issues emerge to be addressed in this way. The CSO advisory group to the Executive Director will play an instrumental role in assisting the design of this mechanism.

UNEP will continue its role in the creation of new and the operation of existing public policy networks related to industry. A key example is the Global Reporting Initiative (GRI), initiated by UNEP and a global network of stakeholders to provide guidelines for sustainability reporting, advancing transparency and public accountability. The GRI will be established as a permanent institution, a UNEP collaborating centre with a multi-stakeholder Board and Advisory Council.

(e) Capacity Building

Improving the effectiveness of CSO contributions at the policy level will require strengthening capacity to participate, especially for NGOs from developing countries and from Central/Eastern Europe and countries with economies in transition. The Civil Society Unit will develop training initiatives to support this, possibly in collaboration with the UN Non-governmental Liaison Service (NGLS). If such training were conducted as part of periodic civil society meetings, the cost implications will be minimal.

5. Strategy Pillar III: Civil Society engagement in programme design and implementation:

In decision GCSS.VII/5, the GC/GMEF directed that 'The strategy should provide clear direction to the secretariat to ensure that all programmes take into account opportunities for multi-stakeholder participation in design, implementation, monitoring of activities, and dissemination of outputs'. It also requested the Executive Director to report to the twenty-second session of the Governing Council on the progress made in the enhancement of civil society engagement in the work of the United Nations Environment Programme.

(a) Institutionalising procedures for engagement

As requested in decision GCSS.VII/5, a more systematic and proactive implementation of the UNEP NGO policy needs to be pursued, to ensure that inclusion and consideration of CSOs in design of activities is a standard requirement. Programme/project planning procedures will require documented consideration of how civil society and private sector will participate in the various stages of the activity. UNEP's programme manual will be amended to provide more detailed guidance on modalities for engagement of CSOs in project/programme design, implementation, and monitoring.

UNEP needs to strengthen the CS Office with human and financial resources, to act as secretariat for the forums and the inter-divisional task group, CS information management, and to develop a training program to address internal and external capacity building, as described above.

The CSO Advisory Group to the ED will play a key role in enhancing programme engagement, in addition to its role at the policy level. As a group they will advise the secretariat on development of engagement guidelines, capacity building needs, and monitoring and evaluation of CSO engagement practices.

(b) Capacity Building

Improving the effectiveness of CSO skills in project design and management in order to strengthen engagement at the programme level will be required. UNEP training projects (eg in environmental law) should accommodate CSO participants, and training programmes can be targeted specifically at CSOs, such as environmental advocacy and awareness raising, and fundraising skills.

A key tool for programme engagement capacity building will be an operational manual for CSOs, to increase awareness of the opportunities for working with UNEP, and build understanding of the policies and procedures for doing so. This will be a particularly important tool for Regional Offices to expand their outreach to and support for CSOs within their regions.

(c) Enhancing Engagement with the Private Sector

UNEP will continue to engage business and industry and related CSOs in multi-stakeholder voluntary initiatives by industry sector. Cross-sectoral voluntary initiatives will also be developed to promote cleaner production and sustainable consumption, working with fellow UN organisations, research partners and stakeholder groups, exapanding and building on the experience of existing initiatives such as the Life Cycle Initiative, Global Reporting Initiative, and UN Global Compact.

In follow-up to the WSSD, UNEP will expand involvement of CSOs in preparation of industry sector reports for Johannesburg+5, building on the consultative process of creating industry sector reports that was completed for WSSD 2002. The reports will indicate progress made with the implementation of the Johannesburg Programme of Action (JPOA). Greater contributions from the developing world will be advanced through regional meetings by sector, organised with UNEP regional offices in order to help industry associations set up regional processes.

(d) Monitoring and evaluation of CS engagement

Learning mechanisms are needed to guide future policy development with respect to civil society engagement. Indicators for monitoring/evaluating quality and impact of multi-stakeholder approaches will be established. This will include substantive reporting on progress to the GC/GMEF and where possible the Environmental Management Group (EMG). A mechanism will also be put in place for ensuring regular feedback from CSOs themselves on their perception of the progress in enhancing UNEP-civil society engagement through this strategy.

UNEP will monitor and evaluate progress of the involvement of industry partners and related stakeholder in its voluntary initiatives through:

- organising annual board and general meetings to examine annual progress reports,

- organising annual roundtable conferences and workshops on topical issues to strengthen industry awareness and involvement, and
- advancing improved reporting along the Guidelines (general, thematic and sectoral) of the Global Reporting Initiative (GRI).

UNEP will also ensure clear guidelines exist for engaging business and industry, disseminating internally and adapting to its mandate the *'Guidelines on Co-operation between the United Nations and the Business Community'*, issued by the UNSG.

6. Strategic Approaches to Implementation

Enhancing civil society engagement in the work of UNEP is not an end in itself. The goal of the strategy is rather to enhance UNEP's capacity to respond to environmental problems world-wide. If the strategy is to contribute significantly to this goal, it must be underpinned with adequate means for effective implementation, in terms of institutional modalities and financial resources. Such means will be obtained through two principal strategic approaches, a medium term plan, and burden-sharing mechanisms.

(a) Medium term plan

As noted in Section 2, the strategy is envisioned to be implemented over a three to four-year period. Institutional changes as proposed, such as the strengthening of the roles of Regional Offices and CS focal points in each Division, operationalising a CSO Advisory Group, and strengthening procedures for project design and implementation, will all require time for detailed planning and mobilising. In terms of the CSO constituency that will be involved at the various levels of implementing the strategy, they will also need to organise their own response.

In order to keep the strategy in focus over this period, for both the internal and external actors, these measures will be incorporated in the medium term plan. This plan will provide the framework to guide implementation, through the identification of roles and timelines, resource needs, outlining strategies to ensure complementarity with the overall UNEP programme of work and budget, and development of strategic partnerships with specific CSOs, governments and agencies.

(b) Burden-sharing mechanisms

Given the goal of enhancing UNEP's capacity to respond to environmental problems world-wide, through enhanced engagement with civil society including the private sector, the responsibility for providing the resources to achieve this will need to, and should, be shared amongst the array of actors who participate in both the implementation and the benefits.

Through the medium term plan UNEP will incorporate activities in its biennium budgetary process as appropriate. Costed work plans will allocate resources dedicated to activities envisioned in the strategy.

Financial allocations separate from the Environment Fund will be required to support implementation of the institutional, capacity building and programmatic measures that cannot be accommodated within the costed work plan. Such funds should not be designed as a small grants facitlity to respond to a myriad of CSO projects, as it would be difficult to administer and there are alternative sources for such funding. These funds, instead, will be designed for targeted use to support implementation of the larger CSO strategy. They will provide a vehicle for donors—including governments, NGOs, foundations and other agencies—to target their funds for the UNEP-Civil Society strategy. At the same time donor agencies will be invited to share the costs of specific activities, such as civil society forums or joint projects with CSOs.

The private sector already bears much of the cost of UNEP initiatives aimed at this sector. With the enhanced engagement of the private sector as envisioned in this strategy, it is expected that such burden-sharing will be made more equitable in future.

A further measure in burden-sharing will be increased efforts to fundraise jointly with CSO partners to obtain the resources needed for implementation of many of the initiatives that emerge during implementation of the medium term plan.

Appendix VII

UNDP

UNDP AND CIVIL SOCIETY ORGANIZATIONS: A POLICY NOTE
ON ENGAGEMENT

> **Issued by UNDP**
> Source: <http://www.undp.org/policy/docs/policynotes/UNDP%
> 20CSO%20Policy.pdf>

I. Introduction

1. The United Nations Charter gives UNDP a powerful mandate to work
   with civil society organizations (CSOs). At the Millennium Summit
   2000, the Secretary General reaffirmed the centrality of civil society
   and its organizations to the mission of the United Nations in the
   twenty-first century:

   > Not only do you (civil society organizations) bring to life the
   > concept of 'We, the Peoples', in whose name our Charter was writ-
   > ten; you bring to us the promise that 'people power' can make the
   > Charter work for all the world's peoples in the twenty-first century.

   Equally, the UNDP focus on sustainable human development that
   places people at the centre of development cannot be achieved without
   the robust engagement of civil society and its organizations. Given the
   collective power of CSOs in building social, economic and political
   agendas—both locally and globally—it is clear that strengthening partnership with CSOs is crucial if UNDP is to remain a relevant and effective development player.

2. World leaders at the Millennium Summit declared the need for more
   equitable globalization the most pressing challenge of the new century.
   A reinvigorated partnership with CSOs is central to delivering the
   promises of the Millennium Declaration within the context of the
   increasingly uneven distribution of costs and benefits associated with
   rapid global economic integration.

3. CSOs are a crucial resource, constituency and partner for UNDP in
   advancing sustainable human development goals and principles. UNDP
   has made significant progress in both broadening and deepening its
   interaction with CSOs at all levels of its work. In particular, UNDP has

developed a valued niche in creating the space with Governments for CSO perspectives to be heard and incorporated into policy and programmes. In so doing, UNDP recognizes that CSOs are not a substitute for government, but are central to sustainable governance.

4. The evolution of CSOs in recent years, the policy imperatives of UNDP, and the context of the new millennium, call for a renewed framework to guide UNDP-CSO engagement. The policy note provides a new set of principles to guide UNDP engagement with CSOs, and highlights policy and programmatic implications. The note has been reviewed and endorsed by the CSO Advisory Committee to the Administrator and has benefited from country office experience.

II. Civil Society: Understanding and Reasons for Collaboration

5. UNDP takes a broad view of CSOs, of which non-governmental organizations (NGOs) are an important part. In this perspective, civil society constitutes a third sector, existing alongside and interacting with the State and profit-seeking firms. Many CSOs have been at the forefront of advocating principles of social justice and equity; but there are also organizations with agendas and values—such as intolerance and exclusion—that do not correspond to those of the United Nations system. In practice, civil society is an arena of both collaboration and contention whose configurations may vary according to national setting and history.

6. UNDP collaborates with CSOs whose goals, values and development philosophy correspond to its own. UNDP also engages with CSOs concerned with (inter)national public policy and governance. The nature of the partnership with CSOs, particularly at the country office level, needs to be rooted in informed analysis and assessment of the country situation including the role, competencies and needs of CSOs.

Why does UNDP engage with CSOs?

7. UNDP interest in partnering with CSOs stems from many considerations. In brief, these are:

   - Improving the condition of the poor and excluded is the ultimate justification for existence of UNDP as a development agency. Collaboration with CSOs that articulate the needs and aspirations of the poor is a sine qua non of good practice;
   - Governments in developing countries cannot on their own fulfil all the tasks required for sustainable human development. This goal requires the active participation and partnership of citizens and their organizations;
   - While external support can help, improved governance must ultimately come from within and be owned by a country and its citizens. CSOs therefore have vital roles to play as participants, legitimizers

and endorsers of government policy and action, as watchdogs on the behaviour of regimes and public agencies, and as collaborators in the national development effort;

– From the human-rights perspective, UNDP, along with member governments, bears duties and obligations towards the poor and excluded who are denied internationally recognized entitlements. To fulfil these obligations, the organization must engage with and involve a range of civic actors in its programmes.

– UNDP positions, public support, work and success in the future are dependent on multi-party trust. In the words of the Administrator:

'You do not buy that [poverty reduction] agenda through loans, you win it through trust. And it is the same asset, trust, that allows us to assemble the partnerships with governments, civil society, labour unions and the private sector that UNDP -everybody's friend - can do.'

8. The increasing sophistication of CSOs places new and more complex demands on UNDP. Over the last decade, CSOs including NGOs, peoples' movements, trade unions, women's federations, formal and informal associations, grass-roots coalitions and indigenous peoples' organizations, have emerged as a powerful force for social justice and equity across and within borders. This is largely a result of the impact of globalization on the intergovernmental system, the changing role of the nation state and the spread of the information age. CSOs have mounted successful campaigns that are effectively shaping the content of national and international agreements—on issues ranging from land-mines and debt cancellation to affordable medication for HIV and AIDS—and have helped to bring about new institutions—including the International Criminal Court and the Permanent Forum on Indigenous Issues. They have also laid the ground for local and global discussions on alternative policy choices—from local 'citizen hearings' on poverty and AIDS to parallel NGO forums at the United Nations conferences, peoples' assemblies and social forums to exchange experiences, debate and propose economic and social alternatives.

9. Most importantly, there is growing recognition, by the United Nations and individual governments, of the role played by CSOs, as well as the private sector, in implementing what is agreed upon at the international level. Global governance is no longer viewed as primarily an intergovernmental concern but one that involves intergovernmental institutions, CSOs, citizens' movements, transnational corporations, academia and the mass media. The emergence of a global civil society reflects a surge in the will and capacity of people to take control of their lives—a fact that governments and intergovernmental agencies cannot afford to ignore.

10. Nowhere is this more evident than in the United Nations over the past decade. The influx of international and national CSOs became highly visible at the Rio Earth Summit and has continued through subsequent United Nations conferences. By the end of 2000, the number of CSOs officially accredited to the Economic and Social Council had more than doubled—to 1900 from about 900 in 1992. CSOs have participated closely in all stages of conference preparation and follow-up, holding parallel forums and lobbying for alternative language and initiatives. Most conference programmes of action bear the imprint of CSOs, many of which have then pursued and monitored government accountability to these commitments at national and international levels.

11. These democratic openings have presented women's organizations, in particular, with extraordinary opportunities for advocacy and policy change. Through the 1990s, feminist ideas of equality and inclusion have had enormous influence across a range of areas—the reproductive health movement, political parties and development practice, for example. Women's organizations at the country and community level have moved into both service delivery and policy advisory roles, and are increasingly involved in delivering vital social services, helping governments to design and implement gender-sensitive programmes.

Box 1. CSOs monitoring government commitments for women's empowerment

Women's rights organizations have a very important role in making the landmark 1979 Convention on the Elimination of All Forms of Discrimination Against Women (the CEDAW Convention) a key instrument of women's empowerment, through advocacy and monitoring their government's implementation of the treaty. The Convention's enforcement mechanism is based on a reporting system, which makes it imperative that NGOs understand and use the reporting mechanism to ensure government accountability both inside the country and at the United Nations. In recent years, civil society advocates of women's human rights have made big strides in their efforts to strengthen CEDAW. A key victory is the wider recognition the CEDAW Committee now accords to the role of non-governmental organizations in monitoring compliance of the Convention. In some countries, coalitions of NGOs, political parties and the government have succeeded in activating CEDAW in domestic political activity and policy formulation.

Why do CSOs engage with UNDP?

12. CSOs' interest in engaging with UNDP depends on the extent to which such collaboration generates mutual added value. From a CSO perspective, some factors that warrant engagement with UNDP are:
    - At the country level, the relationship of trust between developing country governments and UNDP and the ability of UNDP to broker space for government CSO dialogue and engagement;
    - The human development paradigm as a critical entry point and foundation for dialogue, action, joint advocacy and campaigns with civil society;
    - The broad mandate of UNDP, which is not only more holistic compared to other sectoral, issue-specific agencies, but also more in line with the interrelated manner in which many CSOs look at issues of development and conflict;
    - The coordinating role of UNDP in the United Nations system and the United Nations Development Group, both globally and at the country level;
    - The potential of UNDP as an ally and source of resources for CSO human development initiatives;
    - UNDP potential to differentiate itself intellectually from conventional policy advice with the aim of promoting inclusive globalization.

III. Why Update the CSO Policy?

13. At least four developments justify a new CSO policy. First, CSOs are rapidly evolving. They are becoming more capable and demanding in engaging and negotiating terms with other development actors. Second, there are valuable lessons to be drawn from past interaction between UNDP and CSOs. Third, UNDP is undergoing major institutional reform with significant implications for its interface with CSOs. Fourth, the organization has adopted policies, for example on human rights and indigenous peoples, that have major implications for partnerships with CSOs.

Past lessons of CSO engagement

14. UNDP has a rich history of engagement with CSOs in both operational and policy work that cuts across major focus areas. But strategic, mainstreamed partnership, as opposed to episodic, project-driven engagement, remains a central challenge.

15. In the late 1990s, UNDP implemented a global programme dedicated to mainstreaming CSOs in operations and policy development. An internal stocktaking exercise and external mid term evaluation indicate that, despite major constraints, the programme was largely doing the

right things, but lacked adequate engagement with progressive segments of the civil society movement that were required for UNDP 'to be relevant, to compete and to survive'. The programme suffered from inadequate integration across the organization, further impeded by incentives and procedures that push staff to a utilitarian approach towards CSOs to achieve UNDP goals.

16. A corollary lesson is the need to balance CSO involvement in policy arenas with local accountability and civic mobilization on the ground. It is important to have CSOs present at the policy table. But this must not detract from collaboration with CSOs in downstream work. This implies a CSO approach and practice that actively builds links between macro-level policy and pro-poor micro initiatives.

17. Another lesson is to take explicit account of the fact that engagement with civil society, or reducing poverty, promoting human rights and democratic governance, are implicitly political in nature and potentially a source of tension that must be managed with sensitivity, but not used as an excuse for inaction. The policy framework for CSOs respects UNDP collaboration and obligations towards governments but not at the cost of denying CSO rights as claimants. The UNDP reform agenda reinforces and creates improved space for this partnership.

UNDP institutional reform

18. The establishment, in May 2000, of the UNDP CSO Advisory Committee interfacing directly with the Administrator is a major advance in establishing formal status arrangements with CSOs. An expressed intention of this step is to ensure that the organization becomes more open and sensitive to the agendas within civil society.

19. The UNDP CSO Advisory Committee proposed the following priority themes for collaboration:
   – Poverty reduction and sustainable debt;
   – Inclusive globalization—democratizing trade and finance;
   – Conflict prevention and peace building;
   – Human rights and human development;
   – Private sector engagement.
   It also recommended the development of a new policy on CSO engagement and the creation of a policy on engagement with indigenous peoples. The committee emphasized a substantive role for UNDP in cutting-edge analysis and regional debate on the trading regime from a sustainable human development perspective. These recommendations call for country and region-specific CSO agendas.

20. The UNDP reform process has created six focus areas: poverty reduction; democratic governance; crisis prevention and recovery; energy

and the environment; HIV and AIDS; and information, communication and technology for development. To realize the authentic strategic partnerships that UNDP reform has in mind, it is important to understand and negotiate honestly what does and does not fit as an agenda for real UNDP-CSO partnership. The UNDP CSO Advisory Committee provides an important new mechanism for doing so in New York that should be replicated at national and regional levels of the organization.

The human rights dimension to CSO partnership
21. The 1998 policy integrating a rights-based approach to sustainable human development and the 2001 policy on indigenous peoples are of particular relevance to the implementation of the UNDP CSO policy.

Box 2. UNDP human rights policy and CSOs
UNDP support for human rights will respond to national needs and priorities as identified by government as well as by NGOs. UNDP will need to devise policies that enable it to work with civil society organizations and NGOs in such countries. Most important, UNDP must develop a firm policy to ensure that its development programmes do not become vehicles for human rights abuses—for example, in a country that excludes women, indigenous people or ethnic minorities from the benefits of development. In such countries, economic, social and cultural rights provide the obvious entry point for human rights-based sustainable human development programming. But UNDP will have to guard against neglecting political and civil rights and difficult questions of how to incorporate them in programmes in such countries will have to be addressed. From the 1998 policy paper 'Integrating human rights with sustainable human development'.

---

22. A major implication of adopting a human rights-based view of human development is that UNDP acknowledges that it shares obligations with the government. CSOs have legitimate entitlements, codified in international conventions, covenants and laws. People have a right to act as claimants on and monitors of UNDP policies and (implementing) actions, alongside, with and through governments as complementary duty bearers.
23. Correspondingly, UNDP must establish formal means to listen to claimants at the country, (sub) regional and global levels. This must be done not on the basis of need, but as an economic, social, cultural, political and civic right or fundamental freedom. Realistically, citizens

who are most deeply affected by UNDP policy or practice have the greatest legitimacy as claimants.

24. A rights-based philosophy of development challenges CSOs, particularly intermediary NGOs, to reflect on their own obligations as duty bearers. Some CSOs claim a role in policy-making because they are representative of and accountable to certain groups. Others base their claim on their expertise and interest. In their efforts to influence policy, a core issue for CSOs is accountability based on expertise; they should not attempt to act as representatives unless they can demonstrate that they have a constituency that gives a mandate and effective control over policy positions adopted.

IV. Principles and Commitments of CSO-UNDP Engagement

25. At the heart of this policy are five principles and corresponding commitments that together provide a coherent foundation for partnership.

Principle and commitment 1. **Partnership founded on horizontality (equality), trust, inclusion and mutual capability.**
Partnership with CSOs is founded on the principle of a horizontal relationship between parties that, while institutionally different, are of equal standing in promoting the same development objectives, especially poverty reduction though sustainable human development. The relationship is premised on mutual trust that must be earned by both sides. UNDP is committed to investing in enhancing trust with CSOs that share its goals. In doing so, UNDP acknowledges the frequent asymmetry between its capabilities and those of the CSOs with which it wishes to engage. Consequently, UNDP contribution to CSO capacity development remains a cornerstone of its approach to development and partnership.

Principle and commitment 2. **Recognition of obligations as a duty-bearer**
In adopting the principles and a policy on human rights, UNDP implicitly recognizes its responsibility as a duty bearer both towards member governments in terms of supporting fulfilment of their public obligations and simultaneously towards civil society as legitimate claimants on governments and UNDP as a public body. Correspondingly, interacting with civil society is a duty and not an option for UNDP at all levels of its work. UNDP is committed to engaging with CSOs as an expression of their right to development, not simply because of institutional convenience.

Principle and commitment 3. **Negotiation and mutual agenda setting with individual accountability**
Neither UNDP nor CSOs are required to accept or endorse each other's

agendas, interpretations of events or methods. Engagement with CSOs must be founded on the principle of negotiation towards a common interest that recognises complementarity of roles, not a sharing of institutional responsibilities. Each party is individually accountable for its behaviour to its owners or constituencies. While not imposing its own agenda, UNDP is committed to seeking mutual ground for action that respects the agendas of the civil societies where it is present.

Principle and commitment 4. Disaggregation, selection and intellectual differentiation
UNDP recognizes that CSOs are, by their very nature, heterogeneous. This diversity is a valuable development asset that should not be 'homogenized' by CSO engagement with UNDP. To this end, UNDP adopts the principle of respecting CSO diversity. UNDP is committed to enhancing its own insight and capability to differentiate between CSOs while adopting practices that correspond to and respect their differences.

Consistent with its mandate, institutional position and comparative advantages, such as impartiality, UNDP acknowledges the challenge and value added of intellectually differentiating itself in the multilateral system and in its dealings with others. To this end, UNDP is committed to being a distinctive voice and champion of human development based on human rights, continually refining the analytic foundation for its thinking, practice and engagement in dialogue with all its stakeholders. UNDP is also committed to methods of work that are distinctive and that fully realize its comparative advantages, such as respect for national ownership, people-to-people approach, local knowledge and sensitivity, and the ability to facilitate constructive interaction between a range of stakeholders.

Principle and commitment 5. Macro-micro coherence and balance: connecting upstream and downstream
UNDP acknowledges the importance of the principles of coherence and consistency between engagement with CSOs in its in-country initiatives and in international policy work. It is committed to balanced treatment and investment between CSO engagement at local and macro levels, ie, in its operations and policy dialogues, within countries, regionally and internationally.

V. Implications for UNDP and CSOs
26. Adopting and applying the foregoing principles and commitments has practical consequences for headquarters in regional programmes and in country offices. Hands on tools and methods for engagement are in the CSO source book.

A. Strategic partnership

27. A key challenge in implementing the CSO policy will be in effecting a shift from project-driven engagement to strategic partnership. Global and country experience point to the importance of creating an institutionalized forum for UNDP-CSO dialogue and debate on policy directions.

UNDP-CSO committees—global, regional, and local

28. The UNDP CSO Advisory Committee to the Administrator seeks to ensure that senior management at headquarters receives proper guidance on policy issues critical to the future directions of the organization. By having the committee report directly to him, the Administrator sends a clear signal to senior managers and staff of the importance accorded to perspectives. The Committee comprises 14 CSO leaders selected based on the expertise that they can bring to bear on a set of mutually agreed issues. A series of consultations identified the following broad areas of mutual concern: (a) poverty reduction and sustainable debt; (b) inclusive globalization: democratizing trade and finance; (c) conflict prevention and peace-building; (d) human rights and human development; and, (e) private-sector engagement.

29. There are also structured dialogues between members of the committee and the Executive Board on issues including policy options and perspectives in trade, poverty reduction, monitoring the Millennium Development Goals, human-rights based approaches to development and gender-mainstreaming. The UNDP CSO Advisory Committee thus provides a mechanism for mutual agenda setting, policy debate, individual accountability, and ease of access for exchanges between senior managers and civil society leaders on future directions for UNDP. Together these elements provide a sound basis for building a partnership based on principles of horizontality and trust.

30. Country office experience has shown that the creation of local CSO advisory committees ensures local policy relevance and builds UNDP credibility. In situations where relations between the state and civil society might prohibit the establishment of a formal CSO advisory committee, two options could be pursued: (a) informal dialogue with CSOs, and/or (b) discussion of sensitive issues at the regional level. Regional programmes and sub-regional resource facilities (SURFs) can provide impartial space for dialogue which 'stands above' state-civil society tensions and sensitivities that may exist at the country level.

31. Establishing local and regional CSO committees is a critical step in realizing four key principles and commitments of partnership: trust, horizontality, mutual agenda setting and individual accountability.

UNDP is therefore committed to making local and regional CSO advisory committees a regular feature of its partnership of engagement with CSOs at the country and, where appropriate, regional levels. Regional and country office experience has demonstrated the importance of bringing together CSOs to debate and provide both policy and operational advice. Committees or advisory groups have been established around the production and advocacy of National Human Development Reports (NHDR), around particular themes—governance, poverty, human rights, and more recently for the analysis, monitoring and advocacy of the MDGs. The CSO Advisory Committee to the Administrator demonstrates the important synergies that are created when a multidisciplinary committee is established to provide strategic guidance across a range of issues UNDP is grappling with.

Box 3. Zimbabwe Poverty Reduction Forum
The main goal of the Poverty Reduction Forum in Zimbabwe is to provide an arena of debate on issues of poverty reduction that engages a broad representation of civic society with key decision-makers who influence national policies. Created in 1996 with the support of UNDP, the Forum has grown to include a membership of 300 organizations, which brings together NGOs, academics, community-based organizations, trade unions, donor agencies, chambers of commerce, farmers unions, and a growing participation of peoples' organizations. The Forum has influenced a range of national policy issues from poverty reduction strategies to national budgetary processes. It has also provided a critical channel for national debate between civil society and government on structural adjustment processes.

Partnership strategy
32. The revised policy CSOs requires a more strategic approach to engagement, of which a partnership strategy is a key component. An effective UNDP-CSO partnership strategy should build on a mutually set agenda and provide clarity on the desired outcomes and processes. A locally relevant strategy, time frame and resource allocations are important preconditions if country offices are to reach out to CSOs in a credible way.

B. Possible entry points for UNDP-CSO collaboration
33. Drawing from country office experience and a process of UNDP-CSO consultations, the following broad priorities were identified as potential entry points for UNDP-CSO engagement.

Leveraging the relatively trusted relations of UNDP with governments to create the political space for civil society to express alternative views and influence policy dialogue and decision-making at all levels: local, national and global.

Taking a stand on international human rights norms and standards and working with CSOs to realize the rights and obligations they entail for people. These include supporting the societal watchdog functions of CSOs in defending and monitoring the commitments of United Nations Conferences and human rights.

Ensuring genuine CSO engagement in the development, implementation and monitoring of key policy processes.

Initiating multi-stakeholder partnerships among governments, donors and civil society for sustainable human development at all levels (local, national, regional and global).

Supporting the capacity of civil society to articulate demands, offer options and defend the rights of people living in poverty at all levels. This implies supporting the crucial intermediary role played by CSOs in building bridges between local realities and macro-level policy issues.

Facilitating the relational capacity of CSOs to negotiate their concerns with government and business sectors of society.

Jointly identifying 'campaign issues' and mobilizing a broad-based constituency (at local and global levels and especially between South and North) using and advocating greater access to information technology.

Facilitating traditional and horizontal linkages between CSOs that are critical to determining the quality of relationships between communities (otherwise known as bridging social capital). This has been found to be particularly crucial in both preventing and resolving conflict.

Recognizing the differentiated impact of development on diverse vulnerable populations, particularly indigenous peoples, and ensuring that they have a voice in key development policy processes affecting their lives.

Creating an enabling legal and regulatory environment for a vibrant civil society and ensuring the inclusion of CSOs in key legislative processes.

Pursuing these entry points places increasing demands on the range of roles that UNDP is called upon to play.

C. UNDP roles and functions

34. The reform process and the revised CSO policy will make the strongest call on the country and regional capability of UNDP to perform the following broad roles:

Trusted convenor, negotiator and facilitator. Whether negotiating peace and reconciliation processes or facilitating sensitive political dialogues, UNDP is increasingly called on at the country level as a trusted, impartial convenor of multi-stakeholder initiatives. It is at once the organization's strongest asset and most challenging role.

Broker of space for policy options and excluded perspectives. UNDP has an important role to play in ensuring that policy voices and choices are made available to decision-makers. Central to this function is guaranteeing that the perspectives of CSOs and indigenous peoples' organizations are provided the space for expression. In turn, civic engagement in policy processes and choices ensures their eventual sustainability.

Competent enhancer of CSO capacity. UNDP provides a distinct value added not only in developing the internal organisational strengths of CSOs, but supporting and facilitating their networking— among themselves as well as with government and, with business sectors of society.

Enabler of a vibrant civil society. Beyond creating legal and regulatory frameworks for the operation of NGOs and CSOs, UNDP has a broader role to play in facilitating vibrant civic engagement in key national and regional processes for human development.

Disseminator of instructive practice. In collaboration with CSOs, UNDP plays a valuable role in documenting the rapidly evolving trends and developments in civic engagement at the country, regional and global levels.

Implications for competencies

35. To be a trusted interlocutor, country and regional offices must balance enhanced technical competencies, for example, in civil society mapping and CSO selection, with greater attention to 'people' factors in dealing with external relations. In addition to allocating sufficient time to the task, staff aptitudes in terms of negotiation, dialogue and facilitation will become more important.

D. Mechanisms for strategic policy engagement

36. There are several tools and mechanisms to assist in the development of a strategic partnership with CSOs. Briefly, these include:

   CSO mapping

   The rapidly changing nature of CSOs with shifting alliances and evolving institutions that grow and contract in response to social, economic and political imperatives often requires a continuous reading of the civic environment if UNDP is to stay abreast of current trends and developments. Periodic mapping of CSOs enables country offices to stay close to the popular pulse on emerging issues. It also provides the opportunity for a country office to reassess and focus the goals of its partnership strategy: with whom does it partner and to what development end?

Selection process

Wide variations in national CSO history, diverse configurations, inter-CSO relations and state attitude will inevitably require UNDP to select carefully with whom to engage and how. To assist in the selection process, it is important to assess, develop and publish situationally relevant criteria to determine with which actors from civil society to engage and why. Some significant factors are domestic rootedness, demonstrated mandate, legitimacy as claimant, competence and expertise, and accountability.

Multi-stakeholder initiatives

Building on its role of impartial convenor, UNDP has a distinct comparative advantage in facilitating dialogue around sensitive issues that bring together different development actors from society, government and the market to work towards a shared solution. Country office experience in conflict and post-conflict reconciliation processes highlight the value added of bringing CSOs, including indigenous peoples' organizations (IPOs), into all stages of the reconciliation and rehabilitation process.

Creating an enabling environment for CSOs

While the preparation of a legal framework for the operation of CSOs is often associated with an 'enabling CSO environment', it is not necessarily conducive for creating vibrant civic engagement in key national processes. A legal regulatory framework for CSOs is an important but not sufficient condition. Country office experience points to the valuable role that UNDP can play in brokering and creating space to enable full participation of CSOs in national development processes.

Box 4. Capacity 21 in Mexico: creating a space for citizen participation and leadership

Through the Capacity 21 programme in Mexico, UNDP, Government and civil society seek to integrate social issues with the production and conservation of natural resources, harmonize human issues with nature and local matters with national matters in a decentralized approach that advocates renewed citizen participation. Three key themes were thus prioritized in Huatulco and Sierra Gorda: NGO capacity-building to decentralize power and resources, socialization of development and grass-roots leadership. In close partnership with the governments, civil society and grass-roots peasant-farmer communities, UNDP has nurtured an enabling, participatory environment for the adoption of national and local policies. Citizen participation in environmental management was strengthened through the national and regional consultative councils for sustainable development as well as technical councils in the fields of forestry, soils, protected natural areas and river basins. The Capacity 21 programme has contributed to the flourishing of NGOs and to the strengthening of their institutional and administrative planning, evaluation, information, resource management and consensus-building capacities with the promotion of decentralized and inter-sectoral participation.

CSO engagement in UN and UNDP led policy processes

37. A number UNDP-led policy processes, have been, and will continue to be substantially enriched through CSO engagement and mobilization. Three are highlighted below.

    - **Human development reports (HDR)**. The global and national HDRs have become the principal UNDP instruments for stimulating policy debate. CSOs have been most effective in generating local debates on findings from HDRs, translating the report into advocacy strategies and campaigns for effecting policy changes, and bringing about policy studies, poverty assessments and regional and national qualitative indices for monitoring poverty. UNDP is committed to expanding the opportunities for CSO engagement in both the conception and development of advocacy messages and strategies.

    - **Common country assessment and United Nations Development Assistance Framework (CCA/UNDAF)**. As the chair of the United Nations Development Group (UNDG), UNDP has a central leadership role in ensuring that space and opportunity is provided for genuine CSO partnerships in United Nations-led policy processes— from the Millennium Development Goals (MDGs) to the CCA and UNDAF. Though limited to date, country experience with CSO engagement in the CCA/UNDAF process attests to the valued 'peopled perspective' that CSOs bring and their expertise, outreach and ability to build awareness for human development issues. The new CSO policy requires greater participation and engagement of CSOs in these key policy processes. The degree to which genuine partnership can be achieved will depend in large part on the role accorded to CSOs in the conception, implementation and monitoring phases.

    - **The Millennium Development Goals (MDGs)**. Partnerships with CSOs are pivotal for mobilizing public opinion and raising public awareness for the MDGs. In countries across the world, civil society groups have a special interest in one or more of the MDGs. Many have a proven capacity for broad-based mobilization and creating bottom-up demand that holds leaders accountable—skills that will be essential to placing the MDGs at the heart of national debates and development priorities. The role of civil society organizations is crucial not only in campaigning for the goals, but in preparing the analysis for MDG reports, and monitoring progress to generate and sustain political momentum and public interest. They are essential partners for realizing the UNDP mandate of 'Campaign Manager' and 'Score Keeper' of the MDGs.

UNDP engagement in CSO-led policy processes

38. Conversely, UNDP has much to gain in partnering in CSO-led policy processes. This often requires extending engagement beyond well-known organizations of civil society to peoples' movements and grass-roots organizations that are deeply embedded in the creative processes of societal change. As one country office suggested, UNDP should draw inspiration from peoples' movements and support their initiatives rather than simply engage a known range of civil society actors instrumentally in projects and programmes.

Box 5. South Africa poverty hearings: people put poverty on the national agenda

In 1998, a unique series of public meetings enabled the poor throughout South Africa to talk to decision-makers about their experiences of poverty. These meetings were the first stage of the strategy of the War on Poverty Forum, a partnership of CSOs, the Government, UNDP and other donors. The South Africa NGO coalition organized 35 day-long 'Speak out on Poverty' hearings in 29 locations. More than 10,000 people came to the first set of hearings alone. Poor people, most of whom had little or no contact with government representatives, spoke about their experiences and their ideas for improving their lives. Throughout this participatory partnership, the forum put local experiences of poverty on the national agenda. Plans to replicate the 'speak-out' model, which requires little money and is tremendously effective, are now under way elsewhere in sub-Saharan Africa. It also inspired the 'Speak out on AIDS' hearings in South Africa that brought peoples' personal testimony to national, public and policy attention.

E. Mechanisms for operational engagement

39. A series of mechanisms were created in the late 1990s to facilitate the operational engagement of UNDP with CSOs; three are briefly highlighted below. The CSO sourcebook provides more detailed guidance on the mechanisms and their applications.

– **Public information and documentation disclosure policy (IDP)**
IDP is the cornerstone of UNDP operational engagement with CSOs.
The policy, in force since 1997 and assessed in 2001, expresses the
right of citizens and governments to request that UNDP make available all operational programme, project documents and briefs that
UNDP, in the absence of a 'compelling reason for confidentiality', is
required to provide. As a custodian of public funds, UNDP is
directly accountable to its member Governments and to the public in
programme and donor countries. There is a symbiotic relationship
between information sharing and public participation in UNDP-
supported development activities and the quality and sustainability
of these efforts. Requested information should be provided early and
regularly to CSOs, affected parties and the general public. Public
access to information and documentation held or generated by
UNDP will ultimately facilitate the transparency, accountability and
legitimacy of its operations. Beyond the requirement is the principle
of a pro-active approach in which UNDP transparently seeks the
participation and partnership of CSOs. A new oversight panel is in
the process of being established.

– **NGO execution**
Historically, the bulk of UNDP-CSO working arrangements has
taken the form of either a sub-contract within an agency, a nation-
ally executed project or a direct grant. With the introduction of
NGO execution, CSOs can now be engaged directly as an executing
agent with overhead charges. Since the introduction of the modality
in 1998, some 300 projects totalling over $100 million have been
executed in this way. The procedures are currently being reviewed
for simplification and greater accessibility to a broader range of
CSOs.

– **Memorandum of understanding (MoU)**
While not a requirement for UNDP engagement with CSOs, MoUs
can nonetheless be useful in situations which do not require a transfer of resources between the parties but rather a statement of intent
of partnership usually around a particular issue or cause. An MoU
is an agreement that provides a general framework for collaboration
between UNDP and the other party that sets out the broad nature
and scope of the engagement.

– **Small grant facilities of the Bureau for Development Policy (BDP)
and Regional Bureaux**
UNDP has a long-established track record in providing small grants
to community based initiatives which in turn have upstream policy
impact at the district, regional or national levels. At present, two
such mechanisms exist at headquarters: the small grants window of

the Global Environment Facility (GEF) and the Local Urban Initiatives for the Environment (LIFE). Both mechanisms are managed by BDP. At the regional level, the Africa 2000 programme and the South Asia Poverty Alleviation Programme provide small grants to vulnerable local communities for sustainable poverty initiatives.

Resources for CSO-UNDP partnership

40. While substantive policy consultations can have high impact at minimal cost, depending on the nature of engagement, availability of resources can hinder or facilitate partnership. Some of the resources available globally for partnership with civil society found outside country and regional cooperation modalities are:

 – **Thematic trust funds (BDP)**
   Each thematic trust fund (TTF)—for poverty reduction, governance, crisis and recovery, energy and the environment, HIV/AIDS, gender and information and communication technology—outlines strategic services that either directly relate to engaging CSOs or include them as one of key stakeholders in a multi-partner initiative. The funds that most directly engage with CSOs are the Poverty Trust Fund (CSOs are closely integrated into participatory processes for poverty reduction strategies and monitoring and direct empowerment for pro-poor budgeting) and the Governance Trust Fund (particularly regarding local governance issues). The TTFs are managed by BDP in close collaboration with the regional bureaux.

 – **Partnership Facility of the Bureau for Resources and Strategic Partnerships**
   This facility provides small grants for quick disbursement to UNDP country offices to support innovative, highly leveraged partnership initiatives. It is an excellent source of funds for creative partnerships between UNDP and CSOs or for multi-stakeholder partnerships in which CSOs are a critical player. The facility is managed by BRSP in close collaboration with the regional bureaux.

CONCEPT PAPER ON THE ESTABLISHMENT OF A CSO ADVISORY
COMMITTEE TO UNDP

> **Adopted by UNDP**
> **April 2000**

In 1999, UNDP renewed its focus on governance for human development
and sought to systematize its process of consultation with civil society organizations to benefit from the policy and operational advice that this
constituency can offer. It decided to establish a formal committee comprising individuals from representative civil society organizations who will
provide guidance to the Administrator and senior management on key
policy and programming issues.

A series of consultations and workshops with members of the CSO
community to discuss the establishment of a CSO consultative body, to be
known as the CSO Committee, were held in 1999. Based on these consultations, several recommendations came from CSOs on such issues as
membership (duration, criteria for selection, size), function, and funding
requirements and helped to shape the committee. Lessons were also drawn
from examples of CSO/NGO institutional arrangements with other intergovernmental bodies such as the World Bank, UNICEF, UNFPA and the
OECD/DAC.

From these consultations, it emerged that there was a strong preference
for a formal mechanism for civic involvement that also goes beyond traditional advisory bodies. CSOs consulted by UNDP argued for an arrangement that would influence UNDP decision-making processes at
headquarters and country level. Impact would be monitored through periodic evaluations. It was noted that a formal relationship with civil society
at the global level could provide an impetus for civic involvement in difficult country situations and serve to extend good national practice to countries where conditions were not so conducive. CSO leaders also endorsed
the role of UNDP in enabling civil society participation and opening political space at the national level.

The committee met for the first time in May 2000.

Role of the CSO Committee
The primary functions of the CSO Committee are to: provide advice and
strategic guidance to the UNDP Administrator, support and monitor the
implementation of key information policy and advocacy efforts, and pilot
strategic CSO/UNDP initiatives and activities. Within these three broad
areas, the CSO Committee will focus more specifically on:

    A. <u>Providing strategic, policy, and substantive guidance to the
    Administrator and senior management of UNDP.</u>

These activities may include:

- Reviewing and guiding the preparation of an effective operational strategy for UNDP engagement with civil society for the purpose of advocacy, policy dialogue, research and analytical work, and programming.
- Working with UNDP, at headquarters and country office level, to promote effective collaboration with civil society actors and help resolve bottlenecks or conflicts affecting UNDP/CSO collaboration.
- Presenting recommendations and findings to the Administrator to facilitate appropriate policy or procedural changes within UNDP, if required.

B. Supporting and monitoring information and advocacy efforts.
These may include:

- Reviewing the implementation of the UNDP Information Disclosure Policy. Coordinating, sharing and disseminating information related to UNDP-CSO partnerships to relevant partners and internalizing lessons learned within UNDP.
- Advocating within UNDP and outside on issues related to promoting partnerships between various stakeholders as well as those that strengthen participatory policy development.

C. Piloting joint UNDP/CSO initiatives.
These may include:

- CSO/UNDP partnership on conflict prevention and peace-building studies.
- CSO/UNDP partnership in the context of United Nations Development Assistance Framework / Common Country Assessment (UNDAF/CCA) exercises.
- Preparation of periodic CSO evaluation of UNDP practice in participatory engagement.

Meetings

The CSO Committee is expected to convene on an annual basis.

The CSO Committee may wish to convene its meetings to coincide with the annual CSO dialogue with the Executive Board. At present the UNDP Executive Board does not formally recognize or encourage the active participation of CSOs in board sessions, except where they are specifically invited to participate in deliberations and have consultative status with ECOSOC (Rules and Procedures of the Executive Board, Chapter XIII rule 16.3). But this does not preclude the participation, as observers, of CSOs in consultative status.

From 1997–2001, annual informal dialogues were held between Executive Board members and primarily New York or Geneva-based NGOs. At the last such dialogue it was recommended that future participation should be encouraged from southern as well as northern CSO partners of UNDP. Periodic alignment of the two meetings would enable the CSO dialogue with the Executive Board to benefit from the presence of a more diverse and representative CSO constituency.

Structure and Composition

The basic principles guiding membership selection include assembling a committee that has:

I.   The expertise to advise and guide UNDP in substantive policy areas (governance, debt, trade, human rights, poverty reduction, conflict prevention, environment, and gender);

II. The majority of its membership from the South, reflecting UNDP programme country focus;

III. Different types of institutions with which UNDP engages, including (but not limited to): policy-focused CSOs, advocacy and rights-based organizations, indigenous peoples' organizations, peoples' movements, community-based organizations, and trade unions;

IV. Perspective on the many levels at which UNDP operates (local, national, regional and global).

Special attention is also given to balance in gender and regional composition. Finally, ECOSOC status would be considered an asset but not a requirement for committee members.

Based on discussions with CSO partners, it was recommended that UNDP take responsibility for selecting the first group of 12–16 committee members. The internal selection process involved consultations with colleagues in the regional bureaux, with a short list prepared by the Bureau for Development Policy (BDP) and the Bureau for Resources and Strategic Partnership (BRSP) for approval by the Administrator. Externally, this effort was complemented by formal and informal consultations with key CSO partners.

As recommended by CSO partners, a secretariat will be formed for the CSO Committee, ranging in size from three to five individuals. The secretariat will be responsible for assisting with the coordination of activities, including: establishing agendas, (co-) chairing meetings, monitoring funds, and disseminating information. The secretariat will be selected, and its roles and functions clarified at the first meeting of the committee. It will interface with UNDP/BRSP.

Rotation

It is suggested that two-thirds of the initially nominated members serve a three-year term. One-third of the membership will rotate on an annual basis. New members would be proposed by the CSO Committee for review by BDP and BRSP, and approval by the Administrator.

UNDP PROGRAMMING MANUAL: CHAPTER 6: OPERATIONS OF
PROGRAMMES AND PROJECTS

Issued by UNDP
December 2000
Source: <http://www.undp.kz/script_site.html?id=147#81>

[…]

6.0 Operations of Programmes and Projects

1. The present chapter sets out the policies and procedures to be followed in carrying out UNDP-supported programmes and projects. The way a programme or project is carried out is referred to as the management arrangements. The arrangements are worked out during the formulation stage. The approved PSD or project document must include details of these arrangements.

[…]

6.2 Management of programmes and projects

1. In this section, the four types of management arrangements are explained, to enable users to decide which one is the most suitable for a given programme or project. Procedures on how to apply the management arrangements are given in the subsequent sections.

6.2.1 Selection of management arrangements

1. UNDP arranges for its support to programmes and projects to be provided in one of four ways:
   (a) National execution (NEX). This refers to management by a governmental entity and is the norm;
   (b) Execution by a United Nations agency or multilateral development bank;
   (c) Execution by an NGO; or
   (d) Direct execution (DEX). This refers to cases where management is by UNDP itself; it is permitted only in exceptional circumstances.

2. The management arrangements are determined after consultations among the parties during the formulation of the programme or project. The final decision rests with the Administrator in view of his accountability to the Executive Board for the use of UNDP resources. The Administrator has delegated the responsibility for making the decision to the UNDP resident representatives through the Associate Administrator and the regional bureaux directors. The authority to approve UNDP direct execution has been delegated to the Associate Administrator alone.

[...]

5. A single institution is designated to manage each UNDP-supported programme or project. Its main responsibility is to achieve the results expected from the programme or project, and in particular to ensure that the outputs are produced through effective process management and use of UNDP funds.

[...]

6.2.4 NGO execution

1. UNDP seeks to collaborate with national as well as international NGOs that have adequate staff and reasonably sound financial status; have experience in working with external organizations or donors; and, importantly, have the necessary capacities within their fields of expertise to carry out activities and achieve results on behalf of UNDP.
2. Management by a NGO is appropriate in the case of a project that:
   (a) Involves close interaction with target groups such as the poor and vulnerable;
   (b) Would benefit from established contacts with grass-roots associations; or
   (c) Calls for expertise in the use of participatory methods.
3. Some benefits of NGO execution are that it provides expertise in areas where NGOs have a comparative advantage. It offers an opportunity to enhance the dialogue between the government and the civil society organization (CSO) community in the programme country; it also enlarges the range of UNDP partners.
4. An NGO is defined as a non-profit organization, group or institution that operates independently from a Government and has humanitarian or development objectives. The designated NGO may be a national or an international NGO. In either case, the NGO must have the legal status to operate in accordance with the laws governing NGOs in the programme country. For each project, UNDP signs a standard Project Cooperation Agreement with the designated NGO, and this serves as the basic legal agreement between UNDP and the NGO.
5. The UNDP country office must assess the capacity of the NGO to carry out the project. The project document must specify any exceptional support measures required to ensure that the NGO can meet UNDP requirements for managing projects.
6. Normally, the parties use a competitive process to select an NGO to manage a project. Since such designation of an NGO is not a procurement action, the LPAC reviews the proposal to designate the NGO and verifies its competitiveness. The NGO is designated where one specific

NGO is clearly the most suitable to manage the project or when no other NGOs are available or interested. The LPAC minutes must describe the outcome of the review, the alternatives considered and the reasons why the proposed NGO was selected.

7. The designated NGO generally carries out the project activities directly but, if necessary, it may also contract other entities, including other NGOs, to undertake specific activities. This is done through a competitive process in accordance with the description of management arrangements in the project document as reviewed by the LPAC. An NGO is defined as a non-profit organization, group or institution that operates independently from a Government and has humanitarian or development objectives. The designated NGO may be a national or an international NGO. In either case, the NGO must have the legal status to operate in accordance with the laws governing NGOs in the programme country. For each project, UNDP signs a standard Project Cooperation Agreement with the designated NGO, and this serves as the basic legal agreement between UNDP and the NGO.

[...]

Annex 6A
Capacity for Programme and Project Management: Key Considerations

The parties concerned with formulation and design, particularly the UNDP country office, the government, and the institution that will manage the programme or project must review the capacities that will be needed. They first determine which of the tasks listed below apply to the programme or project. For each applicable task, the parties then determine what additional measures need to be taken to ensure that the tasks can performed. The measures must be documented for follow-up action. This may be done, for example, through an action plan, an annex to the PSD or project document or through minutes of a design meeting or workshop.

I. Technical Capacity
Ability to monitor the technical aspects of the programme or project.
1. Undertake regular programme or project visits and monitor progress benchmarks.
2. Ensure that periodic progress and technical reports are received and interpreted.
3. Ensure regular consultations with beneficiaries and contractors.

II. Managerial Capacity
Ability to plan, monitor and co-ordinate activities.
1. Ensure that an annual programme or project review meeting is held.

2. Be able to develop and review an annual work plan.
3. Possess adequate logistical infrastructure: office facilities and space, basic equipment, utilities, communications.

III. *Administrative Capacity*
Ability to procure goods services and works on a transparent and competitive basis.
1. Assess the ability of vendors to provide the required quality, quantity and competitiveness of goods, services and works.
2. Have the authority to enter into contracts.
3. Have standard contracts or access to legal counsel to ensure that contracts establish performance standards, protect UNDP and the institution's interests and are enforceable.

Ability to prepare, authorise and adjust commitments and expenditures.
4. Have written procedures for identifying the appropriate vendor, obtaining the best price, and issuing commitments.
5. Have a system for tracking commitments against budget to prevent overspending and for follow- up on outstanding commitments.

Ability to manage and maintain equipment.
6. Have a property ledger (inventory) to track all important details about property and its cost, annually.

Ability to recruit and manage the best-qualified personnel on a transparent and competitive basis.
7. Be able to staff the programme or project and enter into contract with personnel.
8. Use written job descriptions for consultants or experts.
9. Have standard contracts or access to legal counsel to ensure that contracts establish performance standards and, protect UNDP and the institution's interests.

IV. *Financial Capacity*
Ability to produce programme and project budgets.
1. Track commitments, expenditures and planned expenditures against budget on a consolidated basis.
2. Maintain a programme or project budget showing the timing of planned expenditures, for each year, by quarter.

Ability to ensure physical security of advances, cash and records.
3. Maintain a checking account in a reputable bank and a secure safe for any cash on hand.

4. Have clear procedures on authority, responsibility, monitoring and accountability for handling funds.

Ability to disburse funds in a timely and effective manner.
5. Have written procedures for processing payments to control the risks through segregation of duties, and transaction recording and reporting.
6. Have monitoring controls, such as independent bank reconciliations.
7. Have a means of verifying receipt of goods or performance of services and proper authorisation.
8. Be able to manage the status of expenditures against budget, and the remaining available budget.
9. Have a policy of making payments by their due dates as stated on the invoice or in the contracts and be able to demonstrate performance against this standard.

Ability to ensure financial recording and reporting.
10. Have a reporting system that tracks all commitments and expenditures against budgets by line.
11. Have a reporting system that allows programme or project expenditures to be reported to UNDP quarterly, and which accumulates programme or project-to-date expenditures against budget for management purposes.

The following table describes where to find information on the capacities of a NGO, when NGO execution is considered. It helps the partners to analyse available capacities in accordance with the above list of key considerations for management. (It can of course also be used in cases where the NGO serves as a contractor.)

Table: Sources of information for assessing the capacities of an NGO

What to assess	Types of things to look for
1. Roles and functions – Mission statement or charter – Mandate and policies	– Registration with Government or umbrella NGO – Charter document – Annual report – Policy documents – Legal incorporation documents – Compatibility between the goals of the NGO and purpose of the project
2. Structures and systems – Governing or oversight board – Management structure – Decision-making structure – Financial and budgeting system – Accounting system – Information and monitoring systems – Evaluation and reporting systems – Procurement system – Absorptive capacity – Organizational outreach – Stakeholders – Fund-raising capacity	– Database or profile of NGO – Reports on the annual meeting of the governing body – Accounting system – A bank account or bank statements – Audited finances – Well-designed project and programme documents as well as evaluations and reports – Copies of rules and procedures and examples of compliance – Example of how procurement is done – Evaluation and monitoring reports and newsletters – Minutes of management or decision-making meetings
3. Competencies – Organizational – Specialisation – Individual expertise – Relevant experience – Past performance in achieving results	– Reports and evaluations of projects undertaken – Assessments of performance by beneficiaries, stakeholders and clients of NGO – Catalogue describing specialisation and types and length of experiences to date – Profile of staff, including education and experience background. – Staff turnover

Table: Sources of information for assessing the capacities of an NGO

What to assess	Types of things to look for
	– Reports from participation in international or regional meetings
	– Staff dependency: whether the NGO is dependent on a single person
	– Reports on performance
	– Use of indicators and benchmarks
4. Resources – Operating budget – Facilities and equipment	– Ability to travel and work at project sites – Proper equipment for area of specialisation – Adequate and legal working conditions and work rules – Annual report of operating budget – Computer capability – Library materials – Asset ownership: individual or organizational – Partnerships with national and external NGOs – Reports on technical external support from national or international agencies for operations and capacity-building
5. External support *Additional partnerships:* – Government – Other organizations	
6. Others – Independent assessments – Origin of NGO	– Media reports – Research institutions and case studies on NGO experience – Capacity assessments made by other United Nations entities or bilateral donors having worked with the NGO – Founding documents/membership base

FRAMEWORK OF SELECTION CRITERIA TO ASSESS CSO CAPACITY

> **Issued by UDDP, UNDP and Civil Society Organizations: A Toolkit for Strengthening Partnership (2006)**
> Source: <http://www.undp.org/partners/cso/publications/CSO_ Toolkit_ linked. pdf>

[excerpt]

The intention of this tool is to provide country offices with a broad framework to assess capacity when selecting a CSO partner. It outlines particular criteria to consider within some of the main elements that make up a CSO: mission, organizational structure, leadership, management practices and activities. Most importantly, the tool is to provide guidance for selection and should not be seen as a one size fits *all* approach to selection nor as a score card for CSOs.

As CSOs comprise a full range of formal and informal organizations within civil society, such as non-governmental organizations (NGOs), community based organizations (CBOs), academia, journalist associations, faith based organizations, trade unions, women's advocacy organizations and indigenous peoples' organizations, their capacities, expertise and scope will also vary. Furthermore, every country's civic environment is different. Some countries may have well-established regulatory frameworks that allow for, protect and strengthen the CSO sector, while others may be more repressive. Other factors like a large donor presence and aid flow can create an environment with numerous large scale international NGOs managing vast resources. As national contexts will differ so will their civic environments, the diversity of their national actors, their competence and the role they play in the society. Therefore, these guidelines may have to be adjusted to reflect national and local circumstances. A CSO mapping identifying the CSOs active in a country or sub region may also serve as a useful exercise and complement to this tool.

Before embarking on this exercise it is important that the country office be clear on the kind of work the CSO will be asked to undertake, the purpose of the partnership and the opportunities as well as the limitations of working with CSOs.

CSO capacity assessment tool

PART I. ASSESSING CSO COMMITMENT TO THE UNDP PRINCIPLES OF PARTICIPATORY HUMAN DEVELOPMENT AND DEMOCRATIC GOVERNANCE

1.1 Legal status and history

Degree of legal articulation and biographical indications

INDICATOR	AREAS FOR ASSESSMENT	APPLICABLE DOCUMENTS/TOOLS
1.1.1 Legal status	Is the CSO legally established? Does the CSO comply with all legal requirements of its legal identity and registration?	Name and name of officers Registration with government or umbrella CSO Legal incorporation documents
1.1.2 History	Date of creation and length in existence Reasons and circumstances for the creation of the CSO Has the CSO evolved in terms of scope and operational activity	Annual reports Biographical note on CSO / Media kit—Website

1.2 Mandate, policies and governance

Compatibility between the goals of the CSO with those of UNDP and a sound governance structure

INDICATOR	AREAS FOR ASSESSMENT	APPLICABLE DOCUMENTS/TOOLS
1.2.1 CSO mandate and policies	Does the CSO share UNDP principles of human development? Does the CSO share similar service lines to UNDP? Is it clear on its role?	Mission statement/ Charter document Annual report Policy statements
1.2.2 Governance	Who makes up the governing body and what is it charged with? How does the independent governing body exert proper oversight? Does the CSO have a clear and communicated organizational structure?	Reports on the meetings of the governing body Profile of board members/ trustees Copies of rules and procedures Minutes of management or decision-making meeting Code of Conduct CSO organizational chart

1.3 Constituency and external support

Ability to build collaborative relationships and a reputable standing with other sectors

INDICATOR	AREAS FOR ASSESSMENT	APPLICABLE DOCUMENTS/TOOLS
1.3.1 Constituency	Does the CSO have a clear constituency? Is the organization membership based? Is there a long-term community development vision? Does the CSO have regular and participatory links to its constituency? Are constituents informed and supportive about the CSO and its activities?	Mission-statement-goal Webpage / webforum Newsletter Report of field visits Media coverage Resource center or public assembly space
1.3.2 CSO local and global linkages	Does the CSO belong to other CSO organizations and/or CSO networks in its own sector? Does the CSO have strong links within the CSO community and to other social institutions?	Membership / affiliation in a CSO umbrella Letters of reference Participation in regional / national / international CSO meetings and conferences
1.3.3 Other partnerships, networks and external relations	Does the CSO have partnerships with government / UN agencies / private sector / foundations / others? Are these partnerships a source of funding?	Partnerships agreements with other CSOs Partnerships agreements and/or MoUs Records of funding and list of references Reports on technical external support from national and/or international agencies Minutes of partnership interactions

PART II. ASSESSING CSO CAPACITY FOR PROJECT MANANGEMENT

2.1 Technical capacity	Ability to implement a project	
INDICATOR	AREAS FOR ASSESSMENT	APPLICABLE DOCUMENTS/TOOLS
2.1.1 Specialization	Does the CSO have the technical skills required? Does the CSO collect baseline information about its consituency? Does the CSO have the knowledge needed? Does the CSO keep informed about the latest techniques/ competencies/ policies/trends in its area of expertise? Does the CSO have the skills and competencies that complement those of UNDP?	Publications on activities, specific issues, analytical articles, policies Reports from participation in international, regional, national or local meetings Tools & methodologies Evaluations and assessments
2.1.2 Implementation	Does the CSO have access to relevant information/ resources and experience? Does the CSO have useful contacts and networks? Does the CSO know how to get baseline data, develop indicators? Does it apply effective approaches to reach its targets (i.e participatory methods)	Evaluations and Assessments Methodologies/training materials Use ofTookits,indicators and benchmarks/ Capacity-development tools Databases (of CBOs, partners, etc.)
2.1.3 Human resources	Does the CSO staff possess adequate expertise & experience? Does the CSO use local capacities (financial/ human/other resources)? Does the CSO have a strong presence in the field? What is the CSO's capacity to coordinate between the field and the office?	Profile of staff, including expertise and professional experience Staff turnover Chart of assignments of roles and functions Reports on technical experience from national or international agencies for operations and capacity-building

2.2 Managerial capacity

INDICATOR
2.2.1 Planning, monitoring & evaluation

2.2.2 Reporting and performance track record

2.3 Administrative capacity

INDICATOR
2.3.1 Facilities and equipment

Ability to plan, monitor and co-ordinate activities

AREAS FOR ASSESSMENT
Does the CSO produce clear, internally consistent proposals and intervention frameworks?
Does the development of a programme include a regular review of the programme?
Does the CSO hold annual programme or project review meetings?
Is strategic planning translated into operational activities?
Are there measurable objectives in the operational plan?

Does the CSO report on its work to its donors, to its constituency, to CSOs involved in the same kind of work, to the local council, involved government ministries, etc?
Does the CSO monitor progress against indicators and evaluate its programme/project achievement?
Does the CSO include the viewpoint of the beneficiaries in the design and review of its programming?

Ability to provide adequate logistical support and infrastructure

AREAS FOR ASSESSMENT
Does the CSO possess logistical infrastructure and equipment?
Can the CSO manage and maintain equipment?

APPLICABLE DOCUMENTS/TOOLS
Well-designed project and programme documents as well as evaluations and reports
Action / operational plans
Evaluation and monitoring reports

Reports on performance
Reports to donors and other stakeholders
Internal & external evaluation and impact studies

APPLICABLE DOCUMENTS/TOOLS
Adequate logistical infrastructure: office facilities and space, basic equipment, utilities
Computer capability and library materials
Proper equipment for area of specialisation/inventory to track property and cost

2.3.2 Procurement	Does the CSO have the ability to procure goods, services and works on a transparent and competitive basis?	Standard contracts Examples of how procurement is done Written procedures for identifying the appropriate vendor, obtaining the best price, and issuing commitments
2.4 Financial capacity	*Ability to ensure appropriate management of funds*	
INDICATOR 2.4.1 Financial management & funding resources	AREAS FOR ASSESSMENT Is there a regular budget cycle? Does the CSO produce programme and project budgets? What is the maximum amount of money the CSO has managed? Does the CSO ensure physical security of advances, cash and records? Does the CSO disburse funds in a timely and effective manner? Does the CSO have procedures on authority, responsibility, monitoring and accountability of handling funds? Does the CSO have a record of financial stability and reliability?	APPLICABLE DOCUMENTS/TOOLS Operating budgets and financial reports List of core & non-core donors and years of funding Written procedures ensuring clear records for payable, receivables, stock and inventory Reporting system that tracks all commitments and expenditures against budgets by line
2.4.2 Accounting system	Does the CSO keep good, accurate and informative accounts? Does the CSO have the ability to ensure proper financial recording and reporting?	A bank account or bank statements Audited financial statements Good, accurate and informative accounting system Written procedures for processing payments to control the risks through segregation of duties, and transaction recording and reporting

SIMPLIFICATION OF NGO EXECUTION FOR CRISIS AND POST CONFLICT SITUATIONS

> **Issued by Bureau of Resources and Strategic Partnerships of UNDP**
> **1 August 2004**
> Source: <http://www.undp.org/partners/cso/publications/NGO
> exec_crisis.doc>

Document Name	Simplification of NGO Execution for Crisis and Post Conflict Situations
Language(s)	English—French—Spanish
Responsible Unit	Bureau of Resources and Strategic Partnerships
Creator (individual)	Bruce Jenks – bruce.jenks@undp.org
Subject (taxonomy)	Organizational Procedures, Corporate Systems & Standards, Programme Execution/Implementation
Date created	1 August 2004
Mandatory Review	1 August 2006
Audience	These procedures apply to all UNDP staff at Headquarters and in the Country Offices involved in the creation and management of NGO executed projects.
Applicability	Policy is applicable to all NGO executed projects, in particular to those in crisis and post-conflict countries.
Replaces	Relevant sections in the Programming Manual and Procurement Manual (see table on page 3)
Is part of	To be incorporated into a revised Programming Manual
Related documents	Policy on Engagement with Civil Society Organizations Policy on Engagement with Indigenous Peoples Sourcebook on Building Partnerships with Civil Society Organizations
UN Record Ref.	Not yet available
Queries to	Alejandra Pero, CSO Division, BRSP alejandra.pero@undp.org Patrick Tiefenbacher, Office of Planning and Budgeting, BoM patrick.tiefenbacher@undp.org

I. Background and Context

As UNDP seeks to strengthen its strategic partnerships with key constituencies and be a more responsive partner in the field, the following table reflects suggested revisions to be made to UNDP's NGO Execution Procedures. The suggested revisions are based on an assessment of UNDP's NGO Execution Procedures undertaken in 2001 and a set of regional workshops hosted by the Bureau for Crisis Prevention and Recovery (2002) aimed at strengthening collaboration with civil society organizations

(CSOs) operationally in post conflict environments. Both the assessment and the regional workshops identified some of the operational obstacles and bottlenecks that inhibit an effective partnership between UNDP and CSOs in crisis and post conflict situations and provided some possible recommendations to overcome them.

II. Increased Demand for Operational Collaboration with NGOs

The assessment revealed that over the years there has been a marked increase in use of NGO Execution. The responses from the country offices and many programme staff in headquarters indicate that the reasons for the increased demand lie in the significant advantages for UNDP in collaborating with NGOs, consistent with wider experience in the field. In contrast to the misperception that all NGOs are smaller and weaker partners with little managerial capacity, many UNDP country offices report that in general NGOs are highly desirable partners in many circumstances and in post conflict situations sometimes the only partner.

> **Programme Perspectives: Advantages of NGO Execution to UNDP**
> - Many NGOs demonstrate high quality management capacity, eg technical specialization, operational depth, better performance (ownership & compliance with plans, high quality work, less staff turnover, more efficient use of resources).
> - NGOs are quick to respond, mobile, & positioned to reach communities at grassroots.
> - NGOs share UNDP goals for programme impact & institutional empowerment.
> - Collaboration with NGOs enables UNDP to update its role & multiply programme impacts:
> - Leverage existing NGO relationships & projects with communities.
> - Visibility of NGO partners increases UNDP ability to mobilize resources.
> - UNDP can promote positive relations between government & civil society.

III. Proposed Changes

The proposed revisions address some of the issues raised by both country offices and CSOs to facilitate a more effective operational partnership in crisis and post conflict situations and to promote a more enabling environment between government, UNDP and CSOs. It is important to note, that the following revisions come accompanied by a[n] *Operational Guide on Working with NGOs*.

1. **Pre-Selection:** The proposed change encourages country offices to undertake a CSO mapping of the country. Consequently, a pre-selected roster of CSOs is created with an accompanying assessment of their expertise and capacity to manage a project. This roster can be tapped into particularly in a period of crisis when UNDP is to respond swiftly and effectively. The CSOs selected have been agreed upon by a *Selection Committee*[1] that should be composed of both the Government and UNDP. The criteria for the review of NGOs must include the area of expertise of each NGO, as well as its level of management capacity. All NGOs approved by the Selection Committee are deemed qualified as potential execution agencies for projects in their area of expertise and up to the size commensurate with their management capacity, as determined by the Selection Committee. For pre-selection of NGOs for amounts exceeding the country offices financial delegation, the NGO pre-selection assessment should be forwarded to of the Advisory Committee on Procurement (ACP) in New York. The roster of qualifying NGOs is to be updated annually.

2. **Government Clearance:** Participation and agreement of Government in the Selection Committee will constitute government 'no objection'—on which basis the Resident Representative can sign an advance authorization for a new project executed by an NGO. Also, the rules for obviating government signature for direct execution apply for NGO Execution *mutatis mutandi.*

3. **Project Award:** Once a concrete project has been formulated, specific project proposals from the pre-selected NGOs will constitute the basis for the final selection of the executing NGO by the project appraisal committee. Only an NGO from the pre-selected roster qualifies for this project award, in line with the quantitative evaluation criteria (its expertise, personnel, proposed work-plan and approach).

4. **Advances to the Executing NGO:** Generally, UNDP country offices advance funds quarterly to the executing agency in line with the submitted work-plan. UNDP's advance will cover all commitments by the NGO, and not just cash disbursements, over the period of the work-plan. For projects with annual budgets up to $300,000 the country office can provide one annual advance.

5. **Financial Reporting:** The NGO will provide quarterly financial reports, on which further advances will be based. In the case of an annual advance, the NGO will report semi-annually.

---

[1] The composition of the selection Committee could be modeled after the Contracts, Assets & Procurement (CAP) Committee with additional government representation.

IV. Summary of changes

The matrix outlines the key changes to be made in the NGO Execution Procedures for Crisis and Post-conflict Situations.

Revisions	NGO Execution	Reference to Relevant Manual
Pre-Selection	Selection based on capacity assessment of NGOs and their ability to execute a project or programme. Selection is done by a country office-level Selection Committee with government presence.	Programming Manual Chapter 4.2 & 6.2.4; Procurement Manual Chapter 5.3
Government Clearance	Participation and agreement of government in the Selection Committee will constitute government 'no objection'—on which basis the Res Rep can sign an advance authorization. The rules governing DEX for obviating government signature also apply for NGO Execution.	Programming Manual Chapter 4.2 & 5.5, Annex 6A
Project Award	The project will be awarded to a specific NGO for execution on the basis of a concrete project proposal.	
Advances	Generally on a quarterly basis in line with UN Simplification and Harmonization. For annual budgets up to $300,000 one annual advance.	Programming Manual Chapter 6.5;
Financial Reporting	Generally on a quarterly basis; for budgets up to $300,000 semi-annual financial reporting.	

Appendix VIII

WORLD BANK

INVOLVING NON-GOVERNMENTAL ORGANIZATIONS IN
BANK-SUPPORTED ACTIVITIES

Adopted by the World Bank
February 2000
Document number: GP 14.70
Source:<http://wbln0018.worldbank.org/Institutional/Manuals/Op
Manual.nsf/3c369cae89f572578525705c001d5109/1dfb2471de05b
f9a8525672c007d0950?OpenDocument>

1. Non-governmental organizations and other organizations of civil society (NGOs)[1] are important actors in the development process. These organizations can make important contributions toward ensuring that the views of local people are taken into account, promoting community participation, extending project reach to the poorest, and introducing flexible and innovative approaches. The Bank[2] therefore encourages borrowers and staff members to consult with NGOs and to involve them, as appropriate, in Bank-supported activities, including economic and sector work and all stages of project processing—identification, design, implementation, and monitoring and evaluation.[3]

[1] The term 'NGO' refers to a myriad of different types of organizations. At its broadest, it includes all groupings of individuals that fall outside the public and for-profit sectors, whether legally constituted or informal, established or transient. The term also includes both community-based organizations (CBOs), usually formed to serve the interests of their own members (or community), and intermediary organizations, normally established to serve either the interests of a particular target group (eg, CBOs, poor communities) or the common good (eg, the environment). 'Civil society' is the space between family, market, and state; it consists of not-for-profit organizations and special interest groups, either formal or informal, working to improve the lives of their constituents. Civil society organizations (CSOs) include local and international organizations, business and professional associations, chambers of commerce, groups of parliamentarians, media, and policy development and research institutes. The interests of the Bank coincide with those of many NGOs and CSOs that work in the field of economic and social development, welfare, emergency relief, and environmental protection or that comprise or represent poor or vulnerable people. This document uses 'NGOs' to refer to both NGOs and other organizations of civil society.
[2] 'Bank' incluedes IBRD and IDA, and 'loans' includes credits.
[3] The main purpose of the Bank is to support governments' development programs. In supporting such programs, the Bank should not carry out activities with NGOs without government knowledge and consent. At the same time, with due respect to the prerogative of government as the Bank's primary interlocutor, the Bank has a responsibility to listen to and learn from a range of stakeholders and to make independent, professional, and well-formed judgments.

2. In encouraging collaboration with NGOs, the Bank seeks to (a) enhance the effectiveness of the operations it supports, especially those that focus on poverty reduction or involve environmental sustainability; (b) foster better public understanding of the Bank's activities; (c) foster in borrowing countries a more enabling environment for NGO contribution to national development; and (d) broaden input into Bank policies, analyses, and country strategies. The Bank expects that it will be better able to address these objectives now that it has decentralized many of its activities to the Regional level.

3. NGO involvement in Bank-supported activities implies a cooperative working relationship among the borrowing government, NGOs, and the Bank. In the context of Bank lending, it is important for Bank staff to have an understanding of the nature of the relations between NGOs and the government. Bank staff should be aware that while government/NGO collaboration can enhance the quality of Bank-supported operations, it may not be possible in every country situation.

4. The Bank's agenda has become more complex in recent years as it has given greater prominence to issues of poverty, participation, gender, the environment, governance, capacity building, and implementation quality. The Bank's portfolio is also undergoing a significant shift toward financing in the social sectors and conservation programs—areas in which many NGOs have clear strengths.

5. The Bank concentrates on establishing linkages with those NGOs that (a) possess specialized analytical or operational skills of relevance to the Bank's work, or (b) have extensive grassroots experience and can facilitate reaching and involving poor people. The Bank also aims to maintain open dialogue with NGOs that have significant influence on public opinion or governments in terms of development policy and programs.

6. The characteristics of individual NGOs vary greatly; each has its own strengths and weaknesses. Strengths commonly associated with NGOs include the following:
   (a) social proximity (grassroots and community links);
   (b) field-based development expertise;
   (c) important specialized knowledge or skills;
   (d) the ability to innovate and adapt;
   (e) the ability to bring grassroots experience to discussions of development on a national scale;
   (f) participatory methodologies and tools;
   (g) long-term commitment to and emphasis on sustainability; and
   (h) cost-effectiveness.

Some areas in which NGOs—depending on their experience and structure—might face constraints[4] are as follows:

(a) limited financial, analytical, and management expertise;
(b) limited institutional capacity;
(c) gap between stated mission and operational achievements;
(d) low levels of self-sustainability;
(e) isolation/lack of interorganizational communication or coordination;
(f) capability for small-scale interventions only; and
(g) limited expertise in macro or specific economic issues.

Classification of NGOs

7. The Bank interacts principally with two categories of NGOs: (a) operational NGOs, whose primary purpose is to fund, design, or implement development-related programs or projects; and (b) advocacy NGOs, whose primary purpose is to defend or promote a specific development cause and which seek to influence the development policies and practices of the Bank, governments, and other bodies. The difference between these two groups of NGOs is not rigid, however. While some NGOs concentrate on relief and service delivery and have virtually no analytical or policy function, and some are lobbying NGOs with no operational base, the majority fall somewhere between these extremes. Operational NGOs usually have more field-level experience that is relevant to the Bank; but advocacy groups may also be able to offer valuable grassroots insights and challenge conventional development thinking.

8. Many NGOs have formed networks at the national, regional, and international levels for the purposes of coordinating their activities, enhancing their institutional strength, and disseminating information. Bank staff can benefit from working closely with such networks because they can be a valuable source of information about and contacts within the NGO community.

Information Sharing

9. The Bank aims to be proactive in sharing relevant information with NGOs. At the country level, some country offices have established Public Information Centers (PICs) that provide a comprehensive selection of Bank reports, project documents, procurement materials, and details on scholarships, grants, and recruitment programs, and serve as

[4] See John Clark, *Democratizing Development: The Role of Voluntary Organizations* (Earthscan Publications, London, 1991).

a venue for public outreach activities. Other country offices are translating Project Information Documents (PIDs), other project documents,
and some economic and sector work (ESW) reports into local
languages to make them more accessible to NGOs and the general
public.[5] Much is also being done at the project level; for example, the
design of the Ghazi Barotha Dam Project in Pakistan included the
creation of a Project Information Center near the project site to provide
information in Urdu to local NGOs and communities and to document
the concerns of people affected by the project.

10. When NGOs request information or ask questions about Bank-
supported activities, Bank staff should respond in accordance with the
Bank's disclosure policy.[6] Bank staff should also investigate concerns
voiced by NGOs regarding projects and the application of policies,
provide timely and substantive responses, and meet with NGOs and
affected parties when possible. Similarly, the Bank encourages
borrower governments to be responsive to local NGO requests and
concerns that relate to development policies and programs.

Policy Dialogue

11. The Bank recognizes the value of consulting with NGOs on such
sectoral and operational issues as poverty, environment, social development, participation, and information disclosure. During the formulation of policies, strategies, procedures, and major reports (such as the
World Development Report), Bank staff have sought advice and
comments from relevant specialists inside and outside the Bank, including NGOs. As part of such consultations, Bank staff may make draft
documents available for review by such external specialists and organize opportunities for them to discuss their views and concerns with
relevant Bank staff.

12. The Bank consults with NGOs in other ways, as well: for example, the
NGO-World Bank Committee meets regularly on both a global and
regional basis to discuss issues of mutual concern; and the External
Gender Consultative Group, formed in April 1996 and comprising
NGO representatives and academics, meets with Bank staff to share
information and provide advice on gender-related issues. Country
offices have established systematic interactions with international and
local NGOs to share information, discuss issues of mutual concern,

---

[5] In addition, the Bank encourages NGOs to prepare translations of some of these documents.
[6] The World Bank Policy on Disclosure of Information (World Bank, Washington, DC,
1994); see also BP 17.50, Disclosure of Operational Information, and the Operational
Memorandum Factual Technical Documents, 6/20/94.

and explore possibilities for collaboration. The Bank has organized meetings and workshops that bring together NGOs, Bank staff, and government officials to discuss sectoral issues and identify opportunities for working together.

Operational Collaboration

13. NGOs may be involved in Bank-supported activities in many ways—for example, as informal advisers, consultants, implementing agencies, construction managers, or cofinanciers. When NGOs participate in Bank-financed projects, Bank staff should describe anticipated and actual NGO involvement in the project documentation and should set out in the legal documents any arrangements agreed with the borrower. When the Bank engages NGOs as consultants, it does so either using its own budget or, in exceptional circumstances, acting as executing agency for a trust fund.[7] Borrowers hiring NGOs as consultants, whether using trust funds or the proceeds of Bank loans, select them according to the Consultant Guidelines.[8]

Selecting NGO Partners

14. *Gathering Information about NGOs.* Within the Bank, sources of information about NGOs include staff of the NGO and Civil Society Thematic Team, and NGO/civil society specialists in country and technical departments. The Bank has conducted NGO assessments in a number of countries, and many project and sector reports contain relevant information about NGOs. Additional information about NGOs can be obtained from NGO networks; directories and databases prepared by governments and multilateral, bilateral, and other donors; or informed people in the country.

15. *Establishing Relevant Selection Criteria.* NGO partners should be selected according to the specific skills and expertise required for the task at hand as it relates to the development goals being pursued. The following are some of the qualities that should be considered in selecting individual NGO partners (depending on the nature and purpose of a particular task):
   (a) credibility: acceptability to both stakeholders and government;
   (b) competence: relevant skills and experience, proven track record;
   (c) local knowledge;

---

[7] For the Bank's procedures for engaging consultants, see Bank for Operational Purposes. Further information on the Bank's use of trust funds is available in OP/BP 14.40, Trust Funds.

[8] Guidelines: Selection and Employment of Consultants by World Bank Borrowers (World Bank, Washington, DC, 1997 [revised January and September 1997, and January 1999]).

(d) representation: community ties, accountability to members/beneficiaries, gender sensitivity;
(e) governance: sound internal management, transparency, financial accountability, efficiency;
(f) legal status; and
(g) institutional capacity: sufficient scale of operations, facilities, and equipment.

NGO Involvement in Economic and Sector Work
16. NGOs can provide alternative perspectives in ESW and can promote grassroots participation and consensus-building. Some examples follow.
    (a) Participatory Poverty Assessments (PPAs). NGOs with strong grassroots links and local language skills have been valuable partners in carrying out PPAs.
    (b) National Environmental Action Plans (NEAPs). NGOs and other stakeholders have been consulted in the preparation of NEAPs. In Guinea, the NEAP was prepared entirely by a locally-based national NGO whose community ties and participatory skills helped ensure that the NEAP accurately reflected the needs and opinions of the local population.
    (c) Country Economic Memoranda (CEMs). During the preparation of the Zimbabwe CEM, a participating NGO helped to organize field visits and ensured that the mission had direct contact with the rural poor, thus contributing a first-hand perspective on social issues such as the dependence of the poor on basic services.
    (d) *Country Assistance Strategies (CASs)*. In preparing CASs, the Bank has included NGOs and other participants from civil society in the consultation process.

NGO Involvement in Lending Activities
17. While decisions concerning NGO involvement in lending operations are the responsibility of the borrower, Bank staff may assist borrowers in identifying and assessing NGO partners and, as appropriate, encourage the involvement of NGOs throughout the project cycle. For projects with significant NGO involvement, it may be useful for the borrower to include among the project staff a NGO/civil society specialist whose primary responsibility is to work with NGOs.
18. *Project Identification and Design.* During project identification, NGOs that are familiar with the project area and enjoy ties with the local population can give both the government and the Bank valuable information about local conditions and community priorities. They can also inform local populations about the planned project, organize consulta-

tions with affected people, and work with them to make their voices heard. In many cases, NGOs have provided project ideas, or existing NGO projects have served as models for Bank-financed activities.

19. When Bank staff become aware of NGO concerns about a Bank-financed project, they should report these concerns to their managers, staff working on the project, and specialists in the relevant Network. When proposed projects are potentially controversial, experience has shown that it is often productive to ensure that the public is accurately informed about the project in question and is given the opportunity to voice concerns, which may then be taken into account in project design. For example, during the preparation of the Bangladesh Flood Action Plan, forums were organized in which NGOs, government officials, and others were able to express their views and discuss issues. Although not all differences were resolved, NGOs became more actively involved in the plan, criticisms were more constructive, and discussions led to some modifications in the design of the plan.

20. In projects for which NGO participation during implementation is foreseen, NGOs should also be involved in project design and in the development of priorities and goals. In projects with extensive NGO involvement or community participation, the borrower and the Bank should be prepared to assign additional staff or allow extra time during the project cycle.

21. *Project Implementation, Monitoring, and Evaluation.* When NGOs have responsibility in the implementation of Bank-financed activities, the borrower and the Bank may need to take special measures to enable the NGOs to exercise their comparative strengths. For example, NGOs may have limited financial capability or lack experience with Bank or government procedures. Borrower and Bank staff should ensure that the terms of reference for an NGO-executed activity express clearly the expected timeframe for carrying out the activity and describe areas in which delays may pose risks for project success. Similarly, the borrower and the Bank should be aware of the need to build into the project sufficient time and flexibility to allow NGOs to carry out their responsibilities. It is good practice to organize preimplementation consultations among the government, NGOs, and the Bank.

22. In recent years, NGOs have become increasingly involved in monitoring and evaluating Bank-financed activities. NGOs have been particularly effective in monitoring project impacts on Indigenous Peoples and the environment. Under some circumstances, particularly when the country portfolio contains a large number of projects that involve NGOs, the borrower may wish to consider soliciting the views of representatives of NGOs and other stakeholders as an input into Country Portfolio Performance Reviews and to consider using experienced

NGOs to help monitor the implementation of actions agreed to during such reviews.[9]

23. *Financial Issues.* The Bank may make grants to NGOs, for example, through the Consultative Group to Assist the Poorest, the Special Grants Program, the Small Grants Program, the Global Environmental Facility (GEF), or other programs financed under the Bank's Development Grant Facility.[10] Borrowers and beneficiaries/executing agencies may finance NGO involvement in operations through such sources as loan and credit proceeds, the Project Preparation Facility, the GEF, and the Policy and Human Resources Development Fund and other trust funds.[11] In some cases, NGO activities are funded by cofinancing from other multilateral or bilateral donors or international NGOs.

24. It is often cost-effective to use NGOs. They should not, however, be viewed as a 'low-cost alternative' to other types of implementing entities. The fact that some NGOs cofinance projects or contribute advice or services free of charge has led to some ambiguity about NGOs' status and about how much they should be paid. All parties should understand the exact nature of NGO involvement (eg, informal unpaid adviser, paid consultant to the Bank or the government) from the outset and, as appropriate, establish mutually acceptable fees and overhead costs. NGOs should not be expected to provide contractual services free of charge or to accept fees below market rates.

25. *Procurement and Disbursement.* Bank staff should assist borrowers in ensuring that the NGOs involved in project implementation are well informed about the Bank's procurement and disbursement procedures, including realistic estimates of lead time and areas in which delays are possible. In some projects, Bank staff have found it useful to provide training for NGOs in procurement and disbursement procedures. NGOs and borrower staff should be aware that in a community participation project that involves the procurement of goods or minor works, the procurement procedures should be tailored to the objectives of the project (as allowed under the Procurement Guidelines).[12] Because of the nature of the projects in which NGOs may be involved, it may be appropriate to use local shopping and direct contracting for the provision of small goods and works. When NGOs have a consultant rela-

---

[9] See GP 13.16, Country Portfolio Performance Reviews.

[10] See OP/BP 8.45, Grants.

[11] For information about the Bank's use of trust funds, see OP/BP 14.40, Trust Funds.

[12] See Guidelines: Procurement under IBRD Loans and IDA Credits (World Bank, Washington, DC, 1995 [revised January and August 1996, September 1997, and January 1999]) section 3.15.

tionship[13] with the borrower, the Bank normally expects the use of standard consultant contracts (which are tailored to the needs of a particular project). In addition, NGOs should understand that the Bank accepts the inclusion of reasonable overheads in NGOs' costs and, as appropriate, allows for the provision of advance payments.[14]

Working with Project-Affected People

26. Under Bank-financed operations, borrowers/executing agencies have frequently engaged NGOs to work directly with project beneficiaries and people affected by the project. Such work includes sharing information about the project, soliciting the views and concerns of beneficiaries and affected parties, and promoting the active participation of such people in project activities. Experience has shown that NGOs can be effective in ensuring interaction with affected parties in projects involving involuntary resettlement. In a number of countries, for example, NGOs have consulted with local people, prepared resettlement plans, and monitored pilot resettlement projects.

Capacity Building

27. The Bank seeks to support the strengthening of the institutional capacity of borrowing country NGOs as an important aspect of promoting long-term sustainable development and engaging the national civil society in development activities. In the context of lending operations, a number of strategies have been used to contribute to NGO capacity: consulting with NGOs on their organizational priorities; providing participating NGOs with training and technical assistance; encouraging partnerships between more experienced NGOs and those with less capacity; and promoting networking and information-sharing among NGOs and between NGOs and government. In addition, through the World Bank Institute and country offices, the Bank has directly supported training and capacity-building activities for NGOs.

NGO-State Relations

28. Improved relations between governments and NGOs can contribute to long-term development efforts. Therefore, Bank staff should seek to assist governments to identify areas of complementarity with NGOs working in development. Whenever possible, they should promote constructive working relationships among governments, donors, and

---

[13] See the Consultant Guidelines for details about the selection and use of consultants.
[14] See the Disbursement Handbook, available to Bank staff on the Intranet and to external parties through the Infoshop.

NGOs by, for example, organizing opportunities for dialogue that involve both governments and NGOs, and advising governments on creating an enabling environment for NGOs.

Role of Bank Organizational Units

29. Staff throughout the Bank are involved in activities whose aim is to increase the participation of NGOs and other organizations of civil society in planning, implementing, and monitoring development policy and projects.
30. Country offices gather and maintain information about local NGOs and NGO activities in their country; inform visiting Bank missions about NGOs and NGO activities relevant to their work; organize meetings between local NGOs and visiting mission staff; as appropriate, organize consultations with NGOs and government representatives on policy and sectoral issues; respond to NGO requests for information; and work with the government to promote an enabling environment for NGOs. Many country offices have appointed NGO specialists or NGO liaison officers to act as points of contact and communication with NGOs. These specialists play a lead role in establishing and maintaining effective relations among the Bank, the borrower, and NGOs at the country level--for example, gathering information about NGOs, responding to requests from and disseminating information to NGOs, assisting staff in identifying and assessing NGO partners, organizing systematic consultations with NGOs on country strategy and operational and policy matters, and advising the government on fostering an enabling environment for NGOs.

The NGO/Civil Society Thematic Team consists of Bank staff working on NGO and civil society issues in the Regions and Networks. In collaboration with Regions and Networks, the NGO/Civil Society Unit of the Social Development Family develops and coordinates the Bank's overall relationship with NGOs; provides advice and operational assistance to Bank staff on working with NGOs; promotes within the Bank practices and procedures that facilitate collaboration with NGOs; monitors NGO involvement in Bank-financed activities; disseminates good practice in working with NGOs; coordinates training for staff; assists Bank staff in organizing policy consultations with NGOs; services the NGO-Bank Committee; conducts research on NGO-related issues; maintains an electronic database on NGOs; and responds to NGO requests for information or directs NGO requests to the appropriate Bank staff. In addition, External Affairs builds understanding and support for the Bank across all of its constituencies, including NGOs.

Appendix IX

IMF

GUIDE FOR STAFF RELATIONS WITH CIVIL SOCIETY
ORGANIZATIONS

Issued by the IMF
10 October 2003
Document number: GP 14.70
Source: <http://www.imf.org/external/np/cso/eng/2003/ 101003.
htm>

To: Members of the Staff

Dear Colleagues,

I am pleased to transmit the attached Guide for Staff Relations with Civil
Society Organizations (CSOs).

I welcome the extensive outreach, including to CSOs, that the Fund staff
is already undertaking. The review earlier this year of the IMF's external
communications strategy (SM/03/69, 2/13/03) revealed the increasing depth
of outreach by staff. The Fund's evolving dialogue with CSOs has long
covered a wide range of issues at the global level. Increasingly the dialogue
is taking on a country focus, driven in part by the participatory process
associated with the PRGF and PRSPs, and the IMF's increased emphasis on
national ownership of policies.

In the Board discussion earlier this year, Executive Directors welcomed
the proposal to prepare guidance for staff outreach to civil society organizations that would focus specifically on issues arising in interaction with
civil society that influence the Fund's operational work (Buff/03/32,
3/12/03). The attached guide, which is the result of extensive consultation
with departments and with CSOs themselves, is the result.

The Guide offers a framework of good practices. It is intended to supplement the sound judgment that arises from staff's experience and knowledge
of specific situations. Therefore, it is not mandatory and will not apply in
all situations.

Over time, it is envisaged that the Guide will be revised in light of experience and comments received. To this end, the Guide will be posted on the
Fund's external website with an invitation to comment.

The IMF acknowledges with gratitude the integral role of Professor Jan Aart Scholte, Centre for the Study of Globalisation and Regionalisation, University of Warwick, Coventry, UK in the preparation of this guide. The guide was drafted by Prof Scholte and IMF staff, in consultation with civil society representatives.

Summary

The IMF is committed to being transparent about its work, to explaining itself, and to listening to the people whom it affects. Increasingly, public outreach is an integral part of IMF country work. This guide aims to assist IMF staff in their efforts to build positive relationships with civil society organizations (CSOs). Since individual circumstances surrounding civil society vary enormously between countries, staff must rely substantially on their own assessments of the specific situations that they face. The guide offers a framework that is intended to supplement—not replace—sound judgment and experience.

Definition: What Is Civil Society?

CSOs are highly diverse, so it is very difficult to generalize. For IMF purposes, civil society actors include business forums, faith-based associations, labor movements, local community groups, nongovernmental organizations (NGOs), philanthropic foundations, and think tanks.

Aims of the IMF's Relations with CSOs

- Public outreach: explaining the Fund and its activities
- Policy inputs: obtaining information and insights from nongovernmental sources
- Political viability: gauging forces for and against IMF-supported policies
- Ownership: building national support and initiative toward IMF-backed policies

Basic Parameters

- Priorities: treat public outreach as vital, but (given resource constraints) do not compromise other tasks or hamper relations with government.
- Responsibilities: determine the division of labor for CSO liaison between EXR officials, mission chiefs, and resident representatives on a case-by-case basis.
- Selection: make strategic selections as to which CSOs to engage, but attempt to interact with a broad range of CSOs.
- Timing: meet with CSOs early enough in policy processes that the consultation is meaningful; meet ahead of and between as well as during missions.

- Location: select appropriate sites for meetings, whether IMF offices, government bureaus, CSO premises, or more neutral venues.
- Substance: be as forthcoming as possible with CSOs while strictly respecting confidentiality; don't overplay issues of confidentiality to avoid tough questions.
- Cooperation: consult and collaborate with other multilateral institutions like the World Bank and UNDP that have extensive interaction with civil society.

Process of Meetings

- Preparations: be well briefed about the CSOs to be met; agree a precise agenda in advance; agree explicit ground rules at the outset.
- Proceedings: ensure ample opportunity for questions and comments; debate options; be sensitive to cultural differences; use plain language; if possible use the first language of the majority of participants; avoid impressions of arrogance. Listening is crucial in a good working relationship.
- Follow-up: make a short note of meetings for IMF records; consider a follow-up note to the CSOs; publicize discussions with CSOs (subject to ground rules established); check with CSOs to gauge their impressions of meetings with the Fund.

The Government-IMF-CSO Triangle

The IMF is accountable to its member governments. Dialogue with and transparency toward citizens are important complements to this accountability.

- Keep the initiative with government, whose responsibility it is to engage CSOs. IMF contacts with CSOs supplement, and do not substitute for, government dialogue with citizen groups.
- Handle links with CSOs in ways that do not alienate government. Do not use relations with CSOs to put indirect pressure on governments.
- If a government raises objections to IMF-CSO relations, explain the rationale in terms of the aims identified above. If government resistance persists, refrain from the contacts and refer the matter to headquarters for possible follow-up.
- Where a government is sensitive about IMF engagement with CSOs: (a) inform the national authorities of planned contacts; (b) encourage government officials to help arrange meetings; and (c) invite government representatives to attend the meetings.

Legitimacy Concerns

- In principle, maintain an inclusive approach. Do not deny access without good reason (eg a CSO with malicious intent or a seriously distorted account of itself).

- The legitimacy of CSOs can be assessed in relation to: (a) legality—ie, they are officially recognized and registered; (b) morality—ie, they pursue a noble and right cause; (c) efficacy—ie, they perform competently; (d) membership base; and (e) governance—ie, they operate in a participatory, tolerant, transparent and accountable manner.
- In assessing the legitimacy of CSOs consult government officials, bilateral donor agencies, embassies, local staff in IMF offices, staff of other multilateral institutions, apex civil society bodies, academic specialists, other professional consultants.

Other Important Challenges
- Avoid being manipulated in political struggles. Be aware of CSOs that are closely tied to governments, political parties, commercial enterprises, or media operations.
- Be sensitive that the selection of CSOs to meet—as well as the ways that the Fund conducts and follows up contacts—can have the (unintended) effect of reinforcing (often arbitrary) divisions and inequalities in society.
- Building trust with CSOs can take time and patience. In the beginning, it is usually better to focus discussions on finding and consolidating common ground rather than highlighting areas of disagreement.
- Temper expectations. Encourage CSOs to be realistic about the extent and speed of IMF capacity to solve problems. Be realistic about the degree to which CSO consultations will yield immediately applicable specific policy inputs. Don't expect outreach to win all CSOs over to IMF positions. Some criticism will always exist.

I. Introduction: Nature and Purpose of this Guide
1. This guide aims to assist IMF staff in building positive relationships with civil society organizations (CSOs).[1] In particular, it sets out to help staff to develop interaction with CSOs in a way that enhances the Fund's operational work and contributes to the effectiveness of its support for its member countries.
2. As its designation indicates, the 'guide' offers a framework of good practices. It is not mandatory, and will not apply in all situations. IMF resource constraints in particular may prevent full realization of the aspirations laid out here. In general, the guide is intended to supplement, not replace, sound judgment and experience.

---

[1] On 5 March 2003, the Executive Board of the International Monetary Fund (IMF) reviewed the IMF's external communications strategy. Directors expressed views on relations with civil society organizations, which are reflected in Public Information Notice No 03/33, available at <http://www.imf.org/external/np/sec/pn/2003/pn0333.htm>.

3. Nor does this guide impose a universally and rigidly applicable blue-print. Concrete circumstances of civil society vary enormously among countries, cultures, social sectors, and political climates. The document sets out general principles, but in everyday practice staff must substantially rely on contextual assessments of the specific situations that they face.
4. This guide is not a sole source of advice. IMF staff can also usefully consult—and cooperate with—other multilateral institutions like the World Bank and United Nations agencies that have substantial experience and expertise in civil society liaison.
5. Dialogue with civil society groups is only one part of the Fund's public outreach. By highlighting relations with CSOs, this guide in no way downgrades the importance of IMF contacts with parliamentarians, political parties, subnational authorities, the mass media, and citizens at large.
6. This guide is a living document, subject to periodic amendment in the light of accumulating experience and evolving practices in IMF-civil society relations.

II. Definition: What is Civil Society?
1. Theorists propose widely varying and hotly contested concepts of civil society.
2. For IMF purposes, civil society can be defined as an arena where voluntary associations of citizens seek to shape governance structures and policies.
3. Civil society actors include business forums, faith-based associations, labor movements, local community groups, nongovernmental organizations (NGOs), philanthropic foundations, think tanks, and more. The present guide does not include political parties as part of civil society, given that—unlike the other citizen groups just named—political parties aim to occupy public office. The communications media also are not covered in this guide.
4. CSOs manifest huge diversity in terms of their constituencies, functions, sizes, resource levels, organizational forms, geographical scopes, historical experiences, cultural contexts, agendas, ideologies, strategies, and tactics. It is therefore very difficult to generalize about civil society.
5. Civil society activities are not inherently good or bad. Many CSOs make positive contributions to the political process, but some elements (like racist groups) can be 'uncivil' in their views and conduct.

III. Aims: Why does the IMF Engage with CSOs?
1. Active civil society involvement with global institutions like the IMF is not only an inescapable fact of life in 21st-century politics, but there

are also significant reasons for the Fund to welcome and nurture these relationships.

2. Public outreach (including contacts with CSOs) is an integral part of IMF country work. As a public institution, the IMF is committed to being transparent about its work and to explaining itself to the people whom it affects. Moreover, dialogue with CSOs offers important opportunities to dispel public misconceptions regarding the Fund and its activities.

3. Policy inputs. CSOs can highlight important issues for the formulation, implementation, and review of Fund and Fund-supported policies and programs. CSOs can give the IMF helpful information to supplement official data and insights that may differ from perspectives in official circles. Challenges from CSOs can provoke the Fund to sharpen its thinking and improve its policy advice.

4. Political viability. Discussions with CSOs provide an important gauge of forces for and against IMF-supported policies in a given context. Constructive dialogue with CSOs can help to build mutual understanding and to increase support for Fund-backed measures.

5. Ownership. Dialogue with CSOs can—as an important adjunct to the Fund's accountability to its member governments—significantly enhance 'ownership' of the policies that the IMF advances.

IV. Basic Parameters: How Much, Who, When, Where, What
A. *How much does the Fund engage with CSOs?*

1. The IMF staff is expected to develop constructive relationships with CSOs, together with other forms of outreach such as to the media and parliaments. Staff members should make the necessary judgments to ensure that their other responsibilities do not suffer.

2. Although it is vital for the Fund to extend its relations with a member country beyond public officials, contacts with CSOs must not go so far that they interfere with the IMF's primary relationship with the national government. Discussions of policy alternatives with CSOs should not generate an impression that the Fund is negotiating with CSOs rather than the government.

B. *Who in the Fund staff interacts with CSOs?*

1. IMF staff members are encouraged to meet with CSOs in order to advance one or more of the aims set out in Section III.

2. General coordination of IMF relations with CSOs occurs through the External Relations Department (EXR).

3. Contacts with CSOs concerning general lines of IMF policy are normally handled through the relevant functional and service departments of the Fund, with backing from EXR.

4. Contacts with CSOs concerning the IMF's country-specific surveillance and financial and technical assistance are normally handled through the relevant area department, especially the mission chief and (where one exists) the resident representative for the country, with backing from EXR.

5. The precise division of civil society liaison tasks for a country between the mission chief and the resident representative (where one exists) is determined on a case-by-case basis. In general the resident representative is better placed to develop relations with CSOs.

6. Although this guide focuses on the professional staff of the IMF, the Governors, Executive Directors, and Management of the Fund also have relations with CSOs. The Independent Evaluation Office, too, takes inputs from CSOs.

C. Which CSOs do Fund staff contact?

1. In principle, staff can meet with any and all CSOs in order to advance one or more of the aims set out in Section III.

2. In practice, staff cannot meet all CSOs that have an interest in IMF activities. Nor can the Fund respond positively to every request from CSOs for meetings. In making a strategic selection that ensures that all relevant interests are heard, staff can invoke the following broad considerations:
   (a) Engage with diverse sectors of civil society.
   (b) Aim to alternate the Fund's contacts between different CSOs, rather than always and only meeting the same organizations and individuals.
   (c) Contact locally based associations as well as the local offices of transnational CSOs—the former are often less assertive in approaching the Fund. In particular, staff should not rely on North-based groups to speak on behalf of South-based stakeholders.
   (d) Extend the Fund's dialogue with CSOs beyond elite circles. Contact small enterprise as well as big business, peasants as well as commercial farmers, poor people as well as the affluent, etc.
   (e) Meet with CSOs across the political spectrum. Include critics as well as supporters of the IMF. Consider meeting opponents as well as backers of the current government of a country.
   (f) Reach out beyond civil society circles that look familiar. Formally organized, western-type associations are not always representative of the mainstream in some cultural contexts. In any event, avoid inadvertent favoritism to English speakers in places where English is not the principal language.

3. To attain this diversity of civil society relations, staff may need to undertake proactive outreach. Many CSOs assume that the IMF is not accessible to them and so will not make the first move to seek contact.

4. Some CSOs may decline an invitation to meet with Fund staff. Their reasons might be logistical or principled. It is worth subsequently repeating an invitation as a signal that the IMF's door remains open.
5. Approach umbrella or apex bodies like business federations, labor confederations, NGO forums, and inter-faith councils, including for advice on which among the multitude of CSOs the Fund should meet.
6. Maintain up-to-date lists of names and contact details of the Fund's interlocutors in civil society, particularly at a country level through the resident representative's office. Such lists can be made available to management, missions, EXR (for example, to distribute its *Civil Society Newsletter*), and to inform an incoming resident representative.

D. *When does the Fund interact with CSOs?*
1. In principle, IMF engagement with CSOs can be relevant at all stages of policy formulation.
2. It is important to consult CSOs in the earlier phases of policy formulation, rather than after the key decisions have been taken. Many CSOs respond negatively if they feel that they are being asked to rubberstamp a fait accompli.
3. Peak occasions for Fund contacts with CSOs include the Annual and Spring Meetings, and ad hoc conferences and workshops to discuss general IMF-related policies like Poverty Reduction Strategy Paper (PRSP) consultations and the Heavily Indebted Poor Countries (HIPC) initiative.
4. Many missions allot time to meetings with CSOs: Article IV missions; Use of Fund Resources (UFR) missions (especially as they concern longer-term programs of structural reform); EXR missions; Financial Sector Assessment Program (FSAP) missions; and some technical assistance missions.
5. The resident representative (in countries where one exists) can usefully consult with CSOs ahead of a mission and feed their information and views into the mission's preparation. Such an exercise can broaden the range of options considered and help to assess the viability of proposed policies and programs.
6. It is good to develop relations with CSOs on an ongoing basis—hence between as well as during missions and major conferences. For example, a resident representative could establish a local CSO consultation group and meet with it several times a year.
7. It is fruitful to establish contacts with CSOs outside the mission cycle, so that a relationship already exists when more substantive consultations are undertaken. Well-grounded relations of trust and understanding with CSOs can also have major payoffs when the IMF is called in to address an economic crisis.

E. Where does the Fund meet with CSOs?

1. IMF contacts with CSOs can be direct (face-to-face, telephone, email, etc) or indirect (through the mass media, public speeches, distribution of documents, street demonstrations, etc). In general, meetings in-person are the best way to set up frank and detailed exchanges.
2. Fund officials can also meet CSOs at events organized by other agencies that have well-developed civil society liaison in many countries, such as the World Bank and the United Nations Development Program (UNDP).
3. Meetings could also take place at CSOs' own premises and events. Many CSOs appreciate staff initiatives to bring the IMF to civil society venues. Such visits can also help staff understand the CSO, its size, relations with stakeholders, etc.
4. Sometimes communication may be more constructive if staff meet CSOs at more neutral venues, such as a convention center or a university.
5. Civil society liaison should extend beyond the national capital to other cities, and to rural areas as well as urban centers. CSOs in the national capital sometimes poorly reflect the priorities and perspectives in the country at large.

F. What does the Fund discuss with CSOs?

1. First encounters between the Fund and CSOs often cover general matters: the nature and purpose of the IMF; its organizational structure; concepts and theories of economics that inform the IMF's work; etc. Likewise, in first meetings CSOs often relate basic information about their organization and views.
2. Many conversations with CSOs address broad questions of IMF policy: debt relief programs, capital account liberalization, poverty reduction strategies, exchange rate regimes, control of inflation, etc. EXR can provide staff with summary statements of the latest Fund positions on general policy issues.
3. Many exchanges with CSOs concern country-specific IMF advice related, for example, to macroeconomic targets, adjustments of taxes and subsidies, civil service reform, changes to labor legislation, etc.
4. In discussions with CSOs, staff cannot divulge confidential information and should explain that they are not in a position to do so. Similarly, staff will not be able to discuss sensitive points regarding the state of the Fund's negotiations with a government. Nor can they release market-sensitive information. However, staff should not overplay issues of confidentiality to avoid tough questions.

V. Challenges: Common Problems and How to Handle Them

A. *Keeping initiative with government*

1. The IMF is accountable to the governments of its member countries. Dialogue with and transparency toward citizens represent important complements to this accountability.
2. However, the Fund cannot replace governments in relating with CSOs. IMF contacts with CSOs are a supplement to, and not a substitute for, government dialogue with citizen groups.
3. IMF staff relations with CSOs, therefore, do not substitute for the government's own responsibilities for consultation with civil society. Determining macroeconomic policies and justifying them in discussions with the public (*inter alia* through CSOs) is the responsibility of the national government concerned.
4. Likewise, staff should encourage CSOs to take views and proposals to the relevant national authorities.

B. *Maintaining good relations with government*

1. The IMF has its primary relationships with member governments, and staff should handle links with CSOs in ways that do not alienate the national authorities.
2. IMF discussions with CSOs should not create additional difficulties for the government. Staff should in general not broach issues or make remarks that could put the government in an awkward position.
3. Increasingly, governments understand and accept that the IMF needs to have relations with CSOs; and some governments positively encourage such contacts. If a government raises objections to Fund relations with certain or all CSOs, staff should explain the rationale for such contacts along the lines of Section III. If the difference of views persists, staff should refrain from the contacts and refer the disagreement to headquarters for possible follow-up with the government concerned.
4. Where a government is sensitive about IMF engagement with CSOs, it can be constructive for staff: (a) to forewarn the national authorities of planned contacts; (b) to have government officials help arrange the meetings; and/or (c) to invite government representatives to attend the discussions. With time and experience of IMF-civil society relations, the government may adopt a more relaxed position regarding these exchanges. (In certain contexts, however, close government involvement may deter some CSOs from attending or speaking frankly.)

C. *Getting mired in politics*

1. IMF activities inevitably have political implications. The impacts vary, and may include some consequences that staff do not foresee. Both Fund personnel and CSOs may overestimate the influence of the IMF.

However, most CSOs react skeptically to claims from staff that the Fund is an apolitical institution.

2. That said, IMF officials should strive to be non-partisan and politically non-interventionist. Staff can listen to all sides of debates and avoid the appearance of taking sides.
3. Staff should avoid being manipulated by one side or the other in political struggles: for example, one state against another; government against opposition political parties, or vice versa; employers against trade unions, or vice versa; one religious community against another; one NGO coalition against another; and so on. In this regard, staff should be able to distinguish CSOs that have close ties with governments, political parties, commercial ventures, or media operations.
4. Staff should not use their relations with CSOs to put indirect pressure on governments.
5. Although relations with CSOs can expose the IMF to the political process more directly, these risks are normally well outweighed by the gains of this engagement (as laid out in Section III).

D. *Building trust*
1. Some CSOs harbor considerable suspicion about the IMF and blame the institution for many ills. Conversely, some Fund staff have limited confidence in some or all CSOs.
2. Building trust in these situations takes time and patience. Neither side should expect that a single contact will dissipate accumulated wariness. Indeed, some parties may for some considerable period continue to grasp every opportunity to confirm their suspicions of the other.
3. It is usually better to focus discussions on finding and consolidating common ground rather than emphasizing clashing interpretations and prescriptions.
4. Although polarized confrontations with angry civil society critics of the Fund can be uncomfortable, these exchanges can be useful opportunities to specify differences. Staff can show themselves ready to listen to vociferous opponents, while at the same time politely defending IMF policies. With this clarification of perspectives, third parties are in a better position to decide their own positions for themselves.
5. In circumstances where mutual trust is especially low and opinions are deeply divided, IMF meetings with CSOs might be more constructive when an outside facilitator respected by all sides is used.
6. Trust can also be fostered over time by following many of the 'how-to' suggestions offered in Section IV.

E. *Tempering expectations*
1. Both Fund staff and CSOs can expect too much from their exchanges with each other.

2. CSOs may hold unrealistic expectations about the extent to which and/or speed at which the IMF can solve problems. It is important that staff in these situations explain the depth and complexity of many economic issues, as well as the complexities of decision making at an institution like the IMF. Otherwise CSOs can become disillusioned with the Fund when major improvements are not immediately forthcoming.

3. CSOs may have unrealistic expectations regarding the degree that contacts with Fund staff will influence policy. The fact that staff are open to discussions with CSOs should not be misconstrued to mean that the IMF will necessarily adopt their positions.

4. Fund staff may have unrealistic expectations regarding the degree to which consultations with CSOs provide immediately applicable specific input to the IMF's policy advice. Many of the substantive gains from these exchanges come incrementally and over the long term.

5. Staff should not expect consultations with CSOs to win everyone over to a complete societal consensus behind IMF positions. Some level of critique from civil society circles will always exist.

F. Assessing the legitimacy of CSOs

1. IMF staff are often cautious about engaging with CSOs because of concerns about the possible lack of legitimacy of these bodies.

2. CSOs can accrue legitimacy, and the ability to represent concerns of groups within societies, from a variety of sources. In assessing the extent to which CSOs represent legitimate concerns, it is relevant to consider such issues as their legal status, moral authority, efficacy, membership, and governance.

3. In assessing the legitimacy of CSOs, staff could consult with a wide range of sources, including government officials, bilateral donor agencies, embassies, local staff in IMF resident representative offices, staff of the World Bank and other multilateral institutions (especially their civil society specialists where these exist), apex civil society bodies, relevant academic specialists, and other professional consultants.

4. In a few countries, CSOs operate self-regulatory codes of conduct or certification schemes that can help to identify bona fide associations.

5. The Fund's capacity to assess the legitimacy of CSOs are enhanced to the extent that staff (especially resident representatives, mission chiefs, and EXR officials) build up records of civil society contacts.

6. Outgoing mission chiefs, resident representatives, and other principal Fund contact points with civil society should make a point of giving their successors a briefing on their relations with CSOs.

G. Finding/making time

1. Building relations with civil society requires time and resources, which

must be balanced with other priorities. This is especially challenging in an environment in which IMF member governments expect the Fund to operate within existing staff resources.

2. Staff should treat public outreach (including contacts with CSOs) as an integral part of their overall country work, not as a dispensable lower priority when time is short.

3. Engagement with CSOs can correct misunderstandings, improve policy content, and enhance the political viability of IMF advice. These relations can contribute substantively to the effectiveness of core policy work, and may, over time, actually save staff time and resources.

4. Article IV and program missions could consider adopting a practice of blocking out at least half a day for meetings with CSOs.

5. Resident representatives are likely to undertake the lion's share of relations with CSOs, but it is also highly desirable for their outreach to be supplemented by direct contact between missions and CSOs.

Annex
Process: Holding Meetings with CSOs

This annex contains a number of suggested good practices for running effective meetings and contacts with CSOs. Not all will be practicable or necessary in all circumstances. Many may seem to be 'common sense' or 'common courtesy', but it is helpful to bear them in mind. These are put forward for the benefit of IMF staff; many of the practices, if adopted by CSOs would also contribute to more productive contacts with the Fund.

A. Preparations

1. Well planned meetings can go a long way toward building a productive working relationship.

2. Reply promptly to requests for consultations from CSOs.

3. Maintain an inclusive approach; only deny a CSO access with good reason (for example, if the organization has malicious intent or presents a seriously distorted account of itself).

4. Be well briefed. Review information about the CSOs that will attend. Consult notes of any previous IMF encounters with these groups. Track relevant views and proposals that emanate from civil society congresses. Request relevant materials prepared by CSOs.

5. Agree a fairly precise agenda in advance of the meeting, to encourage a focused discussion of specific questions and propositions.

6. Let both sides have a say in what is discussed. Allow CSOs to raise their issues of concern, even when these matters might not be priorities for, or even seem directly relevant to, the IMF.

7. Distribute relevant IMF documentation to CSOs in advance of a

meeting, where possible in the local language(s). Provide CSOs with the names and job descriptions of the staff that they will meet.

8. Agree explicit ground rules for the meeting at the outset, including how far, in what form, and with whom the proceedings may be discussed outside the meeting. Neither the Fund nor CSOs should misrepresent to others the nature and substance of their consultations.

B. *Proceedings*

1. Where possible, conduct meetings in the first language of the majority of the civil society participants. Linguistic minorities usually appreciate the provision of separate translation.

2. It is normally more time-efficient—especially in the context of mission visits—to meet representatives of a number of CSOs together. However, in-depth and more discreet discussions of specific concerns may require smaller or even one-on-one meetings.

3. Ensure ample opportunity for comments and questions from the CSOs in attendance. Avoid one-way presentations. Take the initiative to ask questions of CSOs about their views and activities. Discussions with CSOs are an occasion for staff to listen, learn, and be influenced as well as to speak and teach.

4. Give all attendees a chance to participate: women as well as men; minority as well as majority ethnic and religious groups; critics as well as supporters of Fund-backed policies, etc.

5. Remember that some CSOs work in new and fragile democratic environments. CSOs that advocate for vulnerable groups can feel at particular political risk. Respect these insecurities and do not expose participants in consultations to reprisals. Report to management any evidence of intimidation of CSO interlocutors.

6. Address CSOs in plain language. Avoid technical terms, institutional acronyms, professional jargon, and other specialized vocabulary.

7. Don't underestimate cultural differences. Without extra efforts at cross-cultural communication, CSOs and Fund officials can leave a meeting with very different understandings of the conversation.

8. Debate options (rather than sell pre-established positions). Frankly discuss the trade-offs between policy alternatives. Honestly explore the negative as well as positive consequences of the various approaches.

9. Be ready to admit ignorance when the answer to a question is not known. Where appropriate, promise to look into the matter and supply a response later.

10. Dress comfortably. Somewhat more casual attire may help to relax the atmosphere in some settings. That said, artificial 'dressing down' can provoke a skeptical reaction. Knowledge of local customs is essential.

11. Avoid impressions of overconfidence. Take the time to answer ques-

tions fully, plainly, and patiently. Few things alienate CSOs (and citizens generally) more than officials who appear arrogant, even if unconsciously.

C. Follow-up

1. Make a short note of meetings with CSOs. Briefly record who was met, what was discussed, what main complaints and/or proposals were heard, and general impressions of the encounter. These notes should be included in the compilation of mission minutes, and briefly summarized in back-to-office reports and periodic reports of resident representatives. The accumulation of data on contacts helps the Fund to build up its capacity for civil society liaison.
2. Mention exchanges with civil society bodies in the formal Staff Reports on missions (or indicate reasons why no such meetings were held).
3. Subject to any ground rules established (see A8 above), publicize discussions with CSOs: on the main IMF website and/or relevant country webpages; in country newsletters where these exist; in EXR's *Civil Society Newsletter*. Consider a follow-up note of thanks for CSOs' input, acknowledging the main points that they have made, informing them of any steps that have been taken or are intended in response to their concerns, and inviting their further comment.
4. Do periodic follow-up checks with CSOs to gauge their impressions of meetings with Fund officials.
5. Conduct periodic reviews through EXR of general IMF liaison with CSOs.
6. The provision of feedback is important. If CSOs perceive that their input is not taken seriously and has no impact, then they are less likely to pursue further consultations with the Fund.

Appendix X

WTO

AGREEMENT ESTABLISHING THE WORLD TRADE
ORGANIZATION

Signed on 15 April 1994
Source: <http:// www.wto.org/English/docs_e/legal_e/04-wto_ e.
htm>

[excerpt]

Article V
Relations with Other Organizations

2. The General Council may make appropriate arrangements for consultation and cooperation with non-governmental organizations concerned with
matters related to those of the WTO.

GUIDELINES FOR ARRANGEMENTS ON RELATIONS WITH NON-GOVERNMENTAL ORGANIZATIONS

Decision adopted by the General Council on 18 July 1996
Document number: WT/L/162, dated 23 July 1996
Source: <http://www.wto.org/English/forums_e/ngo_e/guide_e.htm>

I.   Under Article V:2 of the Marrakesh Agreement establishing the WTO
     'the General Council may make appropriate arrangements for consul-
     tation and cooperation with non-governmental organizations
     concerned with matters related to those of the WTO'.
II. In deciding on these guidelines for arrangements on relations with non-
     governmental organizations, Members recognize the role NGOs can
     play to increase the awareness of the public in respect of WTO activi-
     ties and agree in this regard to improve transparency and develop
     communication with NGOs.
III. To contribute to achieve greater transparency Members will ensure more
     information about WTO activities in particular by making available

documents which would be derestricted more promptly than in the past. To enhance this process the Secretariat will make available on on-line computer network the material which is accessible to the public, including derestricted documents.

IV. The Secretariat should play a more active role in its direct contacts with NGOs who, as a valuable resource, can contribute to the accuracy and richness of the public debate. This interaction with NGOs should be developed through various means such as inter alia the organization on an ad hoc basis of symposia on specific WTO-related issues, informal arrangements to receive the information NGOs may wish to make available for consultation by interested delegations and the continuation of past practice of responding to requests for general information and briefings about the WTO.

V. If chairpersons of WTO councils and committees participate in discussions or meetings with NGOs it shall be in their personal capacity unless that particular council or committee decides otherwise.

VI. Members have pointed to the special character of the WTO, which is both a legally binding intergovernmental treaty of rights and obligations among its Members and a forum for negotiations. As a result of extensive discussions, there is currently a broadly held view that it would not be possible for NGOs to be directly involved in the work of the WTO or its meetings. Closer consultation and cooperation with NGOs can also be met constructively through appropriate processes at the national level where lies primary responsibility for taking into account the different elements of public interest which are brought to bear on trade policy-making.